D0819089

Guide to the National Parks

Southwest

Mountain lion

NATIONAL GEOGRAPHIC

Guide to the National Parks
Southwest

National Geographic
Washington, D.C.

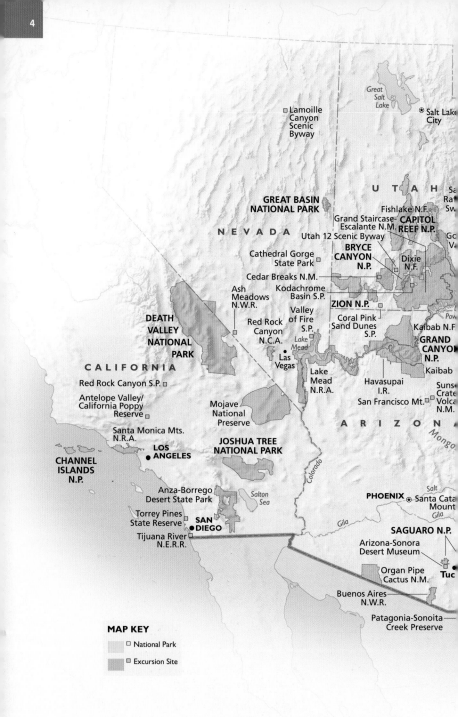

Great
Salt
Lake

✳ Salt Lake
City

U T A H

Sa
Ra
Sw

Lamoille
Canyon
Scenic
Byway

Fishlake N.F.

GREAT BASIN
NATIONAL PARK

Grand Staircase-
Escalante N.M.

CAPITOL
REEF N.P.

N E V A D A

Utah 12 Scenic Byway

Go
V

Cathedral Gorge
State Park

BRYCE
CANYON
N.P.

Dixie
N.F.

Cedar Breaks N.M.

Kodachrome
Basin S.P.

Ash
Meadows
N.W.R.

ZION N.P.

DEATH
VALLEY
NATIONAL
PARK

Red Rock
Canyon
N.C.A.

Valley
of Fire
S.P.

Coral Pink
Sand Dunes
S.P.

Kaibab N.F

Lake
Mead

GRAND
CANYON
N.P.

Las
Vegas

Kaibab

C A L I F O R N I A

Lake
Mead
N.R.A.

Pow

Red Rock Canyon S.P.

Havasupai
I.R.

Suns
Crate
Volca
N.M.

Antelope Valley/
California Poppy
Reserve

San Francisco Mt.

Mojave
National
Preserve

A R I Z O N A

Santa Monica Mts.
N.R.A.

JOSHUA TREE
NATIONAL PARK

LOS
ANGELES

Mongo

CHANNEL
ISLANDS
N.P.

Colorado

Anza-Borrego
Desert State Park

Salton
Sea

Salt

Torrey Pines
State Reserve

PHOENIX ✳

Santa Cata
Mount

SAN
DIEGO

Gila

SAGUARO N.P.

Tijuana River
N.E.R.R.

Gila

Arizona-Sonora
Desert Museum

Organ Pipe
Cactus N.M.

Tuc

Buenos Aires
N.W.R.

Patagonia-Sonoita
Creek Preserve

MAP KEY

▫ National Park

▫ Excursion Site

Cheyenne ⊛

Dead Horse Pt.
State Park

Colorado
N.M.

Colorado
River
Scenic
Byway

White River
N.F.

⊛ DENVER

C O L O R A D O

Colorado

ARCHES N.P.

Grand
Mesa

BLACK CANYON OF THE GUNNISON N.P.

Manti-
La Sal N.F.

Curecanti N.R.A.

Arkansas

CANYONLANDS
N.P.

San Juan
Skyway

GREAT SAND DUNES N.P. & PRES.

en Canyon N.R.A.

Sangre de

Alamosa N.W.R.

Natural
Bridges N.M.

Bluff

MESA VERDE
N.P.

San Juan Mts.

Sangre de Cristo Mts.

onument
alley

Valle Vidal

Canyon de Chelly
N.M.

molovi
ins

Rio Grande
N.W. & S.R.

Cimarron
Canyon S.P.

Enchanted
Circle Area

Rio Grande

⊛ Santa Fe

PETRIFIED
FOREST N.P.

● Albuquerque

El Mapais
N.M. and N.C.A.

Pintail
Lake

N E W   M E X I C O

Pecos

Bosque del Apache
N.W.R.

Bitter Lake
N.W.R.

Oliver Lee
Mem. S.P.

Lincoln

White Sands
N.M.

National

Forest

Living Desert
Zoo & Gardens
S.P.

CARLSBAD CAVERNS N.P.

Kartchner
Caverns
tate Park

UNITED STATES

MEXICO

● El Paso

GUADALUPE MTS. N.P.

T E X A S

Davis Mountains
Loop

0   miles   300
0   kilometers   400

Big Bend
Ranch
S.P.

BIG BEND
NATIONAL
PARK

Rio Grande

Contents

Introduction 8
How to use this guide 10

Arches 14
Excursions: Colorado River Scenic Byway 24, Manti-La Sal National Forest 25, San Rafael Swell 26, Goblin Valley State Park 30

Big Bend 32
Excursion: Big Bend Ranch State Park 46

Black Canyon of the Gunnison 48
Excursions: Grand Mesa 58, Curecanti National Recreation Area 61, Colorado NM 62, White River NF: South 64

Bryce Canyon 66
Excursions: Utah 12 Scenic Byway 76, Kodachrome Basin State Park 78, Grand Staircase-Escalante National Monument 79

Canyonlands 82
Excursions: Dead Horse Point State Park 94, Natural Bridges National Monument 95

Capitol Reef 98
Excursions: Fishlake National Forest 108, Glen Canyon National Recreation Area 110, Bluff Area 112

Carlsbad Caverns 114
Excursions: Living Desert Zoo & Gardens State Park 124, White Sands National Monument 125, Oliver Lee Memorial State Park 127, Bosque del Apache National Wildlife Refuge 130, Bitter Lake National Wildlife Refuge 132

Channel Islands 134
Excursions: Santa Monica Mountains NRA 144, Torrey Pines State Reserve 147, Tijuana River National Estuarine Research Reserve 148

Death Valley 150
Excursions: Mojave National Preserve 162, Antelope Valley/California Poppy Reserve 164, Red Rock Canyon State Park 165, Ash Meadows National Wildlife Refuge 166, Red Rock Canyon National Conservation Area 168

Grand Canyon 170
Excursions: Havasu Canyon Hike 186, Lake Mead National Recreation Area 187, Kaibab National Forest 188, Sunset Crater Volcano National Monument 192, San Francisco Mountain 194

Great Basin 196
Excursions: Lamoille Canyon Scenic Byway 206, Cathedral Gorge State Park 207, Valley of Fire State Park 208

Great Sand Dunes 210
Excursions: Sangre de Cristo Mountains 220, Alamosa National Wildlife Refuge 222, Rio Grande Wild & Scenic River 224, Enchanted Circle Area 228, Valle Vidal 230, Cimarron Canyon State Park 231

Guadalupe Mountains 232
Excursions: Lincoln National Forest 242, Davis Mountain Loop 246,

Joshua Tree 248
Excursions: Anza-Borrego Desert State Park 258, Salton Sea 263

Mesa Verde 264
Excursions: San Juan Mountains 274, San Juan Skyway 278, Monument Valley 281, Canyon de Chelly National Monument 282

Petrified Forest 284
Excursions: El Malpais National Monument & Conservation Area 296, Homolovi Ruins 298, Pintail Lake 300

Saguaro 302
Excursions: Arizona-Sonora Desert Museum 312, Santa Catalina Mountains 313, Kartchner Caverns State Park 315, Patagonia-Sonoita Creek Preserve 316, Buenos Aires National Wildlife Refuge 320, Organ Pipe Cactus National Monument 322

Zion 326
Excursions: Coral Pink Sand Dunes 336, Dixie National Forest 337, Cedar Breaks National Monument 339

Resources 342
Index 346
Illustrations Credits 351
Staff Credits 351

Photos: Cover, Delicate Arch, Arches NP; pp. 2-3, North Rim, Grand Canyon NP; opposite, Guadalupe Mountains NP

More Than a Beloved Desert

MENTION THE NATIONAL PARKS OF THE SOUTHWEST, and most people are likely to focus on a single thought: Desert. Suggest visiting one, and some are likely to focus on a single threshold question: Will there be air conditioning?

They're right, of course, but only in part. Desert does indeed describe most of the vast American Southwest, and the 18 national parks that lie within it preserve great swaths of arid country that can be brutally hot. Pick your desert: Sonoran, Chihuahuan, Great Basin, Mojave. They're all here, each with its distinct cast of leathery-skinned prickly plants and water-shrewd animals. Sand. Bare rock. Alkali flats. Temperatures in the 120s. Whether you visit one of the marquee parks such as Grand Canyon or Death Valley, or the "off Broadway" parks such as Guadalupe Mountains or Petrified Forest, the question is bound to occur: How does anything live out here?

The answers are fascinating, worth the time—and sweat—to investigate. It's one thing to read about the expandable tissue that allows a cactus to absorb and retain quantities of water; quite another to crouch in the heat and touch the waxy surface that protects its precious cargo. Adaptations to desert conditions can astonish us, and certainly they engage active minds, but it is the unexpected beauty that seizes hearts and sometimes takes our breath away. The slickrock domes. The great void of canyons. The graceful span of a sandstone arch, or an oddly balanced rock poised against a vivid sky. The silence. This is what calls to us again and again long after we've left and returned to our burrows of concrete, glass, and steel.

There's more to Southwest parks than the desert, of course. After all, they lie scattered across a region extending from southern California to central Colorado and from Utah to southwestern Texas. Here there are great variations of climate and elevation. Mountain ranges and high plateaus rise from the desert floors. Serpentine cave systems tunnel beneath the surface. River corridors carve into the rock and meander across the land as sinuous oases of shade. The Pacific coast offers its own contrast to the deserts, and in Great Basin you'll even find a tiny glacier.

This blend of ecosystems provides habitat for a variety of plants and animals—from Channel Islands' kelp forests and sea lions to Carlsbad Caverns' nightly cyclone of bats to lizards and snakes, roadrunners and ringtails, javelinas and hummingbirds, elk, and bighorn. Even within parks, the terrain brings into close proximity widely divergent plant and animal communities. Big Bend, for example, combines several canyons of the Rio Grande with a wide sweep of desert and a mountain range. The diversity in birdlife alone runs to 400 species—more than any other

Colorado River running

national park—and there are an astonishing 1,000 flowering plants.

People have been living in the region for thousands of years, a fact highlighted in many of the parks by pictographs, petroglyphs, ruins, and granaries. But perhaps in no other park is man's early presence so keenly and vividly demonstrated as in Mesa Verde National Park, where extensive ruins of impressive ancient dwellings still stand amid the cliffs and atop the mesa. Other sites near some of the parks, such as the Havasupai Indian Reservation along the Grand Canyon, remind us that there are still desert peoples in the Southwest living true to their ancient traditions.

Long before people began living here—or anywhere else, for that matter—the creation story of each park was being written in its rocks. Thanks to the desert, those geologic stories are more apparent in the Southwest than in other regions, simply because there is less vegetation covering the rocks. Most of the parks, including Grand Canyon and Utah's five national parks, demonstrate the awesome power of water and wind to erode solid rock. In other parks, such as Guadalupe and Big Bend, the character of the landscape hinges more on mountain building.

This book does much more than illuminate the natural and human history of the parks. It also offers strategies for visiting them. Itineraries for each park guide you to the sights, identify promising hikes and strolls, and provide estimates of time and distance. There are also excursions to worthwhile sites close to each park, such as national forests, archaeological sites, state parks, and wildlife refuges.

Here, too, you'll find loads of practical travel advice...including where to find a motel with air-conditioning.

—Thomas Schmidt

HOW TO USE THIS GUIDE

Using the Guide

Welcome to the 18 national parks of the Southwest. Whether you are a regular visitor or a first-timer, you have a great treat in store. Each of the parks offers you fun, adventure, and—usually—enthralling splendor. What you experience will depend on where you go and what you do. But exploring an unknown land is best done with a guide, a companion who has tested the trail and learned the lore.

Our coverage of each national park begins with a portrait of its natural wonders, ecological setting, history, and, often, its struggles against environmental threats. You'll understand why a single step off a trail can harm fragile plants, and why visitors are detoured from certain areas that shelter wildlife. Many parks have already suffered from the impact of tourism. Be sure to leave all items—plants, rocks, artifacts—where you find them.

Three of parks have been designated United Nations World Heritage sites for their outstanding scenic and cultural wonders; four of the areas in the book have international biosphere reserve status, signaling the distinctive qualities of their natural environments. Before starting off on your park exploration, use the guide to preview the parks you may want to visit. You'll notice that each park introduction is followed by the following three how-and-when sections:

How to Get There You may be able to include more than one park in your trip. The regional map in the front of the book shows them in relation to one another. Base your itinerary not so much on mileage as on time, remembering that parks do not lie alongside interstates; park roads are usually rugged—and, in summer, crowded.

When to Go The parks of the Southwest are mostly year-round parks. Instead of going in midsummer, when they are hottest and often crowded, schedule your trip for spring or fall (or for June or late August) and time your arrival early on a weekday. In the Southwest, fall can be glorious and autumn vistas coincide with a relative scarcity of visitors, and many of the parks bloom in spring. Winter brings chilly days and cold nights. Consult this heading in each park chapter for details about visitor facilities.

How to Visit Don't rush through a park, give yourself time to savor the beauty. Incredibly, the average time the typical visitor spends in a park is half a day. Often, that blur of time flashes past a windshield. No matter how long you to stay, spend at least part of that time in the park, not in your car. Each park's How to Visit section recommends a plan for visits of one-half, one, two, or more days. Writers devised the plans and trekked every tour, but don't be afraid to explore on your own.

MAP KEY and ABBREVIATIONS

National Park Service system
National Forest Service system
National Wildlife Refuge system
Bureau of Land Management
State Park system
Indian Reservation
Urbanized area

U.S. Interstate
5

Unpaved Road

Railroad / Tram

National boundary

Wilderness Area

U.S. Federal or State Highway
50 33

Trail

Continental Divide

State boundary

National Wild & Scenic River

Other Road
J59

Scenic Byway

Fault Line

Military Reservation

National Marine Sanctuary

POPULATION

- **PHOENIX** above 500,000
- **Albuquerque** 50,000 to 500,000
- Casa Grande 10,000 to 50,000
- Redrock under 10,000

SYMBOLS

- ⊛ State capital
- ⊟ Ranger Station/ Visitor Center/ Park Headquarters
- ▢ Point of Interest
- △ Campground
- ⛱ Picnic Area
- Overlook / Viewpoint
- + Elevation

- ≍ Pass
- Palm Spring
- Falls
- ○ Spring
- Dam
- Intermittent River
- Intermittent Lake
- Dry Lake
- Sand Dunes

ABBREVIATIONS

BLVD.	Boulevard
Cr.	Creek
Ctr.	Center
DR.	Drive
Fk.	Fork
Ft.	Fort
Hdqrs.	Headquarters
HWY.	Highway
I.-s.	Islands
I.R.	Indian Reservation
L.	Lake
MEM.	Memorial
M.	Middle
Mt.-s.	Mount-ain-s
NAT.	National
N.C.A.	National Conservation Area
N.E.R.R.	National Estuarine Research Reserve
N.F.	National Forest
N.M.S.	National Marine Sanctuary
N.M.	National Monument
N.P.	National Park
N.R.A.	National Recreation Area
N.S.T.	National Scenic Trail
N.W.R.	National Wildlife Refuge
Pk.	Peak
Pres.	Preserve
Pt.	Point
R.	River
RD.	Road
Rec.	Recreation
Res.	Reservoir
S.F.	State Forest
S.P.	State Park
S.R.A.	State Recreation Area
S.R.	State Reserve
WILD.	Wilderness

Other features of the Guide:
Excursions The excursions that follow each park entries take you to other natural areas in the region. If time allows, be sure to explore some of these as well. Many of the sites are much less known than the national parks and often less crowded. The distances noted from the parks are approximate and intended for planning purposes only.

Maps The park maps, the excursion maps, and the regional map were prepared as an aid in planning your trip. For more detail on hiking trails and other facilities inside a park, contact the Park Service, phone the park itself, or visit the website. Contact the individual excursions sites to learn more about them. Always use a road map when traveling and hiking maps when walking into the backcountry.

The maps note specially designated areas within park borders: Wilderness areas are managed to retain their primeval quality.

Roads, buildings, and vehicles are not allowed in them. National preserves may allow hunting.

The following abbreviations are used in this book:

NP   National Park
NRA   National Recreation Area
NF   National Forest
NM   National Monument
NWR   National Wildlife Refuge
BLM   Bureau of Land Management
SP   State Park

Information & Activities This section, at the end of each national park entry, offers detailed visitor information. Call or write the park, or visit the park's website for further details. Brochures are usually available free of charge from the parks. For a small fee you can buy a copy of the "National Park System Map and Guide" by writing or calling the Consumer Information Center, P.O. Box 100, Pueblo, CO. 81002; 719-948-3334. Visit the Park Service at: www.nps.gov.

Entrance Fees The entrance fees listed in this book reflect fees at press time. In addition to daily or weekly fees, most parks also offer a yearly fee, with unlimited entries.

For $50 you can buy a National Parks Pass, which is good for a year, from first use, and admits all occupants of a private vehicle to all national parks with a vehicle entrance fee. The pass does not cover parking fees where applicable.

For an additional $15 you can purchase a Golden Eagle hologram to affix to the pass for unlimited admission to U.S. Fish and Wildlife Service, Forest Service, and Bureau of Land Management sites.

People over 62 can obtain a lifetime Golden Age Passport for $10, and blind and disabled people are entitled to a lifetime Golden Access Passport for free, both of which admit all occupants of a private vehicle to all national parks and other federal sites and a discount on usage fees. These documents are available at any Park Service facility that charges entrance fees.

For further information on purchasing park passes, call 888-467-2757 or visit http://buy.nationalparks.org.

Pets Generally they're not allowed on trails, in buildings, or in the backcountry. Elsewhere, they must be leashed. Specific rules are noted.

Facilities for Disabled This section of the guide explains which parts of each park, including visitor centers and trails, are accessible to visitors with disabilities.

Special Advisories
■ Do not take chances. People are killed or badly injured every year in national parks. Most casualties are caused by recklessness or inattention to clearly posted warnings.
■ Stay away from wild animals. Do not feed them. Do not try to touch them, not even raccoons or chipmunks (which can transmit

diseases). Try not to surprise a bear and do not let one approach you. If one does, scare it off by yelling, clapping your hands, or banging pots. Store all your food in bear-proof containers (often available at parks); keep it out of sight in your vehicle, with windows closed and doors locked. Or suspend it at least 15 feet above ground, and 10 feet out from a post or tree trunk.

■ Guard your health. If you are not fit, don't overtax your body. Boil water that doesn't come from a park's drinking-water tap. Chemical treatment of water will not kill *Giardia,* a protozoan that causes severe diarrhea and lurks even in crystal clear streams. Heed park warnings about hypothermia and Lyme disease, which is carried by ticks. In western parks, take precautions to prevent Hantavirus pulmonary syndrome, a potentially fatal airborne virus transmitted by deer mice.

■ Expect RV detours. Check road regulations as you enter a park. Along some stretches of many roads you will not be able to maneuver a large vehicle, especially a trailer.

Campgrounds The National Parks Reservation System (NPRS) handles advance reservations for camp-grounds at the following Southwest parks: Carlsbad, Channel Islands, Death Valley, Grand Canyon, Joshua Tree, and Zion. For a single camp-site, reserve up to five months in advance by calling 800-365-2267, or visiting http:// reservations.nps .gov. Pay by credit card over the phone or Internet. Or, write to NPRS, 3 Commerce Dr., Cumberland, MD 21502. The National Recreation Reservation Service accepts reservations for Arches, Big Bend, Black Canyon of the Gunnison and Bryce National Parks as well as numerous Forest Service and BLM campsites. They can be reached at 877-444-6777, 877-833-6777 TDD, or 518-885-3639 (international callers); or by visiting www.ReserveUSA.com.

Hotels, Motels, & Inns The guide lists accommodations as a service to its readers. The lists are by no means comprehensive, and listing does not imply endorsement by the National Geographic. The information can change without notice. Many parks keep full lists of accommodations in their areas, which they will send you on request. You can also contact local chambers of commerce and tourist offices for accommodations suggestions.

Resources The back of this guide *(see pp. 342–45)* lists additional information: federal agencies, road conditions, state tourism organizations, fishing and hunting divisions, and other helpful phone numbers and websites.

Enjoy your explorations!

Arches

This national park contains more than 2,000 natural arches —the greatest concentration in the world. But numbers have no significance beside the grandeur of the landscape—the arches, the giant balanced rocks, spires, pinnacles, and slickrock domes against the enormous sky.

Perched high above the Colorado River, the park is part of southern Utah's extended area of canyon country, carved and shaped by eons of weathering and erosion. Some 300 million years ago, inland seas covered the large basin that formed this region. The seas refilled and evaporated—29 times in all—leaving behind salt beds thousands of feet thick in places. Later, sand and boulders carried down by streams from surrounding uplands eventually buried the salt beds beneath thick layers of stone. Because the salt layer is less dense than the overlying blanket of rock, it rises up through it, deforming it into domes and ridges, with valleys in between.

Most of the formations at Arches are made of soft red sandstone deposited 150 million years ago. Much later, groundwater began to dissolve the underlying salt deposits. The sandstone domes collapsed and weathered into a maze of vertical rock slabs called "fins." Sections of these slender walls eventually wore through, creating the spectacular rock sculptures that visitors to Arches see today.

The land has a timeless, indestructible look that is misleading. More than three-quarters of a million visitors each year threaten the fragile high desert ecosystem. One concern is a dark crust called crypto-biotic soil composed of algae, fungi, and lichens that grow in sandy areas in the park. Footprints tracked across this living community may remain visible for years. In fact, the aridity helps preserve traces of past activity for centuries. Visitors are asked to walk only on designated trails or stay on slickrock or wash bottoms.

- Southeast Utah, northwest of Moab
- 76,519 acres
- Established 1971
- Best seasons early spring and fall. Wildflowers peak in April and May
- Hiking, rock climbing, wildlife viewing, scenic drives, petroglyphs
- Information: 435-259-8161 www.nps.gov/arch

North Window, Arches National Park

How to Get There

From Moab, take US 191 north 5 miles to the park entrance. From I-70, exit at Crescent Junction and follow US 191 south for 25 miles to the entrance. Airports: 15 miles north of Moab and Grand Junction, Colorado, about 120 miles away.

When to Go

All-year, but spring and fall offer ideal temperatures for hiking in the high desert. Summers are hot, and winters are mild.

How to Visit

Take the **Arches Scenic Drive** at least as far as **The Windows Section.** If possible, carry on to the historic **Wolfe Ranch, Fiery Furnace,** and the **Devils Garden.** Also allow time for hiking at least one of the park's spectacular trails, perhaps to **Delicate Arch** or even **Tower Arch,** in the park's remote **Klondike Bluffs.**

If it's spring, summer, or fall (and you're not bothered by heights), consider joining a naturalist-led 3-hour hike through **Fiery Furnace** *(fee).* It's strenuous, but you'll appreciate the shade in summer's heat. Contact the visitor center for reservations *(recommended)* and tickets.

What Not to Miss

- **Garden of Eden rock formations**
- **Hike from Devils Garden Trail to Landscape Arch**
- **Afternoon hike to Courthouse Towers from the Park Avenue viewpoint trailhead**
- **Delicate Arch at sunset**
- **Ranger-led hike to Fiery Furnace**

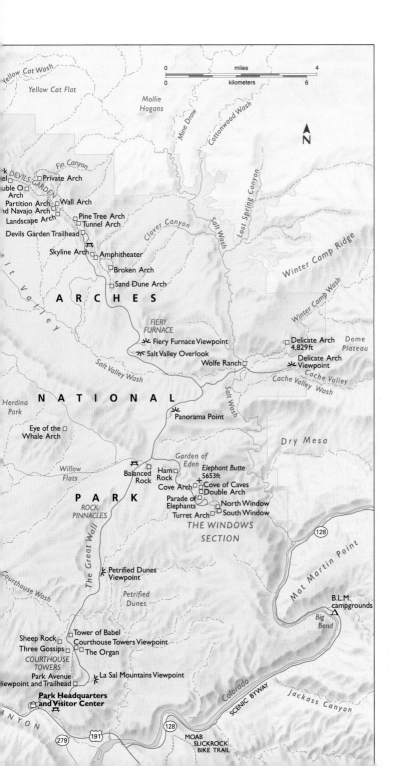

EXPLORING THE PARK

Arches Scenic Drive: 18 miles one way; a half to full day

The scenic drive climbs from the floor of Moab Canyon to Devils Garden, passing through the heart of the park with spur roads leading to The Windows Section, Wolfe Ranch, and the Delicate Arch area. Numerous pull-offs allow leisurely viewing of the park's major features.

From the visitor center the road winds up the canyon wall. Pull off after 2 miles at the **Park Avenue Viewpoint** and **Trailhead** for a view down an open canyon flanked by sandstone skyscrapers.

If you have a willing driver (or don't mind the 320-foot, uphill return climb), walk the easy 1-mile path to the **Courthouse Towers** parking area, where you can be picked up. Interpretive signs

Delicate Arch at sunset

describe nearby rock formations that exhibit the various stages in the birth and death of an arch.

Continue your drive to the beautiful slickrock expanse known as the **Petrified Dunes.** Here you skirt knolls—ancient dunes turned to stone—as the La Sal Mountains rise nearly 13,000 feet in the distance. Farther along, stop at the **Balanced Rock** pull-off where a 0.4-mile trail loops past this classic hoodoo, a strangely eroded rock spire 128 feet high. Edward Abbey wrote his classic *Desert Solitaire* after living in a trailer here as a park ranger.

Just beyond, turn onto the paved road leading to **The Windows.** The road to the right passes a cluster of pinnacles and monoliths called **Garden of Eden** and ends at a parking area fronted by a sandstone wall perforated by several arches. Short trails lead to closeup views of these colossal gateways. The 0.3-mile walk to **South Window,** 105 feet wide, also gives you good views of **North Window** and **Turret Arch.** If time allows walk the half-mile trail for a dramatic closeup look at **Double Arch.**

Retrace your route back to the main road. A bit farther along, a spur road leads 1.5 miles to historic **Wolfe Ranch,** where a Civil War veteran raised cattle around the turn of the 20th century, and **Delicate Arch Viewpoint,** 1 mile beyond the ranch. The distant view of Delicate Arch can be disappointing, so if you have the stamina and at least 2 extra hours consider hiking the **Delicate Arch Trail** from Wolfe Ranch *(see pp. 20–21).* Though it is one of the most rewarding hikes in canyon country, you may be better off saving Delicate Arch for a second day if you plan to take the full drive and other walks.

Return to the main road. Skip the **Salt Valley Overlook** but pull off at **Fiery Furnace,** a dense array of red fins that appear to ignite when the sun is low in the west. Here you see a world standing on end—hoodoos, spires, and slabs 200 feet high. It's easy to get lost in the maze of deeply grooved slots and dead-end passageways. *(Note that visitors who are not part of a guided walk will need a permit to explore Fiery Furnace.)*

Continue your drive 2 miles to the Sand Dune parking lot. Take the 0.2-mile walk to the cool shade of **Sand Dune Arch,** tucked between two fins, but you might want to save **Broken Arch** for another time. As you proceed along the road **Skyline Arch** soon comes into view. In 1940 a great rock mass broke away from the arch, doubling the size of its opening to 45 by 69 feet.

The road ends at the Devils Garden Campground and Trailhead beyond. The **Devils Garden Trail** meanders 7.2 miles to seven major arches, each with its own character. Be sure to save enough time to walk at least as far as **Landscape Arch,** 0.8 mile down the trail. Here a narrow ribbon of stone 306 feet long appears to defy gravity as it floats in a graceful span above a steep dune. It's one of the world's longest freestanding natural arches. From here, take the curving, primitive trail that leads for another mile to **Double O Arch.** If you walk the trail in early morning, watch for the white evening primrose. As the sunlight grows stronger, the flowers wilt, turning the petals pink. Double O Arch is a 160-foot-wide circular arch that hangs above a smaller bore. From here you can walk about half a mile to the rock spire known as the **Dark Angel.**

Delicate Arch Hike: 3 miles round-trip; at least 2 hours

This delightful trail gains 500 feet in elevation as it traverses 1.5 miles of slickrock as smooth and cambered as the back of a whale. It tops out, suddenly and dramatically, at the foot of **Delicate Arch,** a must-see.

As nature writer Edward Abbey put it in *Desert Solitaire,* "If Delicate Arch has any significance it lies, I will venture, in the power of the odd and unexpected to startle the senses and surprise the mind out their ruts of habit, to compel us into a re-awakened awareness of the wonderful—that which is full of wonder."

The hike begins on the grounds of the Wolfe Ranch, which include a weathered corral and a tattered log cabin. Follow the bridge across **Salt Wash** to the cliff on the left, where Ute Indians left petroglyphs. The Ute, who once roamed from the eastern slope of the Colorado Rockies to the canyonlands of southern Utah, camped here, probably trading with Wolfe for provisions.

The trail is ingeniously designed to hide Delicate Arch from view until your very last step. From the valley floor the route threads patches of cryptobiotic soil *(see page 105)* before reaching flat slabs of sandstone, where cairns mark the way. Juniper trees grow from cracks so small the trunks seem to emerge from solid rock. The final third of a mile is a teaser. As the path climbs, it hugs a sandstone fin, then edges along a steep bowl that bars all view of the famous arch. The last few steps require some nerve, but you will be rewarded with a marvelous look at Delicate Arch straddling the edge of a slickrock basin.

Travels by Camelback

You haven't traveled through canyon country until you've done so on a camel. The concept is not as wonky as it sounds: Paleontologists believe that camels originated in North America 40 million years ago, so the animals once likely roamed these high desert plateaus. Some camel species migrated to South America, where they evolved into today's llama and vicuña. Larger species crossed the land bridge to Asia and developed into two distinct species—the single-humped Arabian dromedary and the double-humped Bactrian of central Asia. Today you can enjoy a dromedary ride through the red-rock bluffs of Hurrah Pass, south of Moab, courtesy of Camelot Lodge *(435-259-9721. www.camelotlodge.com).*

Standing 45 feet tall at its highest point, Delicate Arch frames the La Sal Mountains, a fact that gave this extraordinary structure its original name—Landscape Arch. A cartographer's error, however, mislabeled Delicate Arch as Landscape Arch, and vice versa; the oversight was never corrected. The best time to photograph Delicate Arch is near sunrise or sunset. Time your evening hike for the full moon and you may have the thrill of seeing the moon rise above the arch—though the return trip in dim light can be tricky.

Tower Arch Trail: 2.4 miles; 2 hours

Located in the park's remote Klondike Bluffs area, this 1.2-mile one-way trail to **Tower Arch** winds through an intricate landscape of weird sandstone formations, cresting ridge tops now and then for outstanding vistas of the Fiery Furnace, the La Sal Mountains, Book Cliffs, and clusters of towering hoodoos.

To reach the trailhead, drive 1 mile south on the main park road from the Devils Garden parking lot, then turn west on the high-clearance road just past Skyline Arch. *(This unpaved road may be impassable during or after storms.)* Follow the road 7.7 miles through Salt Valley to the turnoff on the left for Tower Arch Trail.

Cairns direct you from the parking lot up a steep rock ridge, and the route soon leads down through a land littered with fins and other rock outcroppings to Tower Arch, which takes its name from the pinnacle standing nearby.

INFORMATION & ACTIVITIES

Headquarters
P.O. Box 907
Moab, Utah 84532
435-259-8161
www.nps.gov/arch

Visitor & Information Centers
Visitor center, on US 191 at the park entrance, is open every day all year-round.

Seasons & Accessibility
Park open year-round. Some unpaved roads may become temporarily impassable after heavy rains. Call headquarters for current conditions.

Entrance Fees
$10 per car per week allows multiple entries; $5 for walk-ins. Yearly fee of $25 is also good at Canyonlands NP, and Natural Bridges and Hoven-weep National Monuments.

Pets
Prohibited on all hiking trails and in the backcountry.

Facilities for Disabled
Visitor center and one of its rest rooms are wheelchair accessible. Rest room and one campsite accessible in Devils Garden Campground. Park Avenue and Delicate Arch Viewpoints are accessible to wheelchairs.

Things to Do
Naturalist-led activities: nature hikes and talks, evening programs *(check park bulletin boards for schedule)*. Also available: geological and historical exhibits, self-guided auto tour, hiking, jeep tours, flight-seeing. Contact park headquarters for concessionaires offering rental and guide services.

Special Advisories
■ Always carry water on hikes—at least a gallon a day per person is recommended in summer.
■ Stay on trails to protect fragile desert soils and plant life.
■ Sandstone slickrock crumbles easily and can make climbing dangerous. Consult a ranger.
■ Overnight backpacking permits required *(free from visitor center)*.

Campgrounds
One campground, Devils Garden, 52 sites with a 7-day limit. Open all year. Winter, first come, first served; March through October, preregister at the visitor center *(open 7:30 a.m.)*. Fees $10 per night. No showers. Tent and RV sites; no hookups. Reservations required for group sites *(tents only)*. Call 877-444-6777, or visit www.Re serveUSA.com. Nearby, the

Balanced Rock, poised above thickets of Utah juniper

BLM maintains 20 campgrounds. Call 435-259-2100, or visit www.blm.gov/utah/moab/rec-frame.html.

Hotels, Motels, & Inns

(Unless otherwise noted, rates are for two persons in a double room, high season.)

In Moab, UT 84532:

■ **Best Western Green Well Motel**
105 S. Main St. 435-259-6151 or 800-528-1234. 72 units. $79–$130. AC, pool, restaurant.

■ **Big Horn Travelodge**
550 S. Main St. 435-259-6171 or 800-325-6171. 58 units. $59–$79. AC, pool, restaurant. www.moabbighorn.com

■ **Cedar Breaks Condos**
Center and 4th E. 800-505-5343. Six 2-bedroom units with full kitchens. $75–$130. AC. www.moabutahlodging.com

■ **Pack Creek Ranch**
(15 miles southeast of Moab, off LaSal Mountain Loop Rd.)
P.O. Box 1270. 435-259-5505. Cabins, houses, bunkhouses. $95–$225, includes breakfast. Trail rides and massages for a fee. AC, pool. www.packcreek ranch.com

■ **Ramada Inn—Moab**
182 S. Main St. 435-259-7141 or 888-989-1988. 82 units. $49–$89. AC, pool, restaurant. www.ramadainnmoab.com

For other accommodations in the area, contact Utah's Canyonlands Region, 805 N. Main St., Moab, UT 84532. 800-233-8824.

Excursions from Arches

Colorado River Scenic Byway

5 miles south of Arches

44 miles; 2 hours Hugging the southeast side of the Colorado River as it winds below sheer cliffs of Wingate sandstone, this route passes isolated side canyons and the spectacular pinnacles known as Fisher Towers. Rafters and kayakers ply the muddy rapids, and sand beaches line the water's edge. The lively town of **Moab** *(Moab Information Center, 805 N. Main St.; see p. 28)* is a base for river runners, mountain bikers, four-wheel-drive enthusiasts, and rock climbers. Also nearby are the red-rock canyons of **Canyonlands National Park** *(see pp. 82–91).*

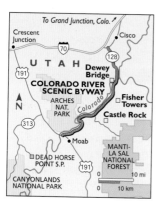

Drive 2 miles north of Moab on US 191, then turn right on Utah 128 for the Colorado River Scenic Byway. A band of roadside vegetation provides a lovely counterpoint to the red and orange hues of the sandstone cliffs. Three miles in, the road passes **Negro Bill Canyon,** named after an early settler. A 2-mile hike up the canyon leads to views of **Morning Glory Natural Bridge.** High across the river from the trailhead lie granaries where the ancestral Puebloans stored crops a thousand years ago.

The **Big Bend Recreation Area** offers a rest spot and sand beaches as the river makes a sweeping U-turn. Above Big Bend the Colorado picks up speed, and rapids begin to riffle the water. Several miles later, the canyon widens, and the road leaves the river. At about Milepost 15, Castle Valley Road heads east, winding up through knolls to **Castle Valley** and views of the high, often snowcapped La Sal Mountains.

Continuing north on Utah 128 for several more miles, you'll see to the south the impossibly slender shape of **Castle Rock,** site of several recent car commercials. At about Mile 21, a 2.2-mile, graded dirt road turns right off Utah 128 toward **Fisher Towers Recreation Site,** with views of soaring rock pinnacles. The 900-foot-high Titan and other pinnacles are remnants of an ancient floodplain. A 2-mile hike crosses to the foot of the spires, ducks through narrow canyons, crosses a steel ladder, and passes convoluted rock formations. The hike ends with spectacular views of adjacent **Onion Creek Canyon**. Five miles beyond Fisher Towers, the road crosses the river near the 1916 Dewey Bridge and heads through desert to I–70 near Cisco.

■ **East-central Utah, from Moab to Cisco** ■ **Road open all year** ■ **Best seasons spring and fall** ■ **Hiking, whitewater rafting and kayaking**

Manti-La Sal National Forest

Stretching south and east from central Utah into western Colorado, Manti-La Sal encompasses wildly divergent habitats, from the slickrock desert canyons near Moab to the lush, high alpine meadows of the La Sal Mountains. Diverse ecologically, this national forest is also diverse geographically. The Manti District lies roughly 150 miles north and west of Arches and embraces the forested Wasatch Plateau. Closer to the park lie two other districts: the Moab and the Monticello.

The Moab District takes in the high country of the La Sal Mountains, some of which are framed famously by **Delicate Arch** *(see pp. 20–21)*. Meanwhile, the Monticello district, located near The Needles section of Canyonlands National Park *(see pp. 82–91)*, preserves some of the area's ancient history.

Medicine Lake in the La Sal Mountains

Countless opportunities exist to explore the contrasting scenery. Start with a drive on the 60-mile-long **La Sal Mountain Scenic Loop**. The drive starts along the Colorado River Scenic Byway *(see p. 24)*, but soon breaks off at the Castle Valley Branch and climbs 4,000 feet into the foothills, forests, and quiet mountain lakes of the La Sals. Return to Moab via US 191.

To the south about 50 miles, the Monticello District also offers a scenic drive, the **Abajo Loop Scenic Backway**—40 miles of rugged dirt roads sometimes unsuitable for passenger cars. This section of the Abajo Mountains is known for its pictographs, petroglyphs, cliff dwellings, and the ruined cabins of early settlers.

■ **1.3 million acres** ■ **Central and southeast Utah and southwest Colorado** ■ **Best seasons late spring–fall** ■ **Camping, hiking, back-packing, mountain climbing, scenic drives** ■ **Contact the national forest, 599 W. Price River Dr., Price, UT 84501; 435-637-2817. www .mantilasal.fs.fed.us**

San Rafael Swell

80 miles
northwest of
Arches

Like a giant bowl inverted, the San Rafael Swell bulges out of the Colorado Plateau, exposing a won-derland of spires, buttes, and contorted canyons. The rock formations here, rivaling those of Canyonlands and Arches National Parks to the east, posed a massively insuperable obstacle to the crossing of southern Utah for 200 years. Today I-70 bisects the swell, giving motorists an easy route over this remarkable geologic feature.

The swell was clearly an impediment in 1776, when the Dominguez-Escalante expedition set off in search of a route to connect the Spanish settlements of New Mexico with southern California. Their efforts opened up the territory, and traffic through the swell increased; tragically, much of it was Indian slaves. Traders met in this area to sell Paiute, Goskute, and Ute women and children as servants in Spanish New Mexico and California. Even though this odious practice had been outlawed by Spain in 1650 and by Mexico at its independence in 1821, it continued into the early 1850s.

Famous western scout Kit Carson carried mail and military dispatches across the swell, while Butch Cassidy escaped into a rock maze here after one of his many robberies. Later on, generations of enterprising cattlemen rounded up and sold off the swell's wild horses; their cattle drives then trampled wide the paths that eventually became the first roads. During the 1950s, miners bumped along these same routes in search of uranium and natural gas.

Today it's four-wheelers kicking up the dust along the swell, plying a tangled network of roads that baffles the best of navigators. *(Please honor the signs prohibiting motorized travel in the swell's wilderness study areas.)* The most popular drive is **Wedge Overlook** and **Buckhorn Draw Road,** which leads to dramatic views of the **Little Grand Canyon** of the San Rafael River. To access the Wedge from I-70, head north 20 miles on Ranch exit 129 to a sign for Wedge Overlook. Turn left at the intersection and drive 6 miles to the parking area. The road drops from the overlook into a narrow slot of sandstone shaded by cottonwoods before reaching **Fullers Bottom,** the put-in for float trips on *(Continued on p. 30)*

San Rafael River

Moab Meanders

Moab, near the confluence of the Green and Colorado Rivers, is outdoor recreation central. Stop first at the **Moab Information Center** (*805 N. Main St.; 435-259-8825 or 800-635-6622*) to talk with seasoned Moabites or pick up publications covering all aspects of canyon country. Outfitters, bookstores, and sporting-goods stores line Main Street; their staff can suggest biking and hiking trails and loop tours.

Mountain Biking

It's hard to resist Moab's two-wheeled trails: Cycling options range from tours of mountain meadows to descents down rolling slickrock to passages through narrow slot canyons.

The challenging **Moab Slickrock Bike Trail** (*2.3 miles E of town, up Sand Flats Rd.*) is a rite-of-passage for fat-tire fanatics, yet it's not for zealots alone: You can sample slickrock touring on the 2.5-mile practice portion before continuing on the trail's 10.5-mile loop. With plenty of diversions to scenic viewpoints of the Colorado River, Moab, and the La Sal range, the normally four- to six-hour ride can easily expand to an all-day adventure.

The 14-mile (one way) **Gemini Bridges Trail** offers views of Arches National Park, the La Sals, and a pair of rock spans, called Gemini Bridges—hundreds of feet long. This easy to moderate ride starts on US 191 roughly 1 mile south of Utah 313, on the way to the Island in the Sky District of Canyonlands National Park.

For the ultimate in back-country biking, consider a multiday trip with vehicle support. A four-wheel-drive vehicle accompanies most guided tours, carrying food, gear, and the occasional bruised, scraped, or breathless biker.

The **White Rim Road** offers a classic tour of canyon country. The 3- to 7-day trip follows a jeep road along the mesa top of Island in the Sky, dropping 1,000 feet to a bench of White Rim sandstone. A maze of canyons lines one side of the trail; towering over your head on the other side are rock walls up to 1,500 feet tall.

If time (and your endurance for steep climbs) is limited, pedal the 21-mile **Shafer Trail Road** with Tag-a-Long Expeditions (*435-259-8946 or 800-453-3292*). This half-day trip descends 1,200 feet of switchbacks through a corner of Island in the Sky. The trip ends at the Colorado River, where the outfitter will meet you for a scenic return to the trailhead.

Biking on the White Rim Road

critical stopover for migrating raptors, shorebirds, and waterfowl. A 1-mile, wheelchair-accessible loop trail spans the wet spots with boardwalks, offers an easy path to the river, and leads to a two-story wildlife-viewing blind.

Moab's Skyway

Across the street from the Matheson preserve is Moab's Skyway *(435-259-7799. www.moab-utah.com/skyway)*. This chairlift ascends nearly 1,000 feet of red rock in less than 12 minutes.

At the top, a wheelchair-accessible boardwalk leads to a viewpoint and several foot trails. One short trail accesses the **Colorado Vista Overlook,** perched above the river gorge far below.

Follow the signs to **Panorama Point,** which offers a grand toss of red-rock spires and sandstone walls. Cliffrose, saltbush, rice grass, rabbit brush, and other plants are scattered across the rock. As you ride back down, look for petroglyphs between Towers 6 and 7, and 2 and 3.

If you'd rather hike back down, follow the **Moab Rim** and **Hidden Valley Trails,** which begin just south of the skyway's upper terminal and descend 7 miles to the base.

Wetlands Preserve

A refreshingly green refuge in a sprawl of red-rock desert, the 890-acre **Scott M. Matheson Wetlands Preserve** *(435-259-4629)* attracts nearly 200 species of birds, amphibians such as the northern leopard frog, and aquatic mammals including beavers, muskrat and river otters.

The preserve is named for a late governor of Utah, who was a tireless champion of conservation. Today it is the only high-quality wetlands area along the Utah shores of the Colorado River.

Conditions within the preserve change dramatically from day to day and from season to season. The best times to visit are spring, fall, and winter, when birds flock to the site, which is a the San Rafael River. This 15-mile, 5- to 6-hour river run is swift but free of rapids; the trip follows the high cliff walls of the canyon you saw at the overlook and ends at San Rafael Campground. Don't continue beyond the campground unless you are very experienced; the rapids are quite dangerous. The river is best floated during spring runoff in May or June. Side-canyon explorations can extend the trip into an overnighter.

A few of the swell's earliest hunters passed through **Black Dragon Canyon,** where they etched a dragonlike image in the walls, along with geometric shapes and animorphic forms. To get there from I-70, drive 14 miles west of Green River, Utah; turn north on a dirt road just past Milepost 145 and follow it for 1 mile. Turn left up a streambed to the canyon mouth; to see the petroglyphs, walk a quarter mile up the canyon.

Goblin Valley Road follows the **San Rafael Reef,** a saw of stone spires that rise 2,000 feet out of the desert and peak at Temple Mountain. The road ends at Goblin Valley State Park *(see below).* A walk through **Little Wild Horse Canyon**—a delightful day hike through a twisting sandstone ravine—begins near the park. Bone-dry most every day, the swell's canyons flash flood with reddish brown torrents of water during sudden rainstorms. Do not enter any of them when rain threatens. Before venturing into the swell, be sure you have the "Trails Illustrated San Rafael" map, or the "USGS San Rafael Desert" topographic map. Carry at least a gallon of water per person per day.

■ **65 miles long, 40 miles wide** ■ **East-central Utah, near the towns of Price and Green River** ■ **Best seasons spring and fall** ■ **Boating, rafting, biking, horseback riding, petroglyphs** ■ **Contact the BLM, P.O. Box 7004, Price, UT 84501; 435-636-3600. www.blm.gov/utah/price/default.htm**

Goblin Valley State Park

100 miles west of Arches

Its wind and water-worn formations make some people laugh. Others shake their heads in wonder at the profusion of spires, balanced boulders, and pedestals. Few places exhibit the appealingly mixed-up topography of Goblin Valley, an out-of-step cutup at the remote south end of that geologic chorus line known as the San Rafael Reef. Goblin Valley's bowl, however, is an ancient sea bottom whose layers of silt, mud, and sand formed this region's rusty red-brown, gray-green, and dark brown bands of sedimentary rock. Softer in some places than others, it erodes unevenly—after cloudbursts you'll see runoff—reshaping before your eyes the vast basin of improbable shapes adults liken to sculptures and young children treat as cartoon creatures come to life.

Remote to begin with, these sunbaked badlands, cliffs, and myriad eroded oddities, surrounded by imposing buttes, impart to hikers, campers, and day-tripping strollers a delightful sense of escape and discovery. If you visit in summer, be prepared for heat. The park is nearly treeless, its campground generally unshaded, and the stone formations radiate warmth long after midday.

As you enter the park, look for the **Observation Shelter** overlooking Goblin Valley. There's interesting geologic information here that corresponds to the unusual shapes before you, and a useful brochure of park trail routes will help you choose a walk. Short, easy footpaths wander down to the Goblins, which range in height from around 10 feet to 20 times that.

Two trails offer rewarding half-day hikes. The 1.5-mile **Carmel Canyon Loop** leaves from the Observation Shelter parking lot, drops into a canyon, and wanders among cliffs and badlands of red siltstone and sandstone in the direction of **Molly's Castle,** a towering, magnificent butte of greenish-gray Curtis Formation sediments.

The **Curtis Bench Trail** from the campground is a bit longer at 2 miles, and though its landscapes are similar to the Carmel Canyon trail, its rumpled up-and-down route is considered by some a more entertaining stroll. One spur leads into Goblin Valley; another winds up to a view of the north-south trending Henry Mountains, rising above 11,000 feet some 30 miles south, and a panorama of the San Rafael Plain.

Only hardy desert plant species, which have learned to survive fiery temperatures and constantly blowing sand, grow in the park's harsh environment. Along your hikes, look for Mormon tea, Russian thistle or tumbleweed, and various cactuses. Higher elevations sustain juniper and pinyon pine.

■ **3,654 acres** ■ **South-central Utah, near town of Green River** ■ **Adm. fee** ■ **Campground with showers, reservations advised in season; call 800-322-3770** ■ **Contact the park, Box 637, Green River, UT 84525; 435-564-3633. www.parks.state.ut.us**

Big Bend

A s the Rio Grande winds south along the Texas-Mexico border, it suddenly veers northward in a great horseshoe curve before continuing its journey. Inside the horseshoe lies the region of Texas known as the Big Bend; Big Bend National Park flanks the river at the southerly tip of the curve. A wild and surprising land, the park remains remote enough that only the dedicated reach it.

Chihuahuan Desert vegetation—bunchgrasses, creosote bushes, cactuses, lechuguillas, yuccas, and sotols—covers most of the terrain. But the Rio Grande and its lush floodplains and steep, narrow canyons almost form a park of their own. So do the Chisos Mountains; up to 20 degrees cooler than the desert floor, they harbor pine, juniper, and oak, as well as deer, mountain lions, bears, and other wildlife. Occasionally, a heavy rain transforms the desert: Normally dry creek beds roar with water, and seeds long dormant burst into fields of wildflowers.

The rocks of Big Bend are a complex lot. Two seas, one after another, flowed and subsided in the region hundreds of millions of years ago, leaving thick deposits of limestone and shale. The present mountains, except the Chisos, uplifted along with the Rockies, roughly 75 million years ago. Around the same time, a 40-mile-wide trough—most of today's park—sank along fault lines, leaving the cliffs of Santa Elena Canyon to the west and the Sierra del Carmen to the east rising 1,500 feet above the desert floor. In the center, volcanic activity spewed layer upon layer of ash into the air and squeezed molten rock up through the ground to form the Chisos Mountains some 35 million years ago.

Big Bend's topographic variety supports a remarkable diversity of life, including 1,200 plant species—some found nowhere else in the world. More species of birds—more than 400—have been counted here than in any other national park.

- Southwest Texas
- 801,163 acres
- Established 1944
- Best seasons spring, fall, and winter
- Hiking, boating, bird-watching, wildflower viewing, scenic drives
- Information: 432-477-2251 www.nps.gov/bibe

Chisos Mountains, Big Bend National Park

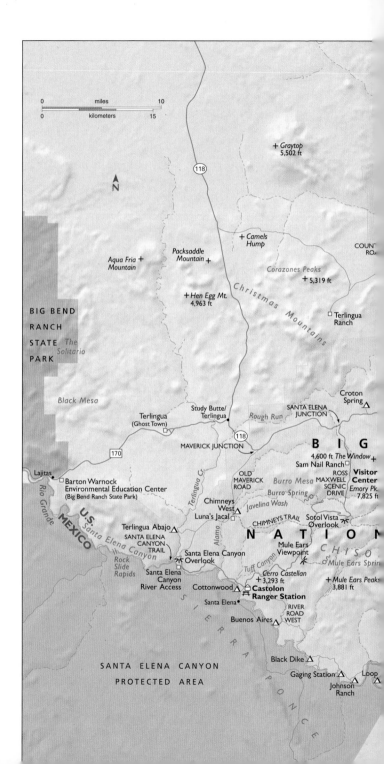

miles 0 10
kilometers 0 15

N

118

+ Graytop
5,502 ft

+ Camels
Hump

Packsaddle
Mountain +

Aqua Fria +
Mountain

Corazones Peaks
+ 5,319 ft

+ Hen Egg Mt.
4,963 ft

Christmas Mountains

□ Terlingua
Ranch

BIG BEND

RANCH

STATE *The*
Solitario
PARK

Black Mesa

Croton
Spring △

Terlingua
(Ghost Town)
□

Study Butte/
Terlingua ●

Rough Run

SANTA ELENA
JUNCTION

118

MAVERICK JUNCTION

170

B I G

4,600 ft *The Window* +
Sam Nail Ranch □

ROSS **Visitor**
MAXWELL **Center**
SCENIC *Emory Pk.*
DRIVE 7,825 ft

Lajitas ●

□ Barton Warnock
Environmental Education Center
(Big Bend Ranch State Park)

Rio Grande

U.S.
MEXICO

Santa Elena Canyon

OLD
MAVERICK
ROAD

Burro Mesa

Burro Spring +

Javelina Wash

Chimneys
West △

Luna's Jacal □

CHIMNEYS TRAIL

Sotol Vista 🔭
Overlook

Terlingua Abajo △

SANTA ELENA
CANYON
TRAIL

*Rock
Slide
Rapids*

Alamo

Santa Elena Canyon
Overlook

N A T I O N

Mule Ears
Viewpoint 🔭

C H I S O

○ *Mule Ears Sprin*

Santa Elena
Canyon
River Access

Tuff Canyon

Cerro Castellan
+ 3,293 ft

Cottonwood △ 🏕 **Castolon**
Ranger Station

+ *Mule Ears Peaks*
3,881 ft

Santa Elena ●

S I E R R A

Buenos Aires △

RIVER
ROAD
WEST

P O N C E

Black Dike △

SANTA ELENA CANYON

PROTECTED AREA

Gaging Station △ Loop
△

Johnson
Ranch

COUNT
RO.

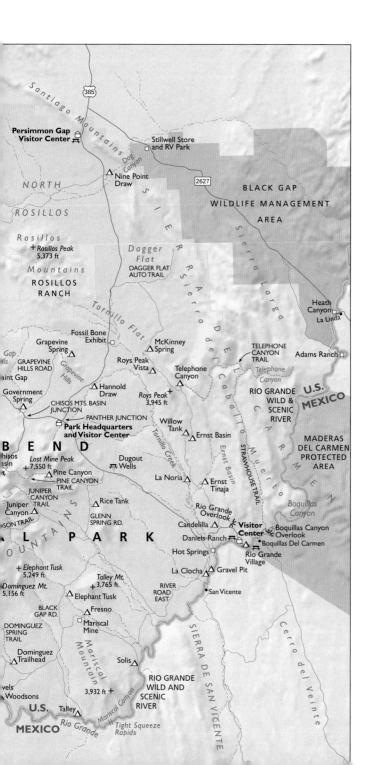

How to Get There

US 385 leads from Marathon to the north entrance of the park; Tex. 118 from Alpine leads to the west entrance; FM 170, from Presidio, joins Tex. 118 shortly before the west entrance. Airports: El Paso (325 miles) and Midland-Odessa (230 miles).

When to Go

All-year park, though fall and winter may be the best seasons. Deciduous leaves turn color in the mountains in autumn; winters are mild. Summer temperatures in the desert can exceed 110°F; the Chisos Mountains remain cooler. If enough rain falls, the desert blooms stunningly in early spring, and again in late summer. Bird-watching is good all year, but especially March through May.

How to Visit

Allow several days, especially if you plan to hike. Explore the **Chisos Mountains Basin** and the **Ross Maxwell Scenic Drive,** engineered to take you past many of the park's geological and scenic highlights. Ideally, devote the better part of a day to each area. With extra time on the second afternoon, or on a third day, drive out to **Rio Grande Village** and the **Boquillas Canyon**

What Not to Miss

- A hike along Lost Mine Trail
- Late afternoon sunset hike on Window View Trail
- Ross Maxwell Scenic Drive
- Old ranch house and windmills at Sam Nail Ranch
- Nature trail at Boquillas Canyon Overlook
- Float trip on the Wild & Scenic Rio Grande

Overlook to experience the river environment and enjoy views of the Sierra del Carmen, particularly spectacular at sunset. On your way in or out, view the landscape and exhibits along US 385 between **Panther Junction** and **Persimmon Gap.** For an extended visit, try more of the many rewarding hikes, drive some dirt roads, and consider a leisurely float trip along the Rio Grande through one of the park's three major canyons.

EXPLORING THE PARK

Touring Chisos Basin: 10 miles; a half day

Start your tour at the visitor center at Panther Junction. Collect maps, information on hiking, and safety tips on avoiding encounters with rattlesnakes, mountain lions, and flash floods. Don't miss **Panther Path**—the 50-yard nature trail near the visitor center entrance whose self-guiding pamphlet provides an excellent introduction to the plants you'll see on much of your trip.

Behind the visitor center lie the **Chisos Mountains,** the southernmost range in the continental United States, and your destination. Turn left out of the visitor center, drive 3 miles, and take another left at Basin Junction. Ahead on the right looms **Pulliam Bluff.** Look closely and you might see in the mountain the profile of a man's face, reclining. Legend relates that the man is Alsate, an important Apache chief whose ghost lives on in the high Chisos Mountains, and whose campfire can occasionally be seen at night.

After 2.5 miles, the jagged summit of **Lost Mine Peak** hoves into view to your left. Spanish explorers, it is told, discovered a rich silver mine near the summit and enslaved Indians to work it. The miners rebelled, killed their overlords, and sealed the entrance to the mine so that it might remain lost forever. As you drive on, the castlelike summit of **Casa Grande**—"big house"—will be straight ahead, a landmark for much of the park.

The road climbs higher into the mountains through a canyon called **Green Gulch:** Watch the vegetation change from desert shrub to sotol grasslands, then to pinyon pine, juniper, and oak woodland. The Chisos form a cooler, moister island in the surrounding desert. Some 10,000 years ago, pinyon-juniper forests extended down to the desert floor, but the trees withdrew to higher altitudes as the climate gradually warmed at the end of the Ice Age.

In about 5 miles the road hits its highest point at **Panther Pass** (5,770 feet), named for the mountain lions that still roam these hills—only the lucky few ever see one. If you have time, park at the nearby trailhead for the **Lost Mine Trail,** a self-guided nature trail with an informative booklet. The panorama from the top, one of the grandest in the park, makes the moderately strenuous 4.8-mile round-trip well worth the trek. But if you're short of time, just hike the 2-mile round-trip to the **Juniper Canyon Overlook,** which offers good vistas of wooded Juniper Canyon to the south and Pulliam Bluff to the northwest.

Beyond Panther Pass, the road descends in hairpin curves to **Chisos Basin,** a 3-mile-wide depression in the mountains chiseled by wind and water. Many of the park's choice hikes start here, from a trailhead west of the ranger station. At the very least, make sure to stroll the easy 0.3-mile round-trip **Window View Trail.** Particularly photogenic at sunset, the **Window** is a V-shaped opening, or "pour off," in the mountains, through which all rain and meltwater from the basin drains. A more challenging trek—**The Window Trail**— descends through desert and shady canyon to the Window itself, offering classic afternoon views of Casa Grande framed by oaks and pines. In summer, take this and other lower elevation hikes in early morning or late afternoon in order to avoid the heat.

The literal high point of many visitors' trips to the park is a hike to the **South Rim** (7,400 feet), a moderately steep 13-mile round-trip that provides unforgettable vistas of much of the park. At **Boot Canyon,** 4.5 miles up the trail to the South Rim, lives an oasis of bigtooth maple, Douglas-fir, and Arizona pine. The gray-and-yellow Colima warbler nests on the canyon floor, its only home in the United States.

Before you hike, check at the Chisos Basin Visitor Center for maps and hiking tips, and make sure you carry plenty of water. At the visitor center, ask also about the presence of peregrine falcons. Several of these endangered birds nest in the Chisos.

Ross Maxwell Scenic Drive: 30 miles one-way; a half day

This trip crosses the heart of Big Bend's Chihuahuan Desert from Santa Elena Junction to Castolon, a dusty old Army post. From there, the route begins to skirt the Rio Grande, sampling the river's distinct water-loving plant and animal communities and offering plunging vistas of some of its canyons. This is an especially reward-ing drive if you can get an early start, when birds and other ani-mals are most active.

Heading south from Santa Elena Junction, **Burro Mesa**—named for the burros that once grazed the top—stands to your right, and the Chisos to your left. After 2 miles, stop at the exhibit on the left for a fine view of the Window framing Casa Grande.

Drive on a little over a mile, then park at the old **Sam Nail Ranch** and stroll the short path to the remains of windmills and a ranch house. The shade of the pecan and willow trees the Nails planted makes a fine resting and bird-watching spot.

Mighty Flier

Fossils of several types of dinosaurs and other ancient creatures have been found in the Big Bend area, including duck-billed dinosaurs and a crocodile estimated to have been 50 feet long. The most amazing, however, is the giant pterodactyl, named *Quetzalcoatlus northropi,* found in Big Bend National Park in 1971. With a wingspan estimated at 36 to 39 feet, it was the largest flying creature ever to exist on Earth. The original fossil wing bones are displayed at the University of Texas Memorial Museum in Austin. Houston's Museum of Natural Science has a full-size model of Quetzalcoatlus's entire skeleton looming over its dinosaur room, giving a hint of the incredible spectacle this monster must have presented as it soared through the skies of what is now West Texas

About a mile beyond the ranch, long walls of rock traverse the landscape. They are dikes, created by molten rock that squeezed up into underground cracks before hardening. The softer rock layers that encased them eventually eroded away, leaving behind the harder, more resistant dikes.

Stop next at the **Blue Creek Ranch** (Homer Wilson Ranch) **Over-look.** A century ago most of Big Bend was cloaked in grasses. But ranchers grazed thousands of cattle, sheep, and goats, destroying the grass and exposing the topsoil to erosion. Creosote, mesquite, allthorn, and other spiny shrubs moved into the damaged areas. Here, and elsewhere in the park, grasses are slowly returning.

Back on the road, take a quick left onto the **Sotol Vista** spur road, named for the ridge's rich growth of sotol, the bright green plant with sawlike teeth on the edges of its leaves. Native Americans roasted and ate the heart of the sotol and fermented it to yield an alcoholic drink. The parking lot at the top provides vistas of the surrounding mountains, and a sign at the end of the loop identifies landmarks.

About 6.5 miles beyond the Sotol Vista spur, an exhibit on the left side of the main road describes how volcanism shaped Big Bend's striking landscape. Farther along on the left, another spur road offers an excellent view of the peaks known as **Mule Ears,** a name explained at a glance. During the 1930s, Army Air Corps pilots drilled by flying planes between the twin peaks.

Another 4.5-mile stretch along the main road brings you to an overlook of **Tuff Canyon,** carved by **Blue Creek** through layers of lava flows, boulders, and compressed volcanic ash called tuff. Stroll the short trail to the right to view the canyon. The trail at the left of the parking lot provides a moderately steep hike down into the canyon, a 0.75-mile round-trip.

The road soon approaches **Cerro Castellan,** another important landmark which rises 1,000 feet above its surroundings. Turn left into **Castolon** to stroll around the old Army outpost built to deter bandits during the 1914-18 border troubles with Mexico. The main building, which was originally the barracks, was converted to a frontier trading post around 1920. Today you can buy cold drinks and picnic there.

After leaving Castolon, the road parallels the Rio Grande, passing the scattered remains of adobe houses dating back to the turn of the 20th century. The occupants once grew food crops and cotton in the Rio Grande's fertile floodplain.

Be sure to stop about 8 miles beyond Castolon, at the parking area for the **Santa Elena Canyon Overlook.** Laden with abrasive silt and gravel, the Rio Grande sculpted the canyon 1,500 feet deep, through the cliffs that tower above the geological trough that forms the bulk of the park.

Drive on to the end of the road, put on some old shoes, and, if the water is low, wade across Terlingua Creek to reach the **Santa Elena Canyon Trail.** The moderate 1.7-mile round-trip trail leads into the canyon, amply rewarding the hiker with striking views.

Descent to Boquillas Canyon: 24 miles; a half to full day

This one-way tour starts at Panther Junction and heads southeast, descending nearly 2,000 feet through the Chihuahuan Desert and terminating near the willows and cottonwoods of the Rio Grande. Before setting off, check at the visitor center for the condition of the Hot Springs road, an enticing spur that leads to a hot springs along the Rio Grande.

About 6.5 miles from the visitor center, turn left onto an unpaved road to see the spring at **Dugout Wells,** formerly the site of a ranch and schoolhouse and now a fine place to picnic and watch for wildlife.

Continuing along the main road, the peak aptly named **Elephant Tusk** will be on your right in the distance, and **Chilicotal Mountain** closer to the road. Far ahead looms the Sierra del Carmen in Mexico. Its striated rock formations are the same limestone and shale as in the cliffs at Santa Elena Canyon.

If you're up to a somewhat rough ride and conditions warrant, take the turnoff to **Hot Springs,** whose mineral waters were valued for centuries. Look for native pictographs on the cliffs along the trail to the springs, just beyond the old motel.

After returning to the main road, pull over at the **Rio Grande Overlook** just past the tunnel on the right and stroll a 50-yard trail for superb views of the Sierra del Carmen, the river floodplain, and part of Boquillas del Carmen village in Mexico. Big Bend bluebonnets bloom profusely here during a well-watered springtime.

Back on the road, continue straight for half a mile, then turn left and proceed another 3 miles to the paved spur road to **Boquillas Canyon Overlook.** Turn left onto the main road, then left again to visit **Rio Grande Village,** an excellent place to watch birds. Don't miss the **nature trail** starting across from site no. 18 in the campground. This easy 0.75-mile loop leads through junglelike floodplain vegetation before climbing onto a ridge that provides terrific views of the river and the Sierra del Carmen.

Journey to Persimmon Gap: 26 miles, one-way; 2 hours

This drive from park headquarters at Panther Junction to Persimmon Gap, the park's northern entrance, follows an ancient trail used by the Comanche on their annual raiding forays into Mexico, and by Army expeditions, settlers, and miners of silver and lead.

The road descends gently to Tornillo Creek and **Tornillo Flat,** one of the park's most overgrazed and poorly recovered areas. The mountains forming the ridge to the east are the Dead Horse Mountains, the Sierra del Carmen's northernmost reach.

Highlights along the way include a view of **Dog Canyon,** through which camels once lumbered in a 19th-century Army experiment, and, near the north end of the Tornillo Creek bridge, an exhibit of fossil mammal bones; the fossils were found in the park in sandstone dating from 50 million years ago.

For an excellent self-guided auto tour, pick up a pamphlet at either end of the road and, if it's springtime, ask whether the giant dagger yuccas are in bloom. (If so, be sure to take the unpaved **Dagger Flat Auto Trail** to see stalkfuls of white blooms weighing up to 70 pounds; if not, skip the detour.)

INFORMATION & ACTIVITIES

Headquarters
1 Panther Junction
Big Bend NP, TX 79834
432-477-2251
www.nps.gov/bibe

Visitor & Information Centers
Panther Junction and Chisos Basin Visitor Centers open daily all year. Contact headquarters for visitor information.

Seasons & Accessibility
Open all year. Check current conditions before heading out on dirt roads.

Entrance Fee
$15 per car per week.

Pets
Prohibited from all trails, public buildings, on the Rio Grande or anywhere off established roadways. May not be left unattended in campgrounds or in vehicles. There are no kennels available.

Facilities for Disabled
Visitor centers and two nature trails are wheelchair accessible. Free brochure.

Things to Do
Free naturalist-led activities include nature walks, workshops, and evening programs. Check park bulletin boards or visitor centers for current schedule. Other activities include hiking, fishing, river-running *(permit required)*, cycling, and nature seminars.

Special Advisories
■ Backcountry camping permits required; free, but must be obtained in person at visitor centers or ranger stations within 24 hours of trip.
■ Backcountry campers should never camp in dry washes, arroyos, or below the high-water mark of any river.
■ Wood fires prohibited, as are ground fires of any kind. Stoves and charcoal fires must be attended at all times.
■ Drink plenty of water, at least a gallon a day, more if hiking in summer.
■ Swimming in the Rio Grande can be dangerous due to drop-offs and strong undercurrents.
■ Climbers should be wary of abundance of unstable rock.

Campgrounds
Three campgrounds with 14-day limit. Open all year, first come, first served. Fees $10 per night. Tent and RV sites. At Rio Grande Village Trailer Park, full hookups only available. Three group campgrounds; reservations through headquarters for groups of ten or more.

Lightning over the Chisos Mountains, Big Bend National Park

Hotels, Motels, & Inns

(Unless otherwise noted, rates are for two persons in a double room, high season.)

INSIDE THE PARK:

■ **Chisos Mountains Lodge**
National Park Concessions, Inc., Big Bend NP, TX 79834. 432-477-2291. 72 rooms, including 6 cottages. $84–$104. AC, restaurant. www.chisos mountainlodge.com

OUTSIDE THE PARK
In Terlingua, TX 79852:
■ **Big Bend Motor Inn**
(FM 118 and 170) P.O. Box 336. 432-371-2218 or 800-848-2363. 86 rooms, 10 with kitchenettes, 4 duplexes with kitchens. $85–$145. AC, pool, restaurant. www.textbest motels.com

■ **Lajitas Resort** (on FM 170) Star Rte. 70, Box 400. 432-424-3471 or 877-525-4827. 70 rooms; 2 houses. $185–$450. AC, pool, restaurants. www .lajitas.com.

In Marathon, TX 79842:
■ **Gage Hotel** (US 90 and US 385) P.O. Box 46. 432-386-4205 or 800-884-4243. 39 units. $69–$225. AC, restaurant, pool. www.gagehotel.com

For a full list of accommodations, contact the Alpine Chamber of Commerce at 432-837-2326; or the Marathon Chamber of Commerce at 432-386-4516. www.marathon texas.net. For more suggestions, visit www.visitbigbend.com.

Adaptation to the Desert

E xcept for high elevation peaks and mesas, the word "desert" defines the vast majority of lands in the Southwest. Adaptation, then, to arid conditions is the prerequisite and primary theme of life for the region's plants and animals. Whether they live in the Chihuahuan, Mojave, or Sonoran Desert *(illustrated below)*, plants and animals have developed many tricks for survival.

As for plants, many annuals produce tough seeds that lie dormant for years. When enough rain falls, they sprint through their life cycle in a matter of weeks. Many perennials also rely on dormancy during drought. The whiplike ocotillo, for example, leafs out and blooms during irregular rains, then goes dormant—a cycle repeated as many as five times a year.

Tiny leaves help shrubs and trees conserve water. Some plants tap deep underground water sources with extremely long roots; others, such as cactuses, cast a broad but shallow net of roots to quickly gather surface water. Expandable tissue stores water for long periods. Thick, waxy skin slows evaporation. Spines provide shade and reflect heat.

Most desert animals simply avoid the intense summer heat.

Organ pipe cactus

Rattlesnake

Javelina

Paloverde

Ocotillo
Cactus wren
Kangaroo rat
Roadrunner
Gila monster

Coyote
Teddybear cholla

Birds may fly to cooler climates. Some reptiles, rodents, bats, and larger animals such as foxes and skunks spend the day in underground burrows or dens. Many are nocturnal. Diurnal mammals, such as the round-tailed ground squirrel, may pass the summer and winter in a state of torpor. The huge ears of jackrabbits cool their blood quickly as they rest in shady places. Kangaroo rats get the water they need from food alone.

Gila woodpecker

Saguaro cactus

Ironwood tree

Elf owl

Prickly pear cactus

Desert tortoise

Mesquite

Gambel's quail

Hedgehog cactus

Bighorn sheep

obe allow

Lupine

Gold poppy

Excursion from Big Bend

Big Bend Ranch State Park

20 mile west of Big Bend

Big Bend Ranch State Park sprawls northward from the Rio Grande, just west of Big Bend National Park. Its 526 square miles—comprising half of Texas's parkland—are composed mostly of desert grassland. The river acts as a long, narrow oasis, providing habitat for an incomparable variety of plants and animals (mountain lions still roam the rocky slopes, and golden eagles cruise the canyons) that otherwise would be absent from this parched land.

Your adventure begins as you drive northwest from Lajitas on FM 170. Known as El Camino del Rio, or the **River Road,** it surely ranks among the most breathtakingly scenic drives in America. With the Rio Grande on one side and the Bofecillos Mountains on the other, the route twists and curls, climbs, and descends for 50 miles of ever changing views of a landscape shaped by ancient seas, continental collision, scarring volcanoes, and eroding rivers. Enjoy the surroundings, but drive with caution. Be especially careful at the road's many low-water crossings, and don't enter water that

Rio Grande flowing through Big Bend Ranch State Park

looks deep or fast-flowing and muddy.

Start at the **Barton Warnock Environmental Education Center** *(432-424-3327. Adm. fee),* near Lajitas, for your introduction to the area's natural history. Walk through the 2.5-acre botanical garden, which displays such typical regional plants as the lechuguilla. Ask center personnel about some of the 32 miles of new park trails and road conditions; also check on upcoming events such as photography workshops, longhorn cattle drives, or horseback rides.

As you follow the River Road, look for the **Closed Canyon Trail,** an easy, shaded walk through a narrow, steep-sided gorge of welded tuff. For something a bit more challenging, drive west a short distance to the West Rancherias Trailhead. There, the **Rancherías Canyon Trail** leads up a canyon past ancient lava flows to a waterfall. Although the entire out-and-back distance is 9.6 miles, beautiful canyonland begins after just 2 miles or so, making shorter walks highly rewarding.

Continue northwest toward Presidio; a few miles past the park's western border, consider turning right onto gravel **Casa Piedra Road** (FM 169), which runs for more than 30 miles into the mountains. *(Large motor homes may have difficulty on this road.)* Listen for desert birds, or at dusk, the eerie howling of coyotes. Mule deer and javelinas (small piglike creatures) are seen often, but it's a lucky traveler indeed who catches even a glimpse of their predator, the mountain lion.

The road leads to Sauceda, where lodging is available in the old ranch headquarters buildings. Beyond Sauceda, you'll find splendid views of the imposing laccolith formation called the **Solitario,** and a lookout point into Fresno Canyon. Two of the park's news hiking/ mountain biking trails are located here. The 7.5-mile Encino loop trail and the 5-mile Horsetrap Trail explore the geologic formation of the Bofecillos Mountains.

Back on the River Road, continue northwest to **Fort Leaton State Historical Site** *(432-229-3613. Adm. fee),* one of two places where you can pay fees and obtain information about Big Bend Ranch.

■ **337,000 acres** ■ **Southwest Texas, near Presidio** ■ **Year-round** ■ **Hiking, rafting, mountain biking, scenic drives** ■ **Adm. fee** ■ **11 primitive campgrounds, 3 river sites, 2 group campsites, dormitory accommodations (30 bunk beds fill up quickly)** ■ **Contact park, P.O. Box 1180, Presidio, TX 79845; 432-229-3416. www.tpwd.state.tx.us/park**

Black Canyon of the Gunnison

Sheer walls of dark gray stone rise more than 2,600 feet above the swift and turbulent Gunnison River to create one of the most dramatic canyons in the country. Deeper than it is wide in some places, this great slit in the Earth is so narrow that sunlight penetrates to the bottom only at midday. The national park protects the deepest, most thrilling 14 miles of the gorge, about 75 miles upstream of the Gunnison's junction with the Colorado River.

Imagine chiseling two parallel walls of hard gneiss and schist running the length of Manhattan and standing higher than two Empire State Buildings stacked atop one another, with water as your only tool. At the inconceivable rate of 1 inch per century, it would take all of human history just to cut through 5 feet of rock. What you see from the rim is the product of two million years of patient work.

The metamorphic rocks exposed at the bottom of the canyon are nearly two billion years old, dating from the Precambrian or oldest era of the Earth. Here and there swirling pink veins of igneous pegmatite shoot through the walls, livening up the canyon's somber appearance.

Native American and white explorers generally avoided the formidable canyon up through the 19th century. In 1900, five men attempted to run the river in wooden boats to survey it as a possible source of irrigation for the Uncompahgre Valley. After a month, with their boats in splinters and their supplies gone, they gave up. But the next year two men ran it in 9 days on rubber air mattresses. A water diversion tunnel was soon in the works; the four-year project, completed in 1909, resulted in a 6-mile-long tunnel through rock, clay, and sand. The labor was so grueling and dangerous that the average period of employment was only two weeks.

- West central Colorado, near Montrose
- 30,244 acres
- Established 1999
- Best months May, June, and September
- Camping, hiking, kayaking, bird-watching, wildlife viewing, auto tour
- Information: 970-641-2337 www.nps.gov/blca

Precambrian-era gneiss and schist along Black Canyon's Gunnison River

Today, three dams upstream have further tamed the Gunnison, but the canyon and its section of river remain wild.

Rim drives and hikes offer plenty of opportunities for peering into the magnificent canyon and marveling at its cliffs and towers of stone. Ravens, golden eagles, and peregrine falcons soar the great gulf of air out in front. On top grows a thick forest of Gambel oak and serviceberry, which provide cover for mule deer and black bear, while farther down the canyon Douglas-firs thrive in the shade, and cottonwoods and box elders find footholds along the river.

How to Get There
The South Rim is located 15 miles northeast of Montrose, via US 50 and Colo. 347. The North Rim is 80 miles by car from the South Rim, via US 50, Colo. 92, and the North Rim Road (15 miles, last half unpaved). Airports: Montrose and Gunnison.

When to Go
Summer is the most popular time to visit. But bring lots of water if you intend to hike at midday on exposed trails. Crisp days in late spring and early fall are ideal for hikes. Winter affords opportunities

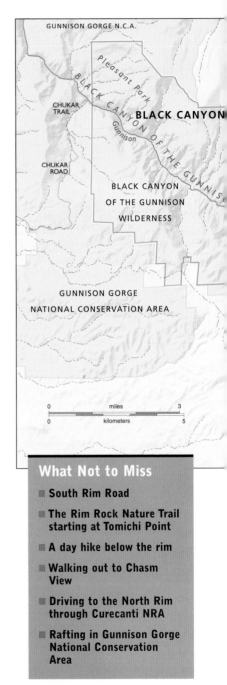

What Not to Miss
- **South Rim Road**
- **The Rim Rock Nature Trail starting at Tomichi Point**
- **A day hike below the rim**
- **Walking out to Chasm View**
- **Driving to the North Rim through Curecanti NRA**
- **Rafting in Gunnison Gorge National Conservation Area**

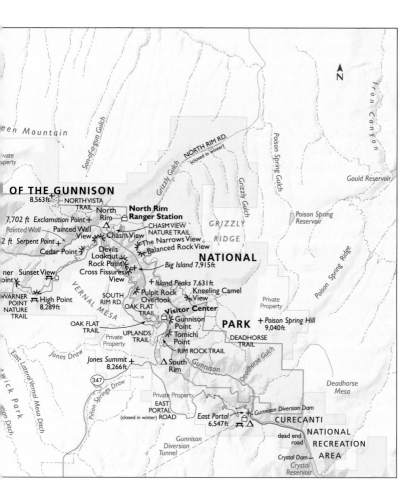

for backcountry camping, cross-country skiing, and snowshoeing. With the rim at 8,000 feet above sea level, winter can set in as early as November and last until April. Snow closes vehicle access to the North Rim; the South Rim road stays open as far as the second overlook year-round.

How to Visit

You can spend most of a day driving the 7-mile one-way **South Rim Road** and exploring its 5 or so miles of trails. Save the afternoon, or a second day, to appreciate the canyon from below by hiking down to the river. With more time, visit the **North Rim** and its 5-mile unpaved drive.

EXPLORING THE PARK

South Rim Road: 7 miles one way; a half to full day

This beautiful drive along the brink of Black Canyon connects Tomichi Point to High Point, with a dozen wondrous scenic overlooks and plenty of chances for short hikes and strolls along the way. One overlook, **Gunnison Point,** is also the location of a rewarding visitor center where exhibits interpret the geology and natural history of the canyon. All these stops offer expansive vistas, but highest on the list of most impressive views and greatest variety of scenery are **Chasm View** and, 2 miles farther along, **Sunset View,** both located along the last third of the drive.

Start at **Tomichi Point,** where a short path leads to a breathtaking vista of the abyss, then drive on to Gunnison Point, which in addition to the visitor center offers a fine network of short hiking trails. If you're inclined to a do a bit of walking begin with the **Rim Rock Nature Trail,** a self-guided interpretive path winding along the rim of the canyon for about a mile from visitor center to campground. The trail gives you excellent views of the vertiginous walls of the eastern part of the canyon and the glinting ribbon of the Gunnison River sluicing down its middle. You walk through a scrubby forest of Gambel oak and sagebrush, studded with pinyon pine and juniper, with its dark purple berries and a cedary look and smell. Breathe in the refreshing air; look for tracks of elk, bobcat, mountain lion, and other rim dwellers; and listen for the scold of Steller's jays.

Painted Wall above Gunnison River

Rather than double back, make a 2-mile loop by following the **Uplands Trail,** which crosses to the opposite side of the road and opens up splendid vistas of the canyon to the north as it returns to the visitor center.

You can extend your jaunt by adding another invigorating loop called the **Oak Flat Trail,** a 2-mile hike that drops below the rim and offers two excellent viewpoints, and winds through thickets of scrub oak, aspen groves, and Douglas-fir.

Hardcore hikers may be interested to note that one of the shortest ways to the canyon floor, the **Gunnison Route,** breaks off from the Oak Flat Trail. It's a mere mile to the river, but it's a tough one—the walk down takes at least an hour. Hikers end up following drainage gullies, which plunge 1,800 vertical feet over scree slopes littered with big rocks. To avoid ankle injuries in some places, crouch and slide. A mounted 80-foot-long chain helps out on one stretch, but the rest is a wild free-for-all. At the bottom, rest and massage your legs, staring up at the spectacular stonework all around. The walk back up—at times a hand-over-hand pull—is harder, of course, than the downhill.

Before driving out along the road, you might look over the schedule of programs posted at the visitor center. Most national parks take justifiable pride in their interpretive activities, but Black Canyon's are a definite cut above the norm. The geology programs in particular are worth going out of your way to attend—check out "Scrap-Booking with the Earth," "Once Upon a Time," "Tales of the Sausage Rock," "Time in the Canyon," or "Muscle, Hammer, and Chisel." In addition, "Canyon Caravan," the excellent ranger-led auto tour along the South Rim, gives visitors a thorough overview of canyon geology.

On the road drive northwest to the aptly named **Pulpit Rock,** which offers a terrific long view of the river knifing its way through the canyon. Other terrific stops along this section of the road include **Cross Fissures View, Rock Point,** and **Devils Lookout**—all with short walks leading to great vistas of the canyon.

Farther along and right beside the road, **Chasm View** overlook perches within about 1,100 feet of the North Rim on the opposite side of the canyon. At this point, the canyon's 1,800-foot depth exceeds its width, and it does indeed look extremely narrow. In fact, no canyon in America is at once so deep, so narrow, and so sheer. The narrowness is a result of the river's steep gradient—within the canyon, the Gunnison drops an average of 95 feet per mile.

The steep gradient is thanks in part to an uplift that wrenched apart the terrain in this section of Colorado some 60 million years ago. This allowed the river to cut through the erosion-resistant Precambrian gneiss and schist that make up the canyon walls. Long after the initial cutting of the canyon began, the Gunnison River

Dryland Shrub

The mountain mahogany (genus *Cercocarpus*) is ingeniously well adapted to dry conditions and relatively poor soils. Like most other arid-land shrubs, mountain mahogany sprouts smaller leaves than shrubs in wet areas, a quality that helps limit the moisture it loses. The plant further reduces exposure to the drying effects of the sun by curling under the edges of its leaves. Its roots have special nodules that serve as homes for certain single-cell bacteria; these bacteria convert nitrogen into nitrate compounds, which then fertilize the plant. The genus name *Cercocarpus* comes from the Greek words for "tail" and "fruit"—a reference to this shrub's wispy, twisted seeds.

swelled with sand and rocky debris carried down from the meltwater of glacial ice, further scouring the canyon. The area's dark gneiss swirls with lines of pink granite and some especially beautiful muscovite.

The Gunnison River through the park consists mostly of extreme white water—Class V and VI—and can be negotiated only by expert kayakers willing to make a number of strenuous portages. (*Those who qualify will need a Park Service permit.*) That said, a number of outfitters in the area offer exciting raft trips below the most severe water, typically ending at the junction of the North Fork Gunnison (*contact the park for a list of approved outfitters*).

The road now bends southwest. Several pull-offs provide views of the magnificent **Painted Wall,** a 2,250-foot sheer cliff decorated with stripes and flourishes of pink and white crystalline pegmatite.

Take the **Cedar Point Nature Trail,** an easy 0.6-mile out-and-back walk, to views of the wall, the river, and islands of stone rising from the canyon depths. This trail also has signs identifying many plants common to the region. Indeed, Black Canyon is remarkably diverse in foliage. Atop or slightly below the rim are clusters of pinyon and juniper, serviceberry, Gambel oak, aspen, Douglas-fir, and adaptable mountain mahogany (*see above*).

Drive on to **High Point,** the end of the road. At an elevation of 8,289 feet, it is the highest point on the rim. From here it is a dizzying 2,689-foot drop to the river. You can take a 1.5-mile round-trip walk out to **Warner Point** for exquisite canyon views to the north.

Turning to the south you can see the verdant farmlands of the Uncompahgre Valley irrigated by water from the Gunnison River. Beyond rise the San Juan Mountains. The trail meanders among pinyon pine, juniper, mountain mahogany, and white-flowering serviceberry. Other plants scattered about include Fendler bush, mule's ear, lupine, and scarlet gilia, the latter bearing lovely tubular flowers.

North Rim Road: 5 miles one way (unpaved); 2 to 3 hours

While it is only 1,100 feet from one side of the canyon to the other, you must endure an 80-mile drive to reach the North Rim from the South Rim—the last several miles of it unpaved along North Rim Road. You can also reach the North Rim from the east side— a 90-mile drive on US 50 and Colo. 92 through the Curecanti National Recreation Area (see p. 61). Either way, you'll find yourself in a remote and awesome spot, a place of wind and coyotes with a wilder, more remote feeling than the South Rim. Even the peregrine falcons, ravens, and red-tailed hawks that wheel from one side of the canyon to the other seem more at home here. So do the climbers, clinging to the cliffs.

The astonishing steepness of the Black Canyon is readily apparent from the half dozen overlooks that punctuate this rim, any of which has the power to take your breath away. This side of the canyon also offers an excellent assortment of hikes, short and long.

Start with a stroll along the 0.4-mile **Chasm View Nature Trail,** a pleasant leg-stretcher which starts along the campground loop road and emerges at two stunning overlooks. along the way, white-throated swifts and violet-green swallows dart from cliffside nests. For a longer hike, try the **North Vista Trail,** a 7-mile round trip that sets off from the North Rim Ranger Station and wanders in and out of scrub forest. In just a mile and a half, a short detour leads to the fabulous and fittingly named **Exclamation Point,** where you'll find staggering views into the depths.

For a more strenuous and even more glorious walk, climb another 2 miles from Exclamation Point to the summit of **Green Mountain,** elevation 8,563 feet. Here the views extend beyond the canyon to Grand Mesa (see pp. 58–60) to the north, the San Juan Mountains to the south, and the West Elk Mountains to the east.

The southern 4 miles of the drive zigzag along the canyon's rim. At **Balanced Rock View** and **Kneeling Camel View,** near the end of the drive, steep unmarked trails wind down side canyons to the river.

INFORMATION & ACTIVITIES

Headquarters
102 Elk Creek
Gunnison, CO 81230
970-641-2337
www.nps.gov/blca

Visitor & Information Centers
Visitor center open daily
except holidays in winter.
North Rim Ranger Station
open in summer only.

Seasons & Accessibility
South Rim open daily, limited
access in winter; North Rim
Road and Ranger Station closed
in winter. Call headquarters for
visitor information.

Entrance Fees
$8 per vehicle per week; yearly
fee $15.

Pets
Pets allowed in park on leash;
not allowed on trails or in
backcountry.

Facilities for Disabled
South Rim: visitor center,
rest rooms, two camping sites;
and Tomichi Point, Chasm
View, and Sunset View Overlooks. North Rim: Balanced
Rock Overlook.

Things to do
Free naturalist-led activities.
Exhibits, scenic drives, hiking,
fishing, kayaking, rock climbing, winter activities. Contact
park headquarters for a list of
concessionaires.

Special Advisories
■ Permits required for all
inner canyon routes, available
at visitor center and North
Rim Ranger Station.
■ Permits required for backcountry camping. Wood
fires prohibited; use camp
stoves only.
■ Stay on trails to protect
fragile vegetation and prevent erosion.
■ When hiking in summer
always bring plenty of water.

Campgrounds
South Rim: 88 sites, $10 per
night, $15 with hookups,
maximum stay 14 days; reservations 5 days in advance only,
call 877-444-6777 or visit
www.ReserveUSA.com. North
Rim: 13 sites, $10 per night,
maximum stay 14 days, no
hookups, no reservations.

Hotels, Motels, & Inns
(Unless otherwise noted, rates are
for two persons in a double room,
high season.)

In Montrose, CO 81401:
■ **Best Western Red Arrow Motel**
1702 E. Main St. (Colo. 50
East). 970-249-9641 or

Scarlet gilia

AC, pool, spa. www.comfort innmontrose.com.

■ **Holiday Inn Express** 1391 S. Townsend. 970-240-1800 or 800-465-4329. 122 units, including 25 suites. $109. AC, pool, spa, exercise room.

■ **Montrose Days Inn** 1655 E. Main St. 970-249-3411. 47 units. $65–$89. AC, pool, sauna, spa.

In Gunnison, CO 81230:

■ **Best Western Tomichi Village Inn** 41883 East Hwy. 50. 970-641-1131 or 800-641-1131. 49 units. $69–$119. AC, pool, hot tub, fitness room, restaurant.

■ **Comfort Inn** 911 N. Main St. 970-642-1000. 58 units, $65–$129. AC, pool, hot tub, fitness center.

■ **Days Inn** 701 W. Tomichi Ave. 970-641-0608 or 888-641-0608. 43 units. $41–$65. AC, hot tub.

■ **Holiday Inn Express** 400 E. Tomichi Ave. 970-641-1288 or 800-486-6476. 50 units. $50–$75. AC, pool, hot tub, fitness center.

800-468-9323. 60 units. $99. AC, pool, fitness center. www.bestwestern.com/redarrow.

■ **Black Canyon Motel** 1605 E. Main St. (Colo. 50 East). 970-249-3495 or 800-348-3495. 49 units. $55–$119. AC, pool. www.toski.com/black-canyon.

■ **Canyon Trails Inn** 1225 E. Main St. (Colo. 50 East). 970-249-3426 or 800-858-5911. 27 units. $58. AC, restaurant.

■ **Comfort Inn** 2100 E. Main St. (Colo. 50 East) 970-240-8000 or 800-228-5150. 51 units, including spa suites. $95–$130.

For other accommodations call the Montrose Visitors & Convention Bureau at 970-240-1414 or 800-873-0244; or the Gunnison County Chamber of Commerce at 970-641-1501.

Excursions from Black Canyon

Grand Mesa

75 miles north of Black Canyon Aptly named, Grand Mesa is one of the largest flat-topped mountains on the planet. But this promontory, lying within Grand Mesa National Forest, is more than just another fine run of high country. Dotted with more than 300 lakes and reservoirs, Grand Mesa offers an uncommon feast of visual and biological diversity. From the floor of Grand Valley to the top of the mesa lie four different biological zones, and sweeping vistas take in alpine peaks, arid valleys, and eroded cliffs.

Visitors will find excellent hiking, camping, and sight-seeing

Mesa Lake, Grand Mesa National Forest

atop the mesa. Mountain bikers can choose from an abundance of dirt roads branching off Colo. 65—itself a scenic byway that crosses the mesa top. Information and a variety of books are on hand at the Grand Mesa Visitor Center at Cobbett Lake, located at the junction of Colo. 65 and FR 121. The quarter-mile self-guided **Discovery Trail** starts right behind the visitor center.

For a splendid day of exploring Grand Mesa on foot, consider hiking the **Crag Crest Trail,** an outstanding 10.3-mile loop that drifts through the rubble of the basalt volcanic cap that covers much of the mesa. Two well-marked trailheads access the route. The western trailhead is located at **Island Lake,** near Grand Mesa

Lodge. To reach the eastern trailhead, follow Colo. 65 east from Island Lake, turn left onto FR 121(marked by signs for Ward Lake), bear left after 1.5 miles, and continue 0.6 mile to the trailhead just past the Eggleston Lake Campground.

From the eastern trailhead, the path rises through forest-and-lake country to a crest barely 4 feet across in some places, with sheer drops on either side and magnificent views of the Book and Roan Cliffs, the West Elk Mountains, the San Juan Mountains, and the Uncompahgre Plateau.

This walk is extremely popular, so those in the mood for solitude will want to get an early start, preferably by 7 a.m. Also note that the exposed nature of Crag Crest makes it a dangerous place during summer afternoons, when lightning strikes are common.

For something far less rigorous, try the half-mile **Land O' Lakes Trail** (*off Colo. 65, just W of Island Lake*). This paved path winds quickly to a splendid overlook, from which you can take in Crag Crest and Ward Lake to the east, as well as the Black Canyon of the Gunnison and the San Juan Mountains to the south.

Aside from the Crag Crest Trail, perhaps the best way to sample the extraordinary scenery and geology of Grand Mesa is to follow gravel **Lands End Road,** which strikes off to the southwest from Colo. 65, several miles west of the Grand Mesa Visitor Center.

In 12 miles the road reaches a small stone "observatory" built on the west rim of Grand Mesa by the Civilian Conservation Corps. Originally touted as a fire lookout, its location offers views of the Gunnison and Colorado River Valleys. The building now serves as a Forest Service visitor center, open in the summer from 10 a.m. to 4 p.m., and sports a small collection of books and brochures. Although it's possible to continue on Lands End Road, making a rather steep drop off the mesa all the way down into Grand Valley, most people prefer to descend via Colo. 65.

Before heading back, take 15 minutes to walk the short, self-guided **nature trail** beside the observatory. In addition to magnificent views, this is a good place to spot golden eagles, Swainson's hawks, and peregrine falcons.

■ **540 square miles** ■ **West-central Colorado** ■ **Best seasons late spring–fall** ■ **Camping, hiking, backpacking, boating, fishing, mountain biking, scenic drives** ■ **Contact Supervisor's Office, GMUG Forest, 2250 Hwy. 50, Delta, CO 81416; 970-874-6600. www.fs.fed.us/r2/gmug**

Curecanti National Recreation Area

40 miles east of Black Canyon

Curecanti's main attractions are its three large reservoirs, created by damming the Gunnison River. The majority of users tend to be boaters, windsurfers, and those in search of fish—one of the reservoirs, **Blue Mesa Lake,** is among the largest Kokanee salmon fisheries in the country. In summer the park offers educational programs, some at the **Elk Creek Visitor Center,** on the shores of Blue Mesa Lake. A descent into the canyon via 232 stairs and a 0.75-mile walking path leads to the dock for Morrow Point Lake's **Pine Creek Boat Dock,** whence a ranger-led boat tours the reservoir. The third reservoir, **Crystal Lake,** features the Gunnison Diversion Tunnel, a national historic civil engineering landmark.

Trails in Curecanti allow casual hikers to enjoy beautiful forests, riparian areas, and sweeping vistas. The flat, easy, 1.5-mile round-trip **Neversink Trail** *(off US 50, 5 miles W of Gunnison on N shore of Gunnison River),* wanders past cottonwoods and willows with views of a fabulous great blue heron rookery. The 5-mile round-trip **Crystal Creek Trail** *(off Colo. 92, approximately 24 miles NW of junction with US 50)* winds through aspen and conifer groves, ending with sweeping views of the Cimarron Valley.

Another worthwhile hike leads 2 miles (one way) to the **Dillon Pinnacles** *(off US 50, 21 miles W of Gunnison, from a picnic area near shore of Blue Mesa Lake).* The trail winds through a long sweep of sage and ends at the base of a stunning set of volcanic pinnacles—oddly shaped towers and spires eroding in the face of wind, rain, and ice.

These points, capped in places by erosion-resistant tuff, are grand reminders of the fiery loads of ash and rock spewed out by the West Elk and San Juan Mountains. At one time, geologists estimate, the blanket of molten rock from these two volcanic centers may have had a volume of 150 cubic miles.

Caution: During summer this walk can be a hot one; bring water *(no drinking water available on any trails)* and hike early in the morning or late in the afternoon.

■ **41,043 acres** ■ **Southwest Colorado, west of Gunnison** ■ **Best months May–Oct.** ■ **Camping, hiking, rock climbing, boating, swimming, fishing, biking, horseback riding, bird-watching** ■ **Contact the recreation area, 102 Elk Creek, Gunnison, CO 81230; 970-641-2337. www.nps.gov/cure**

Colorado National Monument

90 miles northwest of Black Canyon

In a land gorged on geology, Colorado National Monument stands out as one of the great destinations of the high plateaus. Located on the northern edge of the sweeping **Uncompahgre Plateau,** the land here has been eroded into a fantastic collection of towers, spires, and cliffs, all cast in layers of red- to cream-colored rock. This is a place of deep, shadow-laden canyons and sunlit pinnacles, where colors—even moods—ebb and flow with the passing of every sun.

There's a wonderful array of wildlife at this monument, from rock wrens, golden eagles, and pinyon jays to mule deer, bighorn sheep, and mountain lions. As always, those who rouse themselves to explore the monument just after first light stand the best chance of capturing these creatures in memory or on film.

After a stop at the visitor center 4 miles inside the monument's west entrance to orient yourself and pick up a printed guide, take time for the **Rim Rock Drive,** a short tour that offers a variety of outstanding views of both the monument and the great sweep of the Grand Valley, some 2,000 feet below. This route is also suitable for bicycling, but watch for vehicle traffic and fallen rocks.

Grand Mesa viewed from Colorado National Monument

The drive offers a good overview of the monument, but more intimate encounters can be had on any of 13 hikes you'll find along the way. One favorite is the half-mile **Otto's Trail** *(1 mile from the visitor center, on NE side of Rim Rock Drive).* The path begins among clusters of pinyon and juniper, as well as tufts of a stiff, multijointed plant called Mormon tea. Although this growth gets its name from the early Mormon settlers who quickly took to it, Mormon tea has a much longer history of use. Native people relied on it to relieve congestion caused by colds and allergies. Otto's Trail will also introduce you to the single-leaf ash, a favorite for making tool handles, as well as yucca, which native people put to use in everything from rope to sandals.

This is also a good place to catch glimpses of the rock wren. The small, gray to brownish bird can be identified by the odd crook in its tail and by its habit of bobbing while it walks, as if listening to music that no one else can hear. A busy forager, constantly combing stones and boulders for insects, the rock wren issues a pleasant series of trills at a fairly constant pitch.

Otto's Trail ends at an airy, windswept sandstone perch, offering wonderful views of the Grand Valley and the Book Cliffs; in front of you will be the **Pipe Organ** formation, while to the right is Monument Canyon and the 550-foot-tall **Independence Monument.** Many of these spires have not yet fallen to the effects of wind, ice, and water because they are protected by their light-colored, erosion-resistant capstones of the Kayenta formation. This is also a good place to catch sight of white-throated swifts doing a fast dance in and out of the recesses of the canyon, snapping up insects on the wing.

If Otto's Trail leaves you hungry for more, try the quarter-mile **Window Rock Trail,** which affords wonderful views into Wedding Canyon, or the **Alcove Nature Trail,** a self-guided interpretive walk on the Kayenta Bench. For something a bit more ambitious, the **Black Ridge Trail**—a 5.5-mile trek, part of it across BLM lands— leads to inspirational views of Grand Mesa and the mighty San Juan Mountains, far to the south.

■ **20,534 acres** ■ **West-central Colorado, near Grand Junction** ■ **Best seasons spring and fall** ■ **Adm. fee** ■ **Camping, hiking, rock climbing, biking, bird-watching** ■ **Contact the monument, Fruita, CO 81521; 970-858-3617. www.nps.gov/colm**

White River National Forest: South

110 miles northwest of Black Canyon

One word—wilderness—sums up the White River National Forest located south of I-70. This region contains some of the most stirring mountainscapes in all of Colorado, protected by various wilderness districts of the national forest: scenic Maroon Bells-Snowmass, watery Holy Cross, and high-altitude Hunter-Fryingpan. Every single one of them sees an extraordinary amount of summer use, however, so if possible plan your trip for weekdays in the fall, when the traffic is lower.

It would be hard to find a time of year, a road, or even a trail in this region that doesn't offer magnificent scenery. Some of the most rewarding drives include: Colo. 82 from Aspen over Independence Pass to Twin Lakes; US 24 along the east side of Holy Cross Wilderness and south to Leadville; and a network of vehicle-friendly and not-so-friendly dirt roads fanning across many of the old mining districts that first made Colorado a household name.

Few places have been more frequently photographed than **Maroon Bells–Snowmass Wilderness,** a 181,000-acre gem southwest of Aspen. As in all of Colorado's high country, this region owes much of its appeal to glaciers, which carved out long, lovely valleys where streams tumble and aspen quake. Popular entryways and destinations for hikes include **Maroon-Snowmass Trail** and the **West Maroon Creek Trail,** as well as **Buckskin Pass,** all off Maroon Creek Road. Additional trailheads are located south of Aspen at Ashcroft, and west of Aspen near Colo. 133 at Marble. To relieve congestion at the trailheads, use a shuttle bus from Ruby Park in Aspen. Other popular spots such as **Cathedral**, **Snowmass**, and **American Lakes** get so much summertime use that you shouldn't even consider visiting them until after Labor Day.

Holy Cross Wilderness is rich in quiet lakes, tiny ponds, and streams that go from loud torrents to whispers in the course of a single summer. The 10-mile round-trip hike to **Lonesome Lake** *(from the end of FS 703 on E side of Homestake Reservoir)* is a wonderful day trip. Equally unforgettable is the 11-mile round-trip hike to **Notch Mountain** *(S of I-70, off US 24, end of FR 707, at Half Moon Trailhead).*

More lightly visited, the **Hunter-Fryingpan Wilderness** is a perfect destination for those with a penchant for high-altitude walking (8,500 to 12,500 feet). The 8-mile round-trip **Midway Pass Trail** *(off*

Crystal Mill on Crystal River

Colo. 82 at Lost Man Trailhead) offers fabulous panoramas of the Elk Mountains. The same trailhead accesses beautiful South Pass, as well as Lost Man Lake.

The **West Elk Loop Scenic Byway**—a 205-mile loop from Paonia Reservoir and back again—could keep you busy exploring for days. The route passes great runs of aspen and sprawling views. It is also a good way to launch an extended foray into the lovely, 176,000-acre **West Elk Wilderness,** a wonderland of high meadows and eroded volcanic spires and pinnacles.

■ **Central Colorado** ■ **Best seasons summer and winter** ■ **Camping,** hiking, backpacking, rafting, fishing, biking, skiing, wildlife viewing, scenic drives ■ Contact the national forest, 900 Grand Ave., Glenwood Springs, CO 81602; 970-945-2521. www.fs.fed.us/r2/whiteriver/contact_us.html

Bryce Canyon

Perhaps nowhere are the forces of natural erosion more tangible than at Bryce Canyon National Park. Its wilderness of phantom-like rock spires, or hoodoos, attracts around one million visitors a year. Many descend on trails that give hikers and horseback riders a close look at the fluted walls and sculptured pinnacles.

The park follows the edge of the Paunsaugunt Plateau. On the west are heavily forested tablelands more than 9,000 feet high; on the east are the intricately carved breaks where the country drops 2,000 feet to the Paria Valley. Many ephemeral streams have eaten into the plateau, forming horseshoe-shaped bowls. The largest and most striking is Bryce Amphitheater. Encompassing 6 square miles, it is the scenic heart of the park.

Water has been helping carve Bryce's rugged landscape for millions of years and is still at work. Water may split rock as it freezes and expands in cracks—a cyclic process that occurs some 200 times a year. In summer, runoff from violent cloudbursts etches into the softer limestones and sluices through the deep runnels. In about half a century the rim will be cut back into the plateau another foot. But there is more here than spectacular erosion.

In the early morning you can stand for long moments on the rim, held by the mysterious blend of rock and color. Warm yellows and oranges radiate from the deeply pigmented walls as scatterings of light illuminate the pale rock spires.

There is a sense of place here that goes beyond rocks. Some local Paiute Indians explained it with a legend. Once there lived animal-like creatures that changed themselves into people. But they were bad, so Coyote turned them into rocks of various configurations. The spellbound creatures still huddle together here with faces painted just as they were before being turned to stone.

- Southwest Utah, near Hatch, Tropic and Panguitch
- 35,835 acres
- Established 1928
- Best months April–Oct. (some roads closed in winter)
- Camping, hiking, backpacking, cross-country skiing, snowshoeing, bird-watching
- Information: 435-834-5322 www.nps.gov/brca

Hiker on Navajo Loop Trail, Bryce Canyon National Park

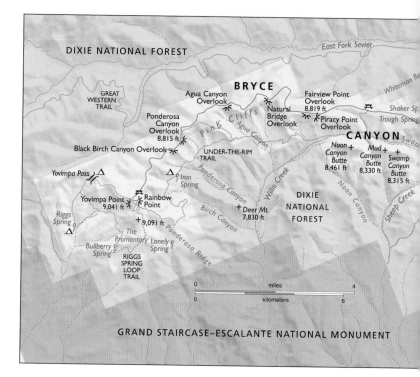

How to Get There

From Zion National Park (83 miles west), follow Utah 9 east, turn north onto Utah 89, then continue east on Utah 12 to Utah 63, which is the park entrance road. From Capitol Reef National Park (about 120 miles to the east), follow Utah 12 southward to Utah 63. Airport: Salt Lake City.

When to Go

All-year park. Wildflowers are at their peak in spring and early summer; the greatest variety of the park's 170 bird species appears between May

What Not to Miss

- ◾ Sunrise: Bryce Point

- ◾ Sunset: Inspiration Point or Paria View

- ◾ Late Afternoon: Sunset Point for shadows and light patterns

- ◾ Nighttime: Walk by flashlight to Wall Street

- ◾ Short hike below the rim on Queens Garden Trail or Navajo Loop Trail

- ◾ Picnic at Rainbow Point

- ◾ Full moon ranger-led walk in summer

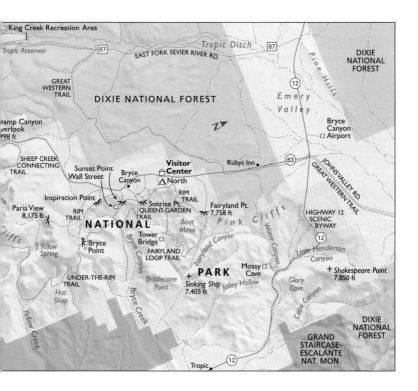

and October. Winter lasts from November through March; snow highlights the brilliantly colored cliffs and provides fine cross-country skiing.

How to Visit

On a one-day visit, tour the **Bryce Amphitheater,** beginning, if possible, with sunrise at **Bryce Point.** If limited time requires choosing between the scenic drive or a walk beneath the rim, take the walk, perhaps on the **Queens Garden Trail.**

If you have more time, drive to **Rainbow Point,** and consider strolling the **Bristlecone Loop Trail** to have a look at some of the park's ancient bristlecone pines. Another enticing option is a moonlight walk among the hoodoos; one promising trail leads into the spires from **Fairyland Point.**

Backpackers would do well to take a couple of days and make the trek from Bryce Point to Yovimpa Point on the **Under-the-Rim Trail.**

EXPLORING THE PARK

Bryce Amphitheater: 8 miles; 2 hours to a full day

Watch sunrise from **Bryce Point,** one of the highest overlooks along the rim of the amphitheater. Drive about 4 miles south of the visitor center, then walk a short distance from the parking lot to the viewpoint. Colors begin to glow even before the sun breaks over the **Aquarius Plateau,** at over 10,000 feet the highest plateau in North America. First light catches the rim of the amphitheater, then drops into the basin, igniting the crowded pillars of rock. From this vantage point you see shallow caves along the rim called the **Grottoes.** Look for the **Alligator,** a sharply incised butte that appears reptilian from above, and the **Sinking Ship,** which resembles a vanishing prow.

Drive back to **Inspiration Point,** bypassing the Paria View turnoff. From the parking lot walk up a short but steep trail to upper Inspiration Point. If the trail looks too ambitious, stay below at the lower viewpoint. Both look over the head of the amphitheater and place you close to the rock formations. No matter what time of day, they provide excellent all-around views.

In the valley below is the small town of **Tropic.** Scottish emigrant Ebenezer Bryce and his wife, Mary, homesteaded nearby in 1875. They grazed cattle in Bryce Canyon but moved away five years later, leaving behind little more than their name.

Continue on to **Sunset Point.** The name is misleading since the viewpoint faces east, limiting sundown views. But the mix of shadows and deep-hued colors makes this an excellent vantage point in the low-angled light of later afternoon. To the left is **Thor's Hammer;** to the right is the **Silent City**—a gridwork of deep ravines that divide turreted walls suggesting the ruins of an ancient metropolis.

Those with time and stamina can follow the **Navajo Loop Trail,** a fairly strenuous 1.5-mile loop into the canyon. The trail drops steeply in a series of tight switchbacks before entering a narrow, steep-walled gorge called **Wall Street.** Several Douglas-firs, two of them 700 years old, grow between the towering cliffs.

Continue down the trail to the junction with **Queens Garden Trail,** the least strenuous trail below the rim. It winds along the bottom of the amphitheater to Queens Garden, then climbs to the rim at **Sunrise Point,** passing weird rock formations and occasional bristlecone pines. From Sunrise Point follow the **Rim Trail** a half mile back to your car at Sunset Point.

Under-the-Rim Trail

No greater pleasure awaits the backpacker than the 22.5-mile Under-the-Rim Trail, a one-way, 2-day trek best taken north to south from **Bryce Point** to **Yovimpa Point.** Stop at the visitor center to obtain a backcountry permit *(fee)* and register for primitive campsites you intend to use.

This hike displays a staggering array of geologic wonders, from the fine cross-bedding of Claron limestone fins and hidden springs flush with wildflowers to the unforgettable **Pink Cliffs.**

View from Inspiration Point

Though some stretches of the trail are rather rugged, an early morning departure will allow you to make the 10 miles to **Sheep Creek** or **Swamp Canyon,** passing through the erosional fantasyland of the **Hat Shop** en route. Along here anyone will appreciate a comment often attributed to pioneer rancher Ebenezer Bryce, for whom the park is named: "It's a hell of a place to lose a cow." The latter portion of the trek climbs rather sharply over several miles to an elevation of 9,100 feet, offering magnificent views to the north and south, from the Pink Cliffs all the way to Navajo Mountain.

Although this hike is renowned for its uncanny rock formations and soaring vistas, there are woodlands to savor as well: ponderosa pine peppered with manzanita and bitterbrush; aspen groves dappled with columbine and Oregon grape; huddles of spruce, fir, and bristlecone pine. Portions of the trail also pass by thickets of Gambel oak, a favorite browse of mule deer and a tree celebrated as one of the few Rocky Mountain species to turn red in the fall.

Along the trail look for a variety of bird life: Steller's jays, Cooper's hawks, northern flickers, violet-green swallows, pygmy nuthatches, vesper sparrows, and broad-tailed hummingbirds. You'll also be sharing the trail with tiger salamanders, as well as tree, sagebrush, and short-horned lizards.

Rainbow Point Drive: 17 miles; 3 hours to a half day

Following the edge of the gently tilted plateau, this scenic drive ascends more than 1,000 feet to Rainbow Point, the plateau's southernmost reach.

Before beginning the drive, be sure to see **Fairyland Point.** Just after you enter the park boundaries, but before the entrance station, a mile-long spur road leads to the Fairyland overlook. The temptation is to leave this for later, but here you see one of the finest vistas in the park. In colorful array, spires and monoliths rise close at hand. Some stand isolated like chess pieces; others group together like a Greek chorus. A short hike down the trail takes you right among them and offers a quick immersion course in the effects of erosion.

When you return to your car, drive past the Sunset Point turnoff *(trailers are not allowed beyond this point)* and on past the Bryce Point turnoff. As the road climbs, you leave the ponderosa pine forest behind and quickly find yourself among the high-elevation blue spruce and Douglas-fir.

Pull in at **Farview Point** for a panoramic view of Table Cliffs and a series of broad platforms stairstepping southeast to the Kaibab Plateau at the North Rim of the Grand Canyon.

Continue south to the **Natural Bridge** pull-off. Here you have a closeup view of a natural arch 85 feet long and 125 feet high. Its bright rusty red contrasts with the deep green of the trees

Hoodoos

The term "hoodoo" originated at Bryce, though its derivation is shrouded in conjecture. It could be a variation of "voodoo" or perhaps an attempted translation of the Paiute term for the formation. Interestingly, a similar-sounding word in ancient Hebrew means "aboriginal person." Because the region's first white settlers included Mormon scholars versed in ancient Hebrew, some people speculate that Mormons may have coined the odd term.

You can see hoodoos in other places, but almost nowhere are they as dramatic as those you'll see in the amphitheaters of Bryce. The Goblin Valley north of Hanksville, for instance, sports fatter, more rounded sandstone hoodoos—features that die-hard Bryce fans refer to as "couch-potato hoodoos."

Natural Bridge

below and the deep azure blue of the sky above.

The next pull-off is **Agua Canyon,** one of the finest vistas in the park. Massive hoodoos stand close to the rim; farther off are the vividly colored Pink Cliffs; and on the far horizon is the domed profile of Navajo Mountain, over 10,000 feet high.

Continue to the end of the road at **Rainbow Point,** the park's highest elevation, 9,115 feet. You might plan to pause at this pleasant spot for a picnic among the thick stands of fir. A pleasant 1-mile walk follows **Bristlecone Loop Trail** to expansive views. A spur trail leads to more views at **Yovimpa Point;** the cliffs that descend from there in stairsteps are named for their rock colors—pink, gray, white, vermilion, and chocolate. A stand of ancient bristlecone pines grows on the edge of the plateau—the oldest has been alive for more than 1,500 years.

Acoustic studies have found that the natural silence in the park equals the quality of a sound studio. The park boasts some of the nation's best air quality as well. But rangers worry that this purity will be threatened by possible development on adjacent lands.

INFORMATION & ACTIVITIES

Headquarters
P.O. Box 170001
Bryce Canyon, UT 84717
435-834-5322
www.nps.gov/brca

Visitor & Information Centers
Visitor center on main road,
1 mile inside park boundary.
Open all year. Call headquarters for visitor information.

Seasons & Accessibility
Park open year-round. Roads
may be closed for short periods
due to snowstorms. Some spur
roads closed in winter for
cross-country skiing. Phone
headquarters for conditions.

Entrance Fees
$20 per car per week. From
mid-May through September,
visitors may leave their cars
near the entrance. From there,
a shuttle system transports
visitors to points throughout
the park.

Facilities for Disabled
Visitor center partially accessible to wheelchairs; all viewpoints and a half-mile stretch
of trail between Sunset and
Sunrise Points also accessible.

Things to Do
Free naturalist-led activities
(summer): prairie dog and
other nature walks, history
and geology talks, evening
programs, night sky programs,
moonlight walks. Also, hiking,
guided trail rides *(inquire at
Bryce Lodge or call 435-679-
8665),* cross-country skiing,
snowshoeing.

Special Advisory
■ Overnight backpacking
allowed only on the Under-
the-Rim Trail near Bryce
Point. Purchase permits for
$5 at visitor center or, in
summer, at nature center.

Campgrounds
Two campgrounds; 14-day
limit. Part of North open all
year. Sunset open May through
Sept. Both first come, first
served. Fees $10 per night.
Showers nearby. Tent and
RV sites; no hookups. Sunset
Group Campground; reservations required; contact park.
Food services in park.

Hotels, Motels, & Inns
(Unless otherwise noted, rates are
for two persons in a double room,
high season.)

INSIDE THE PARK:
■ **Bryce Canyon Lodge**
(South of Utah 12 on Utah 63)
Xanterra Parks & Resorts,
Bryce Canyon NP, UT 84717.
435-834-5361 or 888-297-2757.

Horseback riding below the rim

40 cabins, 70 rooms, 3 suites. $115–$135. Restaurant. Open April through Oct. www.bryce canyonlodge.com.

OUTSIDE THE PARK
In Bryce, UT 84764:
■ **Best Western Ruby's Inn**
(Utah 63) P.O. Box 64000. 435-834-5341 or 800-528-1234. 368 units. $79–$140. AC, pools, restaurant. www.rubysinn.com.
■ **Bryce Canyon Pines Motel**
(Utah 12) P.O. Box 43. 435-834-5441. 46 rooms, 7 cabins, 2 kitchenettes. $65–$125.

Pool, restaurant. www.bryce canyonmotel.com.
■ **Bryce Canyon Resorts**
(On Utah 12). P.O. Box 6. 435-834-5303. 6 cabins, 3 cottages, 58 rooms. $55–$105. AC, pool, restaurant. www.brycecanyon resort.com.

In Panguitch, UT 84759:
■ **Adobe Sands Motel**
390 N. Main St., P.O. Box 593. 435-676-8874. 21 units. $30–$75. AC. Open May through Oct. www.adobesands.com.
■ **Best Western New Western Motel** 180 E. Center St., P.O. Box 73. 800-528-1234 or 435-676-8876. 55 units. $65–$75. AC, pool. www.olwm.com /bwnewwestern.
■ **Color Country Motel**
526 N. Main St., P.O. Box 163. 435-676-2386. 26 units. $52–$68. AC, pool. www.color countrymotel.com.

For other accommodations, contact the Panguitch Chamber of Commerce, P.O. Box 400, Panguitch, UT 84759, 435-676-8585; or the Garfield County Travel Council, P.O. Box 200, Panguitch, UT, 84759, 435-676-1160 or 800-444-6689. You can also visit www.utah.com /bryce/.

Excursions from Bryce Canyon

Utah 12 Scenic Byway

6 miles north of Bryce

122 miles; At least a half day Some of Utah's most outstanding high desert scenery unfolds along this route, which begins near the pale orange spires of Bryce Canyon and ends amid the immense sandstone domes of Capitol Reef. Between these two national parks, this remote highway skirts the northwestern edge of the **Grand Staircase-Escalante National Monument** *(see pp. 79–81)*. Along the way, it snakes along narrow ridge tops, carves through red-rock canyons past prehistoric Native American ruins, and finally ascends 11,000-foot Boulder Mountain for breathtaking views. Only paved in its entirety since 1985, Utah 12 serves as the road-

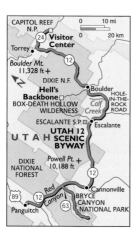

head for many small but scenic side roads offering unparalleled opportunities to delve into one of continental America's last explored frontiers.

The western end of the route begins at the county seat of **Panguitch,** an Old West town dotted with redbrick houses full of Mormon history, and heads southeast toward Bryce Canyon. About 2 miles past the intersection with US 89, the road enters **Dixie National Forest** *(435-865-3700. www.fs.fed.us/dxnf)* and rolls through **Red Canyon,** a fairy-like world of curiously sculptured limestone formations colored brilliant red by iron oxides and accented by large ponderosa pines. Outlaw Butch Cassidy often hid out here.

At 9 miles, the national forest's Red Canyon Campground *(435-676-8815)* offers full camping facilities. As the road ascends to the flats of the Paunsaugunt Plateau, the orange-tinted cliffs and spires of Bryce Canyon appear to the southeast. Twelve miles beyond US 89, Utah 63 branches off toward the park.

Continue east on Utah 12 along the northern reaches of the park into **Water Canyon. Mossy Cave** has a 1-mile round-trip trail to a small cave and waterfall. Beyond the park, the road drops south through the small towns of Tropic and Cannonville, the roadhead for the Cottonwood Canyon Road and Kodachrome Basin State Park *(see pp. 78–79)*.

About 13 miles past Tropic, stop at a pullout for stunning views of the salmon-colored cliffs of 10,188-foot **Powell Point,** an early landmark in Maj. John Wesley Powell's survey of the Southwest. The road continues toward Escalante across the high pastures of the **Table Cliff Plateau.** Seventeen miles beyond the Powell Point pullout, another one provides views of a Fremont granary built high in the cliff face. Primarily hunter-gatherers, the Fremont Indians occupied the area between A.D. 1050 and 1200.

A mile west of Escalante is **Escalante State Park** *(435-826-4466. http://parks.state.ut.us/parks/www1/esca.htm. Adm. fee).* Wide Hollow Reservoir offers good trout fishing, while a 1-mile nature trail leads to a petrified forest, with brightly colored rock logs and a view of Escalante.

Hell's Backbone, a spine-tingling, high-mountain, dirt-and-gravel road accessible in good weather, heads north from Escalante and overlooks **Box-Death Hollow Wilderness** area. Another rugged backcountry road, **Hole-in-the-Rock Road,** cuts south from the Escalante area 18 miles to the twisted slickrock desertscape of **Devil's Garden.** The side road ends at **Hole-in-the Rock,** a spot where in 1879-1880 some 200 Mormon pioneers with 83 wagons and 1,200 head of livestock penetrated a notch in the canyon wall 2,000 feet above the Colorado River.

The 29 miles of Utah 12 between Escalante and Boulder are so dramatic that you might not want to leave the road. But if you ache to put some of the country beneath your feet, pull into Calf Creek Campground *(435-826-5499)* and look for the the **Lower Calf Creek Falls Trail.** This 5.5-mile round-trip trail runs up a side canyon of the Escalante River, through Gambel oak, juniper, and prickly pear. Though the trail is easy and quite flat, it can be extremely hot, especially at midday, when even the high cliffs toward the end of the trail provide little shade. The falls themselves open up in the last 100 yards of the trail as a series of delightful discoveries. From spring through autumn, this trail gets heavy use.

Continue to Boulder, where **Anasazi State Park** *(435-335-7308. http://parks.state.ut.us/parks/www1/anas.htm. Adm. fee)* offers a close-up view of the ancient Pueblo people, who, along with the Fremont Indians, occupied this region in prehistoric times. University of Utah archaeologists uncovered an 87-room village here in the late 1950s, one of the largest ancestral Puebloan communities west of the Colorado River. The state park has re-created a six-room dwelling and museum. From Boulder, the **Burr Trail** *(see pp. 104–105)* leads southeast to Lake Powell and the **Glen Canyon National Recreation Area** *(see pp. 110–13).*

From Boulder, Utah 12 enters a landscape of sagebrush and pinyon pine and ascends the broad flanks of **Boulder Mountain,** which sits on the Aquarius Plateau, the continent's highest plateau. In fall, stands of fire-yellow aspen play against the evergreens. Views from several overlooks, such as **Point Lookout,** are exceptional. The tangled canyons and colored sandstone cliffs of Capitol Reef lie in the foreground, while the imposing Henry Mountains and Navajo Mountain dominate the horizon. From here, Utah 12 descends to the junction with Utah 24 near Torrey and the entrance to **Capitol Reef National Park** *(see pp. 98–107).*

■ **Southern Utah** ■ **Best seasons spring and fall. Check road and weather conditions before taking any unpaved side routes.** ■ **Hiking, nature trails, side roads, prehistoric villages**

Kodachrome Basin State Park

21 miles southeast of Bryce

A pleasing sense of remoteness and desert solitude attracts campers and hikers to 5,800-foot-high Kodachrome Basin's peculiar geology, a meringue of red-rock spires that changes its hues as the sun moves across Utah's arid "color country." Geologists speculate that the park's ruddy towers formed when liquid sand intrusions rose to the surface as a result of earthquake activity and subsequently hardened. The tallest tower stands 156 feet high.

Struck by the park's photogenic character and vivid palette, National Geographic Society visitors in 1948 suggested it be named in honor of the pioneering color film.

If your itinerary doesn't permit an overnight stay amid the juniper and red-rock spires, be sure to treat yourself to a walk on at least one of the park's trails. Take your camera and a park trail map *(available at information kiosks throughout the park).* The half-mile self-guided **nature trail** leaves the campground for a tour of desert plants and Kodachrome's trademark formations. The **Panorama Trail** is an easy 3-mile loop, with several side trails leading to unusual formations, including the graceful **Ballerina Slipper** spire, wide-brimmed pedestals in **Hat Shop,** and the

William Gambel

An accomplished young ornithologist, William Gambel served as assistant to Thomas Nuttal, the author of the first field manual on birds in America. In just a few years of roaming the West in the 1840s, Gambel discovered more than a hundred new species of birds. Along with the Gambel oak, four species of birds and a genus of lizard were named after him. At the age of 28, he died in California, only to have his bones washed from their hillside grave during a gold mining operation.

intriguing **Secret Pass,** a narrow corridor squeezed between high red-rock walls. The main trail continues on to a short, steep spur ending on **Panorama Point,** with its sweeping views of the multihued landscape.

For a short gravel-road adventure (if the weather's dry), continue south about 10 miles to **Grosvenor Arch** a soaring yellow arc split by a supporting spire and named for NATIONAL GEOGRAPHIC magazine's first full-time editor.

■ 4,000 acres ■ Southern Utah, South of Cannonville ■ Year-round ■ Adm. fee ■ Camping, hiking, horseback riding, stagecoach rides, photography ■ Contact the park, P.O Box 238, Cannonville, UT 84718; 435-679-8562. www.utah.com/stateparks/

Grand Staircase-Escalante National Monument

6 miles east of Bryce

This vast, remote, and lightly visited national monument sprawls across southern Utah, from Capitol Reef National Park in the east to Bryce Canyon National Park in the west, and from Utah 12 in the north to the Arizona border in the south. It is the largest national monument outside of Alaska, covering 2,947 square miles—six times the size of Grand Teton National Park.

It is also a controversial monument. Created in 1996 by presidential proclamation over strident local opposition, it is the first to be administered by the Bureau of Land Management, whose commitment to working with neighboring communities may defuse

Red rock, Grand Staircase-Escalante National Monument

the politically charged atmosphere. Ecologically, the monument consists of three main components. From west to east they are the Grand Staircase area southeast of Bryce, the Kaiparowits Plateau south of the town of Escalante, and the Escalante Canyons surrounding the river of the same name.

When geologists talk about the **Grand Staircase,** the word "grand" is no exaggeration. This series of huge cliffs is easily visible from the air, miles above the Grand Canyon. Each colorful face represents a different layer of rock, so climbing the Grand Staircase toward the north will take you on a trek through 200 million years of geologic history. The Vermilion Cliffs are made of Moenave sandstone, the White Cliffs of Navajo sandstone, the Gray Cliffs of younger shales, and the Pink Cliffs of limey siltstone.

Perhaps the best place to see the Grand Staircase geologic formation is from **Grand Staircase Overlook** (*off US 89 Alt., 10 miles S* *of Fredonia).* From that point, it's easy to see the layers of sand-stone, shale, and siltstone stacked up like a staircase.

The **Kaiparowits Plateau** is a high, arid, desolate plateau of very young rock from the late Cretaceous period. Some places contain soils that are poisonous to plants; elsewhere underground coal fires have stained the rock red.

In the **Escalante Canyons** area, water has carved Navajo sand-stone into a maze. The monument contains an almost endless (and often surprising) rendition of a few basic themes: a lush valley, a mass of slickrock, a complicated web of crazy slot canyons.

As for traditional tourist offerings, there are few. Only one devel-oped trail exists: The beautiful **Lower Calf Creek Falls Trail** *(see p. 77),* and the scenic drive on Utah 12 *(see pp. 76–78)* through the monument is stunning, especially the famed stretch between Escalante and Boulder. If you have a four-wheel-drive vehicle, you could combine this stretch with drives on some of the area's rough-and-tumble dirt roads, including **Hells Backbone, Hole-in-the-Rock, Cottonwood Canyon,** or **Dixie National Forest** *(see pp. 337–39)* roads.

People who love this area clearly believe that the best way to see it is to stop at some random point on a road, get out, and walk *(bikes are limited to developed roads).* In a sense, that's the whole point of the national monument: It's a vast and rugged place, sur-prisingly unexplored, its greatest benefits attainable only through first-hand experience.

The shortest drives require at least half a day; longer excursions can take a week or more. Maps for unpaved roads and brochures with guidelines for safely navigating them can be obtained from the Escalante BLM office *(P.O. Box 225, Escalante, UT 84726; 435-826-5499).* Alternatively, begin at one of the monument's four tiny visitor centers in Escalante *(435-826-5600),* Kanab *(435-644-2672),* Boulder *(435-335-7382),* or Cannonville *(435-679-8981).*

Interpretive trails wind through nearby state parks: **Kodachrome Basin State Park** *(see pp. 78–79),* **Escalante State Park** *(see p. 77),* and **Anasazi State Park** *(see pp. 77–78).*

■ **1.7 million acres** ■ **Southwest Utah** ■ **Best months April–June and Sept.–Oct.** ■ **Camping, hiking, backpacking, fishing, hunting, mountain biking, horseback riding, scenic drives** ■ **Contact Escalante Interagency Office, 755 W. Main St., Escalante, UT 84726; 435-826-5600. www.ut. blm.gov/monument**

Canyonlands

From the rim you glimpse only segments of the Green and the Colorado Rivers, which flow together at the heart of Canyonlands National Park. But everywhere you see the water's work: canyon mazes, unbroken scarps, sandstone pillars. The paths of the merging rivers divide the park into three districts. The high mesa known as the Island in the Sky rises as a headland 2,000 feet above the confluence. South of the Island and east of the confluence is The Needles, where red and white banded pinnacles tower 400 feet over grassy parks and sheer-walled valleys. A fine confusion of clefts and spires across the river to the west marks The Maze, a remote region of pristine solitude. A fourth district may be thought of as the rivers themselves.

On every side the ground drops in great stairsteps. Flat bench-lands end abruptly in rock walls on one side and sheer drops on the other. It is a right-angled country of standing rock, and only a few paved roads probe the edges of the park's 527 square miles. Sandstone layers of varying hardness compose Canyonland's visible rock. But the character of the land is largely shaped by underlying salt deposits, which push upward, forming domes that fracture layers of colorful rock at the surface.

Yearly rainfall averages just 8 inches but varies greatly from year to year. Trees that grow here have to be tough and resilient. In drought years, junipers survive by limiting growth to a few branches, letting the others die. Gnarled juniper and pinyon pine take root in the rimlands wherever soil collects, including slickrock cracks and potholes.

The park's isolation and preponderance of backcountry make visiting a spectacular experience, but it may not be for everyone. There are very few traditional visitor facilities and not many paved roads. None of the roads directly link the park's four districts. But patience, a self-reliant attitude, and a four-wheel-drive vehicle can make exploring Canyonlands much easier.

- Southeast Utah, southwest of Moab
- 337,598 acres
- Established 1964
- Best seasons spring and fall
- Camping, hiking, mountain biking, boating, pictographs
- Information: 435-719-2313 www.nps.gov/cany

Hiking Chesler Park Trail in The Needles District

How to Get There

Island in the Sky District: From Moab (35 miles away), take US 191 north to Utah 313 to The Neck entrance road. **The Needles District:** From Moab (75 miles away), follow US 191 south to Utah 211, then west 34 miles to park entrance.
The Maze District: From Green River, take I-70 west to Utah 24, then south to dirt road leading 46 miles to Hans Flat Ranger Station. Airports: Salt Lake City, Utah, and Grand Junction, Colo.

When to Go

Spring and fall are ideal for exploring by foot or vehicle.

How to Visit

Go to **Island in the Sky** for an overview. Next day, go to the **The Needles** to explore classic canyon country. With more time, focus on hiking.

What Not to Miss

- **Grand View Point**
- **Sunrise hike to Mesa Arch**
- **Driving or biking along White Rim Road**
- **A trek on Chesler Park Trail**
- **Rafting in Cataract Canyon**
- **Sunset at Shafer Canyon Overlook**

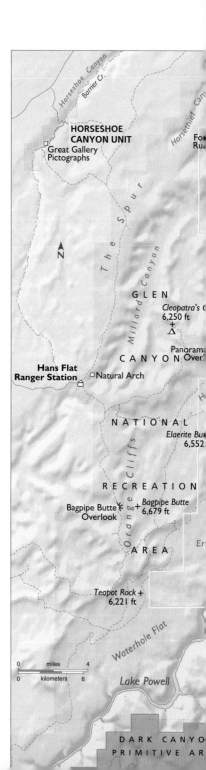

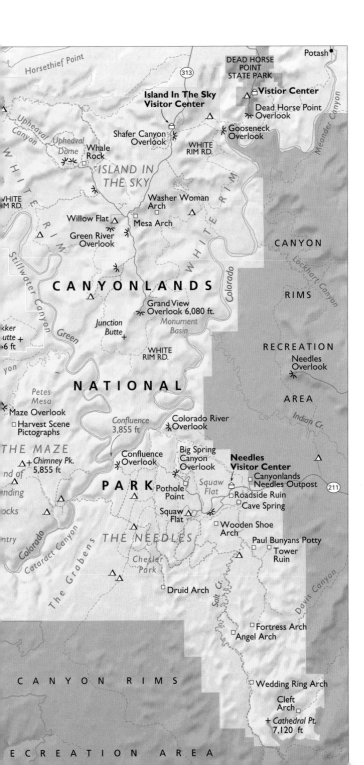

Horsethief Point

Potash

DEAD HORSE
POINT
STATE PARK

313

**Island In The Sky
Visitor Center**

Vistior Center

Dead Horse Point
Overlook

Upheaval
Canyon

Upheaval
Dome

Whale
Rock

Shafer Canyon
Overlook

Gooseneck
Overlook

WHITE
RIM RD.

ISLAND IN
THE SKY

WHITE
RIM RD.

Washer Woman
Arch

Willow Flat

Mesa Arch

Green River
Overlook

CANYON

Stillwater Canyon

Colorado

Lockhart Canyon

RIMS

CANYONLANDS

Green

Grand View
Overlook 6,080 ft.

Junction
Butte

Monument
Basin

RECREATION

Needles
Overlook

WHITE
RIM RD.

NATIONAL

Petes
Mesa

AREA

Indian Cr.

Maze Overlook

Harvest Scene
Pictographs

Confluence
3,855 ft

Colorado River
Overlook

THE MAZE

Chimney Pk.
5,855 ft

nd of

Confluence
Overlook

Big Spring
Canyon
Overlook

**Needles
Visitor Center**

211

nding

ocks

PARK

Pothole
Point

Squaw
Flat

Canyonlands
Needles Outpost

Roadside Ruin

Cave Spring

ntry

Colorado

Squaw
Flat

Wooden Shoe
Arch

Cataract Canyon

THE NEEDLES

Paul Bunyans Potty

Tower
Ruin

Chesler
Park

The Grabens

Druid Arch

Salt Cr.

Davis Canyon

Fortress Arch

Angel Arch

CANYON   RIMS

Wedding Ring Arch

Cleft
Arch

Cathedral Pt.
7,120 ft

kker
utte
6 ft

yon

ECREATION   AREA

EXPLORING THE PARK

Island in the Sky: 40 miles; a half to full day

Just after entering the park, the road crosses **The Neck,** a rock span not much wider than the pavement, which connects the mesa to the rimlands. For a sweeping view of the park's narrow, interlocked canyons and its wide skies, drive right to the end of the road at **Grand View Point Overlook** (6,080 feet). Directly below in **Monument Basin,** stone columns rise more than 300 feet from the canyon floor. Hidden in deep gorges to the south, the Green River joins the Colorado River. During his exploration of the Colorado in 1869, John Wesley Powell scaled the canyon walls at the confluence and discovered a strangely carved landscape. "Wherever we looked," he wrote, "there was a wilderness of rocks." If time allows, take the easy 2-mile round-trip trail that starts at the Grand View parking area and follows the rim.

Drive back the way you came, bypassing Buck Canyon and Muphy Point Overlooks. Turn left onto the road leading to Upheaval Dome, then follow the paved spur road past Willow Flat Campground to **Green River Overlook.** Here you view a wide expanse of canyon country: Below, a quiet stretch of the Green River runs through Stillwater Canyon, with The Maze beyond and the Henry Mountains topping the distant horizon.

Continue on to **Upheaval Dome,** the park's most spectacular geologic formation. A half-mile trail leads to the lip of this anachronistic and puzzling crater, which is a mile in diameter and sports a spire in the center (*hikers with small children should exercise extreme caution approaching the dome*). Trail guides describe the structure of the formation, as well as the many competing theories on its origins. The parking lot offers a good picnic spot shaded by junipers and pinyon pines.

Back on the main road, be sure to pull off at the **Mesa Arch Trailhead.** An easy half-mile loop takes you through a pinyon-juniper woodland to a small natural arch carved from the rim. The curve of the arch frames a magnificent view of the Washer Woman Arch and the La Sal Mountains, snowy in winter. Watch your children at this unguarded viewpoint.

Just before leaving the park, stop at the **Shafer Canyon Overlook.** The short trail leads along a promontory above canyons gouged from miles of layered stone. In late afternoon, the rocks seem to ignite in the low angle of the setting sun.

Potholes

Gems of the desert, potholes are scattered all across canyon country. They come in all sizes and shapes, from the baby bathtubs that dimple Canyonlands' Pothole Point Trail to the giant catchments of the Waterpocket Fold in Capitol Reef National Park. Potholes begin as slight dents in the rock surface. Over time, erosion deepens them enough to hold airborne dust and insect larvae. Add water and you have an aquatic ecosystem.

All life-forms in a pothole are exquisitely adapted to this delicate existence. Ounce per ounce, there's more life in a pothole pool than almost any other place in canyon country. At a newly filled pothole you may see mosquito larvae rise to the surface, then sink back down again. Slender bloodworms resembling lengths of red thread snap and loop in a pulsating rhythm. Gnat larvae, having lost as much as 92 percent of their body weight to dehydration, are capable of swelling to life again when water returns to the potholes.

Tadpoles, too, survive in these temporary pools, which may last a matter of weeks. Tiny horseshoe crab-shaped crustaceans called fairy shrimp tolerate months of drought before a rain shower precipitates their egg production.

Canyonlands pothole

Elaterite Butte, Canyonlands National Park

The Needles: 18 miles; most of a day

The Needles area covers a lattice of canyons, arches, flat-bottomed valleys called grabens, and spectacular sandstone walls notched by rocky spires and columns. To the north, **Island in the Sky** and **Junction Butte** stand silhouetted against the horizon.

Utah 211 will take you directly from Monticello to this district of the park, but along the way you might stop at **Newspaper Rock,** a 200-square-foot chunk of Wyngate sandstone that appears to have been used as a bulletin board for several ancient cultures, beginning 1,500 years ago. Animals, broad-shouldered human figures,

and the occasional snake or river shape are among the hundreds of images scratched into the desert varnish.

Inside the park, stop at The Needles Visitor Center for maps and brochures. Here, a dirt road heads north to the **Colorado River Overlook**. This road makes for rough going; don't take it unless you have a four-wheel-drive vehicle.

Continue on the paved road to the **Roadside Ruin** pull-off. Stretch your legs on a quarter-mile self-guided nature trail that leads to a small but well-preserved granary used by ancient farmers to store corn more than 700 years ago. These people were related to the ancestral Puebloans of Mesa Verde and Chaco Canyon. Pick up an interpretive booklet at the trailhead to learn how they used the native plants for food, medicines, and tools.

From here, drive 0.6 mile to the first road on your left, then turn left again on the next dirt road and follow it 1.1 miles to the parking area and trailhead for the highly engaging, self-guided **Cave Spring Trail.** The cave near the trailhead holds the remains of a cowboy line camp, used as late as 1975 when the last of the cattle were removed from the park. Beyond, you'll find a groundwater spring, pictographs, and maidenhair ferns hanging from the rocks.

Your next stop will be **Pothole Point,** where a half-mile trail leads past depressions in the sandstone that fill with water after a rain. Although the water looks as still as the rock, the depressions often teem with life *(see p. 87)*. Snails, fairy shrimp, and horsehair worms lay eggs that survive the heat of summer encased in dried mud. When the rains come, they hatch in days.

The road ends at **Big Spring Canyon Overlook,** where squat columns of sandstone rise from barren bedrock. Here the 5.5-mile **Confluence Overlook Trail** climbs the far side of the canyon by a ladder and ends at a point 930 feet above the junction of the rivers. This is a popular trail with most park visitors. More scenic is the 2.5-mile **Slickrock Trail,** which begins just before the road ends at the overlook. If time allows, stop here on your return drive for a moderate hike across slickrock balds of Cedar Mesa sandstone.

Turn on the **Elephant Hill** spur, a graded dirt road that leads to the base of a notorious climb for four-wheel drivers. Along the road are great views of The Needles. You see tall fingers of rock arrayed along the skyline, their red and white bands created by the interlayering of ancient river deposits with sand dunes. A shaded area at the end of the graded road makes a good place to picnic.

Henry Mountains Buffalo Herd

The Henry Mountains, located between Canyonlands and Capitol Reef National Parks, support a herd of 360 bison that climb to 11,000 feet in summer. They live on a 150,000-acre preserve near Hanksville where visitors can camp, hike, climb, rockhound, ride horses, and take scenic drives *(high-clearance four-wheel drives only)*. Three primitive campgrounds. Open all year. Information at BLM office *(435-542-3461)* in Hanksville, Utah.

Hikes & Four-Wheel-Drive Routes

To really explore Canyonlands—85 percent of which is backcountry—you must leave your car and proceed on foot, mountain bike, or four-wheel-drive vehicle (for more backcountry activities in the region, see feature pp. 28–29).

In The Needles, **Chesler Park Trail** leads 2.9 miles to a grassland sunk in a wide rock pocket rimmed by colorful spires. **Druid Arch Trail** branches off at Elephant Canyon and leads another 2.4 miles with a short ladder climb to the great arch that resembles a megalithic ceremonial site.

Elephant Hill Trail, a route only for rugged four-wheel-drive vehicles, runs 9 miles to the Confluence Overlook. It begins by climbing Elephant Hill's jaw-clenching switchbacks and 40 percent grade and ends with a half-mile walk to the overlook.

White Rim Road in Island in the Sky is one of the park's most popular jeep roads. Near the entrance, the **Shafer Trail** will take you to it. It follows a broad bench, lunar white along the edge where the red talus has been stripped to bedrock. For more than 80 miles it stays above the inner gorge, 1,200 feet below the Island, as it meanders through prime desert bighorn sheep country.

Northwest of The Maze lies a detached section of the park, the **Horseshoe Canyon Unit,** entered by way of a 3.5-mile trail. You follow an old road into the canyon, then walk up **Barrier Creek** past some of the continent's finest prehistoric rock art. At the **Great Gallery,** ghostly figures painted in red ocher stare through eerie hollow eyes. Archaeologists believe these life-size pictographs may be more than 3,000, perhaps as much as 6,000, years old.

The Maze Overlook can be reached by a 14-mile hike (bring plenty of water) beginning at North Trail Canyon, 3.5 rough miles past Hans Flat Ranger Station. Reaching the trailhead can be an adventure, but the views from the rim of this isolated wedge of canyon country make it worth the effort. And the quiet is as expansive as the vistas. The trail passes north of **Elaterite Butte** for a tantalizing view into the twists and blind alleys of The Maze.

With a high-clearance four-wheel-drive vehicle you can drive the 34 miles from **Hans Flat** to the overlook. This is one of the park's classic jeep routes. Negotiating steep switchbacks allows the driver little chance to sightsee, and with winter snows the route becomes impassable.

INFORMATION & ACTIVITIES

Headquarters
2282 SW Resource Blvd.
Moab, UT 84532
435-719-2313
www.nps.gov/cany

Visitor & Information Centers
Moab boasts a multiagency visitor center *(see p. 28)*. Park visitor centers at Island in the Sky, The Needles, and Hans Flat Ranger Station (near The Maze). Open all year.

Seasons & Accessibility
Year-round, with best seasons in spring and fall. Flash floods from July through September can temporarily close roads. Call for current conditions.

Entrance Fees
$10 per vehicle good for seven days, multiple entries. Annual permit $25, also good at Arches National Park, and Natural Bridges and Hovenweep NMs.

Pets
Leashed at all times. Prohibited on hiking trails, river corridors, and backcountry roads.

Facilities for Disabled
The visitor centers and Moab headquarters are accessible.

Things to Do
Free naturalist-led activities: nature walks, interpretive exhibits. Hiking, boating, rafting *(permit required)*, bicycling. Contact park for list of concessionaires offering mountain biking, hiking, four-wheel-drives, and river-running trips.

Special Advisories
■ Always carry water when hiking—at least a gallon per person per day. Water available near Squaw Flat Campground and at visitor centers.
■ Use care near cliff edges and on slickrock surfaces; falls often fatal.
■ Do not walk on cryptobiotic crust—the fragile, crunchy, black soil that is composed of living plants.
■ Permits required for boating. Permits and reservation fees required for overnight backpacking and four-wheel-drive trips. Available at visitor centers, ranger stations, and park headquarters. For reservations, call (435)259-4351 or visit www.nps.gov/cany/permits.htm.

Campgrounds
Two campgrounds, Squaw Flat and Willow Flat, both with 14-day limit. Open all year, first come, first served; March to October filled by midmorning. Fees $5–$10 per night. No showers. Tent and RV sites;

Mesa Arch sunrise

no hookups. Three group campsites in The Needles, reservations required, contact park headquarters.

Hotels, Motels, & Inns

(Unless otherwise noted, rates are for two persons in a double room, high season.)

In Moab, UT 84532:

■ **Best Western Green Well Motel**
105 S. Main St. 800-528-1234 or 435-259-6151. 72 units. $79–$130. AC, pool, restaurant.

■ **Big Horn Travelodge**
550 S. Main St. 800-325-6171 or 435-259-6171. 58 units. $59–$79. AC, pool, restaurant. www.moabbighorn.com.

■ **Pack Creek Ranch**
(15 miles southeast of Moab, off La Sal Mountain Loop Rd.) P.O. Box 1270. 435-259-5505. Cabins, houses, bunkhouses. $95–$225. Includes breakfast. Trail rides *(fee)*. AC, pool. www.packcreekranch.com.

■ **Ramada Inn—Moab**
182 S. Main St. 435-259-7141. 82 units. $49–$89. AC, pool, restaurant. www.ramadainn moab.com.

In Monticello, UT 84535:

■ **Best Western Wayside Inn**
197 E. Central Hwy. 666. 435-587-2261 or 800-633-9700. 38 units. $64–$69. AC, pool.

■ **Triangle H Motel**
164 E. Central Hwy. 666. 435-587-2274 or 800-657-6622. 26 units. $36–$42. AC.

Excursions from Canyonlands

Dead Horse Point State Park

5 miles east of Canyonlands

Carved mainly by the Colorado and Green Rivers, the vast, labyrinthine wilderness of southeast Utah's canyonlands is so impressive to the appreciative, so provocative to the curious, and so enticing to the adventurous that it's no wonder the panoramas from 5,900-foot-high **Dead Horse Point** are often praised as the most spectacular of any park in the Beehive State.

Add a scenic drive from Moab through sand and sagebrush canyons, past cliffs and spires of liver-hued Kayenta sandstone, and you have one of Utah's most memorable day trips—ending with long views sweeping some 50 miles south across Canyonlands National Park to a horizon steepled by the Henry, La Sal, and Abajo Mountains. Easy walking trails along the rim of the mesa flirt with the edge of the 2,000-foot-deep gorge and lead to a half dozen overlooks of some of the most remote and least accessible public land in the Southwest.

If your time is limited, drive to Dead Horse Point, leave your car, and walk to **Dead Horse Point Overlook,** the park's signature panorama. You can savor the experience of this exhilarating over-look by parking at the visitor center, letting its historical and geo-logical exhibits deepen your appreciation of what you're about to witness, then strolling the 1.5-mile **Main Trail,** skirting the mesa's southeast precipice to the 90-foot-wide "neck" of the promontory. From here stroll the half mile to the overlook and the **Observation Shelter** in the day-use area, where picnic tables command one of the finest views in the Canyonlands region.

From here, the main trail loops back along the mesa's western edge to the **Meander Overlook.** Less well-marked and with trickier footing, this footpath looks down on an exceptionally complex landscape—spires, pinnacles, buttes, and convoluted benchlands and wriggly canyons notorious for disorienting wilderness hikers. Keep walking north and you'll come to the **Rim Overlook,** and then the **Big Horn Overlook,** each claiming a unique section of the panorama. Along the way look for slickrock potholes *(see p. 87)*.

■ **5,362 acres** ■ **Southeast Utah, southwest of Moab** ■ **Best seasons spring and fall** ■ **Hiking, camping, bird-watching, ranger-led activities** ■ **Contact the park, Box 609, Moab, UT 84532; 435-259-2614. www.parks.state.ut.us**

Natural Bridges National Monument

115 miles southwest of Canyonlands

Back in 1883, prospector Cass Hite spent his days wandering the wild, trackless canyons of the Colorado River in search of gold. Although he never hit pay dirt, he did discover a wealth of natural beauty. Hite's precious treasure included three river-carved stone bridges located within an easy walk of one another.

Today, **Bridge View Drive,** a 9-mile loop, takes visitors past all three of Hite's famous bridges: 220-foot-tall **Sipapu,** the world's second largest natural bridge, 210-foot **Kachina,** and the delicate 106-foot **Owachomo.**

Short trails lead from parking areas to bridge viewpoints. Especially worthwhile is the 0.3-mile trail to the overlook for **Horse Collar Ruin,** a uniquely shaped prehistoric structure. The 9-mile **Natural Bridges Loop Trail,** accessible from any of the overlook trails off Bridge View Drive, takes you under all the bridges and past lush desert oases to a canyon bottom etched with the markings of ancient cultures. Watch for white-throated swifts in the skies above the canyon; they also hover along the sheer faces of the rock wall, tending their nests of mud and twigs.

A video and exhibits at the solar-powered **visitor center** located on Utah 275 just inside the monument entrance explain how meandering streams cut through Permian age Cedar Mesa sandstone to carve the natural bridges. Many of the fascinating ranger-guided walks and evening programs focus on cultural aspects of the region's early human occupation, which spanned the period from 7000 B.C. to A.D. 500.

To learn about the area's native plants, including desert sage, pinyon, and juniper—and how they were used as food, tools, and medicine by the ancestral Puebloans—follow the short self-guided **interpretive trail** located just outside the visitor center.

Natural Bridges holds the distinction of being Utah's first National Park Service area. Theodore Roosevelt established the monument four years after the area was featured in a 1904 issue of NATIONAL GEOGRAPHIC magazine.

■ **7,636 acres** ■ **Southeast Utah, 42 miles west of Blanding** ■ **Best seasons spring and fall. Visitor center open May–Sept.** ■ **Adm. fee** ■ **Hiking, scenic drives, ranger-led activities** ■ **Contact the monument, HC 60 Box 1, Lake Powell, UT 84533; 435-692-1234. www.nps.gov/nabr**

Green River

Few rivers in the intermountane West possess a more intriguing mix of natural and cultural history than the Green. For starters, the headwaters of the Green River lie in a phenomenal slice of western Wyoming high country, around Fremont Peak in the Wind River Range. This glaciated region is a place of cold summer nights and lingering snowfields and ice-water streams. Scientist and explorer John Wesley Powell mistakenly identified this slice of high mountainscape as the real source of the Colorado River. "It runs," he said of the Green, "from land of snow to land of sun."

True to Powell's description, the Green moves southward across western Wyoming through the lonely landscape of the Green River Plains, pushing into ever starker places—dry, dreamy waves of domes and pinnacles, ancient lake beds rich in fossils, cliffs, and dunes.

Then on it courses through the slack water of Flaming Gorge to be reborn in the wild tumbles of Colorado's Gates of Lodore. After running back through Utah in an outrageously dizzying series of twists and meanders, the Green finally joins the Colorado River in the sweet, stone bosom of Canyonlands National Park. Along the way is the smell of sedge and meadow grass and the sight of moose, bear, pronghorn, mule deer, and ghostly bands of desert bighorn—with enough geology en route to spin the head of even the most fervent earth scientist.

Many an early explorer stood on high perches and scanned the arid sprawls of the intermountain West for the telltale green of the cottonwood tree; wherever it appeared, water was close at hand. The Green River is no exception. From spring through fall, long, verdant ribbons of Fremont cottonwoods line its banks. Like many other plants here, cottonwood was important to native peoples for both ceremonial and medicinal purposes, helping to break fevers and reduce inflammation. Indeed, various parts of the cottonwood contain salicin and populin—both of which share properties with the active ingredients in aspirin.

Cottonwood seeds have highly specific requirements for germination. They remain viable for only about two weeks, and even then will sprout only on freshly soaked ground—a preference that corresponds to the normal spring flood cycle. With the installation of

Rafting on the Green

upstream dams, however, many places along the Green River no longer enjoy seasonal flooding. In the long term, sad to say, this will severely curtail the extent and growth of cottonwood groves.

For all the history associated with the Green River, none stands out more in the American imagination than the doings of the mountain men. One, Jedediah Smith, roamed the tributaries of the Green. Flouting the stereotype, Smith neither drank nor smoked. Indeed, he was known among his peers for his religious nature—and for his survival of a literally hair-raising experience: Mauled by a grizzly bear and left with his scalp hanging by an ear, Smith told a companion to reattach it as best as he could with needle and thread.

Another legendary pioneer, William Ashley, built two boats of buffalo hides and tossed them in the Green River at Flaming Gorge. He then bobbed and portaged all the way through what is now Dinosaur National Monument. Ashley was largely responsible for hosting those famously boisterous trading-and-resupply parties known as the Rendezvous. Though trappers habitually worked alone or in small groups, once a year for 16 years (from roughly 1825 to 1840) they would gather around company wagon trains laden with goods for some of the biggest bouts of trading, drinking, lying, and fighting imaginable.

Capitol Reef

The unifying geographic feature of Capitol Reef is the Waterpocket Fold. For a hundred miles its parallel ridges rise from the desert like the swell of giant waves rolling toward shore. Exposed edges of the uplift have eroded into a slickrock wilderness of massive domes, cliffs, and a maze of twisting canyons. The fold takes its name from the way depressions in the rock hold water. Imagine hard boulders being washed down a sandstone slope after a storm; at a flat spot or depression the cascading water swirls around them like drill bits to bore into the softer sandstone. Some of these pockets, called tinajas, may end up being 8 or 10 feet deep, though shallower ones are more common. Some hold water permanently, supporting tadpoles, frogs, and various plants as well as providing drinking water for larger animals such as bighorn sheep.

Geologists know the fold as one of the largest and best exposed monoclines on the North American continent. Travelers know it as a place of dramatic beauty and serenity so remote that the nearest traffic light is 78 miles away. And even though its 378 square miles are off the beaten track, the park still attracts nearly 550,000 visitors each year.

Capitol Reef is named for a particularly colorful section of the fold near the Fremont River where sheer cliffs formed a barrier to travel for early pioneers. It reminded them of an ocean reef. Although a highway now crosses the "reef," travel is still challenging for those wishing to see the park's more remote regions.

The southern end of the fold offers fine wilderness backpacking in Lower Muley Twist Canyon and Halls Creek Narrows. Along the park's northern border lies Cathedral Valley, a repository of quiet solitude where jagged monoliths rise hundreds of feet.

The middle region is best known. Here the raw beauty of the towering cliffs

- Southern Utah, near Torrey

- 241,904 acres

- Established 1971

- Best seasons spring and fall

- Hiking, backpacking, mountain biking, scenic drive, petroglyphs, fruit picking

- Information: 435-425-3791 www.nps.gov/care

Temple of the Moon, Capitol Reef National Park

contrasts with the green oasis that 19th-century Mormon pioneers created along the Fremont River, establishing the village of Fruita. Their irrigation ditches still water fruit trees in fields abandoned by Fremont Indians 700 years ago. Mule deer now graze the orchard's grasses and alfalfa, and park visitors get to harvest the apples, peaches, and apricots.

The most striking reminder of the Fremont culture is the rock art it produced. Figures resembling bighorn sheep crowd many petroglyph panels

The last sighting in the park of a native desert bighorn, a subspecies, occurred in 1948. Their disappearance is attributed to overhunting and various diseases caught from domestic sheep. The Park Service reintroduced desert bighorn sheep in 1984, 1996, and 1997. These herds have managed to survive.

How to Get There

From Green River (about 85 miles away), take I-70 to Utah 24, which leads to the east entrance. For a scenic approach, start at Bryce Canyon National Park. Follow Utah 12 over Boulder Mountain to Utah 24, just outside the park's west entrance. Airport: Salt Lake City.

What Not to Miss

- **A hike to Sunset Point for view of Waterpocket Fold**
- **Rim Overlook Trail (from Fruita)**
- **Burr Trail Loop drive**
- **4WD trip into Cathedral Valley**
- **Hiking to Hamburger Rocks (Halls Creek Canyon) or, if with kids, hiking the Surprise Canyon Trail**

When to Go

All-year park. Spring and fall are mild and ideal for hiking. Winter is cold but brief. Back roads can become impassable during spring thaw, summer rains, and winter snows.

How to Visit

On a 1-day visit, take Utah 24 along the **Fremont River** and then the **Scenic Drive** through the park. This section offers fine hiking on nearly 40 miles of developed trails. The best second-day activity is a drive along portions of the **Burr Trail Loop** with a walk to Strike Valley Overlook. For a longer stay, drive the **Cathedral Valley Loop** or hike in one of the more remote canyons of the Waterpocket Fold.

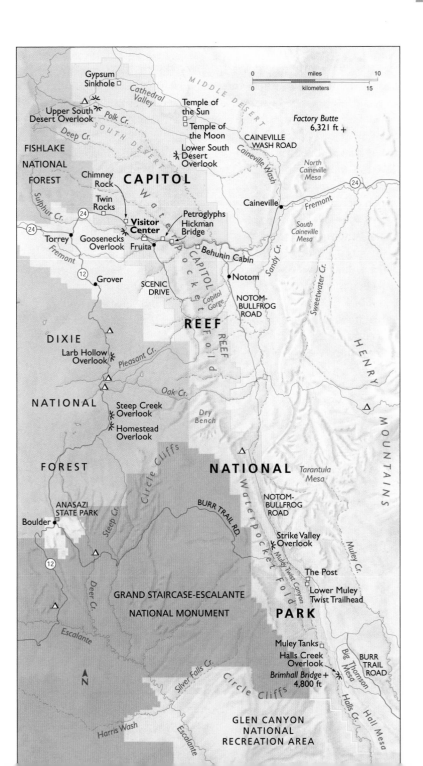

EXPLORING THE PARK

Fremont River & Scenic Drive: 35 miles; a half to full day

Drive east on Utah 24 as you enter the park from the west. Ahead of you rises the eroded west face of the **Waterpocket Fold**, a massive line of cliffs running north and south. After the first few miles, the highway follows the course cut through the rock wilderness by the swift **Fremont River**, named for frontier explorer John C. Frémont. Take the unpaved spur road to the **Goosenecks Overlook**. From the parking area an easy 0.1-mile trail ends above the deeply entrenched meanders of Sulphur Creek. Another short walk takes you to **Sunset Point** for a sweeping view of the Capitol Reef section of the Waterpocket Fold.

Bypass the Chimney Rock turnoff unless you plan to walk the 3.5-mile **Chimney Rock loop trail** or the more ambitious 9-mile **Spring Canyon** route. This follows a deep gorge cutting through fine exposures of Wingate and Navajo sandstones and ends with a ford at the Fremont River to rejoin Utah 24. *(Check on river levels and trail conditions before setting out.)*

Stop at the **visitor center** on the edge of **Fruita**, the remnants of the Mormon frontier community settled in the 1880s and now part

View of the Henry Mountains, from Sunset Point

of the national park. Be sure to see the ten-minute video—the view of the red sandstone cliffs from the theater window is itself worth the stop.

Take the 25-mile round-trip **Scenic Drive** along the rugged face of Capitol Reef. This paved road follows a century-old wagonway known as the Blue Dugway. The old road was used by Native Americans, outlaws, gypsies, and once even the devil himself, according to an early pioneer who chased him off by brandishing the Book of Mormon. Take the short spur road into **Grand Wash.** Look high on the cliff rim for **Cassidy Arch** named for outlaw Butch Cassidy, who reportedly used the canyon as a hideout. A 2.25-mile trail from the parking area leads down Grand Wash through spectacular narrows to the Fremont River. Another trail climbs 1.75 miles to Cassidy Arch. The Scenic Drive ends with a winding 2-mile spur road into **Capitol Gorge.** This was the main road through the reef before 1962. It now ends at a parking area where an easy 1-mile **nature trail** continues down into the canyon to historic inscriptions and a series of natural waterpockets, popular among desert denizens.

Return by the same road to Fruita, then go east on Utah 24, passing well-maintained orchards. Turn in at the **Petroglyphs pulloff.** Here Fremont Indians pecked into the cliff large human figures in headdresses. Since you can view this cliff art only at a distance, binoculars come in handy; spotting scopes are mounted on the main panel boardwalk. The origin of these farmers about A.D. 600 and their disappearance six centuries later are still mysteries. Early settlers found what appeared to be remnants of their irrigation ditches, granaries, and pit houses. One unusual discovery was a brick of tule sugar, grass seeds, and pulverized grasshoppers—thought to have been emergency food.

Continue down the highway a short distance to the **Hickman Bridge** parking area. Stretch your legs with a 1-mile hike up a self-guided **nature trail** that leads under the natural bridge, 125 feet above. For a longer and more arduous hike, take the 2.25-mile **Rim Overlook Trail** along the cliff tops. It ends at a 1,000-foot drop to the Fremont River, providing a good vantage point to view the green pocket of Fruita enclosed in a landscape of tilted rock.

Farther along the road, pull off at the **Behunin Cabin.** This one-room stone cabin was once home to a family of ten. The parents and two youngest children slept inside, the girls in a wagon box outside, and the boys in a nearby rock alcove.

Burr Trail Loop: 125 miles; at least a full day

The drive begins at the visitor center. Go east on Utah 24 to the **Notom-Bullfrog Road.** Paved for the first several miles of its southbound route, the road becomes dirt, skirting the uplift where rock has pushed skyward at 70-degree angles. It crosses several washes that turn into slot canyons where they cut into the east flank of the Waterpocket Fold. At the junction with the **Burr Trail Road,** you must decide whether to make it a half-day trip and return to the visitor center, or to take a full day and complete the loop. If you decide to continue, turn west and climb a series of spectacular

switchbacks to the high rim of the fold. Views of the Henry Mountains to the east, and Burr Canyon straight below, are dramatic.

One of the finest vistas in the park is the **Strike Valley Overlook** in Upper Muley Twist Canyon. Many visitors walk the 2.5 miles from the hikers' parking area to the overlook trailhead through a beautiful canyon with double arches and a large rock window on the rim. High-clearance, four-wheel-drive vehicles can follow the canyon floor to a parking area near the overlook. From there, the trail continues up canyon for another 6.5 miles, passing several large arches.

Those looking for solitude can backpack into **Lower Muley Twist Canyon,** with its miles of fine slickrock wilderness (*free backcountry permits required; available at visitor center*). Bends in the canyon are so tight, early teamsters said, a mule would have to twist itself in order to get through. Also off the Burr Trail are the 2-mile **Suprise** and **Headquarters Canyons** hikes and the 9-mile trail through Halls Creek Canyon to **Hamburger Rocks.**

Burr Trail Road becomes paved as it leaves Capitol Reef and continues west to the town of Boulder. Turn north onto paved Utah 12, which winds up and over Boulder Mountain through a high alpine forest. Here you join Utah 24 about 10 miles west of the visitor center.

Cathedral Valley Circle: 70 miles; a half to full day

A high-clearance, two- or four-wheel-drive vehicle is recommended for this scenic trip (*check unpaved road conditions before setting*

Fragile Ground Cover

Throughout this region you're sure to notice a dark, somewhat lumpy crust on the ground. This so-called cryptobiotic soil is a mix of lichens, mosses, green algae, cyanobacteria, and micro-fungi, and it covers most of the Colorado Plateau.

Cryptobiotic soil is a living web that literally holds the ground in place. The pioneering member of the mix, cyanobacteria, sends out thin filaments surrounded by sticky sheaths that cling to soil particles. Microfungal bodies move in next, tapping nutrients from plant roots and increasing the root system of their host tenfold. Green algae set up shop in the pores of the soil, collecting nitrogen from the air, as do various lichens. Together, the members of this living mulch create the characteristically spongy look and feel of cryptobiotic soil. Dormant during drought, this layer springs to life again after rain.

If your visit to canyon country coincides with recent moisture at the end of a long dry spell, you may witness a remarkable sight: the spongy crust swelling with water.

Despite the ability of this soil to withstand temperatures 50 degrees higher than the surrounding air, it is still surprisingly fragile. A single footstep or tire track can destroy this crust.

out). From the visitor center, follow Utah 24 east for 11 miles. At a marked crossing, turn off Utah 24 and ford the Fremont River. If the river is too high for your vehicle, use the Caineville access to reach Cathedral Valley.

As the road heads north, it passes through the colorful badlands of the Bentonite Hills and follows a mesa called **The Hartnet** to the edge of a 400-foot escarpment overlooking South Desert. On the mesa's opposite side is a spectacular view into **Upper Cathedral Valley.** In this vast open space, keep a lookout for soaring golden eagles riding the thermals. Eroded spires and monoliths of Entrada sandstone jut hundreds of feet from the valley floor like enormous weathered teeth.

The road loops to the south and drops among the unusual formations, following the valley past such landmarks as the **Walls of Jericho,** the **Gypsum Sinkhole,** and the **Temples of the Sun** and **Moon.** The drive ends at Utah 24, near Caineville.

INFORMATION & ACTIVITIES

Headquarters

HC 70, Box 15
Torrey, UT 84775
435-425-3791
www.nps.gov/care

Visitor & Information Centers

Visitor center on Utah 24 at the
park's north end open all year.

Seasons & Accessibility

Park open year-round. Many
roads are unpaved. The scenic
drive may close briefly during
rainy weather and in winter.
Dirt roads may require high-
clearance or four-wheel-drive
vehicles. Contact headquarters
for current conditions.

Entrance Fee

$5 per car per week.

Pets

Permitted on leashes; prohibited from trails, backcountry.

Facilities for Disabled

Visitor center, rest rooms, and
Petroglyphs Trail are accessible
to wheelchairs.

Things to Do

Free ranger-led activities,
evening programs. For information on horseback trips and
jeep tours, contact the Wayne
County Travel Council (800-
858-7951).

Special Advisories

■ Always carry water. Except
for tap water, most water in
park is not drinkable.
■ Watch out for flash floods
between July and September.
■ Overnight backpacking
requires permit, free at visitor
center or from any park ranger.

Campgrounds

Three park campgrounds,
with a total of 70 sites, 14-day
limit, all year, no reservations,
$10 per night. Tent sites at
Cathedral Valley and Cedar
Mesa. Tent and RV sites at
Fruita; no hookups.

   The BLM also has several
backcountry campsites near
Capitol Reef. For permits along
the Burr Trail contact Anasazi
State Park, Grand Staircase
Escalante National Monument
Information Desk, 460 N. Hwy.
12, Boulder, UT. 435-335-7382.
www.ut.blm.gov/monument/.

   Dixie National Forest has a
number of campsites: Contact
Escalante Ranger District,
Escalante Interagency Building,
755 West Main, P.O. Box 246,
Escalante, UT 84726. 435-826-
5400; or Teasdale Ranger District,138 E. Main St., P.O. Box
90, Teasdale, UT 84773. 435-
425-9500. www.fs.fed.us/dxnf
/recreation/campgrounds/camp
index.htm.

Pack trip through Paradise Flats

Hotels, Motels, & Inns

(Unless otherwise noted, rates are for two persons in a double room, high season.)

In Bicknell, UT 84715:

■ **Aquarius Inn** 240 W. Main St. 435-425-3835. 28 units, 6 with kitchenettes. $40. AC, RV park. www.aquariusinn.com.

■ **Sunglow Motel** 63 E. Main St., P.O. Box 68. 435-425-3821. 15 units, most with AC. $35. www.sunglowpies.com.

In Torrey, UT 84775:

■ **Capitol Reef Inn** 360 W. Main St., P.O. Box 100. 435-425-3271. 10 units. $44. Spring-fall. www.capitolreefinn.com.

■ **Wonderland Inn** Utah 12 at Utah 24. 800-458-0216. 50 units. $54–$76. AC, pool.

■ **Comfort Inn & Suites Capitol Reef** 2424 E. Hwy 24. 435-425-3866. 40 units, $73. AC, pool, exercise room. www.gowestindustries.com.

For information on additional lodging, contact the park headquarters or the Wayne County Travel Council, P.O. Box 7, Teasdale, UT 84773. 435-425-3365 or 800-858-7951. Send e-mail to info@capitolreef.org; or visit www.capitolreef.org. Garfield County Tourism Office, 55 S. Main Panguitch, UT 84759. 435-676-1160 or 800-444-6689. www.bryce canyoncountry.com.

Excursions from Capitol Reef

Fishlake National Forest

35 miles west of Capitol Reef

A cool green island of aspen and coniferous forest east of the intersection of I-70 and I-15, Fishlake National Forest sprawls across the very heart of southern Utah's high plateaus. This is an especially comfortable place on hot days, when the slickrock and the pinyon-juniper forests of lower elevations bake in the summer sun.

A number of roads serve as extraordinary gateways into this high oasis, notably the 23-mile **Fish Lake Scenic Byway,** which follows Utah 25 from west of the town of Loa, past Fish Lake and Johnson Valley Reservoir to Utah 72. This beautiful route features abundant coniferous woods and lush meadows. Hearty walkers, might consider a hike along the 4-mile **Pelican Valley Trail** *(just W of Fish Lake, a mile beyond Pelican Overlook),* which climbs steadily some 2,100 feet to the top of the Fish Lake Hightop Plateau. The views are remarkable, with the island uplifts of the Henry, La Sal,

Sunset at Fishlake National Forest

and Abajo Mountains visible far to the east— their feet in the desert, heads in the clouds.

Another terrific drive, the **Beaver Canyon Scenic Byway** (Utah 153), runs east for 17 miles from I-15 at the town of Beaver, meandering along the Beaver River to Elk Meadows at the feet of the beautiful Tushar Mountains. This is an especially fine drive in the fall, when aspen and mountain maple stage their riots of color. Numerous interesting hiking trails thread this area, but most of them must be shared with the whine and rumble of

Kimberly–Big John Road

At altitudes ranging from 6,000 to 11,500 feet, this southwestern Utah dirt road explores Fishlake National Forest's **Beaver District**, ascending the naked slopes of the Tushar Mountains and passing an old mining town. From Junction on US 89, head west on Utah 153 into the national forest, passing Puffer Lake and Elk Meadows, with its downhill ski area.

Near Beaver Canyon, take FR 123 north to the Big John Flat, ascending the Tushar Mountains. Three peaks— Delano Peak, Mount Belknap, and Mount Baldy—soar above 12,000 feet, and a half dozen others top 11,000 feet. On their flanks, high mountain meadows burst with wildflowers in late summer. Their open summits provide sweeping views of south and central Utah. At the northern and eastern flanks of the mountains, the road joins FR 113 and passes **Kimberly,** a turn-of-the-century gold-mining boomtown. The road continues on to I-70.

Junction, Utah, to I-70; 40 miles; Three hours; Summer and fall; Generally passable by high-clearance vehicles; dangerous in wet weather.

all-terrain vehicles. One notable exception is the **Skyline National Scenic Trail** (*24 miles E of Beaver via Utah 153, then quarter mile S of Big Flat guard station*). Running along the broad flank of the Tushar Mountains, this glorious upland hike through wildflower meadows offers soaring views into the Circle Valley, which lies some 5,000 feet below.

■ **1.4 million acres** ■ **Central Utah** ■ **Best seasons summer and fall**
■ **Camping, hiking, fishing, mountain biking, horseback riding, scenic drives**
■ **Contact the national forest, 115 E. 900 North, Richfield, UT 84701.**
435-896-9233. www.fs.fed.us/recreation/forest_descr/ut_r4_fishlake.html

Glen Canyon National Recreation Area

104 miles south of Capitol Reef

Centerpiece to this magnificent recreation area is **Lake Powell,** the world's second largest man-made reservoir. Created by the Glen Canyon dam, which was completed in 1963, the lake is 186 miles long, has 1,960 miles of crenellated shoreline, and offers more water frontage than the entire west coast of the United States. The crown jewel of this lake is **Rainbow Bridge**—a national monument, a sacred Navajo site and the largest natural bridge in the world, rising to 290 feet and spanning 270 feet.

To reach the bridge, you can take a tour boat from Wahweap, Bullfrog, or Halls Crossing. The boat delivers you to a 0.7-mile trail leading directly to the span. Or, you can make the strenuous 14-mile one-way hike from **Navajo Mountain** *(permit required; contact the Navajo Nation Parks & Recreation Dept., 928-871-6647).*

The bridge itself is a splendid sight—a mighty sweep of fine-grained, cross-bedded Navajo sandstone soaring nearly 300 feet above the sandy bottom of Bridge Canyon.

This lovely span of rock started out as a hole punched in a rock fin by a vigorous, sediment-laden stream known as Bridge Creek. The stream's erosional power, combined with constant weathering of the Navajo and Kayenta formations, turned a modest hole into the remarkable span seen today.

Boating

One of the principle pleasures of Lake Powell is to steer a boat along a quiet cove, pausing for a swim before motoring up yet another arm of the canyon. All boaters should follow a detailed map of the lake, preferably one by Stan Jones *(available at Bullfrog Visitor Center, 435-684-7423),* which is updated annually.

Rental houseboats are available for groups of 2 to 20; you can easily spend 3 days to 3 weeks cruising places where few speedboats bother to go. The lake's four marinas all offer boats and supplies: Wahweap, near Page, Arizona; Halls Crossing, 47 miles west of Natural Bridges National Monument; Bullfrog, a ferry ride across the river from Halls; and Hite, the most northern. *(For information call 800-528-6154).*

Lake Powell is also a popular fishing destination. Anglers avoid the summer crowds by renting a boat in late spring or early fall. Fishing is best during the cooler months, when anglers are apt to land northern pike, walleye, large- and small-mouthed bass, crappie, striped bass, and catfish.

Hikes

In the Wahweap area you'll find the 0.4-mile **Horseshoe Bend View Trail** *(5 miles W of Carl Hayden Visitor Center),* which offers a good look at the spot where the Colorado River cuts a horseshoe-shaped bend through layers of sandstone. Parents must keep a close eye on children—there are no guardrails.

Arches, balanced rocks, and natural bridges await along the 3-mile **Wiregrass Canyon Trail** *(6 miles E of Big Water)* to Lake Powell. Along the trail you'll find steep drops created by flash floods, a small natural bridge, small arches high in the canyon wall, and enticing side canyons. *(To reach trailhead from Page, drive N on US 89 to Big Water, turn right between Mileposts 7 and 8, turn right after 0.3 mile onto Smoky Mountain Rd., and continue 4.6 miles to the Wiregrass Canyon Backcountry Use Area pullout.)*

Hole-in-the-Rock Road

Though most visitors to Lake Powell have water-based recreation on their minds, some find driving the region's back roads a grand adventure. The 62-mile Hole-in-the-Rock Road takes you along the once grueling route used by an 1879 Mormon expedition, which consisted of 250 people, 83 wagons, and 1,000 head of livestock. Seeking a shortcut to the San Juan River, where they hoped to establish settlements, the group spent the winter chipping and blasting to enlarge a crack in the rim above the Colorado River. The resulting path dropped 2,000 feet, with a precipitous grade ranging from 25 to 45 degrees.

John Hall, one of southern Utah's earliest pioneers, built a boat for the missionaries that ferried them across the river. For ten years he operated the ferry until people found an easier crossing 35 miles upstream, the present site of Halls Crossing. This road is accessible for high-clearance passenger cars, but the last 10 miles are suited to four-wheel-drive vehicles only.

■ **1.3 million acres** ■ **Southeast Utah, northern Arizona** ■ **Best months March–Oct.** ■ **Adm. fee** ■ **Camping, hiking, boating, houseboating, swimming, fishing, horseback riding, scenic drives** ■ **Contact the recreation area, Box 1507, Page, AZ 86040; 928-608-6200. www.nps.gov/glca**

Bluff Area

181 miles southeast of Capitol Reef

There's a restful air about **Bluff** (population 340), a shady little community tucked into the southeast corner of Utah along the San Juan River. Century-old stone homes reflect the town's Mormon beginnings. Cottonwoods line the streets. Surrounding the town is a rich weave of red-rock formations, enticing locals and visitors alike to explore the area on foot and by raft, bike, or car.

The area's biggest attraction is rafting the silt-laden **San Juan River,** a major artery of the Colorado River. Day trips pass ancient cliff dwellings, petroglyphs, and dramatic rock cliffs. River permits are required; call the Bureau of Land Management in Monticello *(435-587-1532)*. An easier option is to sign on with Wild Rivers Expeditions *(800-422-7654)* for a one-day, 26-mile trip from Bluff to Mexican Hat. Longer trips can be arranged.

Begin your land-based explorations of the Bluff area at **Goosenecks State Park** *(435-678-2238)*, located on Utah 316 southwest of town. The park is famous for its striking view of the entrenched

San Juan River, from Gooseneck State Park

meanders of the San Juan River. Here the river travels through a 1,500-foot chasm, winding 6 miles to advance no more than 1.5 miles as the crow flies.

Return to Utah 261 and head north 5 miles up steeply graded switchbacks. At the top, turn left onto the 3-mile dirt Moki Dugway. This road climbs 1,200 feet up a sandstone cliff to reach **Muley Point Overlook.** Visible below is the **Valley of the Gods** *(accessible from US 163)*, a great spot to end the day with a 17-mile drive.

On another day, consider a visit to the remote archaeological sites of **Hovenweep National Monument** *(NE of Bluff via Utah 262, 970-562-4282)*. The six ancestral Puebloan villages in Hovenweep's canyons were built in A.D. 1200. Camping facilities and ranger-guided tours are available.

■ **Southeast Utah, at intersection of US 163 and US 191** ■ **Best months April–Nov.** ■ **Camping, hiking, rafting, biking, scenic drives, petroglyphs, ancestral Puebloan ruins** ■ **Contact Bluff Visitor Information Center, Hwy. 191, Bluff, UT 84512; 435-672-2220. www.go-utah.com/bl**

Carlsbad Caverns

T he Chihuahuan Desert, studded with spiky plants and lizards, offers little hint that what Will Rogers called the "Grand Canyon with a roof on it" waits underground. Yet, at the northern reaches of this great desert, underneath a mountain range called the Guadalupes, lies one of the deepest, largest, and most ornate caverns ever found.

Water molded this underworld 4 to 6 million years ago. Some 250 million years ago, the region lay underneath the inland arm of an ancient sea. Near the shore grew a limestone reef. By the time the sea withdrew, the reef stood hundreds of feet high, later to be buried under thousands of feet of soil. Some 15 to 20 million years ago, the ground uplifted. Slightly acidic groundwater seeped into cracks in the limestone, gradually enlarging them to form a honeycomb of chambers. Millions of more years passed before the cave decoration began. Then, drop by drop, limestone-laden moisture built an extraordinary variety of glistening formations. Some of these are six stories tall; others tiny, delicate confections.

Cave scientists have explored more than 30 miles of passageways of the main cavern of Carlsbad, and investigation continues. Visitors may tour 3 miles on a paved trail. The Slaughter Canyon Cave provides the hardy an opportunity to play spelunker, albeit with a guide. The park has more than a hundred other caves open primarily to specialists.

Some visitors think the park's most spectacular sight is the one seen at the cave's mouth. More than a half million Mexican free-tailed bats summer in a section of the cave, and around sunset they spiral up from the entrance to hunt for insects. The nightly exodus led to the discovery of the cave in modern times. Around the turn of the 20th century, miners began to excavate bat guano—a potent fertilizer—for shipment to the citrus groves of southern California. One of the guano miners, James Larkin White,

- Southeast New Mexico, 25 miles southwest of Carlsbad

- 46,766 acres

- Established 1930

- Best seasons spring and fall

- Camping, hiking, bird-watching, cave tours, bat flight program

- Information: 505-785-2232 www.nps.gov/cave

Big Room formations, Carlsbad Caverns National Park

became the first to explore beyond the Bat Cave and to and publicize the caverns. He later served as a cave guide, lowering visitors into the caverns in a giant guano bucket.

How to Get There

The park is off US 62/180, 20 miles southwest of Carlsbad and 164 miles east of El Paso, Texas. For the visitor center, turn west at Whites City and drive 7 miles. For Slaughter Canyon, turn west on Rte. 418, 5 miles south of Whites City; drive another 11 miles, *(some of it unpaved),* to the parking lot. Airports: Carlsbad, N.Mex., and El Paso, Tex.

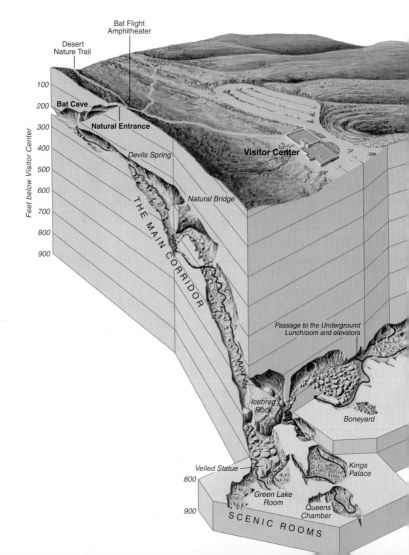

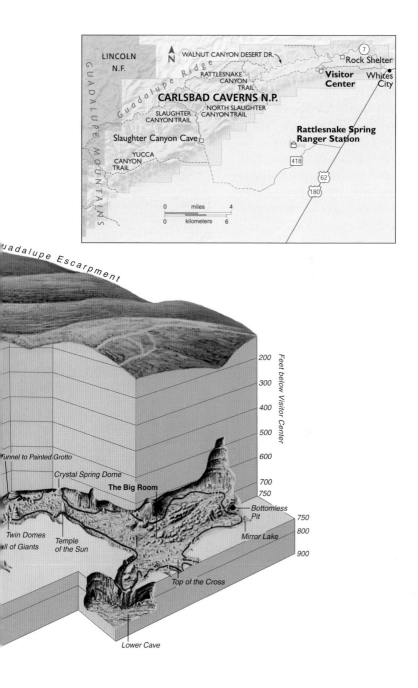

Guadalupe Escarpment

LINCOLN N.F.

WALNUT CANYON DESERT DR.

GUADALUPE MOUNTAINS

Guadalupe Ridge

RATTLESNAKE CANYON TRAIL

CARLSBAD CAVERNS N.P.

NORTH SLAUGHTER CANYON TRAIL

SLAUGHTER CANYON TRAIL

Slaughter Canyon Cave

YUCCA CANYON TRAIL

Rock Shelter

Visitor Center Whites City

Rattlesnake Spring Ranger Station

418

62

180

miles 4
kilometers 6

Feet below Visitor Center

200
300
400
500
600
700
750

Tunnel to Painted Grotto

Crystal Spring Dome

The Big Room

Bottomless Pit

750
800
900

Twin Domes
Hall of Giants

Temple of the Sun

Mirror Lake

Top of the Cross

Lower Cave

When to Go

All-year park. The weather underground remains a constant 56°F. The main cavern gets crowded, especially in summer and on major holiday weekends. Either spring or fall, when the desert blooms, is an excellent time to go. You'll see the bats fly from April or early May through October, sometimes later.

How to Visit

One full day allows you time to tour the main cavern and take a nature walk or a drive before watching the bats fly at sunset.

For a second day's activity, reserve space on a tour of "unimproved" **Slaughter Canyon Cave,** if you're ready for a more rugged caving experience.

At the visitor center, select either the **Natural Entrance Tour** or the **Big Room Tour** (both are self-guided 1-mile walks). Try the first unless you have walking, breathing, or heart problems. It starts at the natural entrance and is mostly downhill, except for one stretch where you climb 83 feet; an elevator whisks you back to ground level. The Natural Entrance Tour is more intimate and may be less crowded than the Big Room.

The **Big Room Tour** begins with an elevator ride directly to

the Big Room, in which you can see most of the types of formations visible in the other sections. If after this tour you want to see more caves, simply take the elevator back up to ground level and proceed with the first half of the Natural Entrance Tour.

Other options include the **Kings Palace Tour,** a 1.5-hour tour led by rangers through the deepest part of the cave open to the public. Or consider taking the **Walnut Canyon Desert Drive,** a 9.5-mile excursion that offers a primer on the park's above-ground flora and fauna.

While waiting for the evening **Bat Flight** to start, you might stall for time by ambling along the half-mile **Desert Nature Trail.**

EXPLORING THE PARK

Natural Entrance Tour: 1 mile; about 1 hour

This tour traces the traditional explorer's route into the cavern, entering through the large historic entrance. To get there, exit the visitor center and follow the path to the right. Once in the mouth of the cave, glance to your right to spot thousand-year-old red and black pictographs high on the wall. You are descending the **Main Corridor,** which, if you keep looking around and up, conveys some of the cavern's enormity—Ceiling height reaches more than 200 feet.

The trail soon passes **Devils Spring.** Here cave decoration continues. As water from rain and snow percolates through the ancient reef, it picks up calcite crystals from the limestone. The water then releases the crystals with each drop, splattering them onto the floor as the water drips—producing a stalagmite—or leaving them on the ceiling as the water discharges carbon dioxide into the cave air—creating a stalactite. You would have heard a lot more dripping 10,000 years ago, when the climate was wetter. Now the Guadalupes receive only about 14 to 19 inches of precipitation a year, and most of the formations are no longer growing.

The trail soon skirts **Iceberg Rock,** a 200,000-ton boulder that crashed down from the ceiling thousands of years ago. After climbing **Appetite Hill,** stroll on past the **Boneyard,** which probably resembles the cavern of 4–6 million years ago, when water filled the chambers. Follow the signs to the **Underground Lunchroom** to have a meal, if you like. To return to the ground level, take the nearby elevator up to the visitor center.

Big Room Tour: 1 mile; 1 hour

A one minute elevator ride from the visitor center provides you with a comfortable descent of 755 feet, or about 75 stories, into the cave system—a distinct improvement over the guano bucket used to convey visitors to the same level during the early 1920s. Follow the signs for the Big Room: For the next hour or so, you'll be circling one gigantic chamber.

The Big Room is the largest single room most visitors will ever see (unless they go to Borneo, where there is a cave with a larger, undecorated chamber), 1,800 feet long at its longest point, and 1,100 feet at its widest. It encompasses 8.2 acres.

To best enjoy the tour, linger, look, listen, and above all let loose

Lechuguilla Cave

In 1986 explorers made one of the most astounding cave discoveries of all time when they broke through rock rubble in an old guano-mining pit in the Carlsbad Caverns National Park backcountry. More than 100 miles of passages have now been mapped within America's deepest limestone cave—1,567 feet. Its rooms contain formations said to surpass Carlsbad's in beauty. Rare speleothems including 20 foot chandeliers as well as gypsum hairs and beards are part of the find. But the previously unseen helictites in the Pellucidar Room may be the cave's treasure.

Already longer and deeper than its better known neighbor, Lechuguilla continues to provide virgin passages to the experts who carefully push through its tight spaces. Access is restricted to scientists and survey teams who will work to protect the cave's integrity.

your imagination. What do the various formations look like to you? Layer cakes? Chinese friezes? Fossilized bonsai? Since the Park Service has removed labels from many of the formations, you can name the fantasyscape yourself.

Near the beginning of the walk, the **Hall of Giants** sports some of the largest formations in the cave, many of them about six stories tall. Look for **Giant Dome,** a 62-foot-high stalagmite, flanked by two 42-foot-high deputies. Appearances are deceptive here because of the immensity of the chamber.

The trail continues along the periphery of the room (resist the call of the shortcut) and leads past a view of the **Lower Cave,** accessible by reserved tour. Farther along, at **Top of the Cross,** rangers sometimes give talks at an amphitheater. Glance up: The ceiling here soars to 255 feet, its highest point above the trail.

The footpath continues through a less ornate area that was once a bat roost. The so-called **Bottomless Pit** has been measured at about 140 feet in depth; it does not lead to other passages. As you proceed, take a good look at sparkling **Crystal Spring Dome,** the cave's largest active stalagmite: Each drop of water adds crystals that make it infinitesimally bigger. Iron carried in the water delicately stains the formations of the **Painted Grotto.** Just a few minutes past the grotto, you will reach the elevator.

In the **visitor center,** don't miss the exhibits on cave restoration. There are also historical photographs here depicting the days of guano mining and early tourism. Then climb the stairs to the **Observation Tower.** Standing high above the ancient reef, you see a striking vista of the reef's seaward side (the slope past the parking lot) and the ancient seabed, called the Delaware Basin. If it's a clear day, the panorama will extend 100 miles or more into Texas.

Other Trails & Sights

■ **Desert Nature Trail**: This easy half-mile loop makes an interesting diversion before the evening bat flight program. The trail's interpretive plaques describe how Indians made use of virtually every plant in sight. The trail starts to the right of the cave's natural entrance.

■ **Bat Flight**: Don't miss the evening cyclone of bats; at its peak, more than 5,000 bats per minute speed out of the cave on their way to consume some three tons of insects. From the visitor center, walk to the amphitheater, at the natural entrance, or drive there by turning right onto the main road, then right again.

■ **Walnut Canyon Desert Drive**: An alternative introduction to the area's natural history. A booklet available at the start guides you along this 9.5-mile gravel loop off the main park road, just before the visitor center.

■ **Kings Palace Tour**: Led by park rangers, this 1.5-hour tour visits four highly decorative rooms, including the Kings Palace, which may be one of the world's most ornate cave rooms. Tour participants descend 830 feet to the deepest part of the cave open to the public. Look for the giant draperies, formed when water trickles down a slanted ceiling. Visitors will also find soda-straw stalactites, columns, and other interesting speleothems. Tours are offered several times a day throughout the year. Make reservations at the visitor center or by calling the park reservation number, 800-967-2283.

■ **Slaughter Canyon Cave**: Be prepared to slip and slide as you explore an "unimproved" cave for two hours by flashlight. Accompanied by rangers, you'll see several types of formations not found in the main cave, after a steep half-mile climb up to the cave's entrance from the parking lot in Slaughter Canyon. The cave is open daily in summer; weekends only in winter. You can make reservations at the visitor center or by calling the park reservation number, 800-967-2283.

INFORMATION & ACTIVITIES

Headquarters
3225 National Parks Hwy.
Carlsbad, NM 88220
505-785-2232
www.nps.gov/cave

Visitor & Information Centers
The visitor center is 7 miles from Whites City; open daily all year.

Seasons & Accessibility
All year park, but above-ground terrain is best to visit in spring and fall when desert wildflowers blossom.

Entrance Fees
No entrance fee for park, but there are fees to enter the cavern and tour the **Natural Entrance** route and **Big Room**: $6 for adults; children ages 6–15, $3; children under 6 free.

To tour **Kings Palace,** an additional fee of $8 for adults; children under age 16, $4; children under 6, free; those under age 4 not permitted.

To tour **Slaughter Canyon Cave,** additional fee of $15 for adults; children under age 16, $7.50; children under age 6 not permitted.

For off-trail caving tour, additional $12 for adults; children under age 16, $6; children under age 6 not permitted.

No charge for **Bat Flight.**

Pets
Not permitted in caves and backcountry. Kennel at visitor center.

Facilities for Disabled
The visitor center and Bat Flight Amphitheater are wheelchair accessible, as is a portion of the Big Room Tour. Picnic area and rest rooms accessible at Rattlesnake Springs.

Things to Do
Ranger-led activities: tours of the main cavern, cavern talks, dusk bat flight programs, flashlight trip into Slaughter Canyon Cave Also available, self-guided Desert Nature Trail and self-guided Walnut Canyon Desert Drive, backcountry trails.

Special Advisories
■ Wear low-heeled, nonskid shoes and bring a jacket.
■ Intense summer thunderstorms may cause floods in low-lying areas, lightning strikes in higher areas.
■ Watch out for rattlesnakes when hiking backcountry trails.
■ Cactuses and other spiny plants can inflict injuries.
■ Baby strollers are not permitted on cave trails.
■ Overnight backpacking permits are required. Pick them up for free at the visitor center.

Mexican free-tailed bats at dusk

Campgrounds

None; backcountry camping only. Food services in park. Campfires prohibited.

Hotels, Motels, & Inns

(Unless otherwise noted, rates are for two persons in a double room, high season.)

In Whites City, NM 88268:
- **Best Western Cavern Inn** 17 Carlsbad Cavern Hwy., P.O. Box 128. 505-785-2291 or 800-228-3767. 63 units. $99. AC, pool, restaurant. www.whites city.com.

In Carlsbad, NM 88220:
- **Best Western Stevens Inn** 1829 S. Canal St., P.O. Box 580. 505-887-2851 or 800-730-2851. 220 units, 28 with kitchenettes. $59–$99. AC, pool, restaurant. www.stevensinn.com.
- **Carlsbad Super 8** 3817 National Parks Hwy. 505-887-8888 or 800-800-8000. 60 units. $49-$65, includes breakfast. AC, pool. www.super8carlsbad.com.
- **Continental Inn** 3820 National Parks Hwy. 505-887-0341. 60 units. $55, includes breakfast. AC, pool.
- **Great Western Inn & Suites** 3804 National Parks Hwy. 505-887-5535 or 800-987-5535. 80 units, 25 with kitchenettes. $58–$110. AC, pool.
- **Quality Inn** 3706 National Parks Hwy. 800-321-2861 or 505-887-2861. 123 units. $60– $90. AC, pool, restaurant. www.choicehotels.com.

For a full list of accommodations, contact the Carlsbad Chamber of Commerce, P.O. Box 910, Carlsbad, NM 88221. 505-887-6516.

Excursions from Carlsbad

Living Desert Zoo & Gardens State Park

25 miles north of Carlsbad

Stop by this nicely designed park on the outskirts of Carlsbad for a fine introduction to Chihuahuan Desert ecology. Set among hills dotted with lechuguilla and sotol overlooking the Pecos River, Living Desert combines the features of a zoo, a botanical garden, and an interpretive center; after a couple of hours here, you'll better appreciate a visit to regional destinations such as Guadalupe Mountains *(see pp. 232–242)* and Carlsbad Caverns National Parks, White Sands National Monument *(see pp. 125–27)*, and Bitter Lake National Wildlife Refuge *(see pp. 132–33)*.

Badger, Living Desert Zoo

Displays in the spacious **visitor center** illuminate a range of subjects, from the Permian reefs that gave birth to Carlsbad Caverns to the adaptational features of desert flora and fauna. Outside, a 1.3-mile **nature trail** loops past exhibits depicting varied habitats, including an arroyo, desert uplands, and the pinyon pine-juniper zone.

In the park **aviary** you'll see birds such as bald and golden eagles, wild turkey, burrowing owl, and greater roadrunner, as well as mountain lion and bobcat. Javelinas live in the nearby arroyo, while in the pinyon-juniper area you'll get close-up looks at badger, porcupine, gray fox, and the appealing little kit fox. Pronghorn, elk, and bison are also residents of the Living Desert. In addition, the park provides a home for a few endangered Mexican gray wolves *(see pp. 128–29)*, which were extinct in the wild until recent efforts to reintroduce them.

Continuing on the nature trail, you'll get closer looks at a few desert snakes than you probably want to have out on a trail somewhere else. Prairie dogs populate a small village near grassy pens, where bison, pronghorn, elk, and mule deer roam.

Like Tucson's Arizona-Sonora Desert Museum *(see p. 312)*, the Living Desert isn't simply a zoo with a hodgepodge of animals from around the world; it's an education-oriented park focused on its own fascinating corner of the Southwest. A visit here is sure to be worthwhile for everyone, from kids to hard-core adventurers.

■ **1,100 acres** ■ **Southeast New Mexico, northwest of Carlsbad off US 285**
■ **Best seasons spring, fall, and winter** ■ **Adm. fee** ■ **Wildlife viewing**
■ **Contact the park, P.O. Box 100, Carlsbad, NM 88221; 505-887-5516.**
www.emnrd.state.nm.us/nmparks/pages/parks/desert/desert.htm

White Sands National Monument

The dazzling sand dunes that cover 275 square miles of New Mexico's Tularosa Valley create one of the most striking sights in the Southwest, but they wouldn't exist if not for a particular series of geologic events. White Sands is one of the few places in the world, in fact, where the right conditions prevail to produce extensive dunes of the bright white mineral called gypsum.

More than 250 million years ago, repeated evaporation of a shallow sea laid down a layer of gypsum, a type of calcium sulfate, in the sedimentary rock that formed here. Much later, after the region had been uplifted into a dome, a section collapsed between fault lines, forming a graben, or basin—a small-scale part of the Rio Grande Rift that cuts across the state from north to south. The sides of this uplifted dome stand as today's San Andres and Sacramento Mountains, to the west and east of what is now called the Tularosa Valley.

As these mountains erode, rain and snowmelt carry the water-soluble gypsum and other minerals into the basin. In most regions, a river would then transport the still dissolved gypsum to the sea—but the Tularosa Valley has no outlet; the minerals build up in ephemeral Lake Lucero, where evaporation leaves them as a powdery white crust of sodium chloride and gypsum crystals. Prevailing strong southwest winds then pick up the gypsum crystals, carrying them northeast where they accumulate as tall dunes. Winds continue to push the sand formations, moving them slowly but relentlessly northeastward at a rate of 30 feet a year.

Forty percent of this gypsum dune field, the world's largest, is protected within White Sands National Monument. Start your visit at the **visitor center,** just off US 70, to learn about White Sands

Yucca at twilight, White Sands National Monument

geology and ecology, then head for take the park's 8-mile (one way) **Dunes Drive.**

For the first few of miles, you'll have dunes on the south and Chihuahuan Desert grassland on the north. Then, where the road enters the dunes, look for the 1-mile **Big Dune Nature Trail,** which loops out across the great waves of sand. While 240 vascular plants grow in the Tularosa Valley, only about 60 can survive in the dune field. A trail booklet, available for a modest fee, identifies plants and explains how they adapt to harsh conditions among the dunes. Animals, mostly shy or nocturnal, are rarely seen. Farther west, the wheelchair-accessible **Interdune Boardwalk** interpretive trail loops for 0.3 mile through an area demonstrating the importance of this habitat.

As you drive, you may note that dunes exist in varying shapes. The first part of Dunes Drive passes through an area of parabolic dunes, where plants anchor the extremities of a formation while its middle is pushed by the wind, creating an inverted U-shape. Later, the road traverses barchan dunes, formed where winds fashion crescent shapes in areas with limited sand, and transverse dunes, created when barchan dunes join in long ridges. Nearer Lake Lucero *(not accessible by the drive)* are dome dunes, low mounds of sand that are the first to form downwind from the gypsum deposits along the lakeshore. After winding through the dunes, the drive makes a short loop at Heart of the Sands picnic area. Here the **Alkali Flats Trail** leads across the dunes to the now dry bed of Lake Otero, a body of water that filled most of the Tularosa Valley in the last ice age but has long since evaporated. This route follows posts across the dunes for a 4.6-mile round-trip.

As long as you park in a designated area, you're free to walk out across the sand anywhere you please, but take plenty of water.

■ **144,420 acres** ■ **South-central New Mexico, 14 miles southwest of Alamogordo off US 70** ■ **Best seasons spring and fall. Occasionally closed for brief periods during military testing at adjacent White Sands Missile Range** ■ **Adm. fee** ■ **Camping, hiking** ■ **Contact the monument, P.O. Box 1086, Holloman AFB, NM 88330; 505-679-2599. www.nps.gov/whs**

Oliver Lee Memorial State Park

175 miles west of Carlsbad

Set at the mouth of spectacular **Dog Canyon,** a deep gash in the side of the Sacramento Mountains, this little gem of a park encompasses the junction of a perennial stream with the arid Chihuahuan Desert—a blend of habitats that hosts a diverse range of plants and animals.

Beginning at the visitor center, the **Dog Canyon Interpretive Trail and Boardwalk** *(half-mile loop)* offers an easy look at the park's natural history. Rio Grande cottonwood, velvet ash, netleaf hackberry, desert willow, and Texas mulberry grow in the riparian zone, while on the drier slopes nearby, you'll see sotol, New Mexico agave, ocotillo, cane cholla, creosote bush, and various prickly pears and yuccas. Along the streambed grow cattail, horsetail, and, at seeps along the canyon wall, maidenhair fern, yellow columbine, and giant helleborine.

Black-chinned hummingbird, ladder-backed woodpecker, violet-green swallow, pyrrhuloxia, canyon towhee, and Scott's oriole are among the park's breeding birds; along the *(continued on p. 130)*

Mexican Gray Wolves

Wolves evoke strong and divergent emotions in humans. Some people look into their expressive eyes and see the very essence of wildness, less an animal than a mystical symbol of freedom. They buy wolf T-shirts, put wolf posters on their walls, and even listen to recordings of wolf calls.

Other people have a seemingly visceral hatred of wolves, looking on them as vicious killers, and on their presence as a threat to humans and domestic animals. Their reaction, on hearing of a wolf in the vicinity, might be to reach for a gun.

Ecologists can afford neither sentimentality nor prejudice when they study our environment. They're likely to look on the wolf as an intelligent animal with an intricate social system that functions as a vital part of certain healthy ecosystems. They see areas in the American West where burgeoning elk populations are overgrazing and damaging their habitat, and they note the absence of a top predator that once preyed on them. They acknowledge that wolves do kill sheep, cattle, and other livestock, but see such attacks as a natural response to human invasion of territory that was once the wolf's, not as evidence of bloodthirstiness.

Unrelenting persecution by shooting, trapping, and poisoning caused the extirpation of the Mexican gray wolf (a subspecies of the gray wolf found in many parts of the Northern Hemisphere) in the Southwest by the mid-20th century. For years the only Mexican gray wolves known to exist lived in zoos and wildlife sanctuaries.

That changed in 1998, when the first wolves were reintroduced into the wild in the Blue Range of eastern Arizona, in what is known as the Blue Range Wolf Recovery Area in Apache-Sitgreaves National Forests. The release of 13 animals in two packs was part of a strategy to have a "viable, self-sustaining population of at least 100 Mexican wolves" in the species' historic range by 2005, according to the U.S. Fish and Wildlife Service's recovery plan.

One hundred wolves don't seem like much of a threat to ranching and commerce in the American Southwest, but livestock growers (and politicians influenced by ranching money) reacted with virulence to the recovery plan. Public hearings often turned into emotional battlefields, with wolf opponents angrily facing off with

Mexican Gray Wolf

wildlife officials. New Mexico counties passed laws forbidding the release of wolves. Livestock growers and local governments filed suit to stop the wolf program, while a coalition of wildlife and conservation groups intervened to support reintroduction.

Despite the controversy, wolf restoration has continued. The program has had ups and downs: A few wolves have been shot, a couple have been killed by mountain lions, and one was killed by a car. As ranchers feared, wolves have killed livestock; in confirmed instances of wolf predation owners have

been repaid by a private environmental group.

Wildlife officials still face mostly hostile crowds at hearings, but there are plenty of people who dream of a time when the howl of the wolf will be heard again in the American Southwest. They believe the nearly 4.4 million acres of the Blue Range Wolf Recovery Area ought to be able to sustain several packs of Mexican gray wolves. They think that a species that has appropriated so much of the world ought to find a way to share part of it with an animal that was here for thousands of years.

trails you might spot crevice spiny lizards, Texas horned lizards, western diamondback and black-tailed rattlesnakes, gray foxes, or javelinas.

The strenuous 5.5-mile **Dog Canyon National Recreation Trail** also begins at the visitor center. It climbs 3,100 feet along the canyon walls to reach FR 90B in **Lincoln National Forest**. At the crest of this imposing escarpment, you'll have a fabulous view of **White Sands National Monument** (*see pp. 125–27*).

■ **640 acres** ■ **South-central New Mexico, 12 miles south of Alamagordo off US 54** ■ **Best seasons spring and fall; spring best for birding** ■ **Adm. fee** ■ **Camping, hiking, bird-watching, wildlife viewing** ■ **Contact the park, 409 Dog Canyon Rd., Alamogordo, NM 88310; 505-437-8284. www.emnrd .state.nm.us/nmparks**

Bosque del Apache National Wildlife Refuge

250 miles northwest of Carlsbad　From fall through spring, tens of thousands of spectacular cranes and waterfowl throng the roadside fields and wetlands of Bosque del Apache, creating one of the country's most exciting wildlife-viewing experiences. Whether it's the wild trumpeting of sandhill cranes or the vision of a huge flock of snow geese put to flight by a passing bald eagle, a wealth of memories reward visitors to this refuge, just minutes off I-25. A 12-mile auto-tour loop, five trails, and several observation platforms make the refuge easily accessible to everyone.

Though Bosque del Apache covers nearly 90 square miles, the focal point of the refuge is the 7,000 acres stretching along 9 miles of the Rio Grande. A *bosque* (Spanish for "woodland") of cottonwoods and willows borders the river, with man-made ponds supplementing the area's natural wetlands. The refuge lies in the western part of the central flyway—a traditional migration route for geese, ducks, and sandhill cranes.

Once the river meandered freely across its flat floodplain, regularly overflowing its banks and cutting new channels to create oxbow lakes and ephemeral marshes rich in wildlife. With much of its flow now impounded by dams or diverted for agriculture, the Rio Grande needs help to provide wetlands habitat.

Bosque del Apache was established in 1939, in part to provide a wintering ground for the then endangered "greater" sandhill crane—a race of a gray, long-legged species that nests from Siberia to Cuba. These handsome, 4-foot-tall birds mate for life, and often are seen in family groups. Their loud *gar-oo-oo* call can be heard for a mile or more. Today, more than 13,000 of these cranes winter here, along with 30,000 geese (mostly snow geese) and more than 60,000 ducks.

Visits to Bosque del Apache are enhanced by extensive volunteer programs, most of which occur from November through March. But even a summer visit can be exciting, when you can search for some of the 115 species of birds that nest here.

Start at the refuge visitor center on the west side of N. Mex. 1, 8 miles south of San Antonio. The 12-mile **refuge tour** sets off nearby, on the east side of N. Mex. 1, and divides into two sections.

The **Marsh Loop** concentrates on waterfowl. The most conspicuous are the huge, cackling flocks of snow geese which gather here from fall through spring. Like many other places, Bosque del Apache has seen significant increases in snow goose numbers in recent years, as the population of this Arctic-breeding fowl has skyrocketed for reasons that are not clear. The 1.5-mile **Marsh Overlook Trail** offers a closer look at the wetlands and perhaps a better chance to spot shorebirds. On the back side of the refuge, the 2-mile round-trip **Rio Viejo Trail** follows an old channel of the Rio Grande with a bosque of young Rio Grande cottonwoods. Nearby, the **River Trail** traces the Rio Grande itself under mature

Smokey Bear

Smokey Bear, the Forest Service symbol of fire prevention, began life in 1944 as an illustrated poster showing a bear pouring water on a campfire. In 1950, after a fire ravaged the Capitan Mountains of Lincoln National Forest, firefighters found a badly burned black bear cub in a tree. Naming him Smokey, after the poster bear, officials eventually sent him to the National Zoo in Washington, D.C. Smokey Bear (not Smokey "the" Bear) became so popular that in 1964 he was given his own zip code. He died in 1976 and was buried in Capitan at **Smokey Bear Historical State Park** *(102 Smokey Bear Rd. 505-354-2748)*. A museum tells his story and that of fire-prevention education.

Rio Grande cottonwoods. In spring and summer, the latter trail can be flooded and buggy.

The greatest numbers of wintering sandhill cranes are usually found along the **Farm Loop** in early morning or late evening, when the birds leave or return from the surrounding fields and croplands. The sight of skeins of calling birds settling in for the night creates the kind of thrilling scene for which the refuge is famed.

Two trails running west of N. Mex. 1 offer Chihuahuan Desert flora and fauna, as well as expansive views of the refuge and the Rio Grande Valley. The **Canyon Trail,** beginning south of the visitor center, makes a 2.5-mile loop through a fairly shady canyon.

The **Chupadera Wilderness Trail,** much more strenuous, leads 5 miles one way to the top of 6,272-foot Chupadera Mountain, gaining 1,700 feet in elevation along a path with no shade and no water. Stamina, preparation, and 6 hours are required. Just a half mile along the way, though, is a vista point with a great view over the refuge—a good destination if you can't do the entire trek.

■ **57,200 acres** ■ **Central New Mexico, 20 miles south of Socorro off N. Mex. 1** ■ **Best months Nov.–March** ■ **Adm. fee** ■ **Hiking, bird-watching, wildlife viewing** ■ **Contact the refuge, P.O. Box 1246, Socorro, NM 87801; 505-835-1828. http://southwest.fws.gov/refuges/newmex/bosque.html**

Bitter Lake National Wildlife Refuge

100 miles north of Carlsbad

Though it may not be as well known as some other southwestern wildlife refuges, Bitter Lake ranks among the best regional birding destinations. Late fall through early spring offers the greatest number of showy species such as sandhill crane, geese, and various types of ducks.

To reach Bitter Lake from Roswell, drive east on US 380 from its junction with US 285 for about 3 miles; drive north on Red Bridge Road 4 miles and turn east on Pine Lodge Road to the refuge. Stop by the office for information, then proceed to the 8.5-mile **auto-tour** route.

Near the start of the drive, a viewing platform offers a look at the lay of the land. The refuge comprises several shallow, man-made impoundments in the flat meander bed of the **Pecos River,** surrounded by scrubby grassland. To the north lies **Bitter Lake,** a seasonal playa, or basin, and the only natural lake on the refuge. All

Mirror Lake

of these "lakes" are fed only by springs, seeps, and rain, and so they often dry up or become mudflats at various times of year. Scenic it may not be, but the area provides a home for more than 350 nesting or migratory bird species.

Bitter Lake lies at the Chihuahuan Desert's northern border, near the western edge of the Llano Estacado's shortgrass plains. Combined with refuge wetlands, this mix of habitats attracts not only a variety of birds, but other wildlife as well. Look for rare spotted ground squirrels, desert cottontails, black-tailed jackrabbits, and mule deer, plus a variety of reptiles, including collared lizards.

From fall through spring, you'll find great numbers of sandhill cranes at Bitter Lake, along with Canada, snow, and Ross's geese, and various ducks. American white pelicans visit in spring and fall. Shorebirds stalk the mudflats and shallow waters, and raptors hunt the grasslands.

■ 24,500 acres ■ Southeast New Mexico, 8 miles northeast of Roswell via Pine Lodge Rd. ■ Best months Nov. and April–May ■ Bird-watching, wildlife viewing, driving tour ■ Contact the refuge, P.O. Box 7, Roswell, NM 88202; 505-622-6755. http://southwest.fws.gov/refuges/newmex/bitter.html

Channel Islands

S trung along a stretch of California coast are five separate pieces of land surrounded by 1,252 square nautical miles of sea. Channel Islands National Park and Channel Islands National Marine Sanctuary protect these islands, the sea around them, and a dazzling array of wildlife.

Two of the islands in this unusual park, Anacapa and Santa Barbara, were earlier designated a national monument, a refuge for nesting seabirds, seals, sea lions, and other long-threatened marine animals. When those islands and three others were joined in a national park, the mission of refuge continued.

Today the park manages a long-term ecological research program that may be the best in the park system. The marine sanctuary, also established in 1980, extends for 6 nautical miles around each island. Among the resources it protects is a giant kelp forest with nearly a thousand kinds of fish and marine plants. The park and sanctuary also guard the area from encroachment by another kind of island—the seagoing oil rigs of the Santa Barbara Channel.

About 70 different species of plants grow only on the Channel Islands, and some plants exist on but one of them. The islands shelter the only breeding colony of northern fur seals south of Alaska. To help native animals, park managers have gotten rid of such nonnative species as burros, rabbits, and house cats gone feral. Efforts to eradicate black rats—descendants of ancestors that jumped ship—are underway, though they have been less successful.

A permanent ranger resides on each of the islands. Reservations are needed for camping. Fishing and diving are strictly regulated and airplanes are asked to keep their distance.

Chumash Indians lived on the Channel Islands until the early 19th century. They traveled from island to island in plank canoes caulked with tar from oil seeps. The

■ Southern California from Point Conception to north of Los Angeles

■ 249,561 acres (125,000 acres underwater)

■ Established 1980

■ Year-round

■ Primitive camping, hiking, boating, swimming, diving, bird-watching, whale-watching

■ Information: 805-658-5730 www.nps.gov/chis

Dolphins gliding through Channel Islands waters

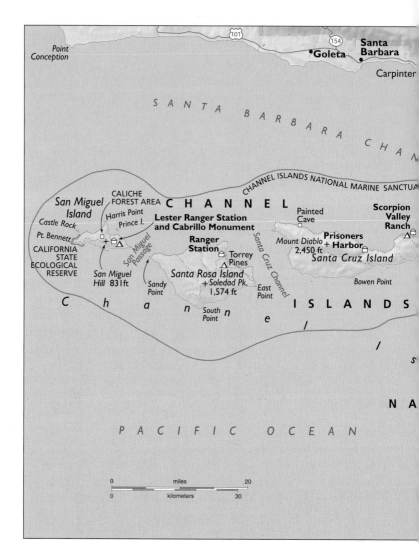

tar from such seeps still appears on mainland beaches, the reason for oil rigs on the horizon.

How to Get There

Take US 101 to Ventura. Northbound, exit at Victoria Ave.; southbound, at Seaward Ave. Follow park signs to the harbor and then to the visitor center on Spinnaker Dr. The nearby Island Packers office provides information on boat and plane schedules to the islands. Airports: Santa Barbara and Los Angeles.

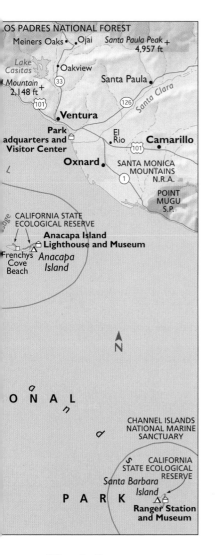

What Not to Miss

■ Dolphin/Whale-watching cruise

■ Cruise to Anacapa Island and view from Inspiration Point

■ Scuba diving off Middle Anacapa

■ Camping overnight on Santa Rosa, Santa Barbara, or San Miguel Island

■ The Caliche forest on San Miguel Island

■ Guided wildlife viewing on Santa Cruz

How to Visit

Your exploration of this unique park depends on your time and resources. Even a short stop at the mainland **visitor center** will give you an understanding and appreciation of the park. For a one-day visit, see the closest island, **Anacapa.** Take all necessities, especially food and water, and dress in layers for all types of weather. Trips to the **other islands** require substantial advance planning (*see Information & Activities p. 142*). The park cautions people from doing more than treading lightly on the islands, which are maintained for the well-being of the residents, both flora and fauna.

When to Go

All-year park. Boat schedules peak in spring and summer, but you should be able to book a trip in any month. Best whale-watching times are late December through March, and July and August.

EXPLORING THE PARK

Anacapa Island: **14 miles from Ventura; a full day**

Before stepping aboard your Island Packers boat for the trip to
Anacapa, take some time to explore the park's **visitor center** in
Ventura. Among the attractions are an indoor marine life exhibit,
a native plant garden, and Chumash artifacts. During the summer,
divers with cameras and microphones drop into the landing cove
on East Anacapa Island to give people on the dock and in the center's auditorium a close-up video tour of the underwater world,
pointing out sea snails and fish such as garibaldi, and taking hold
of an octopus, which squirts ink.

Out on the water, your boat plies the Santa Barbara Channel.
Look for flying fish skipping through the waves and for pelicans
skimming over them. Oil rigs stand on dark stilts. During winter
trips, gray whales may glide by on their annual migrations between
Baja and Alaska. In recent years blue and humpback whales have
also reappeared. And you can expect to have dolphins show up for
a little race with your boat or to frolic about the bow. Orcas (killer
whales) and great white sharks may also be seen, and seals appear
and disappear in the channel waters year-round.

The commercial fishery around and in the park waters is huge,

Seabirds perch Anacapa Island's Arch Rock

particularly for squid and sea urchins. It accounts for 15 percent of California's fishing industry. Protecting the millions earned harvesting urchins is one reason this remains essentially a "sea otter free" area—otters eat sea urchins. Some people, however, would like to reintroduce the otters for ecological balance. The demand for some delicacies, such as white abalone, has all but wiped out those species here.

Approaching the landing cove, the boat passes Anacapa's **Arch Rock** and sails close enough to the rocky coast for you to see resident California sea lions. At the end of the 90-minute voyage (which can be rough), a dinghy transports you to the landing platform. Then you climb 154 steps up a metal-and-concrete stairway to the top of the cliff-girt island.

There you can walk the 1.5-mile **nature trail** on your own or fall in behind a ranger who dispenses island lore: Brown pelicans will wing by in neat formation, and gulls will be everywhere, especially during May and June, when they nest here by the thousands. That plain gray plant (giant coreopsis) is a tree sunflower; in late winter and spring it bursts into glorious gold. You'll also see live-forever plants, which sport purplish flowers, and end at **Inspiration Point.**

The finely ground shells you are walking on are remnants of a Chumash midden. The Chumash once inhabited the four northern islands (San Miguel, Santa Cruz, Santa Rosa, and Anacapa), paddling to the mainland to trade in their tomols, canoes made of driftwood planks. The four islands of the Chumash once formed a single large island, dubbed Santaros by geologists, but water levels have risen since the last great Ice Age and have separated the highlands of Santaros. The fifth island, Santa Barbara, was occupied by a different tribe, the Gabrielino.

Continue along the trail, which skirts the edge of a cliff 150 feet above the sea. Stand well back from the unstable edges. You are ominously warned: *Don't risk your life for a view.*

A building that looks like a Spanish mission church is not what it seems. The structure protects two large water tanks. Vandals who in years past took potshots at the wooden tanks refrain from sniping at a "church." The few buildings date from days when the island lighthouse, now automated, had a crew. Your day ends with a descent to the boat, which picks up passengers about 3 or 4 hours after their arrival; pickup time depends on tide and sea conditions.

Anacapa actually consists of three islets. Most people visit only **East Anacapa.** Scuba divers, subject to strict conservation laws, plunge off **Middle Anacapa** to see the kelp forests or the remains of the *S.S. Winfield Scott,* which sank here in 1853 with no loss of life. The prohibition against fishing (this is one of the park-protected areas) makes this a great place to see various forms of marine life. Divers swim by soft coral stands of red and golden Gorgonians and see such fish as opaleyes, blacksmiths, and bat rays. **West Anacapa** is closed to the public January through October to protect the largest nesting brown pelican population on the U.S. Pacific coast.

Other Islands

If you decide to go to the other islands, your visits will be controlled by weather, regulations, and boat and plane schedules.

■ **Santa Cruz** *(21 miles from Ventura; 60,000 acres)* is the largest of the Channel Islands. The Nature Conservancy runs the western portion of the island and strictly limits visitors *(for a tour call 805-962-9111).* The park owns the east end. When the boat docks at Scorpion Anchorage, passengers disembark with coolers, camping gear, and even kayaks.The campground is just up the creek bed and the launching point for kayaks, Cavern Point, is on the north side. Kayakers can head out around Cavern Point to deep sea caves beneath dramatic cliffs. You can hike the headlands east on a **trail** overlooking Chinese Harbor or climb a 1,500-foot peak, then descend to **Smugglers Cove,** a pretty beach. Of the five, this island has the greatest diversity of habitat. Among its distinctive species are the island oak, the cat-size island fox, and the scrub jay.

■ **Santa Rosa** *(45 miles from Ventura; 53,000 acres)* is an archaeological treasure trove with many Chumash sites. The remains of one human inhabitant have been dated to 13,000 years ago. *(Site visitors must be accompanied by rangers.)* A freshwater marsh sustains waterfowl. Some 195 species of birds may be seen on the island and several animal species, including island foxes and elk.

■ **San Miguel** *(55 miles from Ventura; 9,325 acres),* the westernmost island, is also rich in archaeological sites. Thousands of seals and sea lions crowd its 27 miles of beach to breed and raise pups; as many as 35,000 haul out at times. A 14-mile (round-trip) hiking trail leads to **Point Bennett,** the pinniped-viewing area. A bizarre caliche "forest" spikes a plateau. Caliche—a kind of limey sand—encrusted vegetation that died and decayed, leaving only the

Channel Island Birds

Some 99 percent of California's seabirds find nesting and roosting accommodations in Channel Islands National Park. In fact, like some land birds, including the Santa Cruz Island scrub-jay, and certain seabirds—such as the California brown pelican—nest only on these islands.

The western gull seems especially partial to Anacapa, the largest breeding area in the United States for that bird. In May, thousands of gulls give birth to two or three brown-striped chicks. Their nests are often right next to the path on the easternmost islet, and when you walk by, they will sass you. If they think their chicks are in real danger, they'll take wing and dive-bomb your head.

Santa Cruz Island is known to birders as the only place in the world where the Island scrub-jay can be found. This species can sometimes be found in a grove of eucalyptus trees and other exotic plantings near the landing site at Scorpion Anchorage. If the jays aren't there, you might try finding them by walking about a mile up the seasonal stream to the west to stands of oaks and ironwood trees in the narrowing canyon above.

Among the pelagic species you might see here are sooty shearwater, black-vented shearwater, ashy and black storm-petrels, as well as rhinoceros auklets. The Channel Islands are also home to the Allen's hummingbird.

hollow, calcified sand castings. Once used as a Navy bombing range and missile test site, the island is now administered by the National Park Service, which limits visitors to the beach, ranch, and campground unless accompanied by a ranger.

■ **Santa Barbara** *(52 miles from Ventura; 640 acres),* once a sheep pasturage, has 5.5 miles of nature trails. In springtime, burrows on the island's steep hillsides house the world's largest known breeding population of the remarkable Xantus' murrelet. When a chick is only two days old, it makes a bold foray into night, tumbling down to the sea where it joins its waiting parents. Except for the nesting season, the murrelet will spend the remainder of its life on the ocean. In spring and summer, you can usually see pelicans and sea lions, but don't expect to come across the rock-dwelling island night lizard. It is shy, secretive, and protected; visitors are strictly forbidden to turn over any rock.

INFORMATION & ACTIVITIES

Headquarters
1901 Spinnaker Dr.
Ventura, CA 93001
805-658-5730
www.nps.gov/chis

Visitor & Information Centers
Visitor center in Ventura open daily year-round. Visitor centers on East Anacapa and Santa Barbara also open year-round. Ranger station on San Miguel.

Seasons & Accessibility
Park open year-round. Access to islands subject to unpredictable weather conditions; the channel can be rough. Call headquarters for information.
Anacapa, Santa Rosa, San Miguel, and Santa Barbara: Boat trips offered by Island Packers and Truth Aquatics, the park's authorized concessionaire *(see below)*. Visitors using private boats must obtain landing permits for Santa Rosa and San Miguel from the park. Air service to Santa Rosa via Channel Island Aviation *(see below)*.
Santa Cruz: Island Packers and Truth Aquatics offer day trips to east end. For day trips to west end and permits for private boats, contact well in advance The Nature Conservancy, Santa Cruz Island Project Office, 2559 Puesta del Sol Rd., Santa Barbara, CA 93105

(located at Santa Barbara Museum of Natural History).
805-898-1642.
Boats from Ventura: Contact headquarters or Island Packers, 1691 Spinnaker Dr., Ste. 105B, Ventura, CA 93001. 805-642-1393. www.islandpackers.com. For weekend trips, reserve 3 to 5 days in advance.
Boats from Santa Barbara: Contact Truth Aquatics, 301 Cabrillo Blvd., Santa Barbara, CA 93101. 805-962-1127. www.truthaquatics.com.
Access by airplane: Contact Channel Island Aviation, 305 Durley Ave., Camarillo, CA 93010. 805-987-1301.

Entrance Fee
None.

Pets
Not permitted in park headquarters or on islands.

Facilities for Disabled
Visitor center at Ventura, rest rooms, theater, exhibits, and observation tower accessible. Boats and islands are not.

Things to Do
Santa Barbara Channel: Whale-watching late Dec. through March and June through Sept.
Anacapa: Free ranger-led walks and evening programs; also

wildlife-watching, bird-watching, tide-pool walks, swimming and snorkeling, scuba and skin diving, fishing *(license needed; certain areas closed)*.

Santa Barbara: Nature hikes, marine life observation, bird-watching, tide-pool walks.

Santa Rosa: Free ranger-led nature hike.

San Miguel: Free ranger-led hike to caliche "forest"; also, seal- and sea lion-watching, and tide-pool walks.

Santa Cruz: Hikes, marine life observation, bird-watching.

Special Advisories

■ When hiking on islands, stay on trails and away from cliffs.

■ All birds, animals, tide pools, shells, rocks, and plants are protected; take nothing but photos.

■ Avoid Hantavirus pulmonary syndrome, a potentially fatal virus carried by deer mice, by staying away from cabins and campsites where rodent droppings and burrows are evident.

Campgrounds

All five islands have campgrounds; 14-day limit. Year-round. Reservations and permits required; contact the National Parks Reservation Service *(800-365-2267)*. $10 per night. Tent sites only. Cold shower on Santa Rosa. Drinking water at Scarpton on Santa Cruz. Group camping available. No food services.

Hotels, Motels, & Inns

(Unless otherwise noted, rates are for two persons in a double room, high season.)

In Ventura, CA 93001:

■ **Bella Maggiore Inn** 67 S. California St. 805-652-0277 or 800-523-8479. 24 units. $75–$175. Restaurant.

■ **Brakeyhouse Bed & Breakfast** 411 Poli St. 93002. 805-643-3600. 5 units. $95–$235. www .Brakeyhouse.com.

■ **Country Inn by the Sea** 298 S. Chestnut St. 805-653-1434 or 800-456-4000. 120 units. $99–$129. AC, pool. www.country inns.com.

■ **Four Point Sheraton** 1050 Schooner Dr. 805-658-1212 or 800-229-5732. 175 units. $99–$299. Pool, restaurant. www .fourpoints.com/ventura.

■ **Inn on the Beach** 1175 S. Seaward Ave. 805-652-2000. 24 units. $100–$185. www.innon thebeachventura.com.

For additional lodgings, contact the Ventura Visitor & Convention Bureau at 805-648-2075.

Excursions from Channel Islands

Santa Monica Mountains NRA

25 miles
east of
Channel Islands

Though the Santa Monica Mountains split their city into two parts, a lot of people in Los Angeles don't know about the protected open spaces that range from the knobby dry ridges of the mountains to the coastal beaches crammed with surfers. The Santa Monica Mountains are unique in several ways: A transverse mountain range, the Santa Monicas run east-west, instead of the north-south configuration of most North American mountain ranges; and the climate is a Mediterranean ecosystem, unique in the United States and rare the world over.

Riding through Topanga State Park, Santa Monica Mountains

If you look at a map and follow the direction of this range from the Los Angeles River west toward the Oxnard Plain, it points to the Channel Islands, which are believed to be additional peaks in the Santa Monicas that extend out into the ocean.

The mountains are sandwiched by the thoroughfares of southern California, US 101 to the north and Calif. 1 to the south. Yet the roads and traffic detract only slightly from the beauty of the deep canyons that pour from the mountains into the ocean, from Mugu Lagoon at the northwest end to Topanga and Malibu Canyons to the east. The lagoons are busy with grebes, herons, egrets, sea ducks, sandpipers, and plover, the adjacent beaches are busy with sunbathers and surfers. The canyons, ridges, and hills

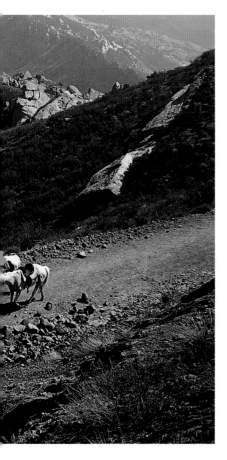

provide essential corridors for wildlife, including mountain lions, deer, and bobcats.

The recreation area was created in 1978 to care for this important region. It comprises state parks, private lands, and reserves managed by dozens of state, federal, and private agencies, all working together to protect the area's features.

Some 500 miles of trails run through the recreation area's pastiche of state and federal lands. If you need advice and maps, stop at the National Park Service headquarters and visitor center in Thousand Oaks *(see below)*.

Topanga State Park *(818-880-0350)* has 36 miles of hiking, riding, and biking trails. Some, such as the 5.3-mile **Rogers Road Trail,** wander through grasslands colored by wildflowers, including golden stars, blue-eyed grass, and mariposa lilies.

Many visitors to **Malibu Creek State Park** *(818-880-0350)* choose to hike or bike the 2.4-mile **Crags Road,** a relatively flat trail following the creek beneath large sycamores and oaks. The trail goes to Century Lake (good fishing) then to the old set of the *M.A.S.H.* television show.

Farther west is **Solstice Canyon** *(off Corral Canyon Rd.),* considered one of the most beautiful canyons in the Santa Monica range. For a short, moderately steep hike, take 1.8-mile **Rising Sun Trail,** which switchbacks up the canyon's west-facing slope before gradually descending to the Solstice Canyon Visitor Center. It leads you down into an old house site with a series of beautiful pools and small waterfalls.

Point Mugu State Park *(818-880-0350),* offers one of the few places on the recreation area where no roads penetrate. At the park's heart is **Boney Mountain State Wilderness Area,** which includes Sandstone Peak, 3,111 feet above sea level. The park has 75 miles of trails and fire roads as well as 5 miles of beach, both rocky and sandy, and the Great Sand Dune at the mouth of Big Sycamore Canyon. To reach the headwaters of Big Sycamore Canyon, head up the 7-mile **Old Boney Trail** from the northern entrance of the park.

■ **150,000 acres** ■ **Southern California, north of Santa Monica on Calif. 1 or US 101** ■ **Best seasons winter and spring** ■ **Camping, hiking, boating, fishing, mountain biking, horseback riding, bird-watching** ■ **Contact National Park Service, 401 W. Hillcrest Dr., Thousand Oaks, CA 91360; 805-370-2301. www.nps.gov/samo**

Grunions

Walking the moonlit sand of a southern California beach near the high-tide line on a summer night, you find yourself tiptoeing among thousands of wiggling silvery fish. Those silver fish are grunions. From March through August, they ride the highest tides of the lunar cycle to the beach. As the surf retreats, the females work their tails into the sand and lay thousands of eggs. The males curl around the females to fertilize the eggs, which remain buried until the next lunar high tide, in about two weeks. The babies then hatch and slip out and venture into the ocean.

Torrey Pines State Reserve

175 miles southeast of Channel Islands

The rarest tree in the United States grows on the craggy coast of southern California just north of San Diego. Here and on Santa Rosa Island grow the few thousand surviving Torrey pines, a gnarly coastal tree with needles long enough to use in knitting. Growing amid greasewood, cactuses and other low-slung shrubbery, they dominate the landscape.

There are three distinct parts to this park: the state reserve; Torrey Pines State Beach *(5 miles S of Del Mar);* and Los Peñasquitos Lagoon Natural Preserve *(just N of the reserve).* To reach the reserve, take I-5 north from San Diego to the Carmel Valley Rd. exit. Go west 1.5 miles, then take a left on Camino Del Mar. Continue a mile to the entrance.

What was once a little pueblo-style inn atop the bluffs is now an informative visitor center with helpful docents. From this high vantage, trails radiate out on the cliff edge and down to the beach. The most popular is **Guy Fleming Trail,** a 0.7-mile loop that gives a great overview of the park: pines, cliffs, beach, and lagoon. The half-mile **Parry Grove Trail** winds through the **Whitaker Memorial Native Plant Garden,** then descends to a bench overlooking the ocean. In January, scan for migrating gray whales. To reach the surf, most visitors take the mile-long **Beach Trail.**

At **Torrey Pines State Beach** you'll see surfers and darting bottle-nosed dolphins. Beach crowds thin to the south in part because there are spots where passage is difficult at high tide. *(Be alert to tide times.)* A few miles south, you round a promontory and arrive at **Black Beach,** which is remote enough that many of the regulars see no need for clothing.

Los Peñasquitos Lagoon is a tidal marsh that curves around the backside of Torrey Pines reserve. It is a valuable piece of habitat, one that birders will recognize as a treasure chest of species rarely viewed in this urbanized stretch of the coastline. Snowy egrets stilt walk in the mudflats, and rare birds such as the light-footed clapper rail nest here amid the pickleweed.

■ **1,500 acres** ■ **Southern California, 15 miles north of San Diego off I-5** ■ **Best seasons spring and summer; whale-watching in winter** ■ **Vehicle fee** ■ **Hiking, kayaking, scuba diving, biking, bird-watching, whale-watching** ■ **Contact California Dept. of Parks and Recreation, 9609 Waples St., Suite 200, San Diego, CA 92121; 858-755-2063. www.torreypine.org**

Tijuana River
National Estuarine Research Reserve

Riding horseback through the brush in Tijuana River National Estuarine Research Reserve, you can explore the river valley, salt marsh, and dune beach of a key stopover on the Pacific flyway, perhaps spotting such endangered species as the light-footed clapper rail and the least Bell's vireo.

The Tijuana River estuary is one of just a few salt marshes that remain in Southern California, where more than 90 percent of wetland habitat has been destroyed. More than 370 species of migratory and native birds depend on this site as a stopover point on the Pacific flyway, and as a breeding, feeding and nesting ground.

There are 27 miles of riding trails in the Tijuana Valley, including paths to the top of **Spooners Mesa** for panoramic ocean views (you can see the Coronado Islands offshore) and a route through **Smugglers Gulch,** once used by Native Americans and rumrunners. Numerous recreational riders use the refuge, including outfitters who lead trail rides.

There are also trails for walkers. Those from the visitor center take you out into prime birding areas around the mouth of the **Tijuana River.** You can explore the creek beds—watch out for quicksand—and then along the beach from the river's outlet to the Mexican border, where a tall fence has been erected in an attempt to keep out illegal immigrants. On the beach, avoid disturbing seabirds nesting on the dry sands and dunes.

This wetland habitat supports a wealth of wildlife. In addition to endangered birds, the refuge is also home to an endangered flower, the salt marsh bird's beak.

Two acres have been planted with native coastal plateau plants near the visitor center at the reserve's north entrance (W off I-5 at Coronado Ave. in Imperial Beach). Twenty years ago car bodies and other trash littered the area. Today upland shrubs such as buckwheat and black sage, as well as dune plants such as sand verbena and evening primrose, line the reserve's paths.

■ 2,500 acres ■ Southern California, 15 miles south of San Diego off I-5 ■ Best seasons spring and fall ■ Walking, guided walks, fishing, horseback riding, wildlife viewing ■ Contact the reserve, California State Parks, 301 Caspian Way, Imperial Beach, CA 91932; 619-575-3613. www.tijuanaestuary.com

Whales and Whale-watching

All up and down the California coast, people climb the headlands or put out in boats in hopes of seeing whales spouting, flipping a fluke, or just showing a little barnacled skin. The whales oblige: They are surprisingly nonchalant about the boats full of humans that chase them around, and sometimes the whales seem actually to show off.

Between November and February, Pacific gray whales—the most commonly seen cetacean along the California coast—head south from their summer feeding grounds in Alaska. Hunted nearly to extinction until international treaties protected them in the 1930s, Pacific grays have bounced back and now number about 23,000. Usually led by pregnant females, followed by adults and adolescents, the whales make the 6,000-mile journey to lagoons along the Baja coast, where the females give birth.

By May, the whales have begun the return migration, now led by newly pregnant females and mothers keeping a close eye on their young ones. The whales often pass within half a mile of shore, much to the delight of the humans who flock to see them.

Humpback whales also migrate to Baja, but they don't come so close to shore; you're more apt to see them from a boat near the Channel or Farallon Islands. Have your camera ready: Acrobatic humpbacks often leap from the water, rolling and smacking their fins.

Looking for whales near Mendocino Headlands State Park

Death Valley

Our largest national park south of Alaska, Death Valley is known for extremes: It is North America's driest and hottest spot (with less than 2 inches of rainfall annually and a record high of 134°F), and it has the lowest elevation in the Western Hemisphere—282 feet below sea level. Even with such extremes, this desert park still receives nearly a million visitors each year.

In 1849 prospectors bound for California's gold fields strayed into the 120-mile-long basin, enduring a two-month ordeal of "hunger and thirst and an awful silence." One of the party died, and the rest came mighty close. One of the last to leave looked down from a mountain at the narrow valley far below and said, "Good-bye, Death Valley."

The forbidding moniker belies the beauty in this vast graben, the geological term for a sunken fragment of the Earth's crust. Here are rocks sculptured by erosion, richly tinted mudstone hills and canyons, luminous sand dunes, lush oases, and a 200-square-mile salt pan surrounded by mountains that soar to 11,000 feet—one of America's greatest vertical rises. In some years spring rains trigger lavish wildflower blooms amid more than a thousand varieties of plants from seven different plant communities.

From 1883 to 1889, wagon teams hauled powdery white borax from mines that have since fallen to ruin, an enterprise that spread word of Death Valley's striking landscapes, its deep solitude, and its crystal clear air.

Far above the valley floor on steep mountain slopes, desert bighorn sheep forage among Joshua trees, scrubby junipers, and pines. Overhead, hawks soar on the thermals rising into vivid blue, usually cloudless skies. As night falls, and temperatures moderate, Death Valley's elusive population of bobcats, kit foxes, and rodents ventures out.

- Southern California, W of Beatty, Nev. on Nev. 374; from the west, Calif. 190 off US 395

- 3.4 million acres

- Established 1994

- Best seasons fall, winter, and spring

- Camping, primitive camping, hiking, auto tour

- Information: 760-786-2331 www.nps.gov/deva

Mile-high view Zabriskie Point in the Amargosa Range

How to Get There

From the west, cross the eastern Mojave Desert via I-15; turn north on Calif. 127 at Baker, then west at Shoshone on Calif. 178 to Furnace Creek. From Las Vegas, take Nev. 160 west to Pahrump; then west on Nev. 372/Calif. 178 to Shoshone and into the park. Airports: Las Vegas, Nev., or Los Angeles, Calif.

When to Go

All-year park. Winter preferred since average summer highs can reach 116°F.

How to Visit

An overnight stay allows time for the valley's vivid sunrises and sunsets, and a visit to the **Death Valley Museum** and **Furnace Creek Visitor Center.** Plan also to visit the **Harmony Borax Works** near the Furnace Creek Campground, to walk **Golden Canyon Interpretive Trail,** and to drive to **Zabriskie Point** for fine views of the valley.

A second day permits exploration of the valley's northern reaches and **Scottys Castle,** the retreat of an early 20th-century millionaire, and nearby **Ubehebe Crater,** blasted out during the region's volcanic past.

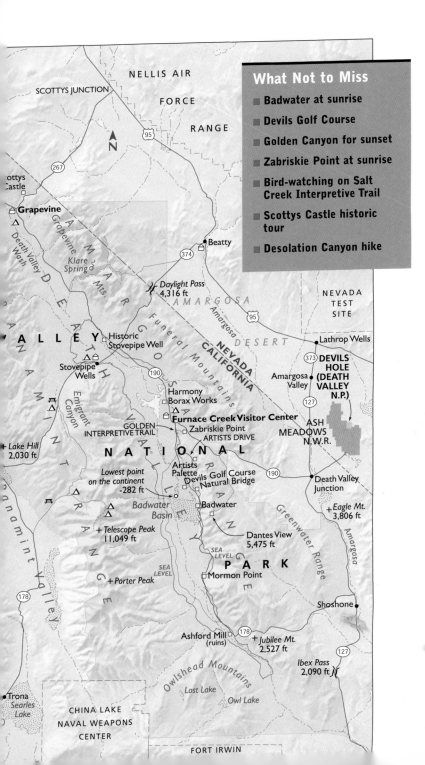

What Not to Miss

- Badwater at sunrise
- Devils Golf Course
- Golden Canyon for sunset
- Zabriskie Point at sunrise
- Bird-watching on Salt Creek Interpretive Trail
- Scottys Castle historic tour
- Desolation Canyon hike

EXPLORING THE PARK

Shoshone to Furnace Creek: 130 miles; 1 to 2 days

From the mining town of **Shoshone**, head west on Calif. 178 through the Amargosa Range to the ruins of **Ashford Mill**. Before you stretches the Death Valley Salt Pan—the residue of a saline lake that existed over 20,000 years ago. Fossils indicate that some seven million years ago the park was a dripping woodland, populated with deer, dwarf horses, tapirs, and rhinos.

Native Americans, most recently the Shoshone, found ways to adapt to the more recent and forbidding desert conditions that exist here now. Rock art and artifacts indicate a human presence dating back at least 9,000 years.

From Ashford Mill to Furnace Creek you travel below sea level, dipping to minus 282 feet at **Badwater** *(27 miles N)*, the Western Hemisphere's lowest point. North of Badwater 4 miles, turn onto the rough road to **Natural Bridge,** an arch spanning a richly tinted conglomerate canyon. A quarter-mile trail to the bridge passes other striking formations.

About 1.5 miles north, look left for the half-mile spur road to **Devils Golf Course,** a meringue of rock salt pinnacles that forms as water evaporates up through the salty crust.

Back on the main road, drive north 5 miles to the 9-mile **Artists Drive** loop road through the Artists Palette, a rumpled terrain of volcanic ash whose yellows, red-oranges, greens, and muted purples challenge plein-air painters. About 4 miles north, the moderate 1-mile **Golden Canyon Interpretive Trail** winds through a canyon that near sunset gleams as if dusted with gold.

Continue north to the Calif. 190 junction and stop at the **Furnace Creek Visitor Center,** which offers exhibits and a bookstore. Check for ranger-guided walks and evening programs *(October– March)* and visit the **Death Valley Museum.** The springs at Furnace Creek oasis produce over a million gallons a day, watering oleanders, palms, and tamarisk trees, and the incongruously verdant fairways of the golf course at the Furnace Creek Ranch.

Next, follow Calif. 190 southeast for a short drive to **Zabriskie Point,** a popular sunrise viewing spot, where rain and wind have shaped rock into dramatic contours. In the soft sandstone are prints left by camels, mastodons, and horses. The promontory commands a broad view of mudstone badlands. To explore them, continue on Calif. 190 for a mile to **Twenty Mule Team Canyon,** where a 3-mile gravel loop road threads through the badlands.

When you return to the highway, turn right, and continue to a 13-mile spur road that leads to **Dantes View,** an overlook perched at 5,475 feet in the Amargosa Range. Here you'll see the lay of the land better than any map can show you. The panorama plunges to Badwater and sweeps across the salt pan to the Panamint Range and 11,049-foot Telescope Peak. Now and then in a wet spring, there will be standing water in the valley. The dark fans flaring at the base of the mountains on both sides of the valley were formed by alluvial sand and gravel washed down through the canyons and spread onto the floor. These materials tend to be darker than the tan muds and sands and white salts of the old lake bed. After taking in the view, you might hike down along the ridge to the south to see the land from different angles.

Furnace Creek to Scottys Castle: 90 miles; a half day

One mile north of the Furnace Creek Visitor Center, walk the quarter-mile paved **Harmony Borax Works Interpretive Trail** to

Stovepipe Wells, Death Valley National Park

the ruins of Death Valley's first successful borax mining venture. Farther north on Calif. 190, follow the 1-mile spur road to **Salt Creek Interpretive Trail,** where spring-fed marshy pools support Death Valley's unusual desert pupfish, descendant of creatures that flourished in the basin's ancient lake at least 12,000 years ago. This is a prime bird-watching area, frequented by many of the 350 species found in Death Valley, including Canada geese, peregrine falcons, hawks, and eagles.

Nearby sand dunes ripple across 14 square miles. At sunrise and sunset the wind-sculptured waves of quartz-grain sand take on a luminous rosy glow. Accessible via paved road near **Stovepipe Wells Village,** these dunes have no established trails; park and walk where you please. Most of the sand is made of quartz fragments, forged deep in the earth, uplifted, then eroded off a mountain range and pushed about by the wind until they drifted here. The deep roots of mesquite trees can get a grip in the dunes, and they attract insects, kangaroo rats, lizards, and larger predators like coyotes, most of which do their work at night.

Next, drive north on Calif. 190 for about 30 miles to Grapevine Canyon and **Scottys Castle,** a Mediterranean-style architectural gem dating from 1922. Once the retreat of a wealthy Chicago couple, the ranch is named for frequent house guest and "desert rat" Walter Scott. Daily on the hour, the Park Service conducts tours through the mansion, which holds original furnishings. In winter, be prepared to wait up to two hours for a tour. While waiting, consider a meal at the castle's restaurant, a picnic outside, or an amble up **Windy Point Trail.**

Eight miles west of the castle is **Ubehebe Crater,** a 600-foot-deep indentation that blew cinder and ash about 2,000 years ago. From the parking lot at its rim, there is a short trail to the rim of the smaller, newer **Little Hebe Crater.**

If you have four-wheel-drive vehicle and some savvy about traveling safely in desert wilderness, visit **Eureka Dunes** at the north end of the park. Wake in the morning to see the light moving down the banded minerals in the surrounding hills, then rapidly sliding down this huge mound of sand. Or drive the **Saline Valley Road,** a very rough track along the west side of the park that leads into Saline Valley. There, you'll find an area of large hot springs that have been delightfully "fixed up" with rock grottos and a desert garden by a group of informal, and often unclothed, vagabonds.

Survival in the Desert

Treat any trip into the desert— even by vehicle—as a wilderness journey. Plan your route thoroughly, and make sure friends know your schedule.

People have survived in the desert since time immemorial by following some simple rules: Carry and conserve water, avoid the heat and sun of midday, and don't panic, whatever happens.

You lose a quart of water per hour walking in 100-degree heat, so drink at least a gallon a day. If you're carrying it, know that water weighs about eight pounds per gallon. Bring more than you think you'll need, and turn back before you've consumed half of it. If you're counting on finding water, bring purifying tablets or a pump to avoid intestinal parasites, and check with rangers to make sure sources you see on the map are really there.

Wear a wide-brimmed hat and sunglasses and slather on the high SPF sunscreen to protect your skin. You will conserve moisture if you wear loose-fitting long pants and long-sleeved shirts.

Plan for cold nights, too. Cotton works best for daytime; for nights, it's wool or synthetic fleece garments that wick away moisture, plus a wind shell.

There are several health conditions that can affect desert travelers and it helps to know the signs. Irritability, muscle cramps, and dark urine signal dehydration. Find some shade, drink water, take salt tablets, breath through your nose, and eat only lightly until you've rehydrated.

If you feel sweaty, cool, fatigued, light-headed, perhaps nauseated, you may have heat exhaustion. Get out of the sun, keep still, and drink liquids in small but frequent doses. Heat stroke is more serious; your skin is dry and hot, you suffer vomiting and headaches, your mind is confused. Your sweat glands have shut down, and your temperature is rising to potentially fatal levels. Remove clothing and cool off if possible by immersing in water or wet towels. Massage arms and legs and drink slowly. Don't take aspirin.

The greatest danger of all is panic. If you get lost or hurt, calm yourself down, find shelter, keep drinking water, and be patient. That's the way denizens of the desert survive.

INFORMATION & ACTIVITIES

Headquarters
P.O. Box 579
Death Valley, CA 92328
760-786-2331
www.nps.gov/deva

Visitor & Information Centers
Furnace Creek, off Calif. 190.
760-786-3220.

Seasons & Accessibility
Open all year. Best seasons
are fall, winter, and spring,
especially if you plan to hike
or go camping.

Entrance Fees
$10 per vehicle per week, or $5
per person entering on foot or
by bike.

Pets
Must be leashed at all times.
Not allowed on trails or in
backcountry.

Facilities for Disabled
The visitor center; Scottys
Castle; and campgrounds at
Furnace Creek, Texas Spring,
and Sunset are all accessible
for wheelchairs.

Things to Do
Free ranger- and naturalist-led
activities available mid-October
to mid-April: nature walks and
talks, evening programs, children's programs. Also, hiking,
nature trails, living history
tours, bicycling, bird-watching,
horseback riding.

Special Advisories
■ Never underestimate Death
Valley's heat. It can make any
emergency life threatening. For
advice on hot weather travel,
consult the Death Valley Guide,
available at roadside kiosks,
ranger stations, and at the
visitor center.
■ Drink plenty of water; one
gallon per person per day is
recommended, two gallons if
hiking. Dehydration is the
second most common cause
of death in the park.
■ Avoid outdoor activity in the
middle of the day. The park
service even recommends
against hiking at all during
the heat of the summer.
■ Emergency radiator water is
available from barrels located
along main park roads.
■ Abandoned mine shafts and
prospect holes pose dangers.
Stay out of abandoned tunnels.
■ Wear a hat and sunglasses.
■ Desert rains, though brief,
cause flash floods. Never ford
washouts, even in a four-wheel-
drive vehicle.

Backcountry Camping
Backcountry camping is permitted at least 2 miles from

Sunrise in Death Valley

.*nps.gov);* all others are first come, first served. Fees: $16 at Furnace Creek; $10 at Sunset, Stovepipe Wells, Mesquite Spring; $12 at Texas Spring; free at Thorndike, Emigrant, Mahogany Flat, and Wildrose.

Hotels, Motels, & Inns
(Unless otherwise noted, rates are for two persons in a double room, high season.)

INSIDE THE PARK:
- **Furnace Creek Inn & Ranch Resort** Furnace Creek, off Calif. 190, P.O. Box 1, Death Valley, CA 92328. 760-786-2345. Inn: 66 units. $270–$370; pool, restaurant, golf course. Ranch: 225 units. $102–$165. Pool, 2 restaurants. www.furnacecreekresort.com.
- **Stovepipe Wells Village Motel** Stovepipe Wells Village, P.O. Box 559, Death Valley, CA 92328. 760-786-2387. 83 units. $59–$99; 14 RV hookups, $20. AC, pool, restaurant.

For additional lodgings, contact the Death Valley Chamber of Commerce, P.O. Box 157, Shoshone, CA 92384. 760-852-4524.

main roads and a quarter mile from water sources. Permits are not required, but those who plan to hike are advised to register at the visitor center and to find out which areas prohibit camping.

Campgrounds
Nine campgrounds in the park, each with a 30-day limit. Furnace Creek, Mesquite Spring, and Wildrose are open year-round; Texas Spring, Sunset, and Stovepipe Wells are open from October to April; Emigrant, Thorndike, and Mahogany Flat are open April to October. Reservations taken only during winter for Furnace Creek (*call National Parks Reservation Service, 800-365-2267; http://reservations*

Water, water

There is, indisputably, a lot of it: Every year, some 200 million acre feet (each enough to flood an acre of land under a foot of water) fall on California, two-thirds of it in the northern half of the state. And therein lies the rub. The water falls in the wrong place. It tends to evaporate or go where no one wants it to go. And most population growth occurs in the south, a land of few rivers and even fewer lakes and streams.

"God," as sociologist Carey McWilliams eloquently put it more than 50 years ago, "never intended Southern California to be anything but a desert…Man has made it what it is."

Humans have mainly made aqueducts. The story of the first is a familiar one to most Californians. A turn-of-the-century Los Angeles business cabal, worried about the impact of drought on land prices, convinced a panicked citizenry to underwrite a 230-mile water canal from Owens Lake. After construction, the water was promptly used to "green up" the San Fernando Valley real estate holdings of the said business cabal. The public still needed water. A new study was commissioned, and a new aqueduct built, this one from Sacramento. More water. More suburban growth.

The pattern persists to this day. Yet as suburban growth continues, many in California have come to question the belief that water needs can be filled by importing more and more water from far reaches of the state. Take the case of metropolitan Los Angeles. Today the region has 45 percent of the population on 6 percent of the state's habitable land—but only .06 percent of the state's total stream flow. With the population predicted to grow from 16 million to 24 million over the next few decades, the region would seem ripe for yet another large-scale public works project.

Yet recent experience suggests otherwise, says UCLA's Martha Davis, who studies water-use issues and the environment. A drought that began in 1987 forced the change. Before then, L.A. water agencies had barely paid lip service to conservation. But in 1990, the three-year drought unexpectedly intensified. For the first time, the Metropolitan Water District mandated water rationing. "The response was dramatic," says Davis. "In 1990, water sales peaked at an all-time high of 2.6 million acre feet; by 1993, these sales had plummeted to 1.5 million acre feet…We have fundamentally changed the water demand curve for the southland. We are supporting more people with less (not more) water."

But can such policies really meet the water needs of L.A.'s future population? Ultimately such questions are resolved not by public policy planners but by politicians.

What Water Does in California

Left undirected and left unrestrained, water has had a profound effect on the topography of California. Four interesting manifestations are:

■ **Underground rivers** (Mojave Desert): Created 15,000 years ago when sedimentation on above-ground rivers hardened to form a sandy "lid."

■ **Alluvial fans** (Death Valley): Formed when periodic downpours loosen hillside rubble and debris and carry it to the bottom, creating fan-shaped mounds. Bajadas, also in deserts, are essentially spread-out, large-scale alluvial fans.

■ **Badlands** (statewide): Sharp features—thin spires, thick columns, and undulating folds—carved into soft sandstone hills by surface runoff.

■ **Underground caves** (throughout Sierra parks): Made by groundwater percolating through soluble rock.

Soda Lake, Mojave National Preserve

Excursions from Death Valley

Mojave National Preserve

112 miles southeast of Death Valley

Of the three great desert parks in California, only Mojave National Preserve encompasses parts of all the region's desert ecosystems; the Colorado Desert from the south, the Mojave Desert's high country, and the Great Basin Desert that stretches across Nevada to the east.

Mojave National Preserve, one of the largest units administered by the National Park Service with over 1.5 million acres, was created under the 1994 California Desert Protection Act. Like most parks set aside in modern times, there are conflicting uses within its borders such as mining and hunting. Private land holdings dot the area and roads and power lines cut through the preserve, giving it a cobbled together look.

There are few amenities for tourists, but the elements lying within its boundaries—sculpted dunes that seem lit from within, volcanic rock formations, desert mountain ranges, and unique limestone caves—make a visit well worthwhile.

Like Death Valley to the north, this is Basin and Range country, where the Earth's surface reflects the process of tectonic plates colliding and overriding one another. As the Pacific plate pushes under North America, chunks of surface have split and tilted up to form several small mountain ranges here. Hot spots and bulges have occurred where magma pushed toward the surface, creating features such as the Cinder Cones and the Hole-in-the-Wall.

Park officials at the Mojave National Preserve Desert Information Center *(760-733-4040)* in Baker will be glad to give you maps and offer suggestions, but there is little in the way of assistance once you move on into the preserve. Among the few developed trails in the park, the **Cima Dome Trail** *(6 miles N of Cima on Cima Rd.)* offers a 4-mile round-trip tramp to the top of 5,755-foot Teutonia Peak, crowned with a crowded stand of Joshua trees.

Heading east from Baker on Kelbaker Road, make a stop the **Cinder Cones,** just 12 miles from town. Visible from the road, the cones are smooth, symmetrical hills of accumulated debris around a vent hole. The oldest cones began forming about 7.5 million years ago. Around the cones you'll find black basalt lava-flow beds.

If you have a four-wheel-drive vehicle, there are roads back into these volcanic beds. Kelbaker Road skirts one of the youngest flows. Continue along Kelbaker Road and you'll see tall, white

dunes to your right—the **Kelso Dunes.** A little over 7 miles past the
town of Kelso, a dirt road on the right leads to a trailhead into the
dune system, which is one of the largest in the country. These are
"living" dunes, moving east from an area called Devil's Playground,
but also living in the sense that there are colorful spring blooms,
coyotes, mice, and sidewinder rattlesnakes. They have even been
described as "singing" dunes, as the loose sand sometimes slides
against itself causing a thrumming noise as it moves.

Hole-in-the-Wall

Back at Kelso, take Kelso Cima Road northwest to Cedar Canyon
Road, then continue 6 miles east to Black Canyon Road. Head
south through **Gold Valley,** one of the most beautiful areas of the
preserve. This is pinyon-pine forest country, with cliff walls favored
by raptors and some strange rock formations shaped by volcanism.

The Hole-in-the-Wall, about 6 miles down Black Canyon Road,
is a pile of rubble on a monumental scale. The material was
expelled some 18 million years ago in a huge volcanic belch by
the Woods Mountains just to the east.

A 2-mile round-trip trail leads through an opening in the cliff
wall and down into the wildly pocketed **Banshee Canyon.** This is
a relatively easy hike except for the beginning: You climb down
through the hole using metal rings imbedded in the rock. A 7-mile
connecting trail winds through a landscape of mesas and boulders
to the Mid-Hills Campground.

Providence Mountains State Recreation Area

In the midst of this new reserve is an old one, Providence Mountains State Recreation Area *(760-928-2586),* where **Mitchell Caverns**
offer some of the state's most interesting cave formations. An
ancient seafloor provided the limestone; several million years ago,
water saturated this rock and slowly dissolved it to form big water-
filled underground chambers that later dried out.

Guided tours *(fee)* are held daily *(Sept.–May)* to look at the
stalactites and stalagmites, draperies, helictites, and popcorn.

■ **1.6 million acres** ■ **Southern California, southeast of Barstow off I-15
or I-40** ■ **Best months Oct.–March** ■ **Camping, hiking, wildlife viewing,
spelunking** ■ **Contact the preserve, 72157 Baker Blvd., Baker, CA 92309;
760-733-4040. www.nps.gov/moja**

Antelope Valley/California Poppy Reserve

165 miles southwest of Death Valley

Every spring Antelope Valley explodes with color, dominated by the brilliant orange of the California poppy. The desert grassland here also welcomes yellow coreopsis, gold fields, and lupine. All of them provide food and cover for mice and kangaroo rats; these creatures, in turn, attract predators such as coyotes, bobcats, and even the occasional mountain lion.

Generally, flowers begin appearing in February, and the bloom can run until May, sometimes into June. Though the reserve ecologists attempt to enhance the blooms through prescribed burns to decrease the impact of non-native grasses, they admit it isn't clear what makes for springtime profusion: It's a guessing game each year. Call the reserve hotline *(661-724-1180)* for the most up-to-date information.

The excellent Jane S. Pinheiro Interpretive Center, open only during the blooming season *(mid-March–May)*, can give you maps and orientation. Seven miles of trails loop around the valley to several higher viewpoints. The 1.5-mile **Lightening Bolt Trail** begins near the interpretive center, passing Kitanmuk Vista Point and leading to Antelope Butte Vista Point. The 1.4-mile **South Loop**

California poppies

Poppy and 1.8-mile **North Loop Poppy Trails** both begin at the center and lead you through fields of poppies.

American antelope, also called pronghorn, are the valley's namesake. Today these animals can be found mostly on the Tejon Ranch Company's private ranch *(661-248-3000. Adm. fee)*, which sprawls across the Tehachapi Mountains northwest of the reserve. During the spring wildflower season it is possible to visit the ranch but you may also be lucky enough to catch a glimpse of the pronghorn along the ranch's borders.

■ **1,745 acres** ■ **Southern California, near Lancaster** ■ **Best months Feb.–May** ■ **Adm. fee** ■ **Wildlife viewing, wildflower viewing** ■ **Contact Mojave Desert Information Center, 43779 15th St. W., Lancaster, CA 93534; 661-942-0662. http://parks.ca.gov**

Red Rock Canyon State Park

115 miles southwest of Death Valley

On the northwest edge of the Mojave Desert where the Sierra Nevada foothills rise from the plains, runoff has cut through sedimentary and volcanic rock to form canyons, leaving colorful traces of red, white, and brown. The layering of different types of rock contributes to the sometimes bizarre formations. Much of the colorful rock can be seen from a car. In many cases you'll need a four-wheel-drive vehicle and a map; talk to park staff about road conditions.

The two natural preserves within the park, **Hagan Canyon** and **Red Cliffs,** are closed to cars, but along the trails you'll find spring wildflower blooms and rarities such as the Red Rock tarweed.

Pick up a brochure at the park's visitor center and hike the half-mile **Desert View Nature Trail.** From this trail another climbs to the ridge above the White House Cliffs. Elsewhere, the **Hagan Canyon Nature Trail** *(1.5-mile loop, off Abbott Dr. near junction with Calif. 14)* visits a dry falls in the canyon, where there are bright red bands of mineral in the cliffs.

■ **27,500 acres** ■ **Southern California, 25 miles north of Mojave on Calif. 14** ■ **Best months late Feb.–May, late Sept.–Nov.** ■ **Adm. fee** ■ **Camping, hiking, rock climbing, mountain biking, horseback riding, wildflower viewing** ■ **Contact Mojave Desert Information Center, 43779 15th St. W., Lancaster, CA 93534; 661-942-0662. http://parks.ca.gov**

Ash Meadows National Wildlife Refuge

25 miles east of Death Valley

One reason for stopping at Ash Meadows is to find out what all the fuss is about. This is the home of the Ash Meadows, the Warm Springs, and the Devils Hole pupfish—three obscure fish that as endangered species have the power to shut down summer-home construction or a big dam-building project. They are minuscule, silver-blue fish with an underslung jaw that have survived in small pockets as the great lakes that once covered the deserts of the Southwest retreated into small corners. These pupfish live here in the desert northwest of Las Vegas, in this small green oasis fed by more than 30 springs.

Although the Ash Meadows and Warm Springs pupfish can be found in many of the springs, the Devils Hole pupfish, the smallest (1 inch), can only be seen in one pool, sunk in a crevasse in the mountainside. This site, which is surrounded by a high fence with barbed wire on top to protect the fish, can be reached by following signs from the refuge headquarters. It holds a few hundred of the endangered little fish.

Springs such as these, isolated in desert uplands, are good candidates for producing endemic species found nowhere else. Biologists count more than 20 unique plants and animals in the area of the refuge in Amargosa Valley, a concentration of indigenous wildlife thought to be greater than anywhere else in the country.

Visitors can take the self-guided 0.7-mile **Crystal Spring Trail,** a boardwalk that begins near the refuge office. Lean over the springs and get a look at the frisky, silvery pupfish against the green mossy bottom. You'll also see threatened plants, such as the Ash Meadows gumplant and ivesia.

Although the springs can discharge up to 2,600 gallons per minute, most of them run in channels no bigger than an irrigation ditch as they meander around the refuge. Beneath the surface is a huge aquifer of "fossil" water that has been flowing underground for thousands of years, and now bubbles up in a series of springs and seeps. Swimming in the springs is prohibited, but you can take a dip in **Crystal Reservoir,** near the visitor center.

■ 22,000 acres ■ Southwest Nevada, 30 miles northwest of Pahrump on Bell Vista Rd. ■ Year-round ■ Hiking, swimming, wildlife viewing ■ Day use only ■ Contact the refuge, HCR 70, Box 610-Z, Amargosa Valley, NV 89020; 702-372-5435. www.r1.fws.gov/desert/ashframe.htm

Bighorn Sheep

With their dignified bearing and crown of curled horn, the desert bighorn sheep are one of the royal families of desert wildlife. They are not easily seen, except with a good spotting scope and a map of watering holes. They stick to the high rocks, avoiding people and livestock, and concentrate on survival and propagation.

Desert bighorn sheep

The bighorns originated in Asia and made their way to North America during the last ice age, when a land bridge existed. The sheep spread throughout the mountain and desert provinces of the West. But then, in the 19th century, the animals' very existence was threatened. First hunters decimated the sheep for food and trophies, then exotic diseases swept through the remaining populations.

To save the bighorn sheep, a small number of refuges such as the **Desert National Wildlife Refuge** *(25 miles N of Las Vegas via US 95, 702-879-6110)* were established in the region stretching from the northern Rockies to the Mexican border. With protection, the great fluctuation in herd size is now caused only by wet and dry cycles. The sheep found on the Desert NWR are smaller in stature than their cousins to the north (the Rocky Mountain and California bighorns), but their distinctive curled horns tend to be larger. These are true horns, which aren't shed; if you find a set in the wild, it's usually attached to a skull.

A ram's horn will form its full distinctive curl by about eight years of age. Like tree rings, the rings, or whorls, on the outside of the horn represent years, the first distinctive ones forming after four years.

During the breeding season *(midsummer–fall)*, you might hear the crack of rams butting heads. They square off at about 20 feet and try to knock each other silly. Lambs are born in February and March, and grow up in nursery groups of ewes, lambs, and young males.

Red Rock Canyon National Conservation Area

120 miles southeast of Death Valley   Gazing up at the multihued sandstone blocks of Red Rock Canyon under a hot summer sun, remind yourself that this was until recently—merely a few hundred million years ago—the bottom of an ocean. Then it became a very dry desert, with drifting dunes piling sand a half mile deep. The sand solidified, and the forces of erosion began to carve it into interesting shapes.

That is the story of much of the sculpted sandstone in the Mojave Desert, but at Red Rock there is a wrinkle that explains why it remains standing tall while other sandstone is worn down: Approximately 65 million years ago, the Earth's crust snapped and overlapped, throwing the harder gray limestone from the long ago ocean floor over the softer and younger red sandstone. You can clearly see the color change of the rock along the Keystone Thrust Fault, and it is the gray cap of limestone that resists erosion.

The canyon sits in the foreground of the Spring Mountains, a tall wall of rock that closes off the west side of the valley. A great many species find refuge here, not because of the colorful rocks, but because there's a little more water flowing in the creeks and canyons. Mountain lions, kit foxes, red-tailed hawks, and kangaroo rats are here. So is a small band of less than 200 desert bighorn sheep *(see p. 167),* who keep to the steeper terrain but can sometimes be spotted at springs. Part of the bighorns' problem is competition from burros, imported animals that have made themselves at home. Two well-known refugees, a desert iguana and chuckwalla, can be found at the **Red Rock Visitor Center.** Both are escapees from Las Vegas, where they were poorly kept "pets" before being brought here for a life of ease.

Human escapees from the city can jump in a car and head west on Nev. 159 for 13 miles to reach the visitor center. Here they'll find exhibits covering geology and natural history. This is also the beginning of a 13-mile **scenic drive** that is the centerpiece of most visits to Red Rock Canyon.

From the numerous pullouts and trailheads, you can join the many short hikes into the area, including the 2.5-mile round-trip **Ice Box Canyon Trail,** the 2.9-mile round-trip **Pine Creek Canyon Trail,** and the short **Calico Hills Trail,** where you'll find deep canyons, natural water-holding tanks, and the remnants of agave roasting pits left by early Native American inhabitants. Ambitious

Petrified Dunes, Red Rock Canyon

hikers can venture from Sandstone Quarry up the 5-mile round-trip **Turtlehead Peak Trail** to the 6,323-foot summit, or along the escarpment atop **Wilson Cliffs,** which back up to the Spring Mountains along the park's western edge.

Though the rock is mostly soft sandstone, rock climbers come here in droves. They work out of the Pine Creek Canyon area, or the Sandstone Quarry, which lies above the scenic loop. There are several outfitters in the area *(contact the BLM for a list).*

The scenic loop area can be extremely busy on weekends, so you may want to shift to less crowded routes at the southern end of the park. You also may want to pay a visit to the cool meadows and old buildings of **Spring Mountain Ranch** *(702-875-4141),* a former cattle ranch that once belonged to Howard Hughes and is now a state park within Red Rock Canyon.

■ **197,000 acres** ■ **Southern Nevada, 13 miles west of Las Vegas on Nev. 159** ■ **Year-round** ■ **Adm. fee** ■ **Hiking, rock climbing, mountain biking, horseback riding, wildlife viewing** ■ **Contact Bureau of Land Management, HCR 33, Box 5500, Las Vegas, NV 89124; 702-515-5350. www.redrockcanyon.blm.gov**

Grand Canyon

The road to the Grand Canyon from the south crosses a gently rising plateau that gives no hint at what is about to unfold. You wonder if you have made a wrong turn. All at once an immense gorge a mile deep and up to 18 miles wide opens up. The scale is so vast that even from the best vantage point only a fraction of the canyon's 277 miles can be seen.

Nearly five million people travel here each year; 90 percent first see the canyon from the South Rim with its dramatic views into the deep inner gorge of the Colorado River. So many feet have stepped cautiously to the edge of major overlooks that in places the rock has been polished smooth. But most of the park's 1,904 square miles are maintained as wilderness. You can avoid crowds by hiking the park's many trails or driving to the cool evergreen forests of the North Rim where people are fewer.

The Grand Canyon boasts some of the nation's cleanest air, with visibility averaging 90 to 110 miles. Increasingly, though, air pollution blurs vistas that once were sharp and rich hued. Hazy days have become more common, with visibility dropping as low as 20 miles. Haze from forest fires and pollen has always been present, but the recent increase is traced to sources outside the park, like copper smelters and urban areas in Arizona, southern California, and Mexico.

It's hard to look at the canyon and not be curious about geology. Some of the oldest exposed rock in the world, dating back 1.8 billion years, lies at the bottom. Exactly how the river formed the canyon is still unclear, but geologists generally agree that most of the cutting occurred within the last five million years.

Beyond its national park status, the Grand Canyon is a World Heritage Site, one of the Seven Natural Wonders of the World and, in Teddy Roosevelt's view, "the one great sight every American... should see."

- Northern Arizona
- 1.2 million acres
- Established 1919
- Best seasons spring and fall. Boating season runs from April–October
- Camping, hiking, bird-watching, wildlife viewing, raft trips, mule rides
- Information: 928-638-7888 www.nps.gov/grca

View of Colorado River from Toroweap Overlook, Grand Canyon National Park

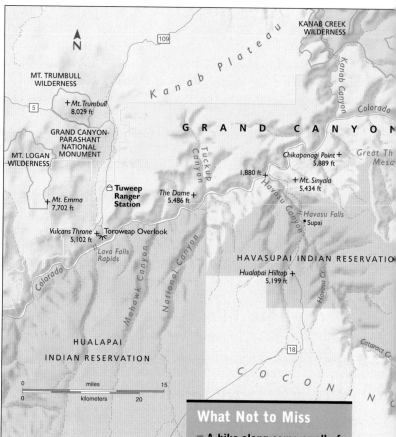

On the map:

KANAB CREEK WILDERNESS

109

K a n a b   P l a t e a u

MT. TRUMBULL
WILDERNESS

5

+ *Mt. Trumbull*
8,029 ft

GRAND CANYON-
PARASHANT
NATIONAL
MONUMENT

MT. LOGAN
WILDERNESS

G R A N D   C A N Y O N

Kanab Canyon

Colorado

Tuckup Canyon

Chikapanagi Point +
5,889 ft

Great Th
Mesa

1,880 ft +

+ *Mt. Sinyala*
5,434 ft

⌂ **Tuweep
Ranger
Station**

The Dome +
5,486 ft

+ *Mt. Emma*
7,702 ft

Havasu Canyon

Havasu Falls
● Supai

Vulcans Throne +
5,102 ft

Toroweap Overlook

*Lava Falls
Rapids*

Mohawk Canyon

National Canyon

HAVASUPAI INDIAN RESERVATIO

Colorado

Hualapai Hilltop +
5,199 ft

Havasu Cr.

HUALAPAI

INDIAN RESERVATION

18

C O C O N I N

Cataract Cr.

miles   15
0

kilometers   20
0

How to Get There
South Rim: From Flagstaff,
Ariz. take US 180 to South
Rim entrance, or take US 89
to Cameron, then Ariz. 64 to
Desert View entrance.
North Rim: Take Ariz. 67 from
Jacob Lake through the Kaibab
National Forest to North Rim
entrance. The two rims are 10
air miles apart but 215 miles by
car, a 5-hour drive. Airports:
Flagstaff, Ariz., and Las Vegas.

What Not to Miss

- ▪ **A hike along some or all of
  Hermits Rest Trail**

- ▪ **Horseback ride or hike
  down Bright Angel Trail
  to Indian Garden**

- ▪ **Visit Hopi Point for sunrise
  or sunset**

- ▪ **Lunching at Grand Canyon
  Lodge overlooking Bright
  Angel Canyon**

- ▪ **Bright Angel Point at
  sunrise or sunset**

- ▪ **Rafting on the Colorado**

- ▪ **A Drive to Point Imperial**

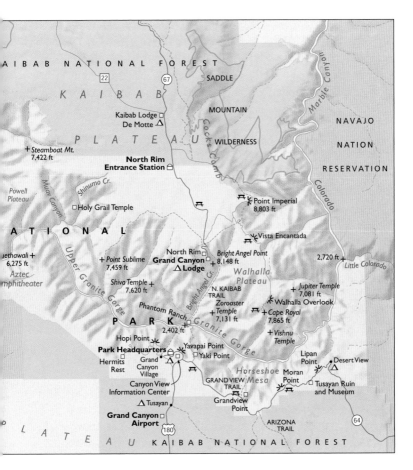

AIBAB   N A T I O N A L   F O R E S T

22   67   SADDLE

K A I B A B

MOUNTAIN

Kaibab Lodge □
De Motte △

+ Steamboat Mt.
7,422 ft

P L A T E A U   WILDERNESS

NAVAJO

NATION

RESERVATION

**North Rim
Entrance Station** ⌂

Powell
Plateau

Cocks Comb

Marble Canyon

Shinumo Cr.

□ Holy Grail Temple

Muav Canyon

□ Point Imperial
8,803 ft

Colorado

Little Colorado

N A T I O N A L

iethawali +
6,275 ft

Aztec
mphitheater

Upper Granite Gorge

× Vista Encantada

North Rim □   *Bright Angel Point*
+ Point Sublime   **Grand Canyon** □   + 8,148 ft
7,459 ft   △ **Lodge**

*Walhalla
Plateau*

2,720 ft +

Shiva Temple +
7,620 ft

N. KAIBAB
TRAIL

+ *Jupiter Temple*
7,081 ft

Bright Angel Cr.

Zoroaster
+ Temple
7,131 ft

× Walhalla Overlook

Phantom Ranch

+ *Cape Royal*
7,865 ft

P A R K

Granite Gorge

2,402 ft

+ *Vishnu
Temple*

Hopi Point ×

Park Headquarters □   × Yavapai Point
□   □ Yaki Point
Hermits   Grand   △
Rest   Canyon
Village

Horseshoe Mesa

Moran
Point

Lipan
Point   • Desert View
△

Canyon View
Information Center

GRANDVIEW
TRAIL

△ Tusayan •

Grandview
Point

□ Tusayan Ruin
and Museum

**Grand Canyon
Airport** □
180

ARIZONA
TRAIL

64

P L A T E A U   K A I B A B   N A T I O N A L   F O R E S T

When to Go

South Rim is open all year; North Rim facilities are closed mid-October to mid-May. Hikers and mule riders to the inner canyon prefer spring and fall; the prime river season is April through October. In summer on the South Rim, midweek is best.

How to Visit

On a 1-day visit to South Rim, take in views along **Hermit Road;** free bus from March–November, private vehicles allowed in winter. On day two, follow **Desert View Drive** for great views of the Colorado River and eastern canyon.

On a longer stay, take the North Rim's **Cape Royal Road.** Hike a backcountry trail. Take a mule ride; or a week-long raft trip through the canyon. Mule rides and rafting require reservations far in advance.

EXPLORING THE PARK

South Rim, Hermit Road: 8 miles; at least a half day; closed to private vehicles March–November

Begin at the **Canyon View Information Center** near Mather Point for a classic panoramic view into the heart of the Grand Canyon. Great solitary buttes rise from narrow ridges reaching out from the distant North Rim. Far below, a green cluster of Fremont cottonwood trees marks **Phantom Ranch,** a lodge and campground reached only by mule or foot. The observation station at nearby **Yavapai Point** explores the canyon's geological history and identifies major landmarks. If bad weather threatens, duck into its glass-enclosed observation room and watch as storm clouds roll in.

Board the free **Hermits Rest Route** bus, which travels along Hermit Road between the information center and Hermits Rest from March through November. Skirting the rim of the canyon for 8 miles, it offers superb views of the Colorado River and the labyrinth of side canyons and broad platforms below the rim. The buses can be crowded at peak times of day.

The first stop is the **Trailview Overlook.** Here you get a hint of the canyon's size. To the south, the historic El Tovar Hotel and Bright Angel Lodge look small and insignificant perched on the brink of the great precipice. Mule strings and hikers file along the Bright Angel Trail as it zigzags 8 miles and 4,460 feet down to the river.

Don't miss **Hopi Point,** a promontory jutting deep into the gorge. Magnificent views 45 miles both eastward and westward make this an ideal spot for watching sunset or sunrise. To avoid crowds, leave the main overlook and walk along the Rim Trail to find your own observation point. Across the river rise the intricately carved walls of **Isis Temple** and tree-topped **Shiva Temple,** described as "the grandest of all buttes."

The bus route continues west, passing Mohave Point and skirting breathtakingly close to **The Abyss,** where a sheer cliff plunges 3,000 feet to a plateau below. From here the road follows the sweep of the rim out to **Pima Point,** where you see the Colorado River threading through the deep gorge. On a still day you can hear the distant rumble of **Granite Rapids** almost a mile below. What looks like a stream from above is a river 300 feet wide that, with its tributaries, drains eight percent of the continental United States.

The road ends at **Hermits Rest,** a limestone building that looks as if Hobbits built it on the canyon's rim; it serves as a curio shop.

View from South Bass Trail

Those with time and stamina can hike partway down the steep **Hermit Trail** to Dripping Springs, 7 miles and 6 to 9 hours round-trip. Here the hermit Louis Boucher raised goldfish in a watering trough at the turn of the 20th century. It's a good place to see some of the canyon's 315 species of birds. Permits are not needed for day hikes, but first ask a park ranger for conditions and advisories. On the return, buses stop only at Mohave and Hopi Points.

For the adventurous, the **Rim Trail** hugs the canyon's edge for nearly 11 miles from Mather Point to Hermits Rest, roughly paralleling Hermit Road. The path is paved to Maricopa Point; the rest is dirt. The trail is generally level except for a steep stretch between the village and Trailview. Short hikes can be combined with rides by catching the shuttle bus at any of the main overlooks. You can also pick up the bus at the the trail's end for an easy return.

South Rim, Desert View Drive: 23 miles; a half to full day

Desert View Drive (Ariz. 64) begins just south of Mather Point and skirts the rim eastward for 23 miles to Desert View, providing numerous pull-offs for long views of the main canyon. In summer, parking at the major overlooks can be a problem, so between March and November only the park shuttle is allowed on the Yaki Point/South Kaibab Trailhead spur road. *(Board at the Canyon View Information Center.)* Along the roadside are shaggy-barked Utah juniper and low clumps of Gambel oak.

Yaki Point provides a fine view of the darkly shining **Granite Gorge,** the innermost canyon. The imposing pyramid-shaped profile of **Vishnu Temple,** 7,533 feet high, dominates the eastern

Kaibab Squirrel

One resident you might possibly encounter along the Grand Canyon's North Rim is the Kaibab squirrel, a great fan of the nuts and inner bark of the ponderosa pine. In spring, the squirrel enjoys a special treat: the fruiting bodies, or truffles, of underground fungi that live on the tree's roots. As squirrels eat this fungi—organisms that are highly beneficial to the tree—the spores pass through the animal's digestive system, spreading the fungi to more pine roots.

The Kaibab squirrel provides a fascinating lesson in allopatric speciation. As the Grand Canyon formed, the Kaibab squirrel became geographically isolated from the region's other tassel-eared squirrels. Eventually it evolved as a distinct subspecies, unable to interbreed with other tassel-eared squirrels.

skyline. The practice of naming major park landforms after world deities began with Clarence Dutton, who published a classic report on the geology of the Grand Canyon in 1882.

On the way back to the main road, you can leave the shuttle and hike the **South Kaibab Trail,** which switchbacks down the west side of Yaki Point. Allot a third of your time for going down and two-thirds for hiking back up. The trail eventually reaches the Colorado River at the bottom of the canyon, but a strenuous 3-mile, 2.5-hour round-trip takes you only partway down to Cedar Ridge. Even though you drop 1,140 vertical feet, none of the major land-forms of the canyon look any closer. Fossil ferns lie exposed in the bedrock on the west side of Cedar Ridge.

Return to your vehicle and follow the main road as it climbs into a tall ponderosa forest. Take the turnoff to **Grandview Point,** one of the finest vistas on the South Rim. From the overlook, **Grandview Trail** drops a rugged 3 miles to Horseshoe Mesa, where miners once worked copper ore from the Last Chance Mine.

Drive farther east to **Moran Point** for the best view of one of the Colorado's major rapids. Here you look directly down on **Hance Rapids;** its rocky 30-foot drop is considered by river guides to be among the most difficult to run. Continue on down the road, and if you need a change of pace, stop at the small **Tusayan Museum.** It displays well-designed exhibits of Native American cultures, and the nearby ruins offer a self-guided tour of an excavated ancestral Puebloan village from A.D. 1185.

Take your time when you reach **Lipan Point,** the finest view of the eastern canyon. Here the Colorado River makes a great bend to the west, where it has carved through the Kaibab Plateau to form the deepest portion of the Grand Canyon. Below, the river makes an S-curve around Unkar Delta, which prehistoric people extensively farmed.

Bypass Navajo Point and continue on to **Desert View,** where you might stop at the snack bar and curio shop. While here, climb the stairs to the top of the 70-foot **Watchtower,** built in 1932. On the tower's walls Native American artist Fred Kabotie painted murals depicting Hopi legends.

North Rim, Cape Royal Road: 23 miles; a half to full day

Averaging 1,000 feet higher than the South Rim, the North Rim's alpine vegetation and more varied vistas appeal to many travelers. Still, you won't find the South Rim crowds here. The focus is the historic **Grand Canyon Lodge,** built in the 1920s on the lip of the canyon and rebuilt after a disastrous fire in 1932. From its Sun Room you'll get an excellent view of **Bright Angel Canyon** incised 11 miles into the plateau and overshadowed by Deva, Brahma, and Zoroaster Temples.

Pick up a self-guiding pamphlet from the box by the log shelter near the parking lot. Follow one of the paved trails to **Bright Angel Point,** which divides a side canyon called The Transept from Roaring Springs Canyon. Listen for the sound of the springs cascading from a cave 3,000 feet below the rim. This is a fine spot for watching sunrise or sunset. Those needing to stretch their legs can take the **Transept Trail,** 1.5 miles along the nearly level canyon rim, or a short hike on the **North Kaibab Trail** (1 mile down takes you 650 feet beneath the rim—and that mile back up feels like 3).

From the lodge, drive north 3 miles to the **Cape Royal Road,** one of the most scenic drives in the park. It passes through forests of spruce, fir, locust, and ponderosa pine mixed with stands of quaking aspen, and through lovely meadows of blue lupine and scarlet bugler. Long-eared mule deer often bound across the road, and you might glimpse the reclusive white-tailed Kaibab squirrel (*see sidebar opposite*) found only in the North Rim forests on the Kaibab Plateau.

Roaring Springs Canyon

Those looking for a dramatic sunrise perch can turn off onto the 3-mile road to **Point Imperial,** at 8,803 feet the highest viewpoint on either rim. Here amid tall evergreens you look across the canyon to the high plateau of the Navajo Indian Reservation. Evidence of a 2000 fire is noticeable in this vicinity (you probably spotted more scars along the first portion of Cape Royal Road). Return to the main road and continue on, passing through the forested Walhalla Plateau. Stop at **Vista Encantada** for superb views of the northeastern canyon and the carved pinnacles of Brady and Tritle Peaks.

The road ends at a parking lot on Cape Royal. A paved half-mile nature trail leads along a narrow peninsula past **Angels Window,** an opening eroded through the rock spur that frames the river below. Watch your children! From the overlook Wotans Throne and Vishnu Temple dominate the foreground. Across the canyon rise the Palisades of the Desert. The unusually broad vista here provides a fine vantage point to watch the sun set and to absorb what naturalist John Burroughs described as Grand Canyon's "strange new beauty."

Carving the Grand Canyon

About 1.8 billion years ago, cataclysmic geological forces crumpled and uplifted ancient sedimentary rock to create a range of high mountains (1). The tremendous heat and pressure recrystallized the rock to schist; molten material from deep inside Earth oozed up and became veins of pink granite. The peaks eroded into a plain (2). A sea submerged the plain, sediments covered it and turned to rock, and magma continued to well up. About a billion years ago, Earth shuddered again, cracking its crust into giant fault blocks that formed a second range of mountains (3), which also eroded away. Much of the canyon's rock visible today (4) accumulated over the schist in the last 600 million years.

In recent geological time (about six million years ago) the young, southward-flowing Colorado River—perhaps later captured by the ancestral Hualapai River encroaching from the west— began to slice into the upper layers and eventually reached the schist 4,000 feet below the rim and continued to cut (5). Wind and water still wear away at the massive gorge, widening and deepening its floor and walls.

Inner Canyon Journeys

Hiking into the Grand Canyon

Traveling by foot is one of the best ways to appreciate the small details of the Grand Canyon—its wonderfully sculptured side canyons, its wildlife, its colorful flowers, its sounds, and its silences. Walking also reveals its grandeur and immense scale. Each of the canyons within the canyon has its own personality; you would need a lifetime to experience them all.

To hike into Grand Canyon's depths, plan ahead and bring the right clothing and gear. If required, obtain a backcountry permit. Water should be the heaviest item in your pack because reliable sources in the canyon may be many miles apart.

Spring offers generally pleasant hiking temperatures, though some roads on the North Rim may still be closed; good conditions return in autumn. In summer the lower part of the canyon becomes an oven; hikers cope by traveling early or late in the day and by drinking extra water. Winter snow and ice can make trails slushy or slippery and close most roads on the North Rim.

The park service publishes a free newspaper, *Grand Canyon National Park's Backcountry Trip Planner,* with lots of good advice, trail information, maps, and permit details; it's available in the park, by mail, and on the Internet. You won't need a permit for day hikes or if you have a reservation at Phantom Ranch in the bottom of the canyon, but all other overnight trips require one.

All trails from the rims offer good day hikes—remember to save two-thirds of your water, energy, and time for the hike back! Many hikers are tempted to go from the South Rim to the river and back in a day, but the distance and elevation change are too great to do this safely; such a trip would be very dangerous in summer.

Park rangers highly recommend that first-time hikers use trails in the Corridor Zone—the **Bright Angel** (7.8 miles) and **South Kaibab** (6.3 miles) **Trails** from the South Rim and the **North Kaibab Trail** (14.2 miles) from the North Rim. Well-maintained and easy to follow, these trails offer spectacular scenery but are sufficiently well trodden for help to be around in case of trouble. All three meet at two footbridges across the Colorado River near Bright Angel Campground and Phantom Ranch. Ask a ranger about current water sources and trail conditions.

If you are fit, you can make a great day-hike loop by descending the South Kaibab Trail 4.4 miles to the **Tonto Trail,** turning left and going 4.1 miles on the Tonto to **Indian Garden,** then ascending the Bright Angel Trail 4.6 miles back to the South Rim. **Plateau Point,** a 3-mile round-trip from Indian Garden, is a popular side trip for those on Bright Angel Trail, offering a 360-degree canyon vista.

A rim-to-rim hike is a grand adventure that takes three days one way. To explore side canyons and attractions such as Ribbon Falls en route requires additional time.

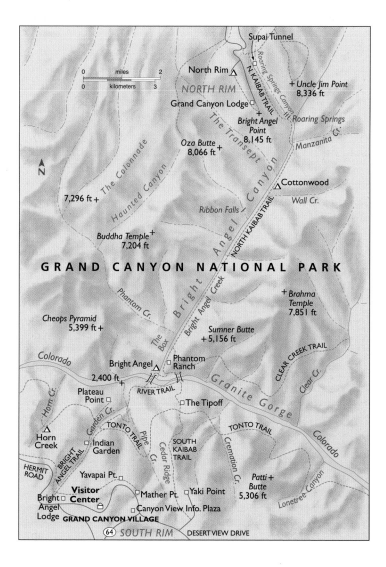

River running in the Grand Canyon

Whether on a large motorized raft or a kayak, a boat expedition is a great way to see the Grand Canyon. Whatever craft you choose, you can look forward to memorable side trips, wonderful campsites, and superb meals. It's hot in summer, but the river is always at hand to cool you off.

Most visitors opt for commercial trips. A skilled crew does the hard work; passengers relax and enjoy. Experienced river runners organize their own trips, but the lengthy permit process is a formidable obstacle. For a list of outfitters or requirements for private trips, contact park headquarters (see p. 184).

Advance reservations are highly recommended, though it is sometimes possible to join a trip on short notice, especially in spring and fall or if there are just a few of you. Boat options are large motorized rafts, small oar rafts, or hard-shelled dories. Kayaks and small paddle rafts can join some raft trips. Motorized rafts travel twice as far in a day as oar-powered craft.

Nearly all trips start at Lees Ferry, just above the Grand Canyon. Some trips stop near Phantom Ranch to take on and let off hikers. Others exchange passengers at Whitmore Wash, where a helicopter usually ferries people in and out. Most trips end at Diamond Creek, the only road access in the canyon, but you can continue to Lake Mead (see pp. 187–88) and the dramatic exit from the Grand Canyon.

White-water boating on the Colorado River

John Wesley Powell

Maps of the American West in the mid-1800s still showed large expanses of unexplored lands, and the one-armed Maj. John Wesley Powell (1834-1902) was destined to help fill in the gaps.

From early childhood, Powell's interest in natural history had taken him on Midwestern field trips. He enlisted in the Union Army at the start of the Civil War, was wounded, and had his right forearm amputated. After the war, as a professor of geology, he led many trips to the Rocky Mountains and other areas of the West to carry out research. A friendly meeting with members of the Ute tribe kindled Powell's passion to study Native American customs and languages.

The idea of exploring the Green and Colorado Rivers intrigued Powell despite legends of earlier expeditions that had perished. He decided to try, selecting a hardy crew who could live off the land under the toughest conditions. On May 24, 1869, Powell set off from Green River Station, Wyoming Territory, with nine men and four boats. He wrote: "What falls there are, we know not; what rocks beset the channel, we know not; what walls rise over the river, we know not." Despite fear of the unknown, near-starvation, abandonment by four crew members (three never to be seen again), and raging rapids that destroyed one boat, the expedition emerged from the Grand Canyon and reached the mouth of the Virgin River in present-day Nevada on August 30. They had traveled more than 1,000 miles providing the first reliable reports of what lay within the canyons of the Green River and the Colorado.

Powell had hoped to accomplish far more scientifically, but loss of instruments and the need to survive had limited his work. So in the spring of 1871 he tried again. This time the trip lasted a year and a half, and he had photographers and a surveyor, who helped provide splendid records of the canyons.

Powell then moved to Washington, D.C. In 1879 he helped create the U.S. Geological Survey and later became its director. He also directed the Smithsonian Institution's Bureau of Ethnology, a post he held for the rest of his life. In 1888, Powell helped found the National Geographic Society. He died in his 69th year and now lies buried in Arlington National Cemetery.

INFORMATION & ACTIVITIES

Headquarters

P.O. Box 129
Grand Canyon, AZ 86023
928-638-7888
www.nps.gov/grca

Visitor & Information Centers

Canyon View Information
Plaza near Grand Canyon
Village open all year. North
Rim Visitor Station open mid-
May to mid-November *(928-
638-7864)*.

Seasons & Accessibility

South Rim open all year. North
Rim roads often close due to
snow mid-November to mid-
May. For current conditions,
call headquarters.

Entrance Fees

$20 per car for seven days;
$10 per person arriving on
foot, bike, or motorcycle.

Pets

Allowed, leashed, on rim trails,
but not below rim. Kennels
available *(928-638-0534)*.

Facilities for Disabled

Visitor center and some shuttle
buses are wheelchair accessible.
Free brochures available. Hermit Road open to vehicles carrying disabled persons, with
permit. Call ahead to make
arrangements *(928-638-0591)*.

Things to Do

Free ranger-led activities: day
and evening nature walks, slide
shows, talks, cultural demon-
strations, and campfire programs. Also, mule trips into
canyon, hiking, bicycling, fishing, river rafting, air tours,
cross-country skiing. Contact
headquarters for list of activities and a list of concessionaires
offering a wide variety of tours.
An IMAX Theater featuring
*Grand Canyon—The Hidden
Secrets* is located a mile south
of the South Rim Entrance, on
Ariz. 64 *(928-638-2468)*.

Special Advisories

■ Be very careful near the
rim; protective barriers are
intermittent.
■ Permits required for
overnight backpacking; $10
fee plus $5 per person per
night. Backcountry Information Center, P.O. Box 129,
Grand Canyon, AZ 86023
(928-638-7875).

Campgrounds

Four campgrounds, 7-day limit.
Three on South Rim, one on
North Rim. Mather open all
year; reservations recom-
mended March to December
*(call 800-365-2267; or visit
http://reservations.nps.gov/)*;
other times, first come, first

served. Desert View open May–Sept., first come, first served. North Rim open mid-May to mid-Oct., reservations recommended *(call 800-365-2267, or visit http://reservations.nps .gov/)*. Trailer Village open all year, 855 sites, reservations recommended *(888-297-2757; for same-day reservations call 928-638-2631)*. Fee $24 per night. Showers at North Rim and near Mather Campground. Tent and RV sites at all campgrounds; hookups only at Trailer Village. Two group campgrounds; must reserve. Food services in park.

Hotels, Motels, & Inns
(Unless otherwise noted, rates are for two persons in a double room, high season.)

The properties inside the park are operated by Xanterra Parks & Resorts *(call or visit 888-297-2757; or visit www.grandcanyon lodges.com)*. Reservations recommended six to nine months in advance. For same-day reservations, try 928-638-2631.

INSIDE THE PARK
South Rim:
■ **Bright Angel Lodge & Cabins** 89 units, 3 suites, some share baths. Cabins $64–$240; rooms $49-$71. Restaurant.
■ **El Tovar Hotel** 78 units. $127–$289. AC, restaurant.
■ **Kachina Lodge** 49 units. $123–

$133. AC.
■ **Maswik Lodge** 278 units. Cabins $66 (June–Aug.); rooms $79–$121. Restaurant.
■ **Thunderbird Lodge** 55 units. $125–$133. AC.
■ **Yavapai Lodge** 358 rooms. $160–$198. Restaurant. Open March to October.

North Rim:
■ **Grand Canyon Lodge** 888-297-2757. 209 units. $91–$121. Restaurant. Open mid-May to mid-October. www.grand canyonnorthrim.com.

In the canyon:
■ **Phantom Ranch** (reached by hiking, mule, or raft trips) *888-297-2757*. April to October. Dorm $28; cabin $75. Mule trip $360, includes cabins and meals. AC, shared showers, restaurant. Reserve up to 23 months ahead. wwwgrand canyonlodges.com. For waiting list call 928-638-2631.

OUTSIDE THE PARK
In Grand Canyon, AZ 86023:
■ **Quality Inn** (on Ariz. 64) P.O. Box 520. 928-638-2673 or 800-999-2521. 232 units. $129–$179. AC, pool, restaurant.
■ **Seven Mile Lodge** (Ariz. 64) P.O. Box 56. 928-638-2291. 20 units. $75–$82. No reservations; first come, first served. AC. Closed January.

Excursions from Grand Canyon

Havasu Canyon Hike

72 miles
west of
Grand Canyon

A hike into **Havasu Canyon** located on the Havasupai Reservation, on foot or on horseback, can be a transformative experience. Towering rock walls enclose **Supai village** and an oasis of lush vegetation, glistening waterfalls, and blue-green pools rimmed by travertine. The beauty and remoteness invoke the dawn of time.

An 8-mile one-way trail, steep at first, descends 2,000 feet from **Hualapai Hilltop** through spectacular canyon scenery to the village. To reach the trail, take Ariz. 66 northwest 28 miles from Seligman or northeast 55 miles from Kingman, then turn northeast and go 60 miles on Rte. 18. No gas, food, or water is available on the road or at the trailhead.

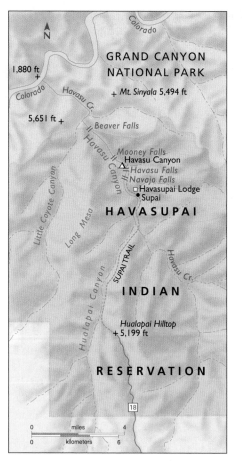

As you enter Havasu Canyon and approach the village, you'll see and hear sparkling Havasu Creek. About 500 Havasupai (from *havasu,* meaning "blue-green water," and *pai* for "people") live in Supai and farm the canyon. They welcome visitors year-round and put them up at Havasupai Lodge (see p. 187) and at a campground.

Navajo Falls is 1.5 miles downstream from Supai. Half a mile farther on, **Havasu Falls** gracefully cascades a 100 feet to a large pool rimmed by travertine. It's an inviting spot for a swim or picnic. Continue another mile beyond the campground to **Mooney Falls,** with its inspiring 196-foot plunge to travertine pools. Havasupai know the falls as "Mother of the Waters."

If you feel like more hiking, an even rougher trail continues downstream 2 miles to small **Beaver Falls** and a good swimming spot just below. Four more miles takes you to the Colorado River at the bottom of the Grand Canyon.

■ **8 miles of hiking or riding mules or horses** ■ **Two days** ■ **Northwest Arizona, about 90 miles from Seligman or 115 miles from Kingman** ■ **Year-round** ■ **Reservations and permission are required for hiking, riding, camping, and lodging** ■ **Contact Havasupai Tourist Enterprise, 928-448-2121 or 928-448-2201**

Havasu Falls, Havasu Canyon

Lake Mead National Recreation Area

250 miles west of Grand Canyon

Impounding the Colorado River created one of the most popular recreation areas in the state of Nevada: Lake Mead. But it wasn't done easily or without cost to the area's wildlife. **Hoover Dam,** a 726-foot-high concrete plug, was completed in 1936 after five years of labor involving some 5,000 workers. It backs up the Colorado River for 110 miles, providing flood control, electricity, drinking water, and irrigation water. It has also contributed to the decline of various species of plants and endangered fish. Yet, while threatening some creatures, damming the river may have helped others.

Lake Mead and its sister reservoir, **Lake Mohave,** along with the the surrounding desert and Arizona's **Shivwits Plateau** are all a part of the Lake Mead National Recreation Area, established in 1964. Most visits start at the **Alan Bible Visitor Center,** just north of Boulder City at the intersection of US 93 and Nev. 166. There, you can pick up maps and advice, and visit an outdoor botanical garden.

Boating on the Lakes

The most common way to explore the area is by boat. If you don't have your own, commercial outfitters offer tours by paddle wheelers or, on the Black Canyon section where the river actually moves, by raft *(contact headquarters for a list of concessionaires)*. You can also rent watercraft at various marinas on the western shore, at Temple Bar, and at Lake Mohave.

Boulder Beach is the most popular launch site. Boaters often head upriver toward **Callville Bay** and **Boulder Canyon,** where they can squeeze into scenic **Wishing Well Cove** or sunbathe at **Sandy Cove.** Farther upriver, the crowds thin and the fishing improves among deep coves of colorful rock adorned with petroglyphs.

Scenic Drives & Hikes

If you are looking for a pebbly beach to sun and swim, or an interesting hike along Lake Mead's shoreline, head north on Nev. 166 from the visitor center. This is **Lakeshore Scenic Drive,** which explores the lake's western shore for 7 miles. It then connects with **Northshore Scenic Drive,** which meanders for another 48 miles. Short hikes along the way include **Northshore Summit Trail** *(0.5 mile round-trip, Milepost 20.5)* and a half-mile loop at **Redstone picnic area** *(Mile 27)* that interprets area geology. Another popular option is a dip in shady **Rogers Spring** *(Mile 40).*

■ 1.5 million acres (NRA); 162,700 acres (reservoir) ■ Southern Nevada and northwest Arizona, 27 miles south of Las Vegas on US 93 ■ Year-round ■ Hiking, boating, swimming, waterskiing, fishing, biking, bird-watching, wildlife viewing ■ Contact the recreation area, 601 Nevada Hwy., Boulder City, NV 89005; 702-293-8907. www.nps.gov/lame

Kaibab National Forest

| 5 miles north of Grand Canyon |

A magical place, Kaibab National Forest is tossed with sweeps of aspen, phalanxes of ponderosa pine, and soaring views, including several that teeter near the edge of the Grand Canyon. It also offers plenty of solitude for those willing to park the car and walk or mountain bike along a network of forest roads and trails. The northern unit of the Kaibab—pronounced KY-bab—covers some 1,000 square miles, a great many of them wonderfully quiet and remote. The Kaibab

Pipe Spring National Monument

This 40-acre monument, on Ariz. 389 near the town of Fredonia, is primarily a historical site, established around an early Mormon fort. However, a half-mile-long nature trail climbs a small set of cliffs (part of the Kayenta formation—not Chinle, as the sign says) for a panoramic view to the south of the Arizona Strip —that area of the state lying between the Grand Canyon and the Utah state line.

The beautiful oasis of Pipe Spring is located at the base of the Grand Staircase (see pp. 79–81). Water percolates through Navajo sandstone and then hits a layer of less permeable Kayenta; at that point it travels horizontally, gathering along the Sevier Fault before finally escaping to the surface at Pipe Spring. One of the few natural springs on the entire Arizona Strip, it has long slaked the thirst of deer, pronghorn, and bighorn sheep, as well as a wide variety of reptiles, including colorful desert spiny lizards, whiptails, and gopher and king snakes. Also fond of Pipe Spring are such avian migrants as orioles, flycatchers, bluebirds, and Say's phoebes.

Plateau is the highest of the five that make up the North Rim of the Grand Canyon; its southern third is contained within Grand Canyon National Park, but much of its northern two-thirds lies within the borders of Kaibab National Forest. The main north-south route across the Kaibab Plateau, Ariz. 67, connects Jacob Lake to the North Rim.

Any visit to the North Kaibab Ranger District should begin with a stop at the Kaibab Plateau Visitor Center (928-643-7298), located at the junction of Ariz. 67 and Ariz. 89A; here you can pick up maps and check road and trail conditions. Backpackers might consider a trip along the 50-mile **Kaibab Plateau Trail,** starting 2 miles east of Jacob Lake on US 89A, which offers hikers a mix of fairly easy walking through stands of Douglas-fir, spruce, and ponderosa pine, broken up here and there by exquisite meadows.

A much shorter walk, the **South Canyon Trail** is a lovely, round-trip hike of 2.5 miles through undulating forested terrain to splendid views of Marble Canyon. To reach the trailhead, go south on Ariz. 67 for just over 26 miles, then turn east onto FR 611 less than a mile past the entrance to DeMotte Campground. Drive 1.4 miles, and turn right (south) onto FR 610; follow this for 7.5 miles to the trailhead sign.

Bird-watchers will find some excellent sites in the Kaibab. At 8,000 feet, **DeMotte Campground** *(on Ariz. 67, 4 miles N of entrance to Grand Canyon NP)* is a favorite staging ground and a good place to spot red-breasted nuthatches, Williamson's sapsuckers, and golden-crowned kinglets. **Fire Point,** just outside the national forest boundary with North Rim views, is located on FR 223 on the west side of the plateau. It is among the very best bird-watching locations in the forest. In the aspen groves look for warbling vireos, mountain chickadees, and brown creepers. The canyon's forested edges bring chances to see the Cassin's finch, green-tailed towhee, band-tailed pigeon, and hairy woodpecker.

Many routes on the Kaibab are suitable for mountain bikes, varying from narrow dirt paths to forest roads that must be shared with the occasional vehicle. A 30-mile stretch of the **Arizona Trail** runs south from US 89A, just east of the Kaibab Plateau Visitor Center, to East Rim. From here follow FR 611 for roughly 6 miles to Ariz. 67. This is ideal for those with a shuttle vehicle.

Jumpup Canyon, Kaibab Creek Wilderness

Another good ride is the easy, 4-mile trek along FR 264 to **Buck Ridge Viewpoint,** which offers excellent views across broken, soaring country all the way to Bryce Canyon *(see pp 66–75)* and Zion *(see pp 326–335)* National Parks. To reach the trailhead, follow Ariz. 67 south from the visitor center for 0.3 mile to FR 461, and turn right. Continue for roughly 4 miles to FR 264, and park.

Finally, consider the 18.6-mile round-trip along FR 233 to **Sowats Point** on the edge of Grand Canyon. To reach the trailhead, turn right off Ariz. 67 onto FR 461, 0.3 mile south of the Kaibab Plateau Visitor Center. Follow this for 5.5 miles to FR 462, turn right, and go 3 miles; turn left onto FR 22 and drive 12 miles, then turn right onto FR 425. Go another 8 miles to FR 233, turn right, and park. *(FR 233 is open to vehicles.)*

■ **1.6 million acres** ■ **North-central Arizona** ■ **Best months April–Nov.; Ariz. 67 from Jacob Lake to North Rim of Grand Canyon closed mid-Oct.– mid-May** ■ **Camping, hiking, fishing, biking, mountain biking, horseback riding, bird-watching, scenic drives** ■ **Contact the North Kaibab Ranger District, Kaibab National Forest, Box 248, Fredonia, AZ 86022; 928-643-7395. www.fs.fed.us/r3/kai/**

Sunset Crater Volcano National Monument

64 miles south of Grand Canyon

Six million years of volcanic activity have given the region around Flagstaff a distinctive appearance that even the most geologically oblivious find impossible to ignore. Symmetrical cones dot the landscape, revealing sites where the earth opened to discharge magma, ash, and cinders. Sunset Crater is the best place to get a close-up look at the area's turbulent past.

Sunset Crater is the youngest known volcano in Arizona. Born in 1064 or 1065, it ceased activity only about 1250, leaving a landscape that today still appears jagged, raw, and scarred. Trees, shrubs, and wildflowers grow but sparsely here, amid a terrain dominated by lava rock and cinders. NASA used the Bonito lava flow to test a lunar vehicle before the 1972 Apollo 17 mission to the moon—testament to its otherworldly look.

As you turn east from US 89 toward Sunset Crater Volcano National Monument, you'll be on Coconino National Forest's **545 Loop.** This 36-mile route passes through both Sunset Crater Volcano and nearby **Wupatki National Monument** *(928-679-2365),* which preserves ruins of a Native American pueblo occupied in the 1100s. These evocative stone buildings tell the story of a people who lived on the Colorado Plateau when Sunset Crater was active.

At the **Sunset Crater Volcano Visitor Center** *(2 miles before W entrance on loop road),* exhibits provide an introduction to the fascinating local geology. **Sunset Crater** and **San Francisco Mountain** *(see pp. 194–95)* are just two of a series of volcanic features that some scientists think are the result of the movement of a tectonic plate over a hot spot. Another theory holds that the slow collision of plates along the Colorado Plateau has created volcanic activity. Other exhibits showcase the plants and animals of the national monument. One wildflower, the pink Sunset Crater beardtongue, is endemic to the San Francisco Mountain area.

Before leaving the visitor center, buy the trail guide for the **Lava Flow Trail,** your next stop. This 1-mile path passes many distinctive volcanic features as it loops to the base of Sunset Crater. You'll see a squeeze-up, xenoliths, a spatter cone, and lava bubbles along the way, and you'll note the difference between jagged aa lava and smoother pahoehoe lava (both terms are Hawaiian in origin).

From the trail you'll have a close view of the slope of Sunset Crater, spangled with the red and yellow cinders that gave it its

Scarlet gilia

name. No climbing is allowed on Sunset Crater—in the past, makeshift trails caused serious erosion on its slopes. The national monument will, however, allow you to climb **Lenox Crater,** just to the west. The trail begins across the road from the Bonito Flow parking area, just west of the Lava Flow Trail parking area. It takes most people about a half hour to climb the half-mile-long path to its top, and another 20 minutes to return.

Less than 2 miles east of the Lava Flow Trail parking area, take the south turn off the main park road to the **Cinder Hills Overlook,** where you'll have a good view of the rugged terrain around Sunset Crater, and of the way vegetation is spreading up its northeast slope. A few miles farther east, the **Painted Desert Vista** looks out to a line of reddish cliffs far to the north, across the sagebrush lowlands of the Colorado Plateau.

To the north, **Strawberry Crater Wilderness** in Coconino National Forest *(928-526-0866)* centers on a cone that erupted at about the same time as Sunset Crater. Hikers prepared for backcountry travel *(there's no water in the wilderness)* sometimes leave from the parking area here to walk 4 miles north to the crater.

A shorter route can be reached by turning east onto FR 546 off US 89 north of the Sunset Crater road. Drive east about 3 miles and take FR 779 to the wilderness area, where a trail leads in a bit more than a mile to the crater.

■ 3,040 acres ■ North-central Arizona, 15 miles northeast of Flagstaff, off US 89 ■ Best seasons spring and fall ■ Camping, hiking ■ Contact the monument, Rte. 3, Box 149, Flagstaff, AZ 86004; 928-526-0502. www.nps.gov/sucr

San Francisco Mountain

80 miles south of Grand Canyon Towering over the region's other volcanic peaks—in fact towering over all of Arizona—San Francisco Mountain rises just north of Flagstaff. Although it is technically a single mountain, its many peaks have earned it the name of San Francisco Peaks. Humphreys Peak, the mountain's and state's highest point at 12,633 feet, stands above neighboring Agassiz Peak, with three other crests over 11,400 feet nearby. The peaks are eroded remnants of a once taller mountain, a volcano that may have risen more than 2,000 feet higher before it destroyed itself.

Humphreys Peak is the heart of Coconino National Forest's **Kachina Peaks Wilderness.** Above tree line here you'll find a few square miles of true alpine tundra, a distinctive and fragile ecosystem. Before heading up to the mountains, visit the excellent **Museum of Northern Arizona** *(3101 N. Fort Valley Rd . 928-774-5213. Adm. fee),* located just northwest of Flagstaff.

Several trails begin just north of town at the **Coconino National Forest Peaks Ranger District** on US 89. Near the office, look for the **Elden Lookout Trail,** a strenuous 3-mile route that ascends almost 2,400 feet to the top of 9,299-foot Elden Mountain. For an easier walk, try 2-mile **Fatman's Loop,** which gains only 600 feet of elevation.

On the east side of San Francisco Mountain, the **Inner Basin Trail** makes a wonderful day hike through a tall coniferous forest in the heart of a huge volcano. To reach it, drive north from Flagstaff on US 89 for 12.5 miles and turn west on FR 552; in a mile, turn right at the sign for Lockett Meadow.

To reach the main trailheads into Kachina Peaks Wilderness, drive northwest from Flagstaff 7 miles on US 180 and turn north on Snowbowl

Road, which climbs 7 miles to parking lots near a downhill ski area. For the strenuous hike to **Humphreys Peak** *(gains 3,300 feet in 4.5 miles)*, park in the left (north) lot and follow the trail across the grassy meadow. *(Check weather forecast before beginning; top portion of the hike is exposed to wind and lightning.)* If you'd prefer an excellent but far easier hike try the 5-mile **Kachina Trail**. Elk are common along this route, and in forest openings you'll have good views toward Flagstaff.

■ **69,120 acres** ■ **North-central Arizona, just north of Flagstaff** ■ **Year-round** ■ **Camping, hiking, biking, skiing** ■ **Contact Peaks Ranger District, Coconino National Forest, 5075 N. Hwy. 89, Flagstaff, AZ 86004; 928-526-0866. www.fs.fed.us/r3/coconin**

Cross-country skiing on San Francisco Mountain near Flagstaff

Great Basin

An Ice Age landscape of glacier-carved peaks rising more than a mile from eastern Nevada's desert floor, Great Basin stands like an island in a sagebrush sea. The park takes its name from the vast region that extends east from California's Sierra Nevada to Utah's Wasatch Range, and from southern Oregon to southern Nevada, encompassing most of Nevada and western Utah. Called the Great Basin by explorer John C. Frémont in the mid-1800s, the region actually comprises not one but at least 90 basins, or valleys, and its rivers all flow inland—not to any ocean.

The park road winds up Wheeler Peak, the second highest mountain in the state of Nevada. When the road ends at 10,000 feet, trails lead to the 13,063-foot summit and to the region's only glacier, near a stand of bristlecone pines.

Great Basin is a young park compared to the likes of a Yellowstone or Yosemite, yet within its confines are some of the world's oldest trees. The bristlecones form the rear guard of a Pleistocene forest that once covered much of the region. Now surviving in scattered stands, some trees are 3,000 years old—alive when Tutankhamun ruled Egypt.

In the flank of the mountain, at an altitude of 6,800 feet, lies Lehman Caves with 1.5 miles of underground passages. These formed when higher water tables during the Ice Age made pockets in the limestone. Park rangers guide visitors past flowstone, stalactites, and delicate white crystals that grow in darkness.

The number of visitors has reached more than 80,000 yearly since 1986, when the cave and neighboring mountains became a national park. They come for the scenic drive and the cave, but also fan out over the park's 65 miles of trails, which offer a chance to see glacial moraines, alpine lakes, and sweeping views of the surrounding Basin and Range country.

- Eastern Nevada, 5 miles west of Baker on Nev. 488

- 77,180 acres

- Established 1986

- Best months late June–Sept.

- Camping, hiking, cross-country skiing, bird-watching, cave tours

- Information: 775-234-7331 www.nps.gov/grba

Wheeler Peak, Great Basin National Park

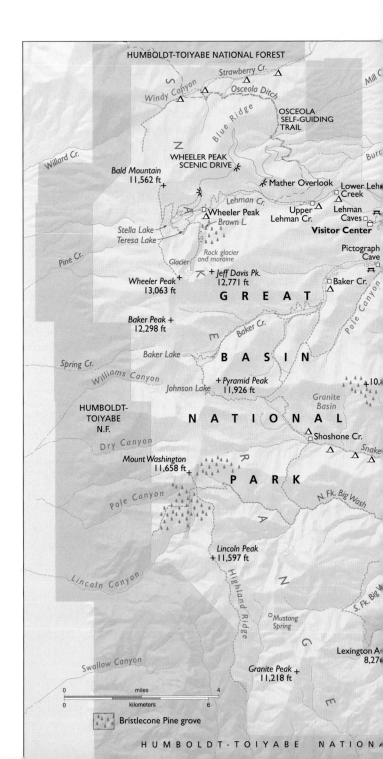

HUMBOLDT-TOIYABE NATIONAL FOREST

Strawberry Cr.

Windy Canyon
Osceola Ditch

Blue Ridge

OSCEOLA
SELF-GUIDING
TRAIL

Willard Cr.

Burr

WHEELER PEAK
SCENIC DRIVE

Bald Mountain
11,562 ft

Mather Overlook

Lower Leh
Creek

Lehman Cr.

Wheeler Peak

Upper
Lehman Cr.

Lehman
Caves

Stella Lake
Teresa Lake

Brown L.

Visitor Center

Pine Cr.

Rock glacier
and moraine

Pictograph
Cave

Glacier

Jeff Davis Pk.
12,771 ft

Baker Cr.

Wheeler Peak
13,063 ft

G R E A T

Baker Peak +
12,298 ft

Baker Cr.

Pole Canyon

Spring Cr.

Baker Lake

B A S I N

Williams Canyon

Johnson Lake

Pyramid Peak
11,926 ft

Granite
Basin

10,

HUMBOLDT-
TOIYABE
N.F.

N A T I O N A L

Dry Canyon

Shoshone Cr.

Mount Washington
11,658 ft

P A R K

Snake

Pole Canyon

N. Fk. Big Wash

Lincoln Peak
+11,597 ft

Lincoln Canyon

Highland Ridge

S. Fk. Big

Mustang
Spring

Swallow Canyon

Lexington A
8,27

Granite Peak +
11,218 ft

0   miles   4

0   kilometers   6

Bristlecone Pine grove

H U M B O L D T - T O I Y A B E   N A T I O N A

How to Get There

From Las Vegas (about 300 miles), take I-15 to US 93, then US 50 to Nev. 487. At Baker, take Nev. 488 to park entrance. From Salt Lake City, Utah (about 250 miles), take I-15 to US 50, then Nev. 487 to Baker and Nev. 488 to park entrance. Airport: Ely, Nev.

When to Go

Great Basin is open year-round, but the upper 8 miles of Wheeler Peak Scenic Drive (beyond Upper Lehman Campground) are usually closed from November to May. In summer, temperatures are generally mild. September and October bring cool weather and fewer crowds. Hikers must beware of sudden thunderstorms that can catch them on exposed ridges anytime of year.

The best time to view Wheeler Peak is in early morning. During winter, visitors enjoy excellent cross-country skiing.

How to Visit

On a 1-day visit, take the **Wheeler Peak Scenic Drive** for dramatic views of high alpine landscapes. On your way back, stop at **Lehman Caves** for a chance to walk underground through intriguing passages.

What Not to Miss

- Scenic road to base of Wheeler Peak

- Overview of whole park on Alpine Lakes Loop Trail to Wheeler Summit Trail

- Lehman Caves Tour (visit Gothic Palace, Grand Palace, Lake Room)

- Baker Lake off Baker Creek Road

OREST

EXPLORING THE PARK

Wheeler Peak Scenic Drive: 12 miles; 1.5 hours to full day

This paved road climbs steeply from the visitor center to Wheeler
Peak Campground at 10,000 feet *(vehicles longer than 24 feet not
recommended)*. Those not used to mountain driving may find both
the view and the drive breathtaking. The road passes from the
tough, drought-resistant pinyon-juniper woodland into the high-
elevation forest of Engelmann spruce, limber pine, and aspen.

Begin the scenic drive near the visitor center. A short trail at the
first pull-off takes you to the historic **Osceola Ditch,** built in the late
1880s to carry water for hydraulic gold mining. Save this for your
next trip, if pressed for time.

Skip the Mather Overlook, but notice the old stand of mountain
mahogany. These usually grow as a shrub but here reach tree
height. Pull off at **Peak Overlook** for spectacular views of Wheeler
Peak on the right and Jeff Davis Peak on the left. The north face of
Wheeler drops 1,800 feet to a glacier below. Snow often dusts the
jagged walls of gray quartzite.

The road ends at Wheeler Peak Campground, where you have
your choice of several fine walks. One of the most popular follows
the 3-mile **Alpine Lakes Loop Trail** past Stella and Teresa Lakes. This
leads you to a dramatic alpine setting with a barren, sawtooth ridge
rising above the smooth surface of the lake.

If time and stamina allow, follow the **Wheeler Summit Trail** to the
ridge above the lakes for an overview of the park and sweeping
views of Great Basin's seemingly endless succession of mountain
ranges. The trail leaves the Alpine Lakes Loop Trail near Stella Lake
and climbs another 3,000 feet to the summit. Once above tree line,
watch for sturdy alpine flowers like primrose and phlox. And be
prepared for harsh weather. A terse entry in the summit register
reads, "Wind took no prisoners."

Just as spectacular is the 3-mile **Bristlecone/Glacier Trail.** This
leaves from Teresa Lake and takes you to Wheeler Cirque, a glacier-
hollowed valley enclosed by sheer cliffs. At the far end lies the
glacier, the Great Basin's only permanent glacier and one of the
southernmost in the country.

Before reaching the glacier be sure to take the **Bristlecone Forest
Loop.** This self-guided nature trail passes ancient trees with
twisted trunks carved and polished by wind-driven snow and ice.
In the 1960s, prior to the creation of the park, the oldest known

Ruby-throated hummingbird hovering over paintbrush

bristlecone pine—a 4,900-year-old tree called Prometheus—was cut down here as part of a climate study. Even after most of its trunk and branches die, a bristlecone pine can continue to survive, sustained by very little moisture. The tree holds onto its needles for 20 to 30 years, assuring stable photosynthesis regardless of environmental stress.

Lehman Caves: 0.6 mile; 1.5 hours

Guided cave tours began here in 1885 with Absalom Lehman, a miner turned rancher. Over the years dozens of legends have grown around his discovery of the cave. One claims he was racing along on horseback when he suddenly dropped through the entrance. He lassoed a tree and managed to hold on until rescued four days later. The hard part was keeping his legs wrapped around the horse to prevent it from falling.

Tour tickets must be purchased one day in advance *(stop by visitor center or call 775-234-7331)*. You have a choice of three

Ivory Towers, Lehman Caves

tours: 90 minutes *($8)*, 60 minutes *($6)*, or 30 minutes *($2)*. The shortest tour visits only the Gothic Palace.

Meet your guide behind the visitor center near the cave entrance. Lehman Caves— a single cavern despite the name—extends a quarter-mile into the limestone and marble that flanks the base of the Snake Range. It is one of the most profusely decorated caves in the region and its attraction lies in the beauty of those formations, well represented in the first room you visit, the **Gothic Palace.** The cave is so filled with columns, draperies, and stalactites that early explorers used sledgehammers to break through them. Because of the cave's manageable scale, you get close-up views of bizarre helictites and delicate aragonite crystals.

The walkway also takes you past fine examples of rare cave shields. These large disks grow from cracks in the ceiling where seeping water deposits minerals in flat, circular forms. Continuing deeper, you reach two of the cave's most beautiful rooms. Rimstone pools and soda straws decorate the **Lake Room;** shields, massive columns, and bacon-rind draperies fill the **Grand Palace.**

A small variety of cave life makes its home here, including pack rats, cave crickets, and the rare pseudoscorpion—an arachnid with scorpionlike pinchers. Bats, however, stay away, finding the cave's vertical entrance too hard to negotiate.

More Great Basin Hikes

Forming a ragged circle around the flanks of Pyramid Peak, the **Baker Lake/Johnson Lake Loop** makes for a challenging, 13.1-mile day hike with a net elevation gain of 3,290 feet. It also makes a good overnight backpacking trip *(pick up a free permit from visitor* *center).* The route starts at 8,000 feet, at the end of the Baker Creek Road, and follows Baker Creek for several miles before switchbacking up into a high cirque on the south side of Baker Peak. There, you'll find the lake, nestled beneath the cliffs.

From here, a primitive trail skirts around the west slope of Pyramid Peak to **Johnson Lake.** Both of these high-elevation lakes are home to four of the five species of trout that inhabit the park's waters, and they will be irresistible to any avid angler. Here, as well as in the park's many creeks, you'll find Lahontan cutthroat, brown, rainbow, and brook trout. Between casts, look for the historic Johnson Lake Mine structures at the east end of the lake. From here, a good trail follows South Fork Baker Creek back down to the trailhead.

An alternate route to Johnson Lake starts from the end of the **Snake Creek Road.** It cuts nearly 4 miles off the round-trip hiking distance, but the trail is quite a bit steeper, rising 2,420 feet over 3.7 miles.

If you're up for an adventure with a high-clearance vehicle, you can negotiate the rugged dirt road *(get directions from visitor center)* into the southern end of the park, where you can take a 3.4-mile round-trip hike to **Lexington Arch,** the main attraction in Arch Canyon at the southern end of the park. From beneath this six-story limestone bridge, believed to have once been part of a cave system, you'll have fine views of Snake Valley to the east.

West and north of the arch lies a remote and wild area penetrated by just a few of the park's visitors. Primitive routes exist along North Fork Big Wash, South Fork Big Wash, and North Fork Lexington Creek, but they are difficult to reach. Ask at the visitor center for advice.

Because many of the park's trails reach elevations above 10,000 feet, you should always be prepared for sudden changes in the weather. If you plan to hike above tree line, be sure to take rain gear and warm clothing. Also, although water is available at the visitor center year-round and at the park's four developed campgrounds during summer, be sure to carry at least one quart of water per person (more for day hikes).

Finally, remember that the alpine world is fragile. At these elevations, plants grow slowly and their margin of survival is narrow. Stay on established roads and trails to avoid inadvertently damaging these areas.

INFORMATION & ACTIVITIES

Headquarters
100 Great Basin National Park
Baker, NV 89311
775-234-7331
www.nps.gov/grba

Visitor & Information Centers
Visitor center and the entrance
to Lehman Caves are located
on Nev. 488 at the northeast
end of park; open daily all year.

Seasons & Accessibility
Year-round park. Snow may
cover high-elevation trails until
late June or July. Some park
roads require four-wheel-drive
vehicles. Call headquarters
about current trail and road
conditions.

Entrance Fees
None for entering the park,
but there are fees for each of
the three cave tours.

Pets
Permitted on leashes except in
visitor center, caves, backcountry, and on trails.

Facilities for Disabled
Visitor center and the first
room in Lehman Caves are
wheelchair accessible, as are
some campsites.

Things to Do
Ranger-led activities include
free nature walks and talks,
exhibits, movie, and campfire
programs. Also available: cave
tours, Wheeler Peak Scenic
Drive, hiking, fishing (license
required), rock climbing, and
cross-country skiing.

Special Advisories
■ Park's high elevation can
cause altitude sickness. People
who have heart or respiratory
problems should take it slowly.
■ Don't count on finding water
sources along the trails; always
carry drinking water when hiking. If you do drink surface
water, first purify it chemically
or filter it.
■ Watch out for rattlesnakes
along hiking trails, especially if
you're hiking below 8,000 feet.
■ Summer thunderstorms are
common; check weather conditions with park before setting
off on a hike.
■ Be careful around the park's
abandoned mine structures.
Never enter a mining shaft
or tunnel.

Backcountry Camping
Those heading out to the
backcountry for an overnight
should stop at the park's visitor
center and complete the free
permit registration form. In
addition to helping to ensure
visitor safety, permits allow the

park to monitor how its resources are being used.

Campgrounds

Four campgrounds, 104 sites, all with 14-day limit, all first come, first served, $10 per night. Baker Creek and Upper Lehman Creek open mid-May through October. Wheeler Peak open mid-June through September. Lower Lehman Creek open all year. Snowstorms may close campgrounds occasionally. No showers. Tent and RV sites; no hookups. Food services in the park. Potable water available year-round at visitor center, and in summer at RV sanitary station, picnic areas, and developed campgrounds.

Hotels, Motels, & Inns

(Unless otherwise noted, rates are for two persons in a double room, high season.)

In Baker, NV 89311:
■ **The Border Inn** (on US 50) P.O. Box 30. 775-234-7300. 29 units. $31–$39. AC, restaurant, RV park. www.greatbasin park.com.
■ **Silver Jack Motel** (on Main St.) P.O. Box 166. 775-234-7323. 9 units, 2 cabins. $34–$60. AC. www.greatbasin park.com.

In Ely, NV 89301:
■ **Bristlecone Motel** 700 Ave. I.

775-289-8838 or 800-497-7404. 31 units. $46–$52. AC.
■ **Best Western Main Motel** 1101 Aultman St. 775-289-4529. 19 units. $65. AC.
■ **Best Western Park Vue Motel** 930 Aultman St. 775-289-4497. 21 units. $65. AC.
■ **Four Sevens Motel** 500 High St. 775-289-4747. 39 units. $35. AC.
■ **Historic Hotel Nevada and Gaming Hall** 501 Aultman St. 775-289-6665. 62 units. $25–$85. AC, restaurant. www.hotel nevada.com.
■ **Holiday Inn** 1501 E. Aultman St. 775-289-8900. 60 units. $89. AC, pool, sauna, restaurant.
■ **Jailhouse Motel and Casino** 5th and High Sts. 775-289-3033 or 800-841-5430. 60 units. $63–$66. AC, restaurant.
■ **Petrelli's Fireside Inn** (2 miles north of Ely) SR 1, Box 2. 775-289-3765 or 800-732-0288. 14 units. $45. AC, restaurant.
■ **Ramada Inn and Copper Queen Casino** 805 Great Basin Blvd. 775-289-4884 or 800-851-9526. 65 units. $85–$90. AC, pool, restaurant.

For a complete list of accommodations contact the White Pine Chamber of Commerce at 775-289-8877.

Excursions from Great Basin

Lamoille Canyon Scenic Byway

230 miles northwest of Great Basin

24 miles round-trip; 2 hours Called the Yosemite of Nevada, Lamoille Canyon in northeastern Nevada is a deep, glaciated trough that descends in one long, gentle curve from the subalpine forests of the Ruby Mountains to the high desert plains southeast of Elko. Dozens of waterfalls spill from the cliffs. Bighorn sheep and mountain goats amble the high country. Hawks and eagles soar overhead.

To get there, follow Nev. 227 east of Elko for 26 miles to the well-marked start of the byway. The Ruby Mountains—a magnificent crest of broad, serrated peaks—seem to burst from the flat valley floor. About 10 miles wide and 100 miles long, the range is composed of a mass of metamorphic and igneous rocks faulted upward about ten million years ago.

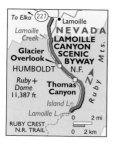

FR 660 leads through **Humboldt National Forest** and dead-ends in Lamoille Canyon, a deep cleft in the mountains straight ahead. To the right of the canyon bulks 11,387-foot **Ruby Dome,** mauled by glaciers. Almost immediately you cross Lamoille Creek, a lush corridor of cottonwoods, willows, and aspens that zigzags up the canyon from the **Powerhouse picnic area** beneath the road. For a quick orientation on the historical and recreational features of the canyon, stop at the interpretive exhibit above the picnic area. A number of the peaks you see ahead top 10,000 feet.

Six miles up the road at **Glacier Overlook,** another exhibit explains the glaciers that moved through here during the ice ages and identifies the spot where the tongues of ice converged. The U-shaped walls of Lamoille Canyon trace the glaciers' paths. Here, too, you may see bighorn sheep on cliffs across the canyon. Continue 2 miles to **Thomas Canyon Campground,** at the mouth of another glacial side canyon. A difficult trail wanders a couple of miles up the broad floor of Thomas Canyon to wildflower meadows and limber and whitebark pine forests.

Take the time to stroll the **Changing Canyon Nature Trail,** which starts 1.5 miles up the road at the pull-off for Hanging Valley. The short loop-trail and its accompanying brochure describe the canyon's formation and identify common plants and animals.

The **Terraces picnic area** is a quiet, off-road spot where you can admire a 1,500-foot cliff of metamorphic rock swirled with light-colored granite that curves for miles along the canyon's east wall. From here, the road coasts over nearly flat meadows, rich with grasses, sedges, and wildflowers. Willow thickets cloak Lamoille Creek's meandering course. Within 2 miles you arrive at **Road's End,** a trailhead beneath an astounding ring of peaks that rise from a forest—and the end of the byway. The elevation here is 8,800 feet, some 2,700 feet above the byway's start.

The **Ruby Crest National Recreation Trail** begins here. It leads into the Ruby Mountains Wilderness, a 90,000-acre tract of lakes, forests, meadows, and glacial peaks where bighorn, mountain goats, and eagles live. But you don't have to hike far to see the backcountry. Island Lake lies just 2 miles away in a glacial cirque.

■ **Northeast Nevada, 25 miles S of Elko** ■ **Best seasons spring–fall, closed in winter** ■ **Camping, hiking, fishing, wildlife viewing, bird-watching** ■ **Contact the national forest, 1200 Franklin Way, Sparks, NV 89431; 775-331-6444 or 775-752-3357. www.fs.fed.us/htnf/humboldt.htm**

Cathedral Gorge State Park

130 miles south of Great Basin

At first the park's main feature—bentonite clay formations—sounds like something only a geologist could love. But you soon adopt a geologist's appreciative eye as you see the ragged remnant of a Pliocene lake bed. If you were standing here three million years ago, you would be buried under water and mud roughly 1,000 feet deep. Over time the lake drained; sediments dried and hardened. The resulting siltstone was eroded by the elements, leaving buff-colored canyons and cliffs.

After Mormon settlers founded nearby Panaca in 1864, ranchers used the chasm as a garbage dump. In the 1890s, a local woman, upon viewing the delicately eroded spires, was reminded of European cathedrals—thus Cathedral Gorge. Later, two Panaca teenagers built a series of ladders through the maze of canyons and crawl ways. By the 1920s, families were coming to picnic and to watch open-air pageants staged at the gorge. It was established as a state park in 1935.

The **visitor center** exhibits cover regional geology and wildlife, including coyotes, bobcats, lizards, and snakes.

Miller Point Trail, Cathedral Gorge SP

A half-mile **loop trail** links the campground and the "caves," actually narrow canyon sections also accessible by car. A 4-mile **trail** leads from the campground through the remote upper gorge among ridgelike fins. The 1-mile **Miller Point Trail** passes between 100-foot-high walls. Off US 93, 2 miles north of the entrance, **Miller Point Overlook** offers views into two side canyons. A **nature loop** along the access road reveals the upper gorge.

■ **1,633 acres** ■ **Southeast Nevada, near Panaca** ■ **Year-round; extreme summer and winter temperatures** ■ **Adm. fee** ■ **Hiking, camping, bird-watching** ■ **Contact the park, P.O. Box 176, Panaca, NV 89042; 775-728-4460. http://parks.nv.gov/cg.htm.**

Valley of Fire State Park

267 miles south of Great Basin

The Valley of Fire seems otherworldly, a surreal realm of stone formations with evocative names like Cobra Rock, Indian Marbles, and Grand Piano. Indeed, the area is named for a phenomenon of cosmic scale: In the morning and the evening, the low slanting sun touches ancient red sandstone formations like a torch, setting them ablaze. On some of the sandstone walls, prehistoric Indians left petroglyphs depicting lizards, eagles, mountain sheep, snakes, and other symbols of life in the desert.

If you've driven northeast from Las Vegas on I-15 and Nev. 169, you'll enter the park through the west gate into a classic scene of the Wild West, where red rocks are set off by skies as blue as Navajo turquoise. Just ahead lie the **Beehives**, sandstone deposits that were shaped in a swirling pattern by the desert's relentless onslaught of heat, cold, rain, and wind. Beyond on the right, a **loop trail** leads to a deposit of petrified wood—evidence a forest thrived here 225 million years ago. You'll see some whole logs, but mostly fragments.

A spur road on the opposite side of Nev. 169 leads to **Atlatl Rock.** Here you climb 84 iron stairs up a sheer wall of rock to see a panel of Native American petroglyphs. Outstanding among the depictions is an atlatl, a notched wooden stick used by prehistoric hunters to throw darts faster and farther. You'll also see concentric circles and bounding mountain sheep.

Driving again on Nev. 169, stop at the **visitor center** to study fine exhibits on the valley's human and natural history. Then take the spur road to **Petroglyph Canyon Trail,** a half-mile, round-trip walk on the sandy floor of a canyon. On the vertical walls look for more prehistoric rock art. The trail leads to **Mouse's Tank,** a water hole or "tank" named for a renegade Paiute Indian of the 1890s, who reportedly murdered two prospectors, fled to the Valley of Fire, and used this remote spot as a hideout.

Continue along the spur road *(closed at sunset)* to **Rainbow Vista,** where you can look out over rock formations tinged in a dramatic splash of reds. Across from Rainbow Vista catch a roller-coaster of a gravel road to an overlook on **Fire Canyon,** a 600-foot-deep gorge.

Back on the spur road, continue north about 3 miles. You will come to a closed dirt road used as a hiking and mountain-biking trail to **Duck Rock** (which looks vaguely like a duck, or perhaps a baseball hat). At road's end stand the **White Domes,** two formations of white silica melting together with red sandstone to create tints of pink and lavender.

Upon returning to Nev. 169 east, you pass the **Seven Sisters,** a gaggle of towering monoliths on the south side of the road. Ahead you'll see a culster of stone cabins built by the Civilian Conservation Corps in the 1930s, later used to accommodate overnight travelers. Then comes the much photographed **Elephant Rock,** reached via a short trail; the chunky rock indeed looks as wrinkled as an elephant's hide.

As you exit the park to the east, straight ahead are the waters of Lake Mead *(see pp. 187–88).*

■ **34,880 acres** ■ **55 miles northeast of Las Vegas on Nev. 169** ■ **Year-round. Summer temperatures exceed 100°F** ■ **Adm. fee** ■ **Camping, hikeing, bird-watching, petroglyphs** ■ **Contact the park, P.O. Box 515, Overton, NV 89040; 702-397-2088. http://parks.nv.gov/vf.htm**

Great Sand Dunes

Visitors to the Great Sand Dunes experience an undeniable sense of wonder, just as happens in so many of our most spectacular national parks. In contrast to the sudden shock of walking to the rim of the Grand Canyon, though, or topping a rise to view Crater Lake, the emotions evoked by this otherworldly landscape arrive in slow motion.

The dunes appear in the distance as you approach, but at first seem dwarfed by their backdrop, the 13,000-foot peaks of the Sangre de Cristo Mountains. Not until you're nearly at their border does their vast scale become apparent: dunes up to 750 feet tall, extending for mile after mile—an ocean of sand hills of breathtaking magnitude.

The dunes sprawl across part of southern Colorado's San Luis Valley, a broad, arid plain between the San Juan Mountains on the west and the Sangre de Cristos on the east. The Rio Grande flows through the valley, and in millennia of meandering has spread a deep layer of sand—eroded from the rock of the surrounding mountains—across its ancient floodplain. Strong prevailing southwesterly winds carry the tiny grains toward the Sangre de Cristos, piling them up against the foothills. The resulting dunes are the tallest in North America, and they cover more than 30 square miles. Adults hike across them and marvel at their beauty; children run and slide down their steep faces.

Winds continually reshape the crests of the tall dunes, and smaller dunes may "migrate" several feet in a week. The dunes show a remarkable permanence of form, though, which geologists attribute to their unusual moisture content. The San Luis Valley receives only about 10 inches of rain a year, but that amount, plus snowmelt and underground water, helps keep the Great Sand Dunes great.

- South-central Colorado, near Fort Garland

- 84,670 acres

- Established 2004

- Best seasons spring–fall. Medano Creek may flow spring– early summer only

- Camping, hiking, backpacking, mountain biking, horseback riding, sand skiing, snowboarding, wildlife viewing

- Information: 719-378-6399 www.nps.gov/grsa

Great Sand Dunes above San Luis Valley

How to Get There

From the east or north, take US 160 west from Walsenburg 59 miles to Colo. 150 and drive north 16 miles. From the south or west, take US 285 to Alamosa and drive 14 miles east to Colo. 150, continuing north to the park and preserve. Airport: Colorado Springs.

When to Go

All-year park. Spring and fall are best; summers are hot and crowded, so visit early or late in the day. Winter snow curtails trips into the high mountains, though the dunes can still be visited.

How To Visit

Start at the **visitor center** then walk out into the dunes. **High Dune** is a popular, moderately strenuous destination. Splash along **Medano Creek,** which meanders along the base of the dunes. Consider another walk along the **Montville Nature Trail** or a hike on the **Mosca Pass Trail.** If you have a high-clearance four-wheel-drive vehicle, and are very careful, you might drive the **Medano Pass Primitive Road,** which leads 11 miles up into the Sangre de Cristos.

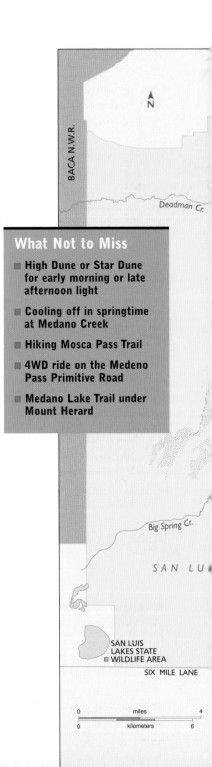

What Not to Miss

- **High Dune or Star Dune for early morning or late afternoon light**
- **Cooling off in springtime at Medano Creek**
- **Hiking Mosca Pass Trail**
- **4WD ride on the Medeno Pass Primitive Road**
- **Medano Lake Trail under Mount Herard**

BACA N.W.R.

N

Deadman Cr.

Big Spring Cr.

SAN LU

SAN LUIS LAKES STATE WILDLIFE AREA

SIX MILE LANE

| 0 | miles | 4 |
| 0 | kilometers | 6 |

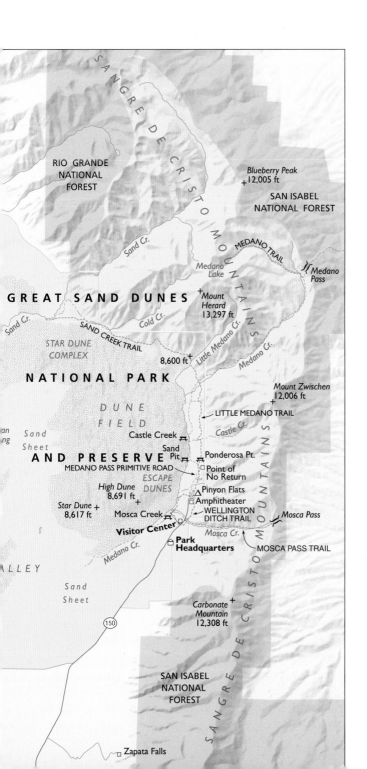

RIO GRANDE
NATIONAL
FOREST

Blueberry Peak
+12,005 ft

SAN ISABEL
NATIONAL FOREST

SANGRE DE CRISTO MOUNTAINS

Sand Cr.

MEDANO TRAIL

Medano
Lake

Medano
Pass

GREAT SAND DUNES

+Mount
Herard
13,297 ft

Sand Cr.

SAND CREEK TRAIL

Cold Cr.

Little Medano Cr.

STAR DUNE
COMPLEX

8,600 ft

Medano Cr.

NATIONAL PARK

Mount Zwischen
12,006 ft
+

DUNE
FIELD

LITTLE MEDANO TRAIL

Castle Cr.

an

Sand

ng

Castle Creek

Sheet

AND PRESERVE

Sand
Pit

Ponderosa Pt.

MEDANO PASS PRIMITIVE ROAD

Point of
No Return

ESCAPE
DUNES

High Dune
8,691 ft

Pinyon Flats
Amphitheater

Star Dune +
8,617 ft

WELLINGTON
DITCH TRAIL

Mosca Pass

Mosca Creek

Visitor Center

Park
Headquarters

Mosca Cr.

MOSCA PASS TRAIL

Medano Cr.

VALLEY

Sand
Sheet

150

Carbonate +
Mountain
12,308 ft

SANGRE DE CRISTO MOUNTAINS

SAN ISABEL
NATIONAL
FOREST

Zapata Falls

EXPLORING THE PARK

The Dunes & Medano Creek: Short hikes; a half day

This park protects most of the dunes in an unspoiled wilderness, but a strange wilderness it is: There's very little plant life, and the majority of wildlife is no bigger than insects or rats. However, six species of insects are unique to the dunes, and more may await discovery. Look out for the circus beetle, which stands on its head when frightened. Kangaroo rats and other water-conserving rodents also live in the sand. Squirrels, bighorn sheep, and even black bears sometimes venture to the edge of the dune field from their usual haunts in the nearby mountains.

A 15-minute video at the **visitor center** offers a good introduction to the geology and history of the park. Rangers in summer present programs here, as well as at other sites and trails. Depending on when you visit, guided events might include nature walks, children's activities, or programs on wildlife, plants, hiking, geology, or the archaeology of the dunes.

Begin your exploration at the Dunes parking lot. The imposing dunes, like buff-brown miniatures of the surrounding Sangre de Cristo crests, rise invitingly to the west. But first take time to discover **Medano Creek.** This small stream flows along the edge of the dunes; the moisture it carries is a vital part of the dune-system environment. Kids may want to build sand castles, or just enjoy a shoes-off walk along the squishy streambed. The wet sand is a good place to look for the tracks of coyotes, kangaroo rats, mule deer, or bobcats. The area's high water table helps preserve the dunes' basic shape, but it's interesting to note that the water table was much higher not so many years ago. Indeed, it was so high that early Europeans approached the dunes by boat.

Today, Medano Creek usually flows only in spring, carrying snowmelt down from the mountaintops. When it contains adequate water, watch for a phenomenon called "surge flow," which occurs when a small, temporary dam of sand upstream collapses, sending down a wave of water that can be up to a foot high.

Next, hike out into the dunes, where you'll quickly learn that walking in the soft sand is more strenuous than you might think. Take your time, and angle up the ridgelines of the dunes, rather than climbing straight up. While it might seem like fun to go barefoot, remember that in summer the sand surface can reach blistering temperatures. Wear protective shoes, as well as a hat, and apply sunscreen. Carry plenty of water if you plan on walking far. One thing you don't need to be concerned about is poisonous animals: There are no snakes or scorpions in the dunes.

You can strike out in any direction, but be sure to keep track of your location. While most people can easily orient themselves by noting the ever present peaks of the Sangre de Cristos, a compass or GPS unit isn't a bad idea for extended hikes. Many people make the 1-mile one-way trip to the aptly named **High Dune,** which towers 650 feet above the floor of the San Luis Valley. You'll find a great panorama at the top, taking in mountains, dunes, and valley. Another mile to the west rises the **Star Dune,** with an equally fine view. "Star" dunes are so named because they have three or more "arms," rather than the single axis of most dunes.

Photography in the dunes is best early and late in the day, when the low angle of the sun creates shadows that accentuate their contours and crests.

A night walk into the dunes can be a little eerie, but thrilling in its sense of solitude and peace. When the moon is out, the dimly lit landscape seems even more haunting.

East of the Dunes: A full day or more

Though the dunes are fascinating and beautiful, there is a certain uniformness about them, and very few plants and animals make their homes there. The same is certainly not true for the foothills and high peaks of the Sangre de Cristo range, a large part of which is now encompassed in Great Sand Dunes National Preserve. (The preserve is administered similarly to the adjoining park, although hunting is allowed.) Here, you can hike or, with the proper vehicle, drive from the scrubby habitat of junipers and pinyon pines, along creeks lined with aspens and cottonwoods, up into forests of ponderosa pine and, even higher, spruce and fir. Alpine tundra tops the tallest summits above tree line, where only grasses, compact shrubs, low wildflowers, and other ground-hugging plants can survive.

East of the main road, just north of the visitor center, you'll find a parking area for three varied trails. The easy, half-mile **Montville Nature Trail** loops into the foothills, where you might spot mule deer, a least chipmunk, a desert cottontail, or a coyote. Black-billed magpies—long-tailed, conspicuous, and raucous—have learned to beg for food *(don't feed them or other wildlife),* and friendly mountain chickadees flit from tree to tree. The **Wellington Ditch Trail** splits off the Montville trail partway around the loop, following an irrigation ditch 1 mile north to the campground.

Also beginning at the Montville trailhead, the **Mosca Pass Trail** follows an old toll road up Mosca Creek, a tributary of Medano, across the national park boundary and into the preserve. You'll walk past cottonwoods and aspens, ascending into a forest of Engelmann spruce and subalpine fir, reaching 9,730-foot Mosca Pass after 3.5 miles; the elevation gain is just under 1,500 feet. For a moderate amount of effort, you'll get a fine overview of the way habitats change with altitude in the Rockies.

Farther north along the park's main road, the **Little Medano Trail** takes off from Ponderosa Point for a 4.5-mile one-way jaunt through grasslands and forests bordering the dunes.

The Little Medano Trail parallels the start of **Medano Pass Primitive Road,** a high-clearance, four-wheel-drive route that follows the national park's eastern border and then climbs to 9,950-foot Medano Pass, 11 miles from the road entrance. This trip offers a nonstrenuous way to explore the high Sangre de Cristos, although certain hazards must be taken into account. The road traverses soft sand for several miles and is not recommended for smaller SUVs lacking wide tires and high-ground clearance. Even large vehicles may need to lower tire pressure to make it through the sand without bogging down. (Air to reinflate tires is near the park amphitheater.) The road crosses creeks several times, which can be problematic during spring high water, and it's closed in winter.

For those without the proper vehicle, an authorized concessionaire(*Great Sand Dune Oasis, 719-378-2222*) operates tours along the Medano Pass Primitive Road from May through September. The narrated, two-hour trips do not climb into the preserve, but remain in the national park, offering a look at areas unseen by most visitors.

Like the Mosca Pass Trail, the Medano Pass road provides a natural-history lesson along with excellent scenery. Ascending from the foothills into lush montane forest is, in effect, like traveling from the southwestern desert to Canada. Ecologists call the different habitats encountered along mountain slopes "life zones"—each an altitudinal band boasting its own related set of plants and animals. Pinyon jays and mule deer, for instance, dwell among the arid-looking habitat of scattered junipers and pinyon pines, while gray jays and bighorn sheep live high on the mountain slopes.

Sand dunes at sunset, Sangre de Cristos in the background

One of the preserve's most popular hikes begins along the Medano Pass road, a half-mile west of the pass. The **Medano Lake Trail** climbs 1,900 feet in 4 miles to reach the lake, strikingly situated in a cirque under 13,350-foot Mount Herard. The trail passes through aspen groves that turn brilliant yellow in fall. The last mile of the trail is rugged, and to have a view westward over the sand dunes you must expend a little more effort, climbing the ridge above the lake. Your reward is a visit to an alpine world of flowery meadows, dense spruce-fir woodland, and wind-stunted trees at timberline, where elk bugle in fall and Clark's nutcrackers give their raucous calls. Listen for the sharp squeaks of pikas, tiny hare that scurry among the rockpiles, sometimes carrying large bundles of plants with their mouths.

INFORMATION & ACTIVITIES

Headquarters
11500 Hwy. 150
Mosca, CO 81146
719-378-6399
www.nps.gov/grsa

Visitor & Information Centers
The new expanded visitor center on Colo. 150 is open year-round with exhibits and viewing area.

Seasons & Accessibility
Park is open year-round. Spring and fall offer ideal temperatures for wandering in the dunes. Summer brings crowds and very hot weather. Temperatures at the surface of the sand can reach 140°F. Contact headquarters for current conditions.

Entrance Fees
$3 per person per week; $10 annual pass.

Pets
Permitted on leashes. Be aware that mountain lions, coyotes, and foxes hunt within the park. Horses not allowed in the dunes area.

Facilities for Disabled
Access to the dunes is difficult for persons with traditional wheeled chairs. Check with the visitor center about borrowing a "sand wheel chair."

Accessible camping sites are available at Pinyon Campground as well as at the Sawmill Canyon Backcountry Campsite along Medano Pass Primitive Road.

Things to Do
Dunes hiking, photography, wildlife viewing, snowshoeing, nature walks, climbing, cross-country skiing, bird-watching, mountain biking on trails away from the dunes. Summer events include sand-castle competitions and kite flying. For four-wheel-drive tours, contact Great Sand Dunes Oasis Campground *(719-378-2222)*.

Special Advisories
■ Shoes are necessary for walking on the dunes as sand can burn bare feet.
■ Carry plenty of water—more than you normally would—for hikes of any length.
■ Wear sunscreen and protective head covering.
■ Permits *(free)* required for overnight camping in the backcountry; fires prohibited.
■ Backcountry camping with horses and pack animals is allowed in most of the park and preserve. Maximum group size: six people and animals within the park; ten in the

preserve. Check with park officials on specific limitations.

Campgrounds
Pinyon Flats Campground, with 88 campsites, open year-round on a first come, first served basis. $10 per night.

Outside the park, San Luis Lakes State Park *(13 miles on Six Mile Ln.)* has 51 campsites. 719-378-2020. $10 per night. Also see Great Sand Dunes Lodge and Campground, below.

Hotels, Motels, & Inns
(Unless otherwise noted, rates are for two persons in a double room, high season.)

In Mosca, CO 81146:
■ **Great Sand Dunes Lodge and Campground** 7900 Hwy. 150 N. Mosca, CO 81146. 719-378-2900 (lodge). 10 rooms. $79–$90. Pool, restaurant. For campground reservations for RVs, cabins, or tepees, call 719-378-2222. www.gsdlodge.com.
■ **Great Sand Dunes Oasis** 5400 Hwy. 150 N., Mosca, CO 81146. 719-378-2222. 100 tent sites $14; RV park $23; cabins $35; Tepees $28. Group sites of 10 or more, $30.

In Alamosa, CO 81101:
■ **Best Western Alamosa Inn** 2005 Main St., Alamosa, CO 81101. 800-459-5123.

53 rooms, including family suites. $59–$90. AC, pool, spa. www.bestwestern.com.
■ **Comfort Inn Alamosa** 6301 US 160, Alamosa, CO 81101. 719-587-9000. 50 rooms. $65–$115. AC, pool. www.choicehotels.com.
■ **Clarion Inn of the Rio Grande** 333 Santa Fe Ave., Alamosa, CO 81101. 800-669-1658. 126 rooms, including suites. $63–$110. AC, pool, jacuzzi, restaurant. www.innoftherio.com.

For other local accommodations, contact the park. For information on locations near the park entrance, call the Alamosa Chamber of Commerce at 719-589-3681, or visit www.alamosachamber.com. For information on lodging near the preserve entrance, call the Westcliffe Chamber of Commerce at 719-783-9163.

Excursions from Sand Dunes

Sangre de Cristo Mountains

30 miles west of Sand Dunes

Stretching from Salida, Colorado, to Santa Fe, the long, lean, slightly independent-feeling Sangre de Cristo Mountains are among the youngest of Colorado's mountain ranges. They boast ten peaks above 14,000 feet and offer visitors a grand expanse of U-shaped valleys, glacially scoured lakes, arêtes, and bowl-shaped cirques.

Centuries before pilgrims arrived at Plymouth Rock, Ute, Comanche, Navajo, and Pueblo Indians lived in the region, later joining the Spanish in 250 years of tenuous farming in the San Luis Valley on the west side of the Sangres.

Despite early development, today there are no asphalt highways, few chairlifts, no rail lines. Happily, much of the range seems destined to stay wild. Approved by Congress in 1993, the 226,455-acre **Sangre de Cristo Wilderness** protects much of its western slope.

Aspens in autumn, Sangre de Cristo Mountains

One of the best ways to appreciate the magnificent Sangre de Cristo Mountains is simply to drive along **US 285,** which offers uninterrupted views of the saw-edged western slope. Along the way, be sure to shift your eyes from the white-capped peaks to the prairie now and then, where you'll almost certainly spy the distinctive white rumps of pronghorn *(see sidebar p. 223).*

For a hike in the high country, consider the 2.5-mile **Williams Lake Trail** (No. 62), which sets off from the base of the Kachina Chairlift at Taos Ski Valley and offers a gentle walk through spruce-fir forest to Williams Lake. The lake sits in the inspiring folds of **Wheeler Peak Wilderness** *(Carson National Forest, 505-758-6200),* home to New Mexico's highest summit, Wheeler Peak (13,161 feet).

To reach the trail, take N. Mex. 150 off US 64 to Taos Ski Valley, watching for signs marking the Carson National Forest and the Wheeler Peak Wilderness. Follow Twining Road for half a mile, then turn left on Phoenix Switchback, driving for just over a mile to the sign for hikers' parking.

Elsewhere, **Santa Barbara Trail** (No. 24) offers another fine day hike. This gradual uphill walk of about 4 miles threads its way through a quilt of spruce, fir, and mountain maple forest, broken here and there by meadows embroidered with mats of harebell, groundsel, paintbrush, and asters. Less than half a mile from the trailhead, the path joins the Rio Santa Barbara and the vegetation expands to include Oregon grape, ferns, thimbleberry, and willow.

The trail continues 1.2 miles, crosses the Rio Santa Barbara via a footbridge, and enters a lush slice of forest. In 2.2 miles, just past the intersection with the West Fork Trail *(bear right),* a wonderful mountain meadow rolls out. Framed by mountains and spruce-fir forest, it is rich with harebell, yarrow, and false hellebore. The display is particularly beautiful during July and August.

To reach the trailhead from N. Mex. 75, follow N. Mex. 73 south 1.5 miles, then turn left onto FR 116 which leads to a parking lot by a campground.

■ **South-central Colorado and north-central New Mexico** ■ **Year-round** ■ **Camping, hiking, boating, fishing, mountain biking, horseback riding, downhill skiing, cross-country skiing** ■ **Contact Rio Grande National Forest, 1803 W. Hwy. 160, Monte Vista, CO 81144, 719-852-5941. www.fs .fed.us/r2/riogrande; or San Isabel National Forest, 1920 Valley Dr., Pueblo, CO 81008, 719-545-8737. www.fs.fed.us/r2/psicc**

Alamosa National Wildlife Refuge

25 miles south of Sand Dunes

Although the San Luis Valley qualifies as a desert environment—receiving on average only 7 inches of rain a year—the snowpack in the surrounding mountains contributes considerably to its groundwater. Throughout much of the 19th century, the valley floor was flush with wetlands, providing habitat for native wildlife and migratory birds. In the past 130 years, however, humans have harnessed much of that water in canals, wells, and various irrigation schemes, drying up many of the wetlands. The Alamosa National Wildlife Refuge attempts to maintain some of what is left.

The Rio Grande River flows along the refuge's southern boundary, and although the refuge has become drier in recent years, managers here help re-create past habitat and conditions through the use of canals and dikes. These wetlands feature a bounty of ducks all year. In spring look for Wilson's phalaropes and northern harriers, and in winter for ferruginous hawks and bald eagles. You can also see American avocets, white-faced ibises, chorus frogs, and black-necked stilts. In the uplands watch for sage thrashers, Brewer's sparrows, and horned lizards.

Like most wildlife refuges, much of Alamosa is closed to the public to maintain quality habitat, yet a 3-mile **auto tour** and the **River Road Walk** offer chances for exploration. This easy trek among willows, birds, and butterflies basically parallels the river for 2 miles; both bikes and leashed dogs are allowed. Stop at refuge headquarters for a map to these self-guided trails, then drive several miles southeast to the **Bluff Overlook,** which provides fine views of the ponds and wetlands and their host of teal, mallard, gadwalls, pintail, and Canada geese.

Twenty miles east of the Alamosa and managed jointly with it, the **Monte Vista National Wildlife Refuge** *(6140 Hwy. 15)* has some of the highest waterfowl-nesting densities in the country. It also provides a resting spot for thousands of migrating sandhill cranes in spring and fall. September and October are also peak months for the 35,000-plus ducks that stop by. A short **auto tour** leads through Monte Vista's mostly man-made wetlands.

■ **11,169 acres** ■ **South-central Colorado** ■ **Best seasons spring and fall**
■ **Hiking, bird-watching, auto tours** ■ **Contact the refuge, 9383 El Rancho Ln., Alamosa, CO 81101; 719-589-4021. www.r6.fws.gov/alamosanwr**

Pronghorn

First comes a flash of white against a backdrop of brown and gray-green grasses. Then it dawns on you: This is a pronghorn, moving as fast as the prairie wind.

Pronghorn have been running for a long time, outpacing predators from saber-toothed tigers to wolves. Millions of years spent on the prairie have endowed the pronghorn with a light-boned, streamlined frame, powered by a large, highly efficient heart. When alarmed, the 80- to 110-pound pronghorn bounds off at 40 to 50 miles an hour, topping 60 miles an hour during short spurts.

They have large eyes and excellent eyesight, as well as a fur of hollow hairs that provides essential insulation. Horns top both male and female; larger horns usually indicate a male.

Pronghorn once browsed across much of North America, their numbers reaching 30 million to 60 million. But overhunting and fence lines reduced their population to an estimated 30,000 in 1920. Today, thanks to conservation efforts, pronghorn number about 60,000 in Colorado alone.

Good places to view the pronghorn in the Sangre de Cristos include the stretches of grassland from Poncha Pass to Saguache along US 285, and on US 40 between Limon and Kit Carson and from Craig to Elk Springs. In winter you can spot herds on either side of Kremmling, along US 40.

Pronghorn on shortgrass prairie

Rio Grande Wild & Scenic River

110 miles south of Sand Dunes

This portion of the Rio Grande in northern New Mexico was one of the original eight streams designated as National Wild and Scenic Rivers in 1968. It's pretty easy to convince yourself the honor was deserved: Simply drive northwest from Taos about 12 miles on US 64, stop at the **Rio Grande High Bridge,** and walk out to the center. Those who know the river only in its placid, irrigation-depleted incarnation downstream will hardly recognize it here, where it's carved a sheer-sided gorge 650 feet deep in the flat surrounding grassland.

To experience its wild side firsthand, consider taking a **float trip** *(permit required)* through a stretch of its celebrated white water. Some sections are remote and exceedingly difficult with rapids rated up to Class VI, but others are easily accessible full- or half-day trips through rapids up to Class IV.

The most popular trips run south from the John Dunn Bridge to the Taos Junction Bridge, about 15.5 miles south of Taos. Commercial outfitters offer various trips along this segment *(contact BLM for a list of licensed outfitters)*. The first 16 miles compose the famed **Taos Box,** a full-day journey through rapids up to Class IV under cliffs hundreds of feet high. It's the most popular white-water run in New Mexico.

Rio Grande Gorge

Two easier stretches follow: the **Orilla Verde** and the **Racecourse.** Both are half-day trips near the town of Pilar and both run through areas where the canyon has widened, and the landscape is more domesticated. The Orilla Verde segment is the more sedate option.

Several mountain-biking and hiking trails provide the opportunity to explore the Rio Grande without getting wet. The **West Rim Trail** *(from US 64 Rio Grand High*

Rio Grande Petroglyphs

Hikers and boaters along the Rio Grande occasionally find examples of Native American rock art called petroglyphs. Unlike painted pictographs, petroglyphs were produced by carving or pecking away at the dark "desert varnish" (a mineral patina) on boulders. Because such art is difficult to date, archaeologists are often uncertain about when it was created. Though some figures are recognizable—handprints, snakes, birds, deer—the exact meanings are elusive.

To see a fabulous collection of rock art, visit **Petroglyph National Monument** (6001 Unser Blvd. NW, Albuquerque. 505-899-0205), located just west of town off I-40. More than 20,000 examples of petroglyphs are preserved here.

Bridge) follows the rim of Taos Box gorge for 9 easygoing miles. Views of the river are spectacular.

Elsewhere, the **Wild Rivers Recreation Area** (3 miles N of Questa, via N. Mex 522 and 378. 505-758-8851. Adm. fee) offers 22 miles of rim and river trails. Several fairly strenuous routes drop all the way to the Rio Grande, then link up with other trails for loop hikes. An easy nature trail at **La Junta Point** (end of the road) remains at plateau level and leads to overlooks of the banded canyon walls—alternating layers of gravel eroded from surrounding mountains and basaltic lava from ancient volcanoes.

Even those not planning to hike should visit La Junta Point for the panorama of the Rio Grande and Red River confluence 800 feet below. A visitor center is open from Memorial Day through Labor Day, and campgrounds and picnic areas are available all year.

Farther north, the **Guadalupe Mountain Trail** (off N. Mex. 378) climbs to the top of an extinct volcano, gaining 1,000 feet over 2 miles and offering vistas of the Sangre de Cristo Mountains.

■ **168 miles long** ■ **North-central New Mexico, north and west of Taos**
■ **Best season May–July** ■ **Camping, hiking, boating, fishing, biking**
■ **Float trip permit required for some sections** ■ **Contact Taos Field Office, Bureau of Land Management, 226 Cruz Alta Rd., Taos, NM 87571; 505-758-8851 or 888-882-6188. www.nm.blm.gov.**

Northern Species, Southern Range

The mountains of northern New Mexico provide a home for several species of animals found at or near the southern edges of their ranges. With summits ranging to 13,161-foot Wheeler Peak (the state's highest point), the uplands of the Sangre de Cristo, Jemez, and San Juan Mountains encompass tundra, mountain meadow, and spruce-fir habitats like those of the northern Rockies.

During the last ice age, which ended only 10,000 years ago, New Mexico had a much cooler and wetter climate. "Northern" habitats, and their associated vegetation and wildlife, were more widespread, reaching down into lower elevations. As the ice retreated and the climate warmed, the distribution of these species shrank, drawing upward to pockets of the environments they needed to survive.

If cooler times return, the animals living in these high-country "refugia" may disperse over a wider range again; if global warming continues, they eventually may disappear from New Mexico entirely. One such species is the snowshoe hare, also called varying hare for the twice-yearly change in its fur color from winter white to summer brown. An uncommon resident of the spruce-fir forests, it might be seen by hikers in the Latir Peak or Wheeler Peak wilderness areas.

Two other inhabitants of the high coniferous woodland are even rarer: The marten, a large tree-climbing weasel that preys on mice and voles; and the boreal owl, a reclusive bird that nests in abandoned woodpecker holes. More common, but still seldom spotted, is the short-tailed weasel or ermine; like the snowshoe hare, it changes color from brown to white as summer turns to fall. Two mammals that are seen much more often are the yellow-bellied marmot and the pika. Marmots can be quite easy to spot on tundra and in subalpine meadows, especially if there are rock piles nearby. The same can't be said of the furtive pika, a chubby little mammal related to rabbits and hare. Also called cony, the pika has short, rounded ears and no visible tail; it occupies rockslides and talus slopes near or above tree line. Its habits of gathering grass for winter food and of giving sharp, loud squeaks have earned it folk names such as "rock farmer" and "calling hare."

It takes a lucky hiker to spot a white-tailed ptarmigan, a

American marten

grouse of the tundra and the stunted woodland just below. Once found more widely in the northern New Mexico mountains, this species is now confined to a few peaks in the Sangre de Cristos. With plumage that molts from summer brown to winter white, the ptarmigan is well disguised, and tends to sit still and let hikers walk past instead of flying or running away.

One species formerly common in northern New Mexico is unlikely to be found no matter how much you try. The boreal toad, a subspecies of western toad, lived in the San Juan Mountains as recently as the mid-1980s. Like so many other amphibians, it has suffered grave population declines over most of its range.

Enchanted Circle Area

110 miles
south of
Sand Dunes

It's not too much to say that there's something for nearly everyone on this route through the Sangre de Cristo Mountains. At one extreme might be simply driving the **Enchanted Circle National Scenic Byway** *(85 miles)*, admiring the views along the 84-mile loop. At the other extreme would be the strenuous hike to the top of **Wheeler Peak,** the highest point in New Mexico and the focal point of the circle.

The activities ranging between these two extremes include rewarding day hikes, national forest campgrounds, interesting wildlife, and historic towns. Summer hiking and mountain biking and winter downhill and cross-country skiing make this a year-round destination. Taos, once home to famed explorer Kit Carson, is now a renowned arts community. It makes an excellent base for venturing into the nearby mountains.

From US 64 north of Taos, N. Mex. 150 leads to Taos Ski Valley resort, start of the most popular trails into the **Wheeler Peak Wilderness** *(see p. 221)*. Driving north on N. Mex. 522, you'll reach Questa. Here, consider a side-trip to **Latir Peak Wilderness** *(N of N. Mex. 563)* for the 5-mile one-way day hike from 9,200-foot **Cabresto Lake** (good fishing) to **Heart Lake,** elevation 11,500 feet.

The scenic byway continues east from Questa on N. Mex. 38, paralleling the Red River past several pleasant campgrounds, including Columbine and the popular 5.7-mile **Columbine Canyon Trail.** From historic **Red River,** N. Mex. 578 leads south to other trailheads for Wheeler Peak Wilderness destinations such as **Horseshoe Lake,** set beside an alpine ridge below Wheeler Peak, with stunted bristlecone pines dotting the stark landscape. To get there, drive to the East Fork trailhead and head out for about 5 miles on the **East Fork** and **Lost Lake Trails.**

N. Mex. 38 crosses 9,820-foot Bobcat Pass to join US 64 at Eagle Nest. From there it's a short drive east to **Cimarron Canyon State Park** *(see p. 231)* and **Eagle Nest Lake** (good fishing for trout and kokanee salmon).

From Eagle Nest it's 31 miles back to Taos on US 64. Three miles east of town, the 6-mile **Devisadero Loop trail** makes a fine, moderate day hike, beginning at El Nogal picnic area.

■ **North-central New Mexico, northeast of Taos** ■ **Best months June–Sept. Campgrounds closed Sept. or Oct.–May** ■ **Camping, hiking, fishing, biking, horseback riding, skiing, wildlife viewing** ■ **Contact Carson National Forest, P.O. Box 558, Taos, NM 87571, 505-758-6200. www.fs.fed.us /recreation/forest_descr/nm_r3_carson.html**

Sangre de Cristo Mountains from Wheeler Peak

Valle Vidal

80 miles south of Sand Dunes

It takes a little effort to get to this parklike valley in the Sangre de Cristo Mountains, but once you're here you'll enjoy one of the most scenic spots in New Mexico. Limited trails make it less of a hiking destination than other areas of the national forest, various regulations restrict public access at different times of year, and the one unpaved access road can sometimes be slick or icy. It's a good idea to contact the Questa Ranger District office when planning a visit.

To reach Valle Vidal, turn east from N. Mex. 522 at Costilla onto N. Mex. 196; continue on FR 1950. You'll pass dry hillsides with scrubby pinyon pine, juniper, and sagebrush as the **Costilla Creek Valley** alternately opens and narrows under tall cliffs. After 19 long miles through private land, you reach the forest boundary. For the next 30 miles or so, you pass through a stunning landscape of rolling hills, with broad meadows bordered by a mixed coniferous forest and some large stands of aspen.

About 2,000 elk roam Valle Vidal. In the Rio Costilla swim Rio Grande cutthroat trout, the only native trout species in the Rio Grande drainage—and New Mexico's state fish. It's estimated that the cutthroat now exists in only about 10 percent of its original range, its population hurt by cattle grazing, dams, interbreeding with non-native trout, and other human-caused factors.

Three miles east of the striking rocky point where FR 1900 diverges north is the trailhead for the **Little Costilla Creek Trail,** which leads north 10 miles to FR 1900. During elk calving season in May and June, the trail is closed to hikers.

Two campgrounds, Cimarron and McCrystal, offer the chance to enjoy Valle Vidal for more than a single day. From the latter, FR 1950 continues about 30 miles east and south to US 64 near the town of Cimarron. Camping is restricted to these two campgrounds; elsewhere in Valle Vidal, you must camp at least a half mile from the road.

■ 100,000 acres ■ North-central New Mexico, 40 miles northeast of Taos ■ Best months July–Sept. Road closed by snow in winter; west side closed May–June during elk calving ■ Camping, hiking, fishing, hunting, horseback riding, wildlife viewing ■ Contact Questa Ranger District, Carson National Forest, P.O. Box 110, Questa, NM 87556; 505-586-0520. www.fs .fed.us/recreation/forest_descr/nm_r3_carson.html

Cimarron Canyon State Park

135 miles south of Sand Dunes

A broad range of outdoorspeople find this beautiful park an appealing destination—none more so than fly fishers, who often line the banks of the **Cimarron River** to cast for stocked brown and rainbow trout. The 8 miles of river running through the park constitute one of the best trout streams in New Mexico; US 64 parallels the river along the narrow canyon; several picnic areas and campgrounds offer parking and easy access.

Set at an elevation of 8,000 feet in the foothills of the Sangre de Cristo Mountains, the canyon is home to elk, mule deer, black bears, porcupines, and Abert's squirrels. Golden-mantled ground squirrels, often mistaken for chipmunks, scamper among the forest of Douglas-fir, white fir, ponderosa pine, and aspen. In wider areas of the canyon, beaver dams produce placid pools. Find a comfortable seat here at dusk and watch the aquatic residents begin their evening activities. Wild turkey and blue grouse walk stealthily through the forest; the latter is seldom seen, but once spotted is often absurdly approachable.

Stop at the **Palisades picnic area** to admire towering cliffs of monzonite, a granitic rock formed below the Earth's surface, now exposed and eroded into spectacular columns. To enjoy both wildlife and scenery, drive west a couple of miles and walk up the **Clear Creek Canyon Trail,** a 5-mile round-trip up a side canyon. This is one of four park trails, most of which follow old logging roads, totaling more than 30 miles.

Fly-fishing, Cimarron Canyon S P

■ 33,000 acres ■ Northeastern New Mexico, 42 miles northeast of Taos via US 64 ■ Best months May–mid-Oct. Wildlife area is popular with hunters; check with park before hiking in fall elk or deer seasons ■ Camping, hiking, fishing, hunting, mountain biking, horseback riding, wildlife viewing ■ Camping fee ■ Contact the park, P.O. Box 185, Eagle Nest, NM 87718; 505-377-6271. www.emnrd.state.nm. us/nmparks/pages/parks/cimarron/ cimarron.htm

Guadalupe Mountains

In West Texas, only about 40 miles southwest of Carlsbad Caverns, lies a gem of a park that few people outside the state have ever heard of, let alone visited. Guadalupe Mountains National Park contains the southernmost, highest part of the 50-mile-long Guadalupe range. From the highway, the mountains resemble a nearly monolithic wall through the desert. But drive into one of the park entrances, take even a short stroll, and surprises crop up: dramatically contoured canyons, shady glades surrounded by desert scrub, a profusion of wildlife and birds.

Some 80 miles of trails can lead the more energetic hiker to Guadalupe Peak, the highest point in Texas (8,749 feet), and to mountaintops with scattered but thick conifer forests typical of the Rockies hundreds of miles to the north. The range's origins may be surprising, too: The Guadalupe Mountains were once a reef growing beneath the waters of an ancient inland sea. That same vanished sea was also responsible for spawning the honeycomb of the Carlsbad Caverns.

Pottery, baskets, and spear tips found in the mountains suggest that people first visited the Guadalupes about 12,000 years ago, hunting the camels, mammoths, and other animals that flourished in the wetter climate of the waning Ice Age.

When the Spaniards arrived in the Southwest in the mid-16th century, Mescalero Apache were periodically camping near the springs at the base of the mountains and climbing to the highlands to hunt and forage. Both the Apache and Europeans spun legends of fabulous caches of gold in these mountains.

As American prospectors, settlers, and cavalry pushed west, the Apache made the mountainous areas their bases and fought to ward off encroachers. By the late 1880s, however, virtually all the Native Americans had been killed or forced onto a reservation.

- Western Texas, 110 miles east of El Paso

- 86,416 acres

- Established 1972

- Best seasons fall–spring, with colorful autumn foliage

- Camping, hiking, horseback riding, bird-watching, wildlife viewing

- Information: 915-828-3251 www.nps.gov/gumo

West face El Capitan, Guadalupe Mountains National Park

NEW MEXICO
TEXAS

Cutoff Mountain⁺
6,933 ft

BROKEOFF MOUNTAINS

Cutoff Ridge

Crow Flats

GUADALU

Gypsum
Sand
Dunes

NATIONA

Shumard Canyo

Williams Ra

Patterson Hills

Quail Mountain⁺
4,962 ft

Cone Peak⁺
5,017 ft

Salt Basin

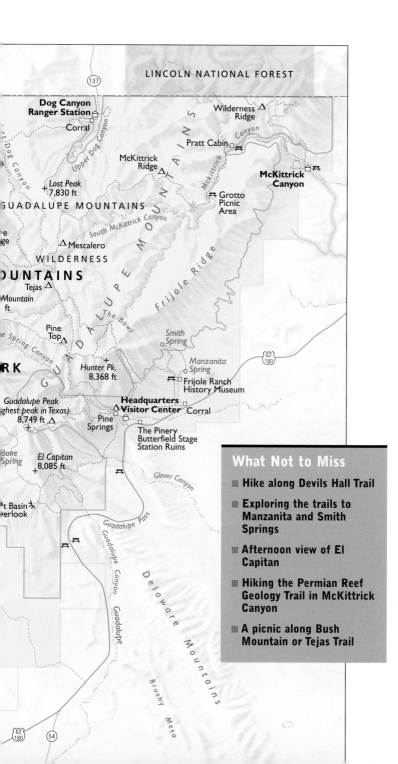

LINCOLN NATIONAL FOREST

Dog Canyon Ranger Station
Corral

Upper Dog Canyon

Wilderness Ridge

Pratt Cabin

McKittrick Canyon

McKittrick Ridge

McKittrick Canyon

Lost Peak
7,830 ft

GUADALUPE MOUNTAINS

Grotto Picnic Area

South McKittrick Canyon

Mescalero

WILDERNESS

Frijole Ridge

OUNTAINS

Tejas

Mountain
ft

The Bowl

Pine Top

Smith Spring

Spring Canyon

Manzanita Spring

Hunter Pk.
8,368 ft

Frijole Ranch History Museum

RK

Headquarters Visitor Center Corral

Guadalupe Peak
ghest peak in Texas)
8,749 ft

Pine Springs

The Pinery Butterfield Stage Station Ruins

Bone Spring

El Capitan
8,085 ft

Glover Canyon

t Basin
erlook

Guadalupe Pass

Guadalupe Canyon

Guadalupe

Delaware Mountains

Brushy Mesa

What Not to Miss

■ Hike along Devils Hall Trail

■ Exploring the trails to Manzanita and Smith Springs

■ Afternoon view of El Capitan

■ Hiking the Permian Reef Geology Trail in McKittrick Canyon

■ A picnic along Bush Mountain or Tejas Trail

How to Get There

Pine Springs-Frijole area (the park's hub) lies off US 62/180, 55 miles southwest of Carlsbad and 110 miles east of El Paso. For McKittrick Canyon, turn off US 62/180 northeast of Pine Springs. For Dog Canyon, go north on US 62/180, then west on Rte. 408, and south on N. Mex. 137, about 105 miles total from Pine Springs. Airports: Carlsbad, N. Mex., and El Paso, Tex.

When to Go

All-year park, but spring and fall are best. In spring, the foliage is fresh and, with enough rain, the blossoms abundant. In late October to mid-November, changing leaves provide splashes of red, yellow, and burgundy.

How to Visit

On a 1-day trip, tour the **visitor center** and **Pine Springs;** take a short hike. On a second day, visit **McKittrick Canyon** for a stroll through a hidden oasis. With more time, add a trip to **Dog Canyon** (3-hour drive) to see a wilder, more isolated area, where trails lead quickly into the high country.

Snow-dusted Texas madrone

EXPLORING THE PARK

Pine Springs-Frijole Area: **A half to full day**

Pick up maps and trail information at the **Headquarters Visitor Center,** where you can also enjoy audiovisual programs on the park's ecology, geology, and history. Fill your water bottles before leaving. Then stroll to **The Pinery** or drive back to the highway, turn left in about 0.1 mile, and park. The stone walls remain from the 1858 Pinery Station of the Butterfield Overland Mail Line—forerunner of the Pony Express. Buy a self-guiding leaflet, if you wish, to learn about the colorful local history.

Return to your car, drive back to the highway, and turn left. Turn left again in about a mile onto a dirt road. Park at the end near the **Frijole Ranch History Museum,** an 1870s ranch house that now preserves artifacts and exhibits that cover some of the park's cultural history.

Be sure to walk the easy 2.3-mile **Smith Spring Trail,** which loops past Smith and Manzanita Springs and—two oases that offer an excellent introduction to the striking contrasts the Chihuahuan Desert can present. Bear to your right at the trailhead.

The thorny plants you see along the trail may seem forbidding, but the Mescalero Apache used a great majority of them for food and for making tools and medicines. Plants include agaves, prickly pear cactuses, walking stick chollas, yuccas and sotols. The Mescalero diet consisted largely of mescal—the heart of the agave plant, one of the succulents with spikes at the tips of the leaves—hence the culture's name.

You'll soon approach **Manzanita Spring,** a promising site for spotting wildlife, especially during the cooler hours of early morning or dusk. Collared lizards, snakes, coyotes, mule deer, and some of the park's 300 species of birds are often seen.

Continue on to **Smith Spring,** a veritable garden of maidenhair ferns, Texas madrone trees (the ones shedding layers of paper-thin bark), alligator juniper (named for its distinctively textured bark), oak, and maple. This, too, is a good spot to keep your eyes open for wildlife. As you loop back to your car, bear left at the fork.

Return to the highway and drive west-southwest about 2 miles, or at least as far as the first pullover, for a superb view of **El Capitan** (8,085 feet), the southern most bluff of the Guadalupes. Late afternoon light shows off this imposing symbol of the region, once the beacon for conquistador, stagecoach driver, and homesteader.

Ancient Reef

The Davis Mountains of western Texas are igneous—that is, built by volcanic activity—but the Guadalupes and other nearby ranges share a more unusual origin. The Apache, Glass, Sierra Diablo, and Guadalupe Mountains are actually remnants of a gigantic reef that surrounded an inland sea 250 million years ago. This horseshoe-shaped reef stretches northward into New Mexico, although most of the formation lies beneath the surface. The reef is unusual because unlike modern coral reefs, it was composed of the skeletons of sponges and algae.

The most famous section of exposed reef is the majestic peak called El Capitan, which towers over the Chihuahuan Desert landscape of Guadalupe Mountains National Park.

McKittrick Canyon: A half to full day

The walls of McKittrick Canyon shelter the only year-round stream in the park, spring fed McKittrick Creek. The water creates a 3-mile-long oasis of grey oak, velvet ash, bigtooth maple, walnut, juniper, and Texas madrone. The canyon itself is nearly 5 miles long and like the park's other canyons, its plant and animal communities reflect a rich mix of desert, canyon woodland, and highland forest. Here, prickly pear cactus and agaves grow a stone's throw from willows and ferns. Farther up the canyon, you'll find stands of ponderosa pine. Mule deer, jackrabbits, coyotes, porcupines, grey foxes, mountain lions and elk all live within the canyon.

Pick up a self-guiding booklet on the area's human and natural history at the McKittrick Canyon Contact Station near the trailheads. For an easy hike (although the trail is rocky and best negotiated in hiking boots), walk the 2.3 miles to the historic **Pratt Cabin.** If you have time, continue another mile through the woods that border the intermittent stream to the **Grotto picnic area.** Because so many of the canyon plants are fragile, please be sure to stay on the trail and out of the stream.

McKittrick Canyon exposes millions of years of geological events. During the Permian era, about 250 million years ago, an inland sea covered parts of West Texas and southeast New Mexico. Along the shore of the sea grew a reef of lime-secreting algae, sponges, other marine organisms, and calcium carbonate precipitated from the water. After millions of years, the climate changed and the ocean dried up; the Capitan Reef loomed hundreds of feet high in a horseshoe 400 miles long. Sediments and mineral salts buried both basin and reef over the next eons. Later, the region began to rise, and erosion slowly reexposed the seabed with part of the fossil reef—today's Guadalupe range—towering above. The Capitan Reef ranks as one of the finest examples of an ancient marine fossil reef found anywhere on Earth.

As you walk into McKittrick Canyon, you are entering the Capitan Reef from the seaward side. To best observe the reef's varied formation and fossils, try the **Permian Reef Geology Trail.** You'll see layers of the ancient reef exposed by centuries of cutting by McKittrick Creek. The trail—4.5 miles one way—climbs the 2,000-foot ridge to a ponderosa forest on the top.

Three more trails on this side of the park make for rewarding day hikes. They all begin from Pine Springs Campground; ask a ranger for details. The 8.3-mile round-trip to the top of **Guadalupe Peak** climbs to the highest point in Texas. (*Because lightning storms can quickly gather on hot summer afternoons, it's best to begin your ascent by 8 a.m. and your descent by 1 p.m. Watch the weather. If you see a storm coming, start down immediately.*) A 9.5-mile loop trail drops into **The Bowl,** a lush area of relict ice age conifer forest, via the Bear Canyon and Tejas Trails. Finally, a 4.5-mile round-trip trail leads through **Devils Hall,** a steep, narrow canyon.

Dog Canyon: A half to full day

Accessibility to the forested high country and its spectacular scenery make Dog Canyon well worth the 3-hour drive from Pine Springs. Ask a ranger to point out Apache mescal roasting pits, still visible among the hip-high grasses, creosote bushes, and succulents. Then picnic and hike; the trails begin past the stables. Popular hikes include the **Bush Mountain Trail,** which, in about 3 miles, leads through open pinyon-juniper woodland to splendid views of the Guadalupes and the Cornudas Mountains, 55 miles to the west. The **Tejas Trail** offers similar views and in about 4 miles climbs into a temperate woodland of Gambel oak, Douglas-fir, and limber and ponderosa pine. This forest is a relict of the plant communities that cloaked the region in the last ice age. It still survives because of the particular, unusual combination of temperature and humidity at this high-altitude site.

INFORMATION & ACTIVITIES

Headquarters
HC 60, Box 400
Salt Flat, TX 79847
915-828-3251
www.nps.gov/gumo

Visitor & Information Centers
Headquarters Visitor Center off
US 62/180 at Guadalupe Pass,
open all year except Christmas.
McKittrick Canyon Contact
Station, off US 62/180 on east-
ern edge of park and Dog
Canyon Ranger Station in the
north open intermittently. Call
headquarters for details.

Seasons & Accessibility
Open year-round but the best
seasons are spring, when wildflower blossoms peak, and
autumn, when deciduous
foliage turns color in the
canyons and highlands. Areas
of the park may be inaccessible
for brief periods in winter due
to snowstorms. Call headquarters for current conditions.

Entrance Fee
$3 per vehicle.

Pets
Not permitted on trails or in
buildings; leashed elsewhere.

Facilities for Disabled
The visitor centers, rest rooms,
and Pine Springs Campground
and amphitheater are wheelchair accessible.

Things to Do
Hikes, horseback trail rides
(no rentals), evening and children's programs.

Special Advisories
■ Rattlesnakes and other potentially harmful desert animals
live here. Watch out!
■ Bring maps if you plan to
hike; the park is managed as
a wilderness, so trail signs
are minimal.

Backcountry Camping
Allowed at designated sites
only; permits required; they
are free and may be obtained
at visitor centers. Backcountry
use permits required to bring
a horse into the park, available
from main visitor center or
Dog Canyon. Horses are not
allowed in the backcountry
overnight; they can be stabled
in Frijole Ranch and Dog
Canyon corrals; reserve space
by calling 915-828-3251.

Campgrounds
Two campgrounds, both with
14-day limit. Open all year,
first come, first served. $8 per
night at Dog Canyon and Pine
Springs. No showers. Tent and
RV sites; no hookups. Two

McKittrick Canyon maple

group campgrounds; reservations are required through headquarters.

Hotels, Motels, & Inns
(Unless otherwise noted, rates are for two persons in a double room, high season.)

In Whites City, NM 88268:
■ **Best Western Cavern Inn,** 12 Carlsbad Cavern Hwy., P.O. Box 128. 505-785-2291 or 800-228-3767. 132 units. $89. AC, pool, restaurant. www.whites city.com.

In Van Horn, TX 79855:
■ **Best Western American Inn** 1309 W. Broadway, Box 626. 432-283-2030 or 800-621-2478. 33 units. $55. AC, pool. www .bestwestern.com.
■ **Ramada, Ltd.,** 200 Golf Course Dr., P.O. Box 1568. 432-283-2780. 60 units. $68. AC, pool.

See also Carlsbad Caverns National Park listings, p. 123.

Excursions from Guadalupe

Lincoln National Forest

10 miles
north of
Guadalupe

Beautiful forests, mountain meadows, wilderness areas, great views, and varied trails are a few of the highlights of this beautiful and varied national forest. The two northern ranger districts, Sacramento and Smokey Bear, are both easily accessible from Alamogordo and offer a scenic byway, a world-renowned observatory, and a fascinating Native American petroglyph site. A third district, the Guadalupe, adjoins Carlsbad Caverns *(see pp. 115–123)* and Guadalupe Mountains National Parks.

If you drive to the Dog Canyon area of Guadalupe Mountains National Park, you'll follow N. Mex. 137 right through the national forest's **Guadalupe Ranger District.** Along the way, consider making a 7-mile detour along FR 276 to **Sitting Bull Falls.** Here, a spring-fed creek cascades over a limestone bluff, dropping into a small pool; the resulting oasis of walnut, cherry, sumac, oak, and willow attracts abundant wildlife—when it's not attracting overabundant people; avoid visiting on summer weekends.

Sacramento Ranger District

From US 54/70 just north of Alamogordo, drive east on US 82 toward the resort community of **Cloudcroft,** set at an elevation of 8,663 feet in the Sacramento Mountains. As you reach the final switchbacks before town *(about 15 miles from US 54/70),* watch for the **Osha Trail** parking lot. This easy, 2.6-mile loop, with interpretive signs, makes a fine introduction to the area, passing through an attractive forest to a good vista of the Tularosa Valley, White Sands National Monument *(see pp. 125–27),* and the San Andres Mountains.

In Cloudcroft, turn south on N. Mex. 130, then west on N. Mex. 6563. Known as the **Sunspot Scenic Byway,** this route certainly is scenic—especially at overlooks where you have views out over the white-sand dunes. In 0.2 mile you'll reach the national forest's Slide Campground and the northernmost trailhead for the 28-mile **Rim Trail,** which follows the edge of the Sacramento escarpment. Few walk the full distance, but intersecting side trails and roads make it possible to hike shorter sections. The scenic byway ends at the **National Solar Observatory** *(505-434-7000)* on 9,255-foot Sacramento Peak. A visitor center is open daily from May through October; tours are self-guided or guided *(Fri.–Sun.; fee).*

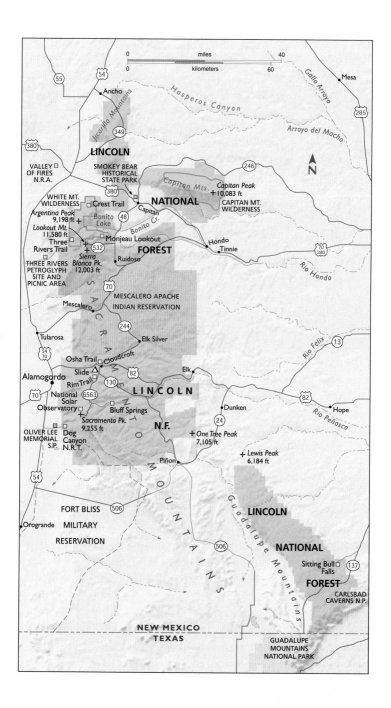

55
54
Ancho
miles   40
kilometers   60
Mesa
Gallo Arroyo
285
Hasperos Canyon
Jicarilla Mountains
349
380
LINCOLN
VALLEY
OF FIRES
N.R.A.
SMOKEY BEAR
HISTORICAL
STATE PARK
246
Arroyo del Macho
N
Capitan Mts.
Capitan Peak
+10,083 ft
NATIONAL
CAPITAN MT.
WILDERNESS
WHITE MT.
WILDERNESS
380
Crest Trail
48
Capitan
Argentina Peak
9,198 ft
Bonito
Lake
Bonito Cr.
Lookout Mt.
11,580 ft
Monjeau Lookout
Hondo
Tinnie
70
380
Three
Rivers Trail
532
FOREST
THREE RIVERS
PETROGLYPH
SITE AND
PICNIC AREA
Sierra
Blanca Pk.
12,003 ft
Ruidoso
Rio Hondo
70
MESCALERO APACHE
INDIAN RESERVATION
Mescalero
S
A
C
R
A
M
E
N
T
O
244
Tularosa
Elk Silver
Rio Felix
13
54
70
Osha Trail
Cloudcroft
Alamogordo
Slide
Rim Trail
82
Elk
National
Solar
Observatory
130
6563
L I N C O L N
82
Hope
Dunken
Rio Peñasco
Bluff Springs
N.F.
24
OLIVER LEE
MEMORIAL
S.P.
Dog
Canyon
N.R.T.
Sacramento Pk.
9,255 ft
+One Tree Peak
7,105 ft
Piñon
+ Lewis Peak
6,184 ft
54
FORT BLISS
506
M
O
U
N
T
A
I
N
S
LINCOLN
Orogrande   MILITARY
RESERVATION
506
Guadalupe Mountains
NATIONAL
Sitting Bull
Falls
137
FOREST
CARLSBAD
CAVERNS N.P.
NEW MEXICO
TEXAS
GUADALUPE
MOUNTAINS
NATIONAL PARK

N. Mex. 532, Lincoln National Forest

Return north on N. Mex. 6563 about 10 miles from the observatory and turn east on FR 164. In 3.7 miles you'll reach **Bluff Springs,** where there's a beautiful waterfall, forests, and fine hiking and mountain biking.

Smokey Bear Ranger District

To begin your exploration of the national forest's Smokey Bear Ranger District take N. Mex. 48 north from Ruidoso about 5.5 miles and turn west on N. Mex. 532. In less than a mile, turn north on FR 117, which climbs steeply alongside Little Creek. *(The upper part of this road can be quite rough at times; check with the district office in Ruidoso, 505-257-4095, about its condition before making the drive.)*

About 5 miles up the road, stop at parking area for the **Crest Trail** and walk at least a short section of this 21-mile path across the high ridges of the Sierra Blancas. Then continue on FR 117 to **Monjeau Lookout** for a panoramic vista of the mountains.

Next, drive back down to N. Mex. 532 and turn west. This winding road toward Ski Apache downhill ski area is one of the most scenic drives in the state. About 9 miles along the way, stop at **Windy Point Vista** for another great view. Near the ski area entrance on the north side of the road, look for the **Scenic Trail,** which climbs 0.6 mile to the Crest Trail *(about 5 miles from the trailhead on FR 117).* Beautiful meadows and coniferous woods make this short trail worthwhile by itself, but it's also used as the route to the top of 11,580-foot **Lookout Mountain,** the highest point in Lincoln National Forest. To reach the summit, turn west on the Crest Trail, proceed for 2 miles and turn south on the 3.4-mile **Lookout Mountain Trail,** which climbs about 1,700 feet.

The most popular trails in the White Mountain Wilderness begin a bit farther north at the Argentina Canyon/Bonito trailhead. To reach it, return to N. Mex. 48 and go north about 4 miles; at the Bonito Lake sign, turn west on N. Mex. 37. In 1.3 miles, turn west onto FR 107 and continue around the lake to the trailhead beyond the South Fork campground.

Here, the **Bonito Trail** and the **Argentina Canyon Trail** start just steps apart. Hikers can combine these trails with a section of the Crest Trail to make a fairly strenuous 6.5-mile loop through the high country. Begin on the Bonito Trail, which follows Bonito Creek through Douglas-fir, white fir, ponderosa pine, oak, and aspen. In the first miles, you pass the remains of two old mines on the creek's south side.

In 1.3 miles, where Bonito Creek and the Bonito Trail turn south, follow the **Little Bonito Trail** west up Little Bonito Creek. Sometimes fairly steep, the trail in 1.2 miles intersects with the Cut Across Trail; continue on the Little Bonito trail for the longer loop. In another 0.3 mile, the Little Bonito Trail meets the Crest Trail. Turn north here, and soon you'll have excellent views as you reach the high point of the hike at 9,100 feet, below Argentina Peak.

After following the Crest Trail for 1.2 miles, turn east on the Argentina Canyon Trail at Argentina Spring. From here, it's a 2.5-mile descent through the canyon to the trailhead. You'll pass through extensive aspen groves and a deep chasm with tall Douglas-firs. This species grows taller than any other tree in the Southwest, and these are suitably impressive specimens.

On the west slope of the mountains, FR 579 *(30 miles N of Alamogordo via US 54)* leads to two promising sites: the **Three Rivers Trail** and the **Three Rivers Petroglyph Site** *(505-525-4300. Adm. fee).* At the petroglyphs, interpretive trails wind past literally thousands of examples of Native American rock art, pecked into the dark desert varnish on basalt boulders by the Jornada Mogollon, a people who lived here between 1000 and 1400. At the end of FR 579, the Three Rivers Trail climbs nearly 4,000 feet in 6 miles, passing through all the significant plant communities in the region —from the Chihuahuan Desert to coniferous forests. At the top, the trail connects with the Crest Trail.

■ 926,000 acres ■ South-central New Mexico, east of Alamogordo and north of Ruidoso ■ Best months April-Nov. High trails and roads often snow covered in winter ■ Camping, hiking, mountain biking, bird-watching, petroglyphs ■ Contact the national forest, 1101 New York Ave., Alamogordo, NM 88310; 505-434-7200. www.fs.fed.us/r3/lincoln

Davis Mountains Loop

135 miles southeast of Guadalupe

74 miles; 2 hours This drive weaves through the ragged Davis Mountains—the "Texas Alps"—and around 8,382-foot **Mount Livermore,** the state's second highest peak. But you'll also see desert, rolling hills, fantastic volcanic formations—and lots of stars.

Start in the frontier village of Fort Davis—at 4,900 feet the state's most elevated town. Its main attraction is the 1854 **Fort Davis National Historic Site** *(432-426-3224),* the first military post on the San Antonio-El Paso Road and a home of the famed African-American buffalo soldiers. Just past the fort, bear left on Tex. 118.

Winding up Limpia Canyon, past walls of jointed lava columns, the drive parallels the cottonwood-lined banks of Limpia (Spanish for "clear" or "clean") Creek. For the next 8 miles through the canyon, you dip along foothills covered with oak woodlands, passing 2,800-acre **Davis Mountains State Park** *(432-426-3337).* Vistas of hills and valleys, intruded by volcanic outcroppings and weathered, rounded slopes, predominate for a few more miles.

Beyond Prude Ranch, you drive out onto a beautiful expanse of Texas grassland. In this open country, you have views of Mount Livermore and the dome that tops 6,809-foot Mount Locke. This is the **University of Texas' McDonald Observatory** *(432-426-3640),* which

Marfa Lights

Although it gained a bit of celebrity when James Dean, Elizabeth Taylor, and Rock Hudson came to town to film the 1955 movie *Giant*, the hamlet of Marfa is best known for the Marfa lights, a phenomenon that's partly a genuine mystery and partly a well-promoted tourist attraction. For well over a century people have been seeing strange, inexplicable lights moving above the desert east of town; theories on their source include glowing rocks, swamp gas, ghosts, secret military experiments, and luminous jackrabbits. If you'd like to look for yourself, there's an official viewing area on US 90 about 9 miles east of town.

boasts a 432-inch telescope, the world's third largest. The observatory visitor center is open daily, and tours are available.

Inspiring mountain views continue as the drive hugs the rim of Elbow Canyon for several miles before winding steadily down past sylvan Madera Canyon, greened by oak, juniper, and pinyon woodlands, toward the high desert.

At the Y-junction, turn left on Tex. 166 into an arid desertscape. Straight ahead looms landmark Sawtooth Mountain, a worn volcanic cone. Opposite its base stands the Rock Pile, a fine example of jointed lava blocks. A couple of miles beyond this, you enter a chaos of volcanism: precipitous slopes, jagged outcroppings, and towering rock peaks. The Davis Mountains, 35 million to 39 million years old, represent one of the largest volcanic centers in the geologic belt stretching from Montana to Mexico.

The peaks subside during the next few miles, yielding to flat, Big Sky country for about 17 miles. Off to the southwest you can see miles into Mexico. The road swings eastward, and as you start to climb again through dun-colored hills, the trees gradually reappear.

Pass a dozen miles of green pastureland before reaching Tex. 17, which leads about 3 miles north to Fort Davis.

■ **Western Texas; loop starts in Fort Davis** ■ **Year-round** ■ **Hiking, historic tours, observatory tours** ■ **Contact Fort Davis Chamber of Commerce, Union Trading Company at Town Square, P. O. Box 378, Fort Davis, TX; 432-426-3015 or 800-524-3015. www.fortdavis.com**

Joshua Tree

Two desert systems, the Mojave and the Colorado, abut within Joshua Tree, dividing California's southernmost national park into two arid ecosystems of profoundly contrasting appearance. The key to their differences is elevation. The Colorado, the western reach of the vast Sonoran Desert, thrives below 3,000 feet on the park's gently declining eastern flank, where temperatures are usually higher. Considered "low desert," compared to the loftier, wetter, and more vegetated Mojave "high desert," the Colorado seems sparse and forbidding. It begins at the park's midsection, sweeping east across empty basins stubbled with creosote bushes. Occasionally decorated by "gardens" of flowering ocotillo and cholla cactus, it runs across arid Pinto Basin into a parched wilderness of broken rock in the Eagle and Coxcomb Mountains.

Many newcomers among the 1.3 million visitors who pass through each year are surprised by the abrupt transition between the Colorado and Mojave ecosystems. Above 3,000 feet, the Mojave section claims the park's western half, where giant branching yuccas—known as Joshua trees—thrive on sandy plains studded by massive granite monoliths and rock piles. These are among the most intriguing and photogenic geological phenomena found in California's many desert regions.

Joshua Tree's human history commenced sometime after the last ice age with the arrival of the Pinto people, hunter-gatherers who may have been part of the Southwest's earliest cultures. They lived in Pinto Basin, which though inhospitably arid today, had a wet climate and was crossed by a sluggish river some 5,000 to 7,000 years ago. Nomadic groups of natives seasonally inhabited the region when harvests of pinyon nuts, mesquite beans, acorns, and cactus fruit offered sustenance. Bedrock mortars—holes

- Southern California, 140 miles east of Los Angeles, 50 miles north of Palm Springs

- 789,745 acres

- Established 1994

- Best seasons fall and spring

- Camping, hiking, rock climbing, mountain biking, wildflower viewing

- Information: 760-367-5500 www.nps.gov/jotr

Joshua trees at sunset

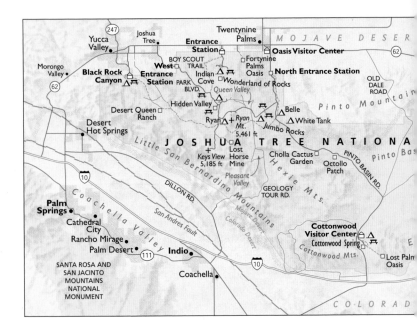

ground into solid rock and used to pulverize seeds during food preparation—are scattered throughout the Wonderland of Rocks area south of the Indian Cove camping site.

A flurry of late 19th-century gold-mining ventures left ruins; some are accessible by hiking trails, or unmaintained roads suited only to four-wheel-drive vehicles and mountain bikes.

How to Get There

The west and north park entrances are at the towns of Joshua Tree and Twentynine Palms. From Los Angeles, take I-10 east to Calif. 62 to Twentynine Palms (about 140 miles total). The south entrance is located at Cottonwood Spring, approximately 25 miles east of Indio off I-10. Call 760-367-5500 for recorded directions. Airports: Palm Springs, Los Angeles.

When to Go

All-year park. Temperatures are most comfortable in the spring and fall, with an average high and low of 85°F and 50°F. Winter brings cooler days, around 60°F, and freezing nights. Summers are hot, with midday temperatures frequently above 100°F, and ground temperatures reaching 180°F. The Mojave Desert zone in the west of the park averages 11 degrees cooler than the Colorado. In

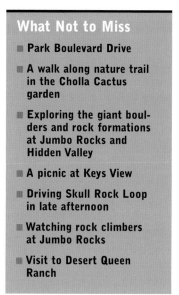

What Not to Miss

- **Park Boulevard Drive**
- **A walk along nature trail in the Cholla Cactus garden**
- **Exploring the giant boulders and rock formations at Jumbo Rocks and Hidden Valley**
- **A picnic at Keys View**
- **Driving Skull Rock Loop in late afternoon**
- **Watching rock climbers at Jumbo Rocks**
- **Visit to Desert Queen Ranch**

winter, snow may blanket the Mojave's higher elevations.

Wildflower blooms usually start in February and peak in March and April, although cactuses may bloom into June. For up-to-date recorded wildflower information, call 760-367-5500.

How to Visit

The park's premier attractions can be enjoyed on a leisurely half-day auto tour along **Park Boulevard**, which loops through the northwestern portion of the park between the towns of Joshua Tree and Twentynine Palms. If the air is clear, take in the side trip to **Keys View,** which overlooks a vast panorama of arid desert basin and range stretching south into Mexico. Also plan to take a second side trip on **Pinto Basin Road,** which stretches to the southeast and crosses the transition zone between the Colorado and Mojave Deserts.

If you plan to explore the park by mountain bike, avoid the main paved roads, which are narrow and without shoulders. Look instead to the park's dirt roads, many of which, like those in **Hidden** and **Queen Valley,** date from the area's 19th-century homestead and gold-mining era. Be sure to acquire reliable route information from headquarters, however, as soft sand and occasional steep climbs can make for arduous pedaling.

EXPLORING THE PARK

Park Boulevard: 64 miles (including side trips); a half to full day

A scenic drive connecting the north and west entrances skirts the sparse Colorado low desert ecosystem, then climbs into the Joshua tree forest and its surrounding plateau of mammoth rocks. Begin at the **Oasis Visitor Center** in Twentynine Palms. Or, if entering from the south, begin at the **Cottonwood Visitor Center** and follow Pinto Basin Road north and east. Both visitor centers provide insights into how plants and animals survive the region's withering heat and aridity, and how its unusual geology was formed, though the Oasis Visitor Center's interpretive displays are more extensive.

The Oasis Visitor Center adjoins the **Oasis of Mara,** a cluster of fan palms (the only palms native to the Southwest desert), Fremont cottonwood, arrow weed, and mesquite shrubs watered by a seeping spring. Take the half-mile path to this scruffy bit of green, which once sustained Native American encampments and later slaked the thirst of prospectors and homesteaders. A minute's stroll leads to a shady respite amid the chatter of birds. (Bird-watchers may want to include a visit to **Cottonwood Springs,** an oasis sheltering many species and located about a mile from the Cottonwood Visitor Center at the south entrance.)

If your schedule allows a full day's visit, take time for short walks along nature trails that offer close-up looks at plant and animal life, or interesting terrain. *(Park brochures describe trail highlights.)* Consider starting early; sunlight playing across Joshua Tree's granite monoliths, peaks, and basins accentuates their contours and colors—especially at dawn and sunset—when rocks are aglow in warm pinks and yellows. On weekends, ask at a visitor center about ranger-led campfire talks, walks, and tours, or check campground bulletin boards.

Continue south from Twentynine Palms on Park Boulevard to the North Entrance Station. The road climbs, skirting the Pinto Mountains that rise to the east. Where the pavement forks *(after about 5 miles),* bear left onto **Pinto Basin Road.** You'll soon enter Wilson Canyon and the transition zone, where the Mojave and Colorado Desert ecosystems join. The sweep of Pinto Basin trending east is in fact an ancient dry lake bed, and a typical Sonoran Desert landscape dominated by the pale creosote bush.

Stroll through the **Cholla Cactus Garden,** a picturesque cluster about 6.5 miles south of the fork and threaded by a short nature

Barrel cactuses

trail interestingly keyed to self-guiding brochures provided there. Known as "jumping" cholla for the tendency of its spiny joints to break off and cling to hapless passersby, the crooked-arm cactus appears velvety but is actually covered by tiny, sharp bristles.

Continue southeast about 2 miles to the **Ocotillo Patch,** where hundreds of the spindly Sonoran Desert plants seem to languish, their rigid gray spines wobbling skyward. After rains in March and April, their tips flame with dense bouquets of blood-red flowers, a lifesaver for hummingbirds migrating north from Mexico (and a highlight of the flowering calendar).

Backtrack northwest to the White Tank Campground and the **Arch Rock Nature Trail.** The easy 0.3-mile path to Arch Rock features interpretive information on how the surrounding geology and the natural arch were formed.

At the fork, turn left to rejoin Park Boulevard and enter the Mojave high desert. Westbound, you'll see mammoth granite formations rising from a sandy plateau. Some 800 million years in the making, worn by eons of weather into the contours of melting ice cream, the **Jumbo Rocks** are a product of this region's seismic restlessness—tectonic tumult evidenced by frequent small temblors that affect the flow of springs watering the park's oases.

Here visitors will likely see climbers scaling the monoliths, for Joshua Tree National Park contains one of America's most accessible, yet challenging, rock-climbing areas. Guidelines designed for safety and the protection of rock surfaces govern climbing within the park. Spectators gather in parking areas to watch the equipment-laden enthusiasts struggle hand over hand up seemingly impossible routes.

Keep an eye out for aptly named **Skull Rock,** which flanks the road as you continue west toward **Hidden Valley,** a scenic garden of huge piled-up boulders resembling animals, human faces, and abstract forms. A popular picnic and camping area, this part of Joshua Tree is heavily populated by the park's trademark branching yucca. Named by early Mormon settlers who saw in its uplifted arms a symbol of the biblical supplicant Joshua, *Yucca brevifolia* can reach 50 feet in height over a life span that may exceed 200 years. Some 25 bird species find protected nesting spots between its short, spiky leaves.

The 1.25-mile **Hidden Valley Trail** follows a circuitous path through a stony maze to a "hidden" bowl where, according to local lore, rustlers once hid with their stolen cattle. The northern portion of this loop requires some scrambling. Also in the Hidden Valley area, the **Desert Queen Ranch** makes a great stop for families. Ranger-led tours show kids what it was like to homestead in America's outback, where families shared bath water once each week. William Keys, arrived in 1910 and acquired the Desert Queen Mine as payment for back wages. Located between Hidden Valley Campground and Barker Dam, Keys's ranch house, schoolhouse, and collection of memorabilia can be visited on the 90-minute tour *(760-367-5555. Fee, reservations recommended).*

There are other worthwhile hiking trails throughout this area, including the scenic 16-mile **Boy Scout Trail**—the trailhead is just west of Hidden Valley Campground—and **Ryan Mountain Trail,** a steep but rewarding 3-mile trek to the top of this 5,461-foot peak. From the top of Ryan, you can see the valleys of the park, and also see the murky edges of smog creeping over the mountains to the west. The encroaching human presence can also be seen by taking take the 6-mile scenic drive up to **Keys View.** Just short of a mile high (5,185 feet), the mountaintop is the park's premier vantage point for motorists. Clear days afford a splendid southerly panorama of Coachella Valley farmlands, the Salton Sea, and Sonoran Desert mountains in Mexico. Across the valley looms 10,804-foot Mount Jacinto, towering above Palm Springs.

Park Boulevard continues northwest through the Joshua tree forest to the West Entrance Station and the town of Joshua Tree.

Unpaved spur roads lead from Park Boulevard to various rewarding spots for visitors with mountain bikes, vehicles with high clearance, or four-wheel drive. If you have four-wheel drive, you might consider taking the 18-mile round-trip **Geology Tour Road,** which turns south off Park Boulevard just west of Jumbo Rocks and explores **Pleasant Valley.** Informative stops are numbered at intervals along the route. You can pick up a brochure at the visitor center or at the head of the road.

Desert Tortoise

A generation ago, you'd see the distinctive, yellowish rectangular shields of the desert tortoise shell all over the Mojave Desert. But the tortoises' diet of desert grasses has been curtailed by the continuing disappearance of habitat. Many have fallen prey to an upper respiratory tract infection and young turtles are hunted down by ravens. They are now listed as a threatened species.

It is against the law to handle these creatures. Under dire circumstances, such as a tortoise on a highway, you may move it just off the road. Approach the tortoise slowly; if you spook one, it may void its essential water. For advice, call Joshua Tree Tortoise Rescue *(760-369-1235).*

INFORMATION & ACTIVITIES

Headquarters
74485 National Park Dr.
Twentynine Palms, CA 92277
760-367-5500
www.nps.gov/jotr

Visitor & Information Centers
Oasis Visitor Center, off
Calif. 62 near Twentynine
Palms and the north entrance.
Cottonwood Visitor Center,
off I-10 at south entrance. Both
visitor centers open daily.

Seasons & Accessibility
Open year-round.

Entrance Fees
$10 per vehicle, good for seven
consecutive days; $25 for
annual pass.

Pets
Permitted on leashes. Not
allowed on trails or in backcountry (more than 100 yards
from the road). Must be
attended at all times.

Facilities for Disabled
The Oasis Visitor Center's
interpretive displays, garden,
and bookstore are all wheelchair accessible, as are the
quarter- and half-mile loop
trails to the adjoining Oasis of
Mara. The Keys View wheelchair viewpoint is just below
the summit. The Cap Rock

Nature Trail *(half-mile loop
from parking area)* and the
Bajada Nature Trail *(quarter-
mile loop)* are also wheelchair
accessible. No campsites are
officially accessible, however
the Belle or White Tank camping areas have accessible
restrooms.

Things to Do
Free ranger-led activities held
weekends year-round, including
tours to Keys Ranch homestead.
Also, interpretive exhibits, self-
guided cactus garden trails,
auto touring, bicycling *(on
established roads only)*, hiking,
rock climbing, horseback
riding on approved trails, bird-
watching. All-terrain vehicles
and off-road motorized travel
and bicycling prohibited.

Special Advisories
■ Always carry water, even on
short hikes. Recommended:
one gallon per person per day,
two gallons if hiking.
■ Campfires are prohibited in
the backcountry. Collecting
vegetation is prohibited, so
bring your own firewood for
campground fires.
■ Rock climbers should regard
all fixed protection found in
place as unsafe.
■ Use extreme caution around
old mine workings. Never enter

abandoned tunnels or shafts.

■ Hikers should carry a compass and a good topographic map. Established trails can be obscured, and park landscapes have few prominent features. Even experienced backcountry hikers sometimes find the park disorienting.

■ Archaeological sites and remains may not be disturbed in any way.

■ Climbing within 50 feet of Native American rock art is prohibited.

■ Registration required for backcountry camping; permit required for those with horses *(760-367-5545)*.

■ Avoid camping in washes, which are subject to flash floods, from even distant mountain cloudbursts.

Campgrounds

Nine campgrounds, all with 14-day limit from September through May, and a 30-day limit from June through August. Open all year on first come, first served basis. Fees for individuals and groups up to six: None to $10. Group camping (site maximums vary from 20 to 70) available at Cottonwood, Indian Cove, and Sheep Pass by reservation only. Call the National Parks Reservation Service *(800-365-2267. http://res ervations.nps.gov)*. Fees from $10 to $30. Horses permitted at Black Rock.

Hotels, Motels, & Inns

(Unless otherwise noted, rates are for two persons in a double room, high season.)

In Twentynine Palms, CA 92277:

■ **Best Western Gardens Motel** 71487 Twentynine Palms Hwy. 760-367-9141 or 800-528-1234. 84 units, 12 with kitchenettes. $85. AC, pool, spa.

■ **Motel 6** 72562 Twentynine Palms Hwy. 760-367-2833 or 800-466-8356. 124 units. $50. AC, pool.

In Indio, CA 92201:

■ **Quality Inn** 43-505 Monroe St. 760-347-4044. 62 units. $69–$99. AC, pool, spa.

■ **Royal Plaza Inn** 82-347 Hwy. 111. 760-347-0911 or 800-228-9559. 99 units. $69–$110. AC, pool, restaurant.

In Yucca Valley, CA. 92284:

■ **Oasis of Eden Inn & Suites** 56377 Twentynine Palms Hwy. 760-365-6321 or 800-606-6686. 40 units. $70–$199. AC, pool, spa.

For other accommodations, contact Twentynine Palms Chamber of Commerce, 6455 Mesquite Ave., Unit A, Twentynine Palms, CA 92277. 760-367-3445.

Excursions from Joshua Tree

Anza-Borrego Desert State Park

60 miles south of Joshua Tree

New to the desert? At first you may be dismayed by the seeming emptiness of Anza-Borrego. The park sprawls across more than 900 square miles of rock and grit, and hundreds of washes and canyons. But soon the vast space, the pure light, and the silence flood your soul—healing antidotes to the noise of civilization.

The "empty" park turns out to contain riches—oases of palm trees, bighorn sheep, and eroded badlands. Paradoxically much of the park's terrain was shaped by the one element of nature conspicuous by its absence: water. A desert cloudburst can deepen a canyon by a few feet in just a few hours.

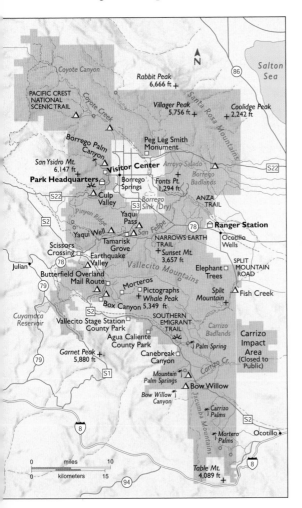

Spring is the time of year to see this desert at its showy best. But good timing is vital when it comes to catching the primroses, sand verbenas, and ocotillos in bloom. Between February and April, the blossoms start to open, depending on elevation, rainfall, and weather. They usually peak in March. To receive a personal alert about the wildflower season, send a self-addressed, stamped postcard to the park. Naturalists will mail it back about two weeks before the desert bursts into full flower.

Humans have dwelled in this desert for more than 5,000 years. Native Americans left petroglyphs and pictographs on rock walls. The first outsiders to see the region were a party of Spaniards led by Juan Bautista de Anza in 1774. The park takes its name from Anza, and from the Spanish word for "lamb," *borrego,* referring to desert bighorn sheep.

To explore, approach the **visitor center** *(2 miles W of Borrego Springs on Palm Canyon Dr.)* from any of several scenic routes: Montezuma Valley Road (Rte. S22) from the west, Borrego-Salton Seaway (Rte. S22) from the east, or Rte. S2 from the southeast.

The underground center presents two slide programs and information on the park's 60 species of mammals, 225 birds, and 60 reptiles and amphibians. In the gardens outside grow native shrubs and trees (helpfully identified), and a pond contains endangered desert pupfish, Ice Age holdovers that can live in both fresh and salty water, at temperatures from near freezing to 108°F.

The pupfish pond is at the start of the **Borrego Palm Canyon Trail** *(W end of Borrego Palm Canyon Campground).* The first mile of this trail is a self-guided walk that introduces the park's notable features—alluvial fans, ocotillos, dry washes, Cahuilla morteros (holes in boulders where Native Americans ground seeds), and scurrying lizards. Another half mile brings you to a grove of native California fan palms, whose trunks are sheathed in skirts of dead leaves that evoke Hawaiian hula dancers. Indians once ate the fruits and used the frond fibers for sandals and baskets.

Two other short trails begin at the visitor center: the **All Access Trail,** which is wheelchair accessible, and the 1.2-mile **Borrego Springs Trail** to the campground.

To explore more of the park, head east on Rte. S22. After a couple of miles you can turn north on Di Giorgio Road for a side trip to **Coyote Canyon.** *(The route is suitable only for hikers, horseback riders, and four-wheel-drive vehicles.)* Here you'll find a stream, surprisingly lush vegetation, and part of the historic Anza Trail. Farther east on Rte. S22 stands a pile of rocks called the **Peg Leg Smith Monument,** honoring a colorful, 19th-century prospector who claimed to have found a gold mine—and then lost it in the rugged terrain. The faker inspired the annual Peg Leg Liar's Contest *(held on Sat. closest to April 1);* anyone is invited to tell a tale, as long as none of it is true. Behind the monument rises Coyote Mountain, whose metamorphic rocks hold deep red garnets.

Continue to Font's Point Road for a side trip to view the gullies and ragged ridges of the **Borrego Badlands,** which were carved by countless thunderstorms. Font's Point itself is being eroded away by rain and faulting. North of Rte. S22 lies **Clark Dry Lake,** the desiccated basin of a lake that existed 20,000 years ago. Its clay bottom conceals the eggs of tadpole shrimp that hatch when flood waters penetrate the soil. Ahead rise the Santa Rosa Mountains, where rain has washed rocks and sand down from the slopes, forming classic alluvial fans. These ragged mountains are so young that they are still rising. The Santa Rosas lie along the active San Jacinto Fault.

To visit the center of the park, known as the **Yaqui Pass Triangle,** take Rte. S3 south from Borrego Springs toward Calif. 78. Along here the **Mescal Bajada Overlook** shows off a bajada (ba-HA-da), a sloping plain created when a series of alluvial fans blend together at the base of desert mountains. Just ahead, the **Cactus Loop Trail** leads you among hundreds of teddybear cholla, beavertail, and hedgehog cactuses.

At Calif. 78, turn east to the **Narrows Earth Trail,** where a short walk reveals how mighty mountains are reduced to grains of sand. In this small canyon you'll view a fault line and rocks 100 million years old.

If time permits, continue on Calif. 78 to Ocotillo Wells, then turn south on Split Mountain Road to the **Elephant Trees Nature Trail,** named for a herd of chubby trunked trees with wrinkly bark.

Another major park route is the old **Southern Emigrant Trail,** which you pick up where Rte. S2 joins Calif. 78 at Scissors Crossing. Over this trail have passed Spanish explorers, frontier scout Kit Carson, and passengers on the Butterfield Overland stage. After driving through Earthquake Valley, turn east on the marked dirt road for a side trip to the **Butterfield Overland Mail Route Historical Monument.** You'll come to **Foot and Walker Pass**—terrain so steep that stagecoach passengers had to get off and push the coach over the ridge. Here you can walk in wheel ruts dating from the 1850s. Farther along lies a short trail to morteros and a rutted spur road leading to a 1-mile trail to Native American pictographs.

Back on Rte. S2, proceed to **Box Canyon.** During the Mexican War in 1847, the Mormon Battalion conquered this dead-end canyon, using only axes and a pry bar to hack out a wagon trail.

Sunset in Anza-Borrego Desert State Park

After that, thousands of soldiers, travelers, and gold-crazed emi-
grants poured across California on the two rough trails below you.

Continue to the **Vallecito Stage Station,** originally built in 1857
and authentically reconstructed. Ahead, take a side trip on the
bumpy road to **Palm Spring,** where trails lead to oases shaded by
California fan palms. Take a moment to rest here, as stagecoach
travelers did more than 130 years ago.

One more route is the **Montezuma Valley Road** *(Rte. S22, SW of
visitor center);* turn north on the dirt road to the Culp Valley primitive camp area. A trail leads west of the campground about 0.75
mile to **Peña Spring,** whose waters lure deer, coyotes, and many
birds, including quail. Another short, marked trail leads to a lookout on the Borrego Valley and the Santa Rosa Mountains. At 3,400
feet this spot offers a retreat from the hot desert floor.

At Mountain Palm Springs in the southern corner of the park,
you'll find the **Pygmy Grove** and **Southwest Grove Trails;** the former
is a 1-mile round-trip, the latter, 2 miles.

■ **600,000 acres** ■ **Southern California, 85 miles northeast of San Diego
on Calif. 78** ■ **Best months Oct.–May** ■ **Adm. fee** ■ **Camping, hiking,
mountain biking, horseback riding, wildflower viewing, natural hot springs,
pictographs** ■ **Contact the park, 200 Palm Canyon Dr., Borrego Springs,
CA 92004; 760-767-5311. http://parks.ca.gov**

Fragrant Trees of the Desert

Although the spring bloom of the desert wildflowers gets all the press, much of the glorious fragrance that accompanies it is provided by flourish of the desert trees. Visitors to **The Living Desert Zoo and Gardens** (*Portola Avenue, Palm Desert. 760-346-5694*) can get a look (and perhaps a sniff) of all the most common species.

■ **Blue paloverde** (*Cercidium floridum*) has a pale green trunk, spiny olive-green twigs, and sparse foliage. Short and willowy, it is often found along stream and wash banks, performing a vital service in preventing erosion. Once a year it bursts into bright yellow bloom. Desert burros can be seen champing on its soft wood in stupid delight.

■ **Desert smoketree** (*Dalea spinosa*) is one of the great landscape treasures of the Palm Springs area. It owes its mystical image—a fog-shrouded tangle of wooden antlers—to its evanescent foliage. Until its third year its twigs are thickly coated with gray hairs, which explains the tree's ghostly appearance under the summer moon. It flowers precisely in the dead heat of summer, when tourists have departed.

■ **Desert catalpa** (*Chilopsis linearis*) was once used to make hunting bows. Fittingly known as the bow willow, it has long, thin, light green leaves and is willow-like in appearance. It often stands—hunches, rather—over washed-out culverts and ditches throughout the Colorado Desert. Its remarkable flowers are showy pink spikes with white and yellow spots in the throat. Later in the summer the heat draws out their subtle fragrance, like that of sweet violets.

■ **Desert ironwood** (*Olneya tesota*) more than lives up to its name. With a specific gravity of 1.14, a piece of it will sink in water. Its notable red-brown bark peels in long downward strips, and it has gray leaves. If you are in the desert in early summer you will witness its remarkable flowering, a flourish of thousands of indigo and rose-purple blooms with a subtle perfume.

■ **True mesquite** (*Prosopis juliflora*) is among the Colorado Desert's dominant flora. It has dark, reddish brown bark and slim, smooth twigs like tendrils waving at the bottom of the sea. Its usefulness to a range of inhabitants is legendary. Its scent—piney and smoky— is the desert's own.

Salton Sea

13 miles south of Joshua Tree

The Salton Sea is the product of a colossal accident: In 1905 an irrigation dike on the Colorado River gave way and, over the course of two years, poured water into the arid Imperial Valley creating the largest lake in California.

Centuries ago, the Colorado River fed into a much larger lake that reached to the base of the Santa Rosa Mountains in the west. When the Colorado changed course around 1500, rerouting itself to the Gulf of California, the lake dried up and disappeared. Four hundred years later, the water was back, and birds came with it. The rich habitat around the southern end of the lake harbors many birds, and a 1,785-acre **wildlife refuge** created here in 1930 is now an important stop on the Pacific flyway.

But there are problems here, and they underline how unnatural is this desert lake that sits on the San Andreas Fault 232 feet below sea level. With no outlet the lake's water evaporates in the broiling heat and leaves its minerals behind. It is saltier now than the Pacific Ocean and is growing more so all the time. Water still flows into the Salton Sea, but not directly from the Colorado; rather, it filters through farm fields and arrives loaded with impurities. There is so much agricultural runoff that the lake has risen, gradually drowning the marshes of the refuge where birds feed. Refuge managers have been forced to plant crops for the birds.

The pale blue lake stretches north for 35 miles into a treeless desert landscape, which seems not to discourage boaters, anglers, or swimmers. Generally, the water at the north end of the lake is cleaner. The fish in the lake are introduced species, including sargo, orangemouth, corvina, and Gulf croaker from the Gulf of California and the popular sport fish tilapia, which was brought in from the neighboring irrigation canals.

Check with officials at the refuge or **Salton Sea State Recreation Area** *(North Shore. 760-393-3052. http://parks.ca.gov. Adm. fee)* on the northeast side of the lake for health advisories regarding swimming or eating fish. Various bacteria and viruses, including avian botulism, have affected fish and bird health in recent years.

■ **380 square miles** ■ **Southern California near Mexican border** ■ **Best months Oct.–June** ■ **Camping, hiking, boating, fishing, bird-watching** ■ **Contact Sonny Bono Salton Sea National Wildlife Refuge, 906 W. Sinclair Rd., Calipatria, CA 92233; 760-348-5278**

Mesa Verde

At Mesa Verde, Spanish for "green table," ancient multi-storied dwellings fill the cliff-rock alcoves that rise 2,000 feet above Montezuma Valley. Unique for their number and remarkable preservation, the cliff dwellings cluster in sandstone canyons that slice the mesa into narrow tablelands fingering southward. Here, and on the mesa top, archaeologists have located some 600 dwellings dating from about A.D. 550 to 1300.

The sites, from mesa-top pit houses and multistoried dwellings to cliffside villages, document the dramatic changes in the lives of a prehistoric people that archaeologists once dubbed the Anasazi. They are now more accurately called the ancestral Puebloans, and 24 Native American tribes in the Southwest today consider themselves descendants of these ancestral people. Some 40 pueblos and cliff dwellings are visible from park roads and overlooks; many of these are open to the public.

Beginning about A.D. 750, the ancestral Puebloans grouped their dwellings in mesa-top pueblos, or villages. About 1200 they moved down into recesses in the cliffs. Massive overhanging rock has so sheltered these later villages that they seem to stand outside of time, aloof to the present. In 1888 two cowboys tracking stray cattle through snow stopped on the edge of a steep-walled canyon. Through the drifting flakes they could make out traces of walls and towers of a great cliff dwelling across the canyon. Novelist Willa Cather, a later visitor, described the scene: "The falling snowflakes sprinkling the piñons, gave it a special kind of solemnity. It was more like sculpture than anything else…preserved …like a fly in amber."

Climbing down a makeshift ladder to the deserted city, the excited cowboys explored the honeycombed network of rooms that they named Cliff Palace. Inside, they found stone tools and pottery and other artifacts. Later investigators

- Southwest corner of Colorado
- 52,122 acres
- Established 1906
- Best seasons mid-May–mid-Oct.
- Camping, hiking, archaeological tours
- Information: 970-529-4465 www.nps.gov/meve

Cliff Palace, Mesa Verde National Park

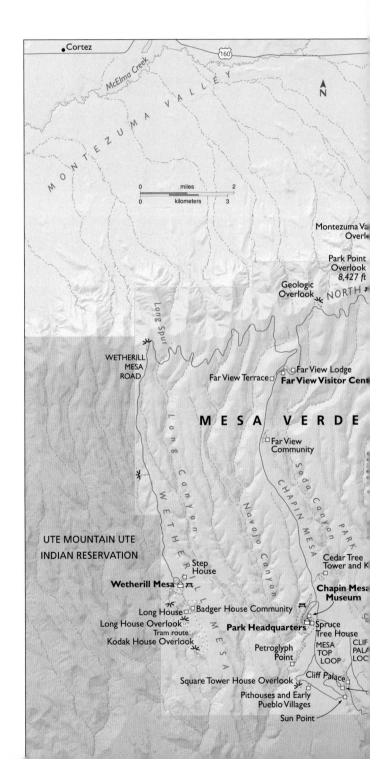

Cortez

160

McElmo Creek

MONTEZUMA VALLEY

MONTEZUMA

N

miles 2
kilometers 3

Montezuma Va
Overl

Park Point
Overlook
8,427 ft

Geologic
Overlook

NORTH

Long Spur

WETHERILL
MESA
ROAD

Far View Terrace

Far View Lodge

Far View Visitor Cent

MESA VERDE

Far View
Community

Long Canyon

Soda Canyon

CHAPIN MESA

PARK

WETHER

Navajo Canyon

UTE MOUNTAIN UTE
INDIAN RESERVATION

Step
House

Cedar Tree
Tower and K

Wetherill Mesa

Chapin Mesa
Museum

Long House

Badger House Community

Long House Overlook
Tram route
Kodak House Overlook

Park Headquarters

Spruce
Tree House

MESA
TOP
LOOP

CLIF
PALA
LOC

Petroglyph
Point

Square Tower House Overlook

Cliff Palace

Pithouses and Early
Pueblo Villages

Sun Point

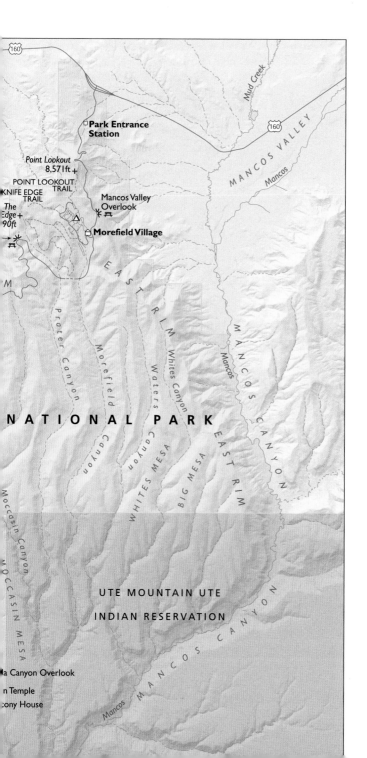

160

Mud Creek

Park Entrance
Station

160

MANCOS VALLEY

Mancos

Point Lookout
8,571ft +

POINT LOOKOUT
TRAIL

KNIFE EDGE
TRAIL

The
Edge +
90ft

Mancos Valley
Overlook

Morefield Village

E A S T   R I M

Prater Canyon

Morefield Canyon

Whites Canyon

Waters Canyon

Mancos

M A N C O S   C A N Y O N

N A T I O N A L   P A R K

WHITES MESA

BIG MESA

E A S T   R I M

Moccasin Canyon

M O C C A S I N   M E S A

UTE MOUNTAIN UTE

INDIAN RESERVATION

MANCOS CANYON

Canyon Overlook

Temple

cony House

Mancos

learned that these rooms had been uninhabited for some seven centuries.

Why the Mesa Verde people eventually left their homes may never be known. Indeed, they lived in the cliffside dwellings for only about the last 75 to 100 years of their occupation of Mesa Verde. Early observers guessed warfare, and the evidence for this is still being debated. Archaeologists also think they may have been victims of their own success. Their productive dry farming allowed their populations to grow perhaps as high as 5,000. Gradually woodlands were cut, wild game hunted out, and soils depleted. Years of drought and poor crops may have been aggravated by village squabbles. By the end of the 13th century the ancestral Puebloans had left the plateau, never to return.

How to Get There

From Cortez, take US 160 east for 8 miles to the entrance of the park, then follow the winding park road 15 miles to Far View Visitor Center and 5.5 miles farther to park headquarters area, which includes the museum and main cliff dwellings. Trailers prohibited past Morefield Village. Airports: Cortez and Durango, Colo.

What Not to Miss

- Chapin Mesa Museum
- Petroglyph Point Trail
- Cliff Palace overlook from Mesa Top Loop Road
- View from Square Tower House
- Sun Point Overlook
- Ranger-led cliff dwelling tour
- Stargazing from Mancos Overlook

When to Go

All-year park. Wetherill Mesa, Far View Visitor Center, Cliff Palace Loop, Balcony House, and many services are closed in winter. Wildflowers bloom from April through September. In winter, cross-country skiing is allowed on parts of Mesa Top Road when conditions permit.

How to Visit

On a 1-day visit, begin early and stop first at the **Far View Visitor Center,** open mid-April to mid-October, to purchase tickets. Then go to the **Chapin Mesa Museum** for an overview; and then visit nearby **Spruce Tree House.** From there take the Cliff Palace Loop of **Mesa Top Road.** In the afternoon, follow the **Mesa Top Loop.**

EXPLORING THE PARK

Chapin Mesa Museum & Spruce Tree House:
2 hours to a half day

Before descending to the sites, go through the **Chapin Mesa Museum,** located at the Spruce Tree House Trailhead and park headquarters area. Here you pick up self-guiding booklets to the major sites and view a 25-minute video. Excellent dioramas bring to life the changing world of the Mesa Verde people. Also displayed are some of the Southwest's finest artifacts and Native arts and crafts. During summer, pick up a self-guiding booklet to **Spruce Tree House** and walk the paved quarter-mile trail to the park's best preserved site.

Here you will see the skillful building techniques and stonework of the ancestral Puebloans; 90 percent of the stonework is original. Rangers will be on duty to answer questions. *(Mid-Nov.–early March, when the park is less crowded, rangers lead guided tours.)* The cliff dwelling, built in an alcove more than 200 feet wide, housed 60 to 100 people. Three of its eight kivas—underground ceremonial rooms—have reconstructed roofs. At one of them, you may climb down the ladder through the smoke hole into the dark chamber below. Either now or later—if time and stamina allow—take the 2.8-mile **Petroglyph Point Trail,** a self-guided nature walk that branches off the Spruce Tree House Trail. Register and pick up a guidebook at the trailhead. The trail offers a good place to stretch your legs, familiarize yourself with plants and their prehistoric uses, and see one of the park's largest petroglyphs, a panel 12 feet across.

Mesa Top Loop Road: **12 miles; a half day**

Dotted with wayside interpretive exhibits, two 6-mile loops wind through Chapin Mesa's fire-scarred pinyon-juniper woodland. If you purchased tickets, begin your tour by turning onto the Cliff Palace Loop and driving to the parking area at **Cliff Palace.** A short trail takes you to a striking view of the largest cliff dwelling in North America: The 150-room site once housed more than a hundred people. A park ranger will meet you at the overlook and guide you down a quarter-mile trail to tour the dwelling.

Continue driving to the **Balcony House** parking area. This 40-room dwelling is one of the highlights of the park. But it is not for everyone. Rangers guide adventurous groups up a 32-foot ladder to an easily defended ledge site and a panoramic view of Soda Canyon. To leave Balcony House, you must crawl through a tunnel on your hands and knees.

Keep going along the road to its junction with the **Mesa Top Loop** and turn left. The road and its trails lead to **Square Tower House,** the park's tallest dwelling; the **Late Pithouse** and **Early Pueblo Sites,** examples of Mesa Verde's earliest permanent dwellings; and **Sun Point Overlook,** which offers views of a dozen cliff dwellings. Last, stop to scratch your head over **Sun Temple,** an enigmatic, D-shaped structure built by skilled masons but never inhabited. Archaeologists speculate it may have been a ceremonial center or perhaps an observatory.

Wetherill Mesa: **13 miles; a half day or more**

Accessible only in summer, the **Wetherill Mesa Road** starts on the west side of Far View Visitor Center, where you stop to purchase tickets for the 1.5-hour tour of **Long House.** The steep road takes you to sites opened to the public in 1972 after an extensive archae-

Long House, Wetherill Mesa

ological study. Under sponsorship of the National Geographic Society and National Park Service, several major cliff dwellings and mesa-top sites were excavated.

Drive to the kiosk area and park. From here take the half-mile, self-guided walk to **Step House,** named for its prehistoric stairway. The site is unusual, for pit houses have been uncovered next to a multistoried pueblo built in the same alcove. Return to the kiosk area and take the mini-train to the head of **Long House Trail.** Rangers lead groups down the quarter-mile trail to the park's second largest cliff dwelling—150 rooms with 21 kivas, an unusually high number. Gustaf Nordenskiöld, a Swedish scientist, excavated portions of Long House and other sites in 1891, publishing the first scientific report on Mesa Verde.

You can extend your visit by taking the mini-train to the half-mile, self-guided trail that threads through the sites of **Badger House Community.** These excavated pit houses and pueblos show the contrast between life on the mesa top and that in the canyon alcoves below. The mini-train will return you to the kiosk area.

INFORMATION & ACTIVITIES

Headquarters
P.O. Box 8
Mesa Verde, CO 81330
970-529-4465
www.nps.gov/meve

Visitor & Information Centers
Far View Visitor Center at northwest section of park open daily mid-May to mid-October. Chapin Mesa Museum at southern end of park, located 21 miles from entrance, open daily year-round.

Seasons & Accessibility
Park is open year-round, but most visitor facilities and services are available from the middle of May to the middle of October only. Spruce Tree House open all year; Cliff Palace open early April to early November; Balcony House open mid-May to mid-October; Wetherill Mesa open summer only. During the winter, snow or ice may prompt the park to close Mesa Top Road. For current weather and road conditions, contact headquarters.

Entrance Fees
$10 per car per week. Additional tickets required for tours of Cliff Palace, Balcony House, and Long House; available at Far View Visitor Center for a small fee.

Pets
Permitted on leashes, not in buildings, in sites, or on trails.

Facilities for Disabled
Visitor center, museum, half-mile trail at Wetherill Mesa, some campsites, and most rest rooms are wheelchair accessible. Site tours are not accessible, but most major cliff dwellings can be viewed from the mesa-top roads and overlooks. Free brochure.

Things to Do
Ranger-led activities: archaeological walks, tours of Balcony House (spring–fall), Spruce Tree House (fall–spring), and Long House (summer only); evening campfire programs. Also available: wayside exhibits, archaeological museum, self-guided tours, and limited hiking (registration required for two trails), cross-country skiing, and snowshoeing.

Special Advisories
■ Visits to the cliff dwellings are strenuous. Wear sturdy shoes and use caution, especially if you have heart or respiratory problems.
■ Hold onto your children on cliff trails and canyon rims.
■ Backcountry camping is not allowed in the park.

Campgrounds

One campground, Morefield, with a 14-day limit. Open mid-April to mid-October. First come, first served. Fees $19–$25 per night. Showers within 1 mile of campground. Tent and RV sites; 14 hookups. Morefield Group Campgrounds available first come, first served. Food services in park (mid-April–mid-Oct.).

Hotels, Motels, & Inns

(Unless otherwise noted, rates are for two persons in a double room, high season.)

INSIDE THE PARK

■ **Far View Lodge** Mesa Verde Co., P.O. Box 277, Mancos, CO 81328. 800-449-2288. 150 units. $101–$113. Restaurant. Open mid-April to mid-March.

OUTSIDE THE PARK
In Cortez, CO 81321:
■ **Anasazi Motor Inn** 640 S. Broadway. 970-565-3773 or 800-972-6232. 86 units. $50–$71. AC, pool, restaurant. www.AnasaziMotorinn.com.
■ **Best Western Sands** 1120 E. Main St. 970-565-3761 or 800-528-1234. 80 units. $62–$102. AC, pool. www.bestwestern .com.
■ **Best Western Turquoise Inn and Suites** 535 E. Main St. 970-565-3778 or 800-547-3376. 77 units. $80–$129. AC, pool.

■ **Econolodge** 2020 E. Main 970-565-3474 or 800-424-6423. 70 rooms. $36–$89. AC, pool.

In Durango, CO 81301:
■ **Strater Hotel** 699 Main Ave. 970-247-4431 or 800-247-4431. 93 units. $139–$205. AC, restaurant. www.strater.com.
■ **General Palmer Hotel** 567 Main Ave. 970-247-4747 or 800-523-3358. 39 rooms, including suites, $98–$275. Victorian hotel, AC. www .gphdurango@yahoo.com.
■ **Budget Inn** 3077 Main Ave. 970-247-5222 or 800-257-5222. 35 rooms. $37–$118. AC, pool, hot tub. www.budgeinndur ango.com.

In Mancos, CO 81328:
■ **Mesa Verde Motel** 191 Railroad Ave., P.O. Box 552. 970-533-7741 or 800-825-6372. 15 units. $59. AC, hot tub.

For further suggestions, contact the Cortez Chamber of Commerce at 970-565-3414; or the Durango Chamber of Commerce at 800-525-8855.

Excursions from Mesa Verde

San Juan Mountains

25 miles northeast of Mesa Verde

Try to condense the most satisfying vacation of your life into a single sentence and you'll know what it's like to sum up the San Juans, the largest mountain range in the American Rockies. Plain and simple, you would be hard pressed to find a more awe-inspiring collection of peaks, wilderness areas, hikes, drives—and even towns—than you'll discover in this southwestern corner of Colorado. A day in the San Juans may begin at dawn with the climb of a Fourteener, continue with a soak in natural hot springs, and end with a plate of crawfish étouffée at a Cajun restaurant. Though this area is increasingly popular, it's still possible to spend long days roaming the wilds without ever feeling crowded.

The San Juans remain a wild range; here you'll find six federal preserves, totaling nearly one-third of Colorado's three million acres of federally designated wilderness. **Lizard Head Wilderness** (41,193 acres) flanks the western edge of the San Juans near Telluride. **Mount Sneffels Wilderness** (16,565 acres) and its neighbor, the **Uncompahgre Wilderness** (102,721 acres), both lie outside Ouray. Farther east, near Creede, you'll find **La Garita Wilderness** (128,158 acres). To the south, the 158,790-acre **South San Juan Wilderness** beckons with 180 miles of lightly used trails. Finally, the **Weminuche Wilderness** (487,912 acres) sprawls along the range's southwest flanks.

Much of this sublime alpine terrain is tied together by 86 miles of the **Continental Divide Trail,** accessible from various points including Wolf Creek Pass near Pagosa Springs and the Molas Pass Area south of Silverton.

Exploring by Vehicle

The **San Juan Skyway** *(see pp. 278–280)* makes a 236-mile loop through the mountains and high deserts of the San Juan region, sampling a wide variety of habitats and terrains.

Another good route, designed primarily for four-wheel-drive vehicles, is the 65-mile **Alpine Loop Byway.** This figure-eight drive circles two volcanic calderas and passes some abandoned tramways and mill sites. It also climbs Cinnamon Pass to views of three Fourteeners: Handies (14,048 feet), Redcloud (14,034 feet), and Sunshine (14,001 feet). The loop is accessed in Ouray from US 550,

in Silverton from Colo. 110, and in Lake City from Colo. 149. Each of these towns offers jeep rentals and guides. An excellent guidebook to the route is *Alpine Explorer,* available from the San Juan Mountains Association *(970-385-1210).*

Hiking in the Weminuche Wilderness

Colorado's largest and perhaps most spectacular natural landscape lies in this wilderness at the heart of the San Juan Mountains. Within its soaring sweep of high country (average elevation 10,000 feet), elk graze in summer and ptarmigan stand camouflaged against the rocks of the tundra. High use has led to the prohibition of camping, campfires, and the grazing of recreational livestock in some areas, so check with the Forest Service before setting out.

If you're in the mood for a dose of the alpine, head to **Crater Lake,** a sparkling gem nestled in the trees below 13,075-foot North Twilight Peak. The 5.3-mile, one-way **Crater Lake Trail** *(Molas Pass area, S of Silverton off US 550 near Milepost 63)* climbs 1,650 feet through wildflower meadows revealing views of the area's most beautiful lakes and summits.

North of Silverton, the **Highland Mary Trail** climbs 1,650 feet in 3.5 miles and crosses numerous creeks and marshes before topping out at seven shimmering high-altitude lakes. To reach the trailhead, follow Colo. 110 east out of Silverton 5 miles to the old town of Howardsville. Turn right onto FR 589, then continue 4 miles up

Cunningham Gulch to the remains of the Highland Mary Mill. After an earnest climb of 500 feet in the first half mile, you'll reach the **Cunningham Gulch Trail;** the left fork quickly leads to the register for the **Highland Mary Trail.**

In the Pagosa Springs area, look for the **Fourmile Falls Trail,** which climbs 750 feet in 3 miles to a 300-foot "bridal veil" falls that spills over a black precipice. This relatively easy trail is suitable for all ages and passes through a mix of flower-filled meadows, stands of aspen, marshes, and the occasional dark, quiet forest of fir and spruce. To reach the trailhead from Pagosa Springs, head north onto Rte. 400 off US 160. Continue 8.4 miles, then bear right onto FR 645 (Fourmile Road) and follow it to the end. The trail starts at the parking lot.

Boating the Dolores River

Considered by many to be one of the most sublime destinations in the West, the Dolores River starts high in the San Juans near Telluride, runs south to its namesake town, then follows a curving path north to the Colorado River near Moab, Utah. Along the way, it sweeps through ponderosa pine parklands and sunbaked slickrock canyons, reveals 250 million years of geologic history, and offers excellent fishing and white-water boating for every ability.

Although most of the water from this river is diverted for irrigation, the Dolores remains one of the few southwestern rivers to host at least three different multiday trips. In early spring, when the waters from McPhee Dam are released, boaters flock to the river's two most popular canyons, Dolores and Slick Rock.

Well-known for harboring the region's most challenging rapid, Snaggletooth, **Dolores Canyon** begins sliding south with a gentle 19-mile section cradled by stands of ponderosa pines and soaring canyon walls. This quiet start to the canyon, from Bradfield Bridge to Dove Creek Pump Station, is accessed north of Cortez, Colorado, via US 666 and Rte. R16. When water flows are less than 1,000 cubic feet per second, white-water boaters bound for Snaggletooth must instead portage their rafts around this rapid and the 9 miles of churning water below it.

After leaving the tumult of Dolores Canyon, the river enters sculpted sandstone near the tiny town of Slick Rock, Colorado. Aptly named, **Slick Rock Canyon** is a twisted run through multicolored rock. Most boaters allow 3 days to travel this 48-mile section, then take out at the small village of Bedrock.

Access to Slick Rock Canyon is from Dove Creek on US 666, some 18 miles north on Colo. 141. Bedrock sits in the Paradox Valley, near the Utah state line, on Colo. 90. For information about water releases and boating requirements, call 970-385-1354; for current water flow information, call 800-276-4828; for estimated release dates, check out www.doloreswater.com.

■ **10,000 square miles** ■ **Southwestern Colorado** ■ **Best months Jan.–Feb., July–Aug.** ■ **Camping, hiking, backpacking, mountain climbing, boating, fishing, mountain biking, horseback riding, cross-country skiing, snowshoeing, wildflower viewing, scenic drives** ■ **Contact San Juan National Forest, 15 Burnett Ct., Durango, CO 81301; 970-247-4874. www.fs.fed.us/r2/sanjuan**

Chimney Rock Archaeological Area

Driving through the green sweep of ranchland between Pagosa Springs and Durango, you can hardly miss it: A 7,900-foot-high sandstone spire silhouetted against the sky, centerpiece of religious practices that governed the area's ancestral Puebloans about a thousand years ago. A tour led by the San Juan Mountains Association *(970-385-1210 Oct.–mid-May; 970-883-5359 the rest of year)* is a great way to view the unique prehistoric sites that straddle the mesa in Chimney Rock Archaeological Area.

The tour visits a great kiva, an excavated village, and several unexcavated pit houses, as a guide describes the challenges ancestral Puebloans faced. You'll also learn about archaeoastronomy, and how the people who lived here conducted complex calculations based on their observations of the night sky.

A highlight is the **Great House** at the edge of the mesa, offering views of the San Juan Mountains to the east and the Piedra River Valley below, as well as **Chimney Rock** and its smaller neighbor, **Companion Rock.** This pair may have lured early religious leaders to the area, where they created the highest, most northeastern of all ancestral Puebloan sites. The dwelling was situated so that its inhabitants could watch the moon rise between the two pinnacles every 18 years.

San Juan Skyway

15 miles northeast of Mesa Verde

236 miles; 1 to 2 days As its fanciful name implies, the San Juan Skyway flirts with the heights, climbing to more than 10,000 feet three times as it charts a ragged loop through the mountains and high deserts of southwestern Colorado. Starting a few miles from Cortez, this spectacular route heads north into the heart of the San Juans, pausing at Telluride, and then descending to Ridgway. From there, the route bends south over the crest of the San Juans and passes through the historic mining towns of Ouray and Silverton. It drops into red-rock canyons near Durango, then sails west across the desert to Mesa Verde.

Just east of Cortez, turn north onto Colo. 145 for 7.5 miles, then turn left onto Colo. 184 to visit the **Anasazi Heritage Center** *(970-882-4811),* an innovative museum depicting the evolution of the ancestral Puebloan culture. Self-guided trails lead to ruins.

Back on Colo. 145, you follow the Dolores River *(see pp. 276–77)* into the San Juan Mountains. About 10 miles from Rico,

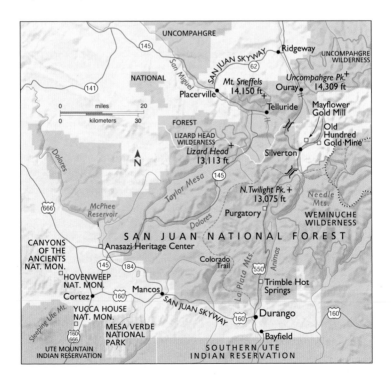

Durango-Silverton train

13,113-foot Lizard Head Peak appears off to the left—an isolated column of rock jutting from a broad, rounded mountaintop. A couple of miles farther, pull over at **Lizard Head Pass,** 10,222 feet, for an incredible view of the toothy San Juan crest, which soars 3,000 feet above the road.

Below the pass, the road stops at a T-intersection. Turn right to visit the booming ski town of **Telluride,** which boasts a magnificent downtown district of Victorian buildings plus a 365-foot waterfall that spills from the cliffs behind town.

From Telluride, Colo. 145 and the San Miguel River burrow down through sedimentary layers into a canyon lined by vermilion sandstone cliffs. At Placerville turn right on Colo. 62 and climb 11 miles to the **Dallas Divide.** As you top the pass, a spine of naked rock heaves into view, slicing upward from gentle foothills. Most of these San Juan peaks exceed 12,000 feet.

From the divide, glide back down to Ridgway, at the base of

14,150-foot Mount Sneffels, then continue south along US 550 and the Uncompahgre River toward a deep cleft in the mountain front. At **Ouray,** multicolored cliffs squeeze the valley against the base of 14,000-foot peaks. Consider soaking at **Ouray Hot Springs** *(970-325-7073)* or visiting to **Box Canyon Falls,** a spectacular plume of white water that drops from the cliffs above town.

From Ouray, US 550 switchbacks up into the mountains along the flank of **Uncompahgre Gorge.** There's no bracing yourself for what comes just beyond top the rim of the gorge. There, vivid red peaks burst into view, with broad smears of orange and red gravel streaming down their flanks into the dark surrounding evergreens. The road climbs nearly to tree line before arriving at 11,075-foot **Red Mountain Pass,** then drops into **Silverton.**

Incorporated in 1876, Silverton retains its rickety historic look. While you knock around town, the **Durango & Silverton Narrow Gauge Railroad** *(970-247-2733)* might come chuffing up the valley on one of several daily runs between Silverton and Durango.

Continue south on US 550 to **Molas Pass,** with its fine view of the West Needle Mountains, the Grenadier Range, and other peaks rising over tiny Molas Lake. The road winds along the contours of the mountains for several miles to Coal Bank Pass, then tilts downward and drops 4,000 feet in elevation to the plateau and canyon country around **Durango.**

The cliffs give out before you arrive in Durango, an 1880s railroad town that boomed while the San Juan mines were in full swing. Elegant brick and stone Victorian buildings line its downtown streets. At the end of Main Street, you'll find the yellow 1882 train depot, a historic landmark and starting point for the narrow-gauge railroad to Silverton.

From Durango, follow US 160 west through a rolling terrain of minor canyons and mesas. The La Plata Mountains rise to the north over a dark forest of low-growing trees. After about 23 miles the broad dome of **Sleeping Ute Mountain** appears on the western horizon. **Mesa Verde** stands to the left. You pass Mancos and drive about 8 miles across a flat, grassy plain to Mesa Verde National Park and Cortez.

■ Southwest Colorado ■ Best months June–Oct. ■ Camping, hiking, boating, fishing, biking ■ Contact San Juan National Forest, 15 Burnett Ct., Durango, CO 81301; 970-247-4874. www.fs.fed.us/r2/sanjuan/

Monument Valley

157 miles southwest of Mesa Verde

Few thrills compare with driving north on US 163 across the endless sagebrush and red-sand desertscape of northern Arizona and coming upon Monument Valley. Immense mesas, buttes, and pinnacles of raw sandstone rise like phantom ships on a silent sea.

The drive begins just south of Kayenta on US 163, which shoots past a 7,096-foot rock monolith named **Agathla.** Just after 6 miles, an overlook on the right offers good views of Agathla and its neighbor, **Owl Rock**—a red-sandstone formation with protruding "ears." At Milepost 15 the large formations of Monument Valley come suddenly into view.

After crossing the Utah border at Mile 21, Rte. 42B leads 4 miles east to **Monument Valley Navajo Tribal Park** *(435-727-3353. Adm. fee).* At this intersection Native Americans sell jewelry, pots, and samples of delicious Navajo fry bread. After a mile the side road dips back into Arizona and comes to the valley **visitor center,** site of a small museum, campground, gift shop, and the roadhead for a 17-mile, dirt **loop-trail** into the formations. Jeep tour operators sell off-road excursions from the parking lot, but you can also guide yourself with a booklet from the visitor center. The ride is rough,

Red-sandstone buttes of Monument Valley

and recommended for high-clearance vehicles only. **John Ford Point,** 3.5 miles along the drive, celebrates the director who filmed such Westerns as *Stagecoach* here. Three miles beyond you'll see the figures of **Totem Pole** and **Ye B Chai,** thin pinnacles that seem far too fragile to be rock.

Heading back west and crossing US 163, Rte. 42B continues to **Goulding's Lodge** *(435-727-3231),* a haunt of Ford and John Wayne when filming here. Return to US 163 and go 5 miles north to the drive's end at **Mexican Hat,** a small town on the San Juan River named for a precariously balanced rock formation reminiscent of a large sombrero.

■ **Arizona-Utah border between Kayenta, Ariz. and Mexican Hat, Utah**
■ **Best months April–Nov.; Visitor center open all year; campground open summer only** ■ **Adm. fee** ■ **Scenic drive, guided hikes** ■ **Contact the park, P.O. Box 93, Monument Valley, UT 84536; 801-727-3287**

Canyon de Chelly National Monument

141 miles southwest of Mesa Verde

One of the most famously scenic landscapes in the Southwest is found within this off-the-beaten-track national monument, managed cooperatively by the National Park Service and the Navajo Nation, within whose reservation lands it lies. In this red-rock wonderland, sheer cliffs of sandstone tower hundreds of feet over broad canyon bottoms, the walls dotted with niches containing the ruins of ancient dwellings.

Dozens of Navajo families live and farm within the park, continuing a history of occupation by Native Americans dating back at least 2,000 years. Because of this unique juxtaposition of geological wonder and living culture, travel within Canyon de Chelly (pronounced SHAY) is more limited than in most parks. Two roads wind along canyon rims, offering superb vistas, and one trail leads down to the canyon floor; otherwise, visitors must be accompanied by a Navajo guide.

Though named for its main canyon, the park also encompasses another major canyon, **Canyon del Muerto,** and smaller side canyons. Together, the main canyons form a rough V-shape with the park visitor center at its point, 3 miles east of the small town of Chinle. Exhibits and a film at the **visitor center** will provide background on the long history of the park; you can also get information here on guided tours. Most visitors take four-wheel-drive auto tours along the canyon floor, though for those with time, horseback rides afford a quieter experience.

South Rim Drive follows the rim of Canyon de Chelly for 18 miles, passing some of the park's most famous scenes along the way. Near the beginning is **Junction Overlook,** a viewpoint of the confluence of the two major canyons. A few miles farther, turn north to the trailhead for the **White House Trail,** the only place you can enter the canyon without a guide. This 2.5-mile round-trip path leads from the canyon rim 500 feet down to a ruined dwelling occupied by Puebloan people about a thousand years ago. South Rim Drive ends at the amazing spectacle of **Spider Rock,** an eroded pinnacle rising 800 feet above the canyon floor.

Side roads along the 17-mile **North Rim Drive** lead to views of several ruins, including **Mummy Cave Ruin,** one of the park's largest structures, with living and ceremonial buildings flanking a central tower, all beneath an overhanging bluff. Nearby is the overlook at **Massacre Cave,** where in 1805 Spanish soldiers killed 115 Navajo who were trapped on a ledge on the canyon wall.

■ **83,840 acres** ■ **Northeast Arizona, just east of Chinle off US 191**
■ **Best seasons fall and spring. Canyon access sometimes closed by snow in winter** ■ **Camping, scenic drives, horseback tours, guided tours—permit and fee required for hiking and guided driving tours** ■ **Contact the monument, P.O. Box 588, Chinle, AZ 86503; 928-674-5500. www.nps.gov/cach**

Canyon Cliffs

The tall cliffs of Canyon de Chelly were formed as rivers cut into sandstone rising with the uplift of the Colorado Plateau. The process began more than 60 million years ago, though the main canyon formation occurred over the past two million years. Canyon-cutting continues today, with erosion caused by rain, ice, and wind-carried grit. In places in the upper canyons, the walls stand about 1,000 feet above their parent streams.

The dark streaks on the red cliffs are "desert varnish," created by microscopic organisms that take minerals from airborne dust particles and deposit them on the rocks.

Petrified Forest

A sun-swept corner of the Painted Desert draws more than 575,000 visitors each year. While most come to see one of the world's largest concentrations of brilliantly colored petrified wood, many leave having glimpsed something more. The 147 square miles of Petrified Forest open a window on an environment more than 200 million years old, one radically different from today's high desert.

Where you now see ravens soaring over a stark desert landscape, leathery-winged pterosaurs once glided over rivers teeming with armor-scaled fish and giant, spatula-headed amphibians. Nearby ran herds of some of the earliest dinosaurs. Scientists have identified several hundred species of fossil plants and animals in Petrified Forest.

The park consists of two main sections. Located in the south are the major concentrations of the famous petrified wood; in the north rise the colorful banded badlands of the Painted Desert. Giant fossilized logs, many of them fractured into cord-wood-size segments, lie scattered throughout, like headstones bearing a deceased's likeness.

Much of the quartz rock that replaced the wood tissue 200 million years ago is tinted in rainbow hues. Many visitors cannot resist taking rocks, despite strict regulations and stiff fines against removing any material. To see if the petrified wood was actually disappearing at an alarming rate, resource managers established survey plots with a specific number of pieces of wood; some were completely barren in less than a week.

The problem is not new. Military survey parties passing through the region in 1851 filled their saddlebags with the petrified wood. As word of these remarkable deposits spread, fossil logs were hauled off by the wagonload for tabletops, lamps, and mantels. In the 1890s gem collectors began dynamiting logs searching for amethyst

- Northeast Arizona, 25 miles east of Holbrook
- 93,533 acres
- Established 1962
- Year-round
- Camping, hiking, wildlife viewing, petrified logs, petroglyphs
- Information: 928-524-6228 www.nps.gov/pefo

Long Logs Area, Petrified Forest National Park

and quartz crystals. To prevent further destruction of its unique bounty, the area was designated a national monument in 1906 and then gained national park status more than a half century later.

How to Get There

If you are traveling west on I-40, exit south into the park. When leaving the south end of the park, the road joins US 180. Follow US 180 for 19 miles to Holbrook and back to I-40. If you are traveling east on I-40, take the US 180 exit. The south entrance is 19 miles from Holbrook. After driving through park, leave via I-40. Airport: Flagstaff.

When to Go

All-year park. Summer's dramatic clouds and thunderstorms enhance the beauty of the landscape. Fall, with its milder weather, also attracts many visitors. Winter in the high desert can be cold with brief snowstorms, but moderate afternoon temperatures are not uncommon. The desert blooms colorfully in spring; winds can be high.

How to Visit

The park is laid out along a north-south road that offers pullouts, overlooks, and many

What Not to Miss

- **A stroll along Long Logs Trail from Rainbow Forest Museum**
- **Blue Mesa Trail**
- **Pintado Point—highest point along Painted Desert Rim**
- **A hike in the Painted Desert Wilderness**
- **Puerco Indian ruins and petroglyphs**

opportunities for short hikes and strolls. You'll find informative exhibits at both the **Painted Desert Visitor Center,** at the north end of the road, and the **Rainbow Forest Museum,** at the south end.

Most of the features at Petrified Forest are on a scale best appreciated by leaving the car. Plan enough time to walk among the fossil logs and Painted Desert badlands.

For a half-day visit, follow the park road from the **Rainbow Forest Museum** to **Pintado Point** and beyond to the Painted Desert Visitor Center.

If you can stay longer, include a walk to **Agate House,** take the trail into the **Blue Mesa** badlands, and consider a hike in the **Painted Desert wilderness.**

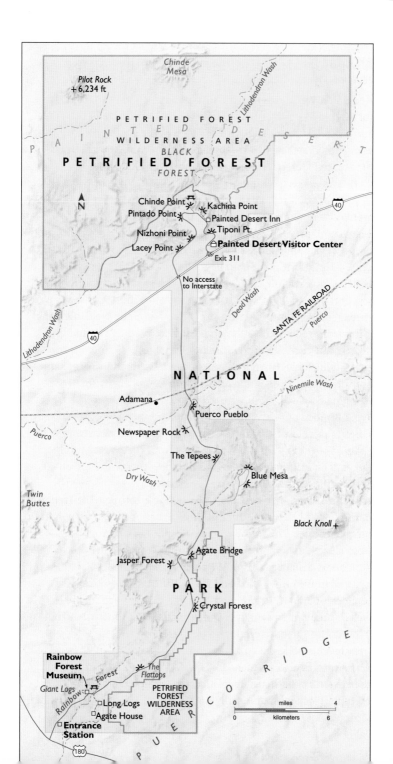

EXPLORING THE PARK

Rainbow Forest to Painted Desert Road:
28 miles; a half to full day

A scenic drive connecting the south and north entrances passes through high desert grasslands broken by unexpected escarpments and bare hills banded in pastels. Begin at the south entrance with a stop at the **Rainbow Forest Museum.** (Or, from the north, begin at the Painted Desert Visitor Center and reverse this tour.)

Be sure to see the dioramas of the Triassic landscape and the displays of fossils and early dinosaurs. The most common fossil animals are members of the phytosaur group, including *Nicrosaurus gregorii.* Some of these carnivorous giant reptiles grew up to 30 feet long and weighed five tons. They showed many of the same adaptations to an aquatic predatory lifestyle as modern crocodiles. Long, narrow jaws were lined with sharp teeth to capture fish and other prey, a long tail powered quick bursts of underwater speed, and eyes and nostrils were located atop the head, allowing Nicrosaurus to remain submerged as it awaited its victim.

The museum sits in the **Rainbow Forest,** one of four major concentrations of petrified logs called "forests." Behind it winds the half-mile **Giant Logs Trail** *(closes 15 min. before park);* the largest fossil log is Old Faithful with a 9.5-foot diameter.

Continue your drive north, bypassing three turnoffs—Crystal Forest, Jasper Forest, and Agate Bridge, unless you have plenty of time. Take the 3-mile spur road that climbs **Blue Mesa.** You loop through strange badlands layered in blue, purple, and cream colors that change with weather and time of day.

Return to the main road and drive north through **The Tepees,** bare, conical hills whose reddish hues are produced by iron and other minerals. The trail to the **Newspaper Rock** petroglyphs has been closed, making them difficult to see from the overlook above.

A short distance beyond is **Puerco Pueblo,** one of the largest prehistoric sites in the park. Here you see the partially excavated remains of an ancestral Puebloan village abandoned about 1380 as well as many fine petroglyphs of animals and geometric designs pecked into the outcropping rock.

Scientists believe a chiseled circle here was used by the Native Americans as a solar calendar. The week preceding and following the advent of the summer solstice, the sun interacts with this petroglyph. Early in the morning on the day of the summer solstice, rangers guide observers to the place where a shaft of sunlight pierces and fills the very center of the ancient symbol.

The road crosses the intermittent Puerco River, which divides the park in two. No permanent streams flow in Petrified Forest, and fewer than 9 inches of precipitation fall each year, half in summer thunderstorms. After crossing I-40, the drive reaches the edge of a volcanic escarpment overlooking a particularly colorful section of the Painted Desert.

Pull off at **Lacey Point,** the first of eight overlooks. Here the bare Chinle slopes are tinted in the chalky shades of a Navajo rug. The colors are especially vivid when the sun shines on sediment still wet from a thunderstorm.

Continue on to the sweeping panoramic vista at **Pintado Point**— the highest along the Painted Desert rim. Below lies Lithodendron Wash, braiding through the red badlands of the Black Forest. In the distance stands the dark profile of Pilot Rock, at 6,234 feet the park's highest point.

The scenic drive ends at the **Painted Desert Visitor Center,** which is the park headquarters located at the north entrance. Here, you can view an orientation film and see models and bones of some of the large prehistoric reptiles found in the area. During the Triassic period, when park fossils originated, dinosaurs were just beginning the development that would see them dominate the later Jurassic period, so the true dinosaurs were less impressive than their relatives. Take some time to study the exhibits here, even if you're eager to move on.

Roadside Trails

From the Rainbow Forest Museum, a half-mile spur road *(closes 30 min. before park)* takes you to the start of the 0.6-mile Long Logs loop and the 1-mile round-trip Agate House trail. At **Long Logs,** you will see the largest concentration of petrified wood in the park, with logs up to 120 feet long—many crisscrossed in logjams. As you walk the trail here, you're bound to marvel at the way organic material has been duplicated in rock: woodgrain, knotholes, and beetle borings, all in astonishingly fine detail. Note how logs are broken so smoothly and evenly that they seem to have been cut across with a saw.

The majority of the park's petrified wood comes from tall conifers called Araucarioxylon. These ancient trees grew more than

200 million years ago in distant highlands, where floods or perhaps mudflows uprooted them. Tumbled and abraded, the fallen trees washed into logjams and were quickly buried by silt and ash. Silica-laden water percolated through the wood, replacing organic tissue with multicolored quartz. Not only tree trunks were buried by those Triassic streams, of course. Fossils of ferns, cycads, giant horsetails, and other plants are common in the park. Many animals have been unearthed, as well, including snails, insects, fish, and amphibians.

Next, if you have time, strike out on the 1-mile paved trail to **Agate House.** During the 1930s crews restored one of the rooms in this eight-room dwelling built more than 800 years ago by ancestral Puebloans. The prehistoric structure was of wood and adobe; the reconstruction uses concrete to stabilize the walls.

Farther north, off the Blue Mesa spur road, look for **Blue Mesa**

Petrified tree trunk, Long Logs area

Trail, which makes a 1-mile, 45-minute loop through the park's badlands. The trail is paved and nearly level except for one very steep section. Even if you can't take the full hike, a walk of just 100 feet leads to good views of the intricately eroded mesa. Of all the landscapes in the park, this is probably the most strikingly other-worldly. The bluish color here derives from manganese oxide in the clay, while the rusty maroon color comes from iron oxide.

For a longer hike, walk through the rugged beauty of the **Painted Desert wilderness** at the north end of the park. The trail begins at **Kachina Point** behind the old **Painted Desert Inn,** originally built as a roadside inn, now open daily as a historical site. Once in the flats below the rim, the trail disappears, requiring you to do your own route-finding. Look for the **Black Forest,** an area of dark fossilized wood, and **Onyx Bridge.** Finding the bridge can be an adventure since there are no landmarks to guide you.

INFORMATION & ACTIVITIES

Headquarters
P.O. Box 2217
Petrified Forest, AZ 86028
928-524-6228
www.nps.gov/pefo

Visitor & Information Centers
Painted Desert Visitor Center
at north entrance, just off I-40,
and Rainbow Forest Museum
near south entrance, just off
US 180. Painted Desert Inn
National Historic Landmark,
2 miles from north entrance,
also has archaeological displays
and historical information.

Seasons & Accessibility
Open all year; extended hours
May through August. Snow
or icy roads may close park
temporarily in winter.

Entrance Fees
$10 per car, good for seven
days. $5 per biker, good for
seven days.

Pets
Pets are permitted on leashes,
but they are not allowed in
public buildings, wilderness
areas, or on the Giant Logs
Trail. Horses are permitted
throughout park in groups of
six or fewer when accompanied
by riders, but grazing is prohibited within the park, and there
is no available water.

Facilities for Disabled
Visitor centers, museum, and
rest rooms are wheelchair
accessible.

Things to Do
Free ranger-led, year-round
activities: nature talks, wildlife
viewing, and bird-watching.
Also available, a film, interpretive exhibits, self-guided auto
tours, hiking, horseback riding
(no rentals in area).

Special Advisories
■ Stay on trails to prevent
damage to the fragile desert
environment and to avoid personal injury from sharp edges
of petrified logs.
■ Take nothing from the park
but memories, not even a tiny
piece of petrified wood; small
pieces taken by each of many
visitors quickly add up to tons.
■ Carry water when you hike;
none is available outside developed areas.
■ Do not approach any wildlife;
as cute as they are, park animals may carry bubonic
plague, Hantavirus, and rabies.
■ Permits are required for
overnight camping in the
Painted Desert Wilderness.
They are free and can be picked
up at the visitor center or at the
museum up to one hour before
park closing.

Painted Desert

Campgrounds
None inside the park, but food service available.

Hotels, Motels, & Inns
(Unless otherwise noted, rates are for two persons in a double room, high season.)

In Holbrook, AZ 86025:
- **Best Inn** 2211 E. Navajo Blvd. 928-524-2654 or 800-551-1923. 40 units. $41–$45. AC.
- **Best Western Adobe Inn** 615 W. Hopi Dr. 928-524-3948. 54 units. $40–$60. AC, pool.
- **Comfort Inn** 2602 E. Navajo Blvd. 928-524-6131. 61 units. $63–$75. AC, pool, restaurant.
- **Days Inn** 2601 Navajo. 928-524-6949. 54 units. $58–$70. AC, indoor pool, restaurant.
- **Holbrook Comfort Inn** 2602 E. Navajo Blvd. 928-524-6131 or 800-228-5150. 61 units. $64–$74. AC, pool, restaurant. www.comfortinnnav.com/hotel/av420.
- **Holiday Inn Express** 1308 E. Navajo Blvd. 928-524-1466. 59 units. $89. AC, indoor pool.

For additional accommodations, contact the Holbrook Chamber of Commerce, 100 E. Arizona St., Holbrook, AZ 86025. 928-524-6558. www.ci.holbrook.az.us.

Mogollon Rim

A portion of the southern edge of the Colorado Plateau is marked with geologic certitude by the Mogollon (moge-ee-YONE) Rim, an escarpment that runs from central Arizona southeast to the White Mountains. Cut by ancient rivers and recent erosion, the rim ranges from a few hundred feet high to around 2,000 feet in its central section, where cliffs rise above the Verde River and Tonto Creek watersheds.

The Mogollon Rim reaches its greatest glory in the Payson area. Here Ariz. 260, coming from Camp Verde, drops off the Colorado Plateau and then rises again on its way east to Heber. Trails, roads, and recreation areas offer countless ways to experience the landscape both below and above the rim in this vicinity.

Hikers on edge of Mogollon Rim

For backpackers, the **Highline National Recreation Trail** runs for 51 miles below the rim, from a trailhead just east of Pine to another on Ariz. 260 about 25 miles east of Payson. For drivers, FR 64 (Control Road) also runs from near Pine to Ariz. 260, paralleling the Highline trail on the south. The trail and the road pass through the area burned by the Dude Fire of July 1990, which raged across 24,000 acres of forest. This fire also destroyed the cabin of famed western author Zane Grey, who used the Mogollon Rim as a writing and hunting retreat in the 1920s.

Beginning at the trailhead near Pine, the 8-mile **Pine Canyon Trail** heads north up a beautiful canyon and climbs the rim to Ariz. 87; walking 2 miles to **Dripping Springs** is a fine day hike.

To visit **Hellsgate Wilderness**, drive 12 miles east of Payson on Ariz. 260, turn south on FR 405A, and continue less than a mile to the trailhead.

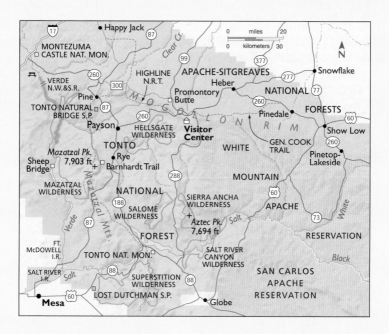

From here the route drops roughly 1,500 feet in 6 miles into a canyon on Tonto Creek.

Ariz. 260 ascends the rim about 30 miles east of Payson; near the top you'll find the Forest Service's **Mogollon Rim Visitor Center,** open from May through September. Forest Road 300 travels west from here along the top of the rim, with side roads and trails leading to some breathtaking vistas. The easy, scenic **Rim Lakes Vista Trail** begins on FR 300 just off Ariz. 260 and runs along the edge of the rim for 3.5 miles. FR 300 parallels the rim all the way to Ariz. 87, north of Strawberry. So, too, does a segment of the 138-mile

General Crook Trail, which stretches from Dewey *(E of Prescott)* to Pinedale *(between Heber and Show Low).*

This route was blazed in 1872 by Gen. George Crook, who traveled the rim in a campaign to subdue Apache tribes.

General Crook preferred to ride mules, which were more surefooted than horses; today visitors can walk or ride a mountain bike along Crook's historic route.

For more information on the region, contact Black Mesa Ranger District, Apache-Sitgreaves National Forests, 2748 Hwy. 260, Overgaard, AZ 85933. 928-535-4481. www.fs.fed.us/r3/asnf.

Excursions from Petrified Forest

El Malpais National Monument & Conservation Area

138 miles east of Petrified Forest

You'll find the word "badlands" scattered all over the map of the American West, applied to places that early settlers shunned because of their rugged terrain or sparse vegetation. *El malpais* is Spanish for "the badland," and there's a special reason the phrase was used for this area of northwest New Mexico: Over a period of more than 100,000 years, ending only about 3,000 years ago, repeated volcanic eruptions left an expanse of cinder cones and lava flows covering hundreds of square miles of an intermountain plain here.

El Malpais, which protects much of this area, is managed cooperatively by the National Park Service (administering the 115,000-acre national monument) and the Bureau of Land Management (responsible for the adjacent 263,000-acre El Malpais National Conservation Area). These intermingled lands—including two BLM wilderness preserves, Cebolla and West Malpais—form a tract offering recreational opportunities from sight-seeing to cross-country backpacking.

Lava tube cave, El Malpais National Monument

From I-40 just east of Grants, take N. Mex. 117 south; in 10 miles the BLM's El Malpais Ranger Station on the east side of the road can provide maps and information on the conservation area and the national monument. Just a mile or so farther south, follow a dirt road west to the **Sandstone Bluffs Overlook** for a fine panorama of the volcanic region. Green junipers and pinyon pines dot the vast jumble of black lava immediately below this long, picturesque sandstone ridge. Off to the west rise the **Zuni Mountains,** an uplifted dome of ancient granite, stripped by erosion of the younger rocks that once lay atop it. To the north stands 11,301-foot Mount Taylor, a volcano that may have blown apart in a violent explosion like that of Mount St. Helens in 1980.

Interpretive signs explain regional geology and identify different varieties of lava, such as rope-like pahoehoe and the sharp, jagged aa. Although there's no established trail, you can walk along the ridge—formed from the compacted dunes of a desert that existed here more than 200 million years ago—to experience its strikingly eroded contours.

Back on N. Mex. 117, continue south 5 miles to the east trailhead for the **Zuni-Acoma Trail.** This 7.5-mile route leads to N. Mex. 53 on the west side of the national monument. With a car shuttle you can hike one way; otherwise it's an out-and-back walk *(not advised).*

Though this trail has little change in elevation, it's by no means easy. You'll be walking across sharp, uneven lava (very sturdy hiking boots are a must), on a route with no water and little shade; for most of its length the trail is marked by lava rock cairns that can be hard to see. With those cautions in mind, you should hike at least a little of the Zuni-Acoma Trail just to get a feel for this remarkable landscape.

The trail takes its name from two Native American peoples whose pueblos were connected centuries ago by a trade route; some of the cairns and rock-fill "bridges" across lava gullies were put in place by Native Americans hundreds of years ago. Many different eruptions poured lava onto the surface at El Malpais. As you continue west, you'll cross lava flows up to 115,000 years old.

In 2.5 miles, N. Mex. 117 reaches the parking area for **La Ventana Natural Arch** in the El Malpais National Conservation Area. This impressive rock span is eroded from a sandstone bluff. A very short and fairly steep trail leads to the arch, but you don't have to walk all the way to enjoy this 165-foot-long formation. Continue south on N. Mex. 117 to see **The Narrows,** where the highway seems to be squeezed by lava flows on the west and 500-foot-tall sandstone bluffs to the east.

From I-40 at Grants, you can take N. Mex. 53 south 16 miles to the west trailhead for the Zuni-Acoma Trail. By hiking less than a mile east you can see both the **El Calderon Flow,** the oldest lava in El Malpais, and the much younger Twin Craters Flow.

Heading west 4 more miles on N. Mex. 53, you'll reach the **El Calderon Area,** where trails through stands of ponderosa pines lead to the El Calderon cinder cone and **Junction Cave,** a quarter-mile-long lava tube.

Lava tubes form when the surface of flowing lava, exposed to cooling air, hardens into a crust while liquid lava continues to flow inside. Properly prepared people (with gloves, hard hats, and three flashlights per person) are allowed into the cave.

The national monument's El Malpais Information Center, a few miles west of El Calderon, offers maps and advice. Continuing west on N. Mex. 53, you'll reach the privately owned and operated **Ice Caves and Bandera Volcano** *(888-423-2283. Adm. fee).* Inside the main cave (another lava tube), ice that forms during winter is insulated from intense summer heat; over time, a layer of permanent ice has been formed.

■ **378,000 acres** ■ **Northwest New Mexico, just south of Grants off N. Mex. 117** ■ **Best seasons fall and spring; summer heat can make hiking unpleasant. Some dirt roads impassable after rain** ■ **Primitive camping, hiking, cave exploration** ■ **Contact the monument, 123 E. Roosevelt Ave., Grants, NM 87020; 505-783-4774. www.nps.gov/elm**

Homolovi Ruins State Park

65 miles west of Petrified Forest

Four major ruins on Arizona's nearly treeless high desert grassland at Homolovi (HO-mo-low-vee) composed an important farming and trading settlement built by the Hisat'sinom, ancestors of the Hopi people, who lived here from about A.D. 1200 to 1400.

The settlement's name means "place of the little hills" or "where the hills come down toward the river" (in this case, the Little Colorado River). Since excavation began in 1896, archaeologists have identified over 340 sites including pit houses, kivas, campsites, places of agricultural activity, petroglyphs, and "lithic scatters" of hand-worked stone and potsherds.

Homolovi is now a center of research for the late migration period of the Hisat'sinom, who grew their crops in the rich flood plain and along the sandy slopes. The Hopi still consider

Homolovi and other pre-Columbian sites to be parts of their homeland, and they continue to make pilgrimages to those places. While archaeologists continue to investigate Homolovi and, in consultation with the Hopi, unravel its history, park visitors are welcome to explore the ruins on foot.

At an elevation of 4,850 feet, the park is open year-round, but winter often brings treacherous highway conditions to surrounding mountains. If possible, plan your visit for June or July, when you can watch over the dusty shoulders of archaeologists working key sites. Selected findings from each summer's work are displayed during Archaeology Day, when the scientists complete their season.

Introduce yourself to Homolovi at the **visitor center,** where exhibits chronicle the site's history and display significant artifacts recovered here.

Then tour the two main ruins, **Homolovi I** and **II,** by following self-guided trails posted with interpretive information developed in cooperation with the Hopi. At wheelchair-accessible Homolovi II, a collapsed pueblo believed to have enclosed a thousand chambers, five rooms and a rectangular ceremonial kiva chamber have been excavated and stabilized. They provide an authentic, if fragmentary, picture of the adobe trading and cotton-growing center, which peaked in population between 1340 and 1380. Catastrophic flooding is believed to have caused Homolovi's abandonment, driving its people north to Hopi Mesas.

If you have a bit more time, consider a short hike along the park's **Tsu'vö Trail,** a half-mile nature trail that loops between the Homolovi's twin buttes. It is also an archaeological trail, leading past milling stone areas and petroglyphs The name means "path of the rattlesnake" in Hopi.

Contact the park for information on half- and 1-day workshops *(fee)*—some offering college credit—that are offered throughout the year. Subjects range from storytelling, traditional seed planting, gardening, and harvesting presented by Hopi elders, to ranger-led wildlife-viewing field trips.

■ **4,500 acres** ■ **5 miles northeast of Winslow via I-40 and Ariz. 87**
■ **Year-round, best months June and July** ■ **Hiking, wildlife viewing, ancient ruins, guided archaeological tours** ■ **Contact the park, HC 63, Box 5, Winslow, AZ 86047; 928-289-4106. www.azstateparks.com**

Pintail Lake

70 miles south of Petrified Forest

Permanent wetlands are few and far between on the Colorado Plateau, so this artificial lake and marsh area ought to be on the itinerary for bird- and wildlife-watchers in the Mogollon Rim or White Mountains area. Created in 1977 as an innovative solution for wastewater treatment, Pintail Lake now boasts a shoreline ringed with cattails, bulrushes, and sedges, as well as nesting islands that are home to variety of waterbirds.

Accessible to all by means of a barrier-free trail and viewing stations, Pintail does indeed often have northern pintail swimming across its waters, along with other ducks including mallard, cinnamon teal, gadwalls, northern shovelers, and ruddy ducks. The pied-billed grebes you'll see here resemble ducks, but belong to a completely different order; note the thoroughly unduck-like bill on this little brown diver. The black birds with white bills are American coots; again, though convergent evolution has caused them to look like ducks, they're not waterfowl, and in fact are more closely related to cranes.

Watch for other wetland-loving species on or around the lake, including black-crowned night-herons, great blue herons, soras, killdeer, belted kingfishers, black phoebes, marsh wrens, and song sparrows. Shallow parts of the lake attract flocks of shorebirds in spring and fall migration—an unusual sight in this area. Bald eagles are common winter visitors, and sometimes a peregrine falcon zooms through, hoping to pick up a quick duck dinner.

In the pinyon pines and one-seed junipers around the lake you'll find bushtits, bridled titmice, mountain chickadees, and Bewick's wrens. Out in the grassland to the east, northern harriers fly low in winter looking for rodents. Elk, mule deer, and even pronghorn might appear in this broad meadow at any time of year; the best chance of seeing these large mammals, as is usually the case in wildlife observation, comes in the early morning or late in the afternoon.

■ **57 acres** ■ **East-central Arizona, 4 miles north of Show Low, off Ariz. 77** ■ **Best seasons fall and winter** ■ **Hiking, bird-watching, wildlife viewing** ■ **Contact Lakeside Ranger District, Apache-Sitgreaves National Forests, R.R. 3, Box B-50, Pinetop-Lakeside, AZ 85929; 928-368-5111. www.fs.fed.us/r3/asnf**

Meteor Crater

For one of America's natural wonders, Meteor Crater often has a delayed impact on the observer. Once you grasp that it's more than 4,000 feet from one rim to the other, and that the hole is as deep as a 60-story building is tall, the mental image of the event that occurred here 50,000 years ago can be staggering.

A meteor, or a small group of them, made of iron and nickel and with a diameter of 150 feet, was traveling between 30,000 and 40,000 miles per hour when it struck this spot with a force equivalent to 20 million tons of TNT.

Rock at the impact area was vaporized, and 175 million tons of rock scattered to cover the surrounding plain for more than a mile in all directions. Chunks of rock were thrown for up to 24 miles.

So great was the pressure that bits of graphite in the meteors were converted into tiny diamonds.

Meteor Crater (*35 miles E of Flagstaff, 928-289-5898*) amply justifies a side trip off I-40, whether you simply marvel at its magnitude or take time to consider the site's scientific significance.

Exhibits in the visitor center illustrate its formation, and as you visualize the impact you can't help but be awed by the forces at work.

Visitors surveying Meteor Crater

Saguaro

Symbol of the American Southwest and North America's largest cactus, the saguaro's imposing stature and uplifted arms give it a regal presence. Perhaps that's why this burly giant, whose only bits of exuberance are seasonal blossoms and figlike fruits at the tip of its limbs, has been dubbed the "desert monarch."

Carnegiea gigantea is the trademark of the Sonoran Desert, whose basins and ranges rumple 120,000 square miles of northwestern Mexico, southern Arizona, and southeastern California. Saguaro National Park is comprised of two sections. The westerly Tucson Mountain District embraces about 24,000 acres of the hotter, drier, less-vegetated "low" Sonoran ecosystem, which occurs below 3,000 feet. Thirty miles east, on the other side of Tucson's urban sprawl, is the 67,000-acre Rincon Mountain District, which occupies loftier ground and has a cooler, slightly wetter "high desert" environment. Most of it is inaccessible save by foot or on horseback. Here the terrain inclines from saguaro forests into nearly pristine woodlands of oak and pine. Hikers pressing on to higher elevations find Douglas-fir, ponderosa pine, and solitude.

The Sonoran Desert's extreme temperatures, perennial drought, frequent lightning, banshee winds, and voracious predators keep the saguaro forever at the limit of its endurance. Odds against survival rival a lottery: Though the cactus annually produces tens of thousands of pinhead-size seeds—some 40 million over a life that may last two centuries—few ever even sprout. Even fewer seedlings achieve the grandeur of towering 50 feet and weighing up to 16,000 pounds.

Though the saguaro may be the park's centerpiece, after wet winters the spring wildflower display can be breathtaking.

- Southern Arizona: Rincon Mountain District east of Tucson; Tucson Mountain District west of the city

- 91,440 acres

- Established 1994

- Best seasons spring–fall

- Backcountry camping, hiking, biking, horseback riding, bird-watching, wildlife viewing

- Information: 520-733-5153 (Saguaro East); 520-733-5158 (Saguaro West) www.nps.gov/sagu

Saguaro cactuses in dusty Saguaro National Park

The brilliant gold of Mexican poppy is often the first-noticed bloom, while penstemons, lupines, desert marigolds, brittlebushes, and globe mallows contribute their lively colors of red, lilac, blue, and yellow. Many trees, shrubs, and cactuses also bloom, including creosote bushes, paloverdes, ocotillos, chollas, and hedgehog cactuses. Saguaro blooms in early summer, a hot time to visit the region.

How to Get There

Saguaro West (Tucson Mountain District): From Tucson take Speedway Boulevard west to Gates Pass Road, turning right on Kinney Road. *(Buses, RVs, and towed vehicles not recommended on Gates Pass; instead take Ariz. 86W from Tucson to Kinney.)*
Saguaro East (Rincon Mountain District): Take Broadway Boulevard east from central Tucson to Old Spanish Trail. Airport: Tucson.

When to Go

All-year park, but fall through spring are the best seasons. From October through April, temperatures reach the upper 60s to mid-70s and can drop below freezing overnight. From May through September, highs routinely exceed 100°F. July

What Not to Miss

- Bajada Scenic Loop Drive
- Hiking Sendero Esperanza Trail
- Driving Cactus Forest Road
- A picnic at Mica View
- Hike Hugh Norris Trail to the highest point in Tucson Mountains

through September is characterized by brief but fierce thunderstorms. Saguaros begin blooming nightly in late April, and keep blooming into June.

How to Visit

On a 1-day visit, begin early and view the **Arizona-Sonora Desert Museum** before heading to Saguaro West; then pause at the **Red Hills Visitor Center** for an overview. Take the **Bajada Scenic Loop Drive,** stopping en route to walk the paved **Desert Discovery Nature Trail.** Return to Tucson, continuing east to Saguaro's Rincon Mountain District. Take the **Cactus Forest Drive** and walk the **Desert Ecology Trail.** For a scenic rest stop along the drive, visit **Mica View picnic area.**

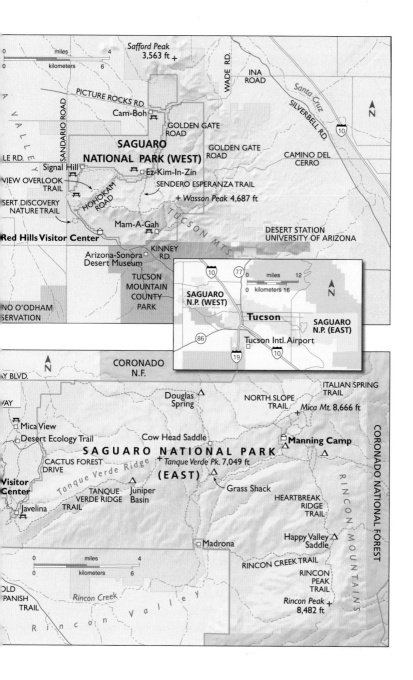

Safford Peak
3,563 ft

INA
ROAD

WADE RD.

Santa Cruz

SILVERBELL RD.

10

PICTURE ROCKS RD.

SANDARIO ROAD

Cam-Boh

GOLDEN GATE
ROAD

SAGUARO
NATIONAL PARK (WEST)

GOLDEN GATE
ROAD

CAMINO DEL
CERRO

Signal Hill

Ez-Kim-In-Zin

LE RD.

VIEW OVERLOOK
TRAIL

SENDERO ESPERANZA TRAIL

Wasson Peak 4,687 ft

SERT DISCOVERY
NATURE TRAIL

HOHOKAM ROAD

Mam-A-Gah

TUCSON MTS.

DESERT STATION
UNIVERSITY OF ARIZONA

Red Hills Visitor Center

Arizona-Sonora
Desert Museum

KINNEY
RD.

10   77

SAGUARO
N.P. (WEST)

miles   12
kilometers 16

N

TUCSON
MOUNTAIN
COUNTY
PARK

Tucson

SAGUARO
N.P. (EAST)

NO O'ODHAM
SERVATION

86

19

Tucson Intl. Airport

10

CORONADO
N.F.

Y BLVD.

N

ITALIAN SPRING
TRAIL

Douglas
Spring

NORTH SLOPE
TRAIL

Mica Mt. 8,666 ft

VAY

Mica View

Desert Ecology Trail

Cow Head Saddle

Manning Camp

SAGUARO NATIONAL PARK

CACTUS FOREST
DRIVE

Tanque Verde Ridge

Tanque Verde Pk. 7,049 ft

(EAST)

CORONADO NATIONAL FOREST

Visitor
Center

Javelina

TANQUE
VERDE RIDGE
TRAIL

Juniper
Basin

Grass Shack

HEARTBREAK
RIDGE
TRAIL

RINCON MOUNTAINS

Madrona

Happy Valley
Saddle

RINCON CREEK TRAIL

RINCON
PEAK
TRAIL

OLD
PANISH
TRAIL

Rincon Creek

Rincon Valley

Rincon Peak
8,482 ft

EXPLORING THE PARK

Saguaro West: Tucson Mountain District:

About 25 miles; a half day

The drive west through Tucson Mountain County Park takes you past the excellent, zoolike **Arizona-Sonora Desert Museum** *(see p. 312),* whose 12 acres include every Sonoran Desert life zone and most of its animals and plants. It's well worth a stop.

Continue on Kinney Road to the **Red Hills Visitor Center,** where an orientation slide show and desert life exhibits will enhance your understanding of what you'll encounter here and in Saguaro East. Walk the center's **Cactus Garden Trail,** a paved path through an unruly crowd of cactuses: hedgehog, barrel, fishhook, chainfruit cholla, and prickly pear.

Saguaros thrive in the coarse, absorbent soil of bajadas, long desert mountain slopes of eroded rock, gravel, sand, and clay, where a mature plant's shallow, wide-ranging roots can absorb up to 200 gallons from one rainstorm, enough to last a year. The 9-mile **Bajada Loop Drive,** beginning at the visitor center, explores one of these life zones It passes through some of the finest stands of saguaro found anywhere, with the giant cactus growing in amazing profusion on the hillsides. About 1 mile west of the visitor center, look left for the **Desert Discovery Nature Trail,** a half-mile path across a bajada at the base of the Tucson Mountains.

Hook right onto Hohokam Road. *(Part of the loop is one way; enter here to drive it all in one direction.)* About 1.5 miles from the turnoff, **Valley View Overlook Trail** winds up about half a mile to panoramas of the Avra Valley—a rugged, cactus-studded landscape. Unpaved Golden Gate Road turns off about a mile farther on and passes a pleasant picnic area near the head of **Sendero Esperanza Trail,** a moderately strenuous, popular half-day hike into the mountainous backcountry.

Backtrack on Golden Gate Road past Hohokam Road to **Signal Hill picnic area,** where rocks are etched with centuries-old Hohokam petroglyphs. Archaeologists believe the symbols, chipped through a brown patina of iron-manganese oxide called "desert varnish," signify territorial claims, clan migrations, personal accounts, visions, and pure artistic whimsy.

Continuing through ironwood and palo verde, the loop closes at Sandario Road, an alternative route back to Tucson via Picture Rocks, Wade, and Ina Roads to I-10.

The Mighty Saguaro

Standing up to 50 feet tall and weighing eight tons or more, the saguaro seems to dominate the Sonoran Desert environment; with its tough skin and abundant spines, it exudes strength and vigor.

What we see in a full-grown saguaro, in fact, represents victory over long odds. The huge cactus begins as a seed the size of a pinhead, which must avoid being eaten by hungry animals. Next, it has to find a favorable germination site; young saguaros do best in the shelter of a "nurse" plant such as a paloverde or creosote bush. The tiny seedling then has to escape rodents, javelina hooves, and the boots of careless hikers; it may take 25 years to reach 2 feet in height.

After 50 years, the saguaro may overtop a person standing beside it, and as it continues to grow it exhibits marvelous adaptations to its arid surroundings. Its roots can spread 50 feet in all directions, the better to soak up water quickly. Woody ribs support its weight, but their flexibility, along with the cactus's pleated skin, allows tremendous expansion in volume. A saguaro may take in 200 gallons of water during one rainstorm.

During a life that may span 200 years, a saguaro can produce 40 million seeds. If only one survives to become an adult, the plant will have replaced itself by the time it dies—and that's all nature asks.

Hikers viewing saguaro cactuses

Saguaro East: Rincon Mountain District:
About 25 miles; a half day

Higher elevations here create Sonoran Desert environments different from Saguaro West's lowland desert zone. A steady, east-trending incline slants up into the roadless Rincon Mountain wilderness area, which is dotted with forests of oak, pine, and fir accessible only by foot or on horseback.

Make your first stop the **Saguaro East Visitor Center** at park headquarters. If you plan to hike into backcountry, this is the place to acquire trail guides, maps, and permits. Outside, signs identify some of the more common plants you'll see as you explore the park. In spring, you'll soon become accustomed to the chugging call of the cactus wren and the sharp *whit-wheet* of the curve-billed thrasher, common around the entrance area.

If time is limited, pick up a guide to the **Cactus Forest Drive** and take the 8-mile loop, which winds through rolling desert and across several washes. Many of the saguaros are more than 150 years old. About 2 miles along the route, look left for a gravel road

Englemann's hedgehog bloom

Sabino Canyon

Just minutes from Saguaro East, but a world away in climate, vegetation, and wildlife, beautiful Sabino Canyon beckons with its towering cliffs, waterfalls, seasonal swimming holes, and lush (for the desert) riparian zone of cottonwoods, Arizona sycamores, alligator junipers, and Arizona walnuts.

Free of vehicular congestion *(private vehicles banned),* the canyon offers hikers unfettered access to its charms. The area is still very popular, however, and often crowded. Arrive early and avoid weekends.

A tram service *(520-749-2861.* *Fee)* runs 3.8 miles up the canyon and into adjacent **Bear Canyon,** making it possible to plan a variety of short hikes and outings.

The Forest Service **visitor center** operates a bookstore and offers guided bird-watching hikes and other natural history programs. Drop by for a schedule or to pick up some advice about promising hiking routes.

One fairly strenuous, 13.4-mile hike ascends Sabino Canyon, follows the **East Fork Trail,** then wanders down into Bear Canyon.

To reach the area, follow Sabino Canyon Road north from Tanque Verde Road in northeastern Tucson.

leading to scenic overlooks at **Mica View picnic area,** a pleasant place to stop. About a mile farther, the quarter-mile paved **Desert Ecology Trail** is designed to illustrate the crucial role of water in desert ecosystems. The flat trail runs alongside a wash that sits dry as powder most of the year. This area receives only about 11 inches of rain a year; the top of Mica Mountain, which you can see peeking over the flank of Tanque Verde Ridge to the east, gets as much as 21 inches. What you are likely to remember most from this 20-minute amble, however, is the desert's perfect stillness.

Near the south end of the Cactus Forest loop road, consider walking part of the **Tanque Verde Ridge Trail,** which heads south and then east from the Javelina picnic area. In return for 3 miles or so of fairly vigorous uphill hiking, you'll experience cactus desert, the grassland above, and a bit of oak-juniper forest on the ridge. You'll have good views of Rincon Peak to the east and Tucson below to the west. In the grassland zone, look for sotol, which was used by Native Americans to weave mats and other objects.

INFORMATION & ACTIVITIES

Headquarters
3693 S. Old Spanish Trail
Tucson, AZ 85730
520-733-5158 (Saguaro West)
520-733-5153 (Saguaro East)
www.nps.gov/sagu

Visitor & Information Centers
Saguaro West Red Hills Visitor
Center off Kinney Road.
Saguaro East Visitor Center
(park headquarters) on Old
Spanish Trail. Open daily.

Seasons & Accessibility
The park is open year-round.
Best seasons are fall, winter,
and spring, when temperatures
are moderate. Summers are
brutally hot. Desert wildflower
blooms can be spectacular in
spring. Call headquarters for
current conditions.

Entrance Fees
Saguaro West: None.
Saguaro East: $10 per vehicle.

Pets
Not permitted on trails, in
the backcountry, or in any
of the park's public buildings.
Elsewhere they are allowed,
but only on leashes.

Facilities for Disabled
All visitor centers, nature trails,
and roadside picnic areas are
accessible for wheelchairs.

Things to Do
An abundance of ranger-led
activities including nature
walks and talks. Hikes and
night walks, scenic drives, trail
walks, bird-watching and
wildlife viewing, picnicking,
bicycling, backcountry hiking.
Horsebacking riding is permitted on some of the trails.

Special Advisories
■ Avoid open and low-lying
areas during thunderstorms,
when lightning and flash floods
pose a danger.
■ Stay on trails. Abandoned
mine shafts in Saguaro West
can make off-trail hiking and
riding hazardous.
■ Always carry a flashlight at
night to avoid encounters with
rattlesnakes, scorpions, and
Gila monsters.
■ There is no water at picnic
areas or along most trails. If
hiking, carry at least one gallon
of water per person per day;
more if hiking during summer.
■ Backcountry camping is
allowed only at designated sites.
Use permits must be obtained
at visitor centers in advance of
each trip.

Campgrounds
Four backcountry campsites
in Saguaro East, accessible by
trail. Campground in Tucson

Saguaro cactuses at dusk against a stormy sky

Mountain County Park, next to Saguaro West.

Hotels, Motels, & Inns

(Unless otherwise noted, rates are for two persons in a double room, high season.)

In Tucson, AZ:

■ **Arizona Inn** 2200 E. Elm St., 85711. 520-325-1541 or 800-933-1093. 85 rooms, 3 houses. $280–$3,500. AC, pool, restaurant. www.arizonainn.com.

■ **Best Western** 1015 N. Stone Ave., 85705. 520-622-8871 or 800-528-1234. 79 units. $59–$99. AC, pool, restaurant. www.bestwestern.com.

■ **Comfort Suites at Sabino Canyon** 7007 Tanque Verde Road, 85701. 520-298-2300.

90 units. $59–$164. AC, pool. www.comfortsuites.com.

■ **Ramada Foothills Inn & Suites** 6944 E. Tanque Verde Rd., 85715. 520-886-9595 or 888-546-9629. 113 units. $129–$199. AC, pool, sauna.

■ **Tucson East Hilton** 7600 E. Broadway, 85710. 520-721-5600 or 800-445-8667. 233 units. $145–$200. AC, pool, restaurant. www.hilton.com.

For more lodgings, contact Tucson Metropolitan Chamber of Commerce. 520-792-1212.

Excursions from Saguaro

Arizona-Sonora Desert Museum

5 miles south of Saguaro West

No one interested in nature who visits southern Arizona should miss the Arizona-Sonora Desert Museum. You may be eager to get to a park or wildlife refuge or to hit the trails in a national forest, but you'll be better prepared if you see this renowned Tucson attraction first.

As soon as you enter the gate, you'll realize that the name "museum" hardly fits the scene before you. Part zoo, part botanical garden, and part mini-nature preserve, the museum spreads over 21 acres, with 2 miles of walking paths that connect a series of exhibits ranging from naturalistic open-air displays of mountain lions, black bears, and ocelots to close-up views of tarantulas, scorpions, and other invertebrates. Among the most popular is the walk-in **hummingbird aviary,** where seven species of these glittering feathered jewels zoom past visitors, sometimes perching practically within touching distance.

American Kestrel

The **"Life Underground"** exhibit features nocturnal creatures you'd ordinarily have little chance to spot in the wild, including Merriam's kangaroo rats, lyre snakes, banded geckos, and kit foxes.

If you ever thought a cactus was a cactus, you'll learn better at the museum's **Cactus Garden,** where dozens of species grow alongside other Sonoran Desert plants. You'll see how the paloverde tree uses its green trunk and branches for photosynthesis, and how the spiny and usually dead-looking ocotillo has adapted to grow leaves immediately after rain and shed them quickly when drought returns. The **Desert Garden** shows how native plants can be used for decorative landscaping; at certain times of year the flowering plants here teem with butterflies.

■ **21 acres** ■ **Just west of Tucson, adjacent to Saguaro National Park, Tucson Mountain District** ■ **Best months Nov.–April** ■ **Walking, wildlife viewing** ■ **Adm. fee** ■ **Contact the museum, 2021 N. Kinney Rd., Tucson, AZ. 85743; 520-883-2702. www.desertmuseum.org**

Santa Catalina Mountains

At once imposing and inviting, the Santa Catalina Mountains command the horizon northeast of Tucson, their picturesque granite spires promising great scenery, and even greater vistas, for those who reach their high country. From trailheads at the base, some with elevations of less than 3,000 feet, hiking trails climb all the way up Mount Lemmon, its conifer-clad summit rising to 9,157 feet.

Instead, most opt for the **Sky Island Scenic Byway,** which ascends along 27 winding miles to within a short stroll of the peak's crest. Thanks to the road, and to its proximity to the city of Tucson, Mount Lemmon is by far the most-visited high point of southern Arizona's sky island ranges.

The great range of elevation spanned by the scenic byway means you can start the morning with a walk along a desert path through saguaros and ocotillos and in less than 2 hours find yourself in a forest of white firs, Douglas-firs, and aspens. Birders love this varied topography, for it means they can fit into an easy day trip sightings of typical desert birds such as cactus wrens and Gambel's quails as well as mountain species such as Steller's jays.

Those keen to hike might start with a visit to **Catalina State Park** *(off Ariz. 77 W of the range, 520-628-5798),* which offers short loop trails and trailheads for treks into the mountains. The 2.3-mile **Canyon Loop** makes a nice early morning desert walk through mesquite scrub. For something more challenging, continue from the Canyon Loop on the **Romero Canyon Trail;** in 1.1 miles you'll reach the boundary of the **Pusch Ridge Wilderness** and soon cross a divide into Romero Canyon. Backpackers can keep going from here to the top of Mount Lemmon. Elsewhere in the park: the ruins of a village of the Hohokam people who are believed to be the ancestors of today's Tohono O'odham Indians.

For those who would rather drive, Sky Island Scenic Byway *(toll),* angles northeast from Tanque Verde Road 2.5 miles east of Sabino Canyon Road and climbs steadily for more than 6,000 feet to the summit of Mount Lemmon. The road quickly reaches **Molino Basin** and enters a zone that receives roughly double the precipitation of Tucson, a fact that accounts for the change in vegetation here. Farther along, stop at one of the picnic areas in woodsy **Bear Canyon** or pull over at **Windy Point** for the view of Tucson and picturesque rock formations of gneiss and granite.

West face, Santa Catalina Mountains

Rose Canyon Lake is a popular trout fishing spot with good birding among ponderosa pines. The Palisades Visitor Center offers maps of the area and dispenses hiking advice. Near Summerhaven, a spur road leads south to **Marshall Gulch picnic area** and trails into **Wilderness of Rocks,** with its stunning granite formations.

Back on the main road, continue past the ski area the last couple of winding miles to the top of Mount Lemmon, where trails lead to various nearby lookout points.

■ 265,142 acres ■ Southern Arizona, near Tucson ■ Best seasons summer (high country) and winter (desert) ■ Camping, hiking, fishing, biking, bird-watching ■ Contact Santa Catalina Ranger District, Coronado National Forest, 5700 N. Sabino Canyon Rd., Tucson, AZ 85750; 520-749-8700. www.fs.fed.us/r3/coronado/scrd

Kartchner Caverns State Park

45 miles southeast of Saguaro East By the time Kartchner Caverns State Park opened in 1999, excitement about this underground wonder had built to almost rock-concert proportions. Calls to the reservation number jammed local phone lines and tours were booked weeks in advance. The beautiful formations contained within the cave would themselves have merited such attention, but the story behind its opening added even more to its renown.

In 1974, two spelunkers exploring the Whetstone Mountains made a discovery that all cave hunters dream of: a pristine cave never before seen by humans, full of gorgeous, colorful speleothems (the technical term for cave formations). Fearing damage to the fragile cave ecosystem, whether from deliberate vandalism or carelessness, they kept their find a secret for four years before telling the landowning Kartchner family. What followed were years of hush-hush meetings with conservation agencies and state officials before the site was added to the Arizona state park system in 1988 and word reached the public.

Preparing for visitor access meant elaborate planning and meticulous construction aimed at preserving this "living" cave. During construction, workers found a number of fossils, the most impressive of which were the bones of a giant Shasta ground sloth estimated to have lived 80,000 years ago.

Impressive displays at the **visitor center** offer an introduction to cave formation and ecology—preparation for the awe-inspiring journey into the earth that follows. Tours enter "rooms" sculpted by water flowing through crevices in the limestone of the Whetstone Mountains. When the water table dropped around 200,000 years ago, leaving the cave dry, moisture began seeping in from above, dissolving the limestone and redepositing it as speleothems such as stalagmites, stalactites, flowstones, draperies, and the striped formations known as cave bacon. Kartchner is especially rich in soda straws: thin, delicate shapes that hang from the ceiling. The cave contains the longest soda straw seen in any U.S. cavern, an incredible 21 feet 2 inches. (It isn't on the tour, but visitors can see a model in the visitor center.)

The centerpiece of the cave is a 58-foot-tall column called **Kubla Khan.** Arizona's tallest cave column, it ascends in layer after rounded layer—a giant's multiscoop ice-cream cone, perhaps. Kartchner holds the first known examples of formations called "turnip" shields, as well as several other unique or rare formations and mineral occurrences.

The tour visits two large rooms, **Rotunda** and **Throne,** on its quarter-mile route. Eventually the trip will be expanded to include the **Big Room,** larger than the other two chambers combined.

Not everything in the caverns is inanimate. More than a thousand cave myotis bats inhabit the Big Room in summer, the females giving birth to pups and nursing them until they can leave the cave on their own. Bat guano provides nutrients for invertebrates such as mites, isopods, spiders, and crickets, all adapted to live in this dark ecosystem. Visitors are unlikely to see any of the cave critters, though, with the exception of occasional bats leaving the cave at dusk or returning at dawn.

The trail is fully wheelchair accessible, with only short steep sections, so nearly everyone can experience the grandeur of one of the most significant North American cave discoveries of the 20th century—a natural spectacle that's a secret no longer.

■ **550 acres** ■ **Southeast Arizona near Benson** ■ **Year-round** ■ **Adm. fee; reservations recommended** ■ **Camping, hiking, guided tours** ■ **Contact the park, P.O. Box 1849, Benson, AZ 85602; 520-586-4100 (information), 520-586-2283 (reservations). www.pr.state.az.us/Parks/parkhtml/kartchner.html**

Patagonia-Sonoita Creek Preserve

50 miles south of Saguaro East

Ranked among the top birding sites in the country, The Nature Conservancy's Patagonia-Sonoita Creek Preserve protects a beautiful stretch of one of the finest riparian habitats remaining in southeastern Arizona. Pick up a trail map at the visitor center, ask about recent wildlife sightings, and start with the short, self-guided **nature trail** just outside. Longer trails branch out toward the north. On Saturdays at 9 a.m., you might tag along on a guided walk to get acquainted with the preserve's trails, flora, and fauna—which includes not only birds but also deer, badgers, foxes, coyotes, javelinas, and racoons.

The **Creek Trail** winds along Sonoita Creek, past imposing specimens of Fremont cottonwood, some over 100 feet tall and thought to be 130 years old. Botanists consider this assemblage of venerable cottonwoods to be among the best in the state. In spring and summer, listen for the high whistles of the gray hawk, which nests regularly along Sonoita Creek. Other notable breeders include yellow-billed cuckoos, broad-billed hummingbirds, gilded flickers, Bell's vireos. The preserve is also known for hosting a variety of fly-catchers, from the common black phoebe to the thick-billed king-bird, the latter found in the United States only in southern Arizona.

The Creek Trail intersects the **Railroad Trail** near the north end of the preserve and leads directly back to the visitor center.

■ 850 acres ■ Southeast Arizona, near Patagonia off Ariz. 82 ■ Best months April–May and Aug.–Sept. Closed Mon.–Tues. ■ Guided walks, bird-watching, wildlife viewing ■ Contact the preserve, 150 Blue Haven Rd., Patagonia, AZ 85624; 520-394-2400.

Hikers at Patagonia-Sonoita Creek Preserve

Southeast Arizona Birding

There's no more enthusiastic group of nature lovers than birders, whose zeal to add new species to a life list (a record of all the different types of birds seen) spurs them on to spend vacations traveling around the country and, in many cases, around the world. To many of them, southeast Arizona ranks as the No. 1 birding destination in the United States, rivaled only by the lower Rio Grande Valley of Texas.

Well over 400 kinds of birds have been spotted in the region south and east of Phoenix; of that number, several dozen either occur nowhere else in the country or are found more easily here than elsewhere.

Two factors primarily explain this avian richness. First is the great environmental diversity of southeast Arizona. A birder can easily walk a desert wash at dawn, move on to a riparian woodland in late morning, spend the afternoon in an oak savanna, and finish the day in a forest of pine, fir, and Douglas-fir.

Second is the region's proximity to Mexico. Many birds range only slightly across the U.S.-Mexican border, either as regular breeders or as strays.

The list of local specialties includes some that are fairly common and easily seen, such as Harris's hawks, Gambel's quails, blue-throated hummingbirds, magnificent hummingbirds, Mexican jays, bridled titmice, curve-billed thrashers, painted redstarts, and yellow-eyed juncos.

A little searching, or luck, is usually required for others, including zone-tailed hawks, Montezuma quails, whiskered screech-owls, violet-crowned hummingbirds, Strickland's woodpeckers, buff-breasted flycatchers, northern beardless-tyrannulets, sulphur-bellied flycatchers, Mexican chickadees, olive warblers, and rufous-winged sparrows. And every birder hopes for a sighting of one of the regional rarities, such as ruddy ground-doves, buff-collared nightjars, plain-capped starthroats, black-capped gnatcatchers, blue mockingbirds, eared trogons, flame-colored tanagers, or yellow grosbeaks.

Some of the sites covered in this guide rank among the most famous birding locations in North America. Every experienced birder has heard of **Cave Creek Canyon** in the Chiricahua Mountains, The Nature Conservancy's **Ramsey Canyon Preserve** in the Huachucas, the **Patagonia-Sonoita Creek Preserve** *(see pp. 316–17)* near

Elf owl nesting in a saguaro

Patagonia, and **Madera Canyon** in the Santa Rita Mountains, to name only a few of the hot spots.

The regional birding itinerary also includes some smaller places that probably only birders would think of visiting. One of the smallest is the **rest area on Ariz. 82** just southwest of Patagonia, often called the "most famous rest area in America" (among birders, anyway). A flycatcherlike bird called rose-throated becard, rare in the United States, nests along the creek across from the rest area parking area, and hundreds of birders have had their first sighting of the species here. The becard builds a bulky, football-size nest that hangs from the tip

of a branch, usually near water. *(If you look for this bird, don't cross fence onto private property beyond.)* The rest area also hosts uncommon birds such as gray hawks and thick-billed kingbirds.

Most travelers don't put sewer ponds high on their list of must-see destinations; birders often do, though, for the waterfowl and shorebirds these artificial wetlands can attract. On Ariz. 90, some 3 miles east of Ariz. 92, the **Sierra Vista wastewater ponds** offer a viewing platform overlooking marsh vegetation where ducks and swallows often congregate. Beautiful yellow-headed blackbirds winter here in large flocks, and marsh wrens are also present in winter.

Birders in the Kartchner Caverns area *(see pp. 315–16)* drive another mile south and turn west into Coronado National Forest's **French Joe Canyon,** a rugged area in the Whetstone Mountains *(a high-clearance vehicle needed for primitive entrance road).* Here the rufous-capped warbler, an extremely rare bird in the United States, has been seen in recent years; the even rarer Aztec thrush has been found as well, and the elusive Montezuma quail is sometimes spotted in the grassland mouth of the canyon.

Buenos Aires National Wildlife Refuge

54 miles southwest of Saguaro West There's a de facto conservation champion hiding in the grasslands of the Altar Valley, along the Mexican border in south-central Arizona. It takes the form of a chunky, cinnamon-colored bird that almost vanished from the Earth, and whose future remains far from secure.

The bird is the masked bobwhite, a subspecies of the northern bobwhite quail familiar throughout the eastern United States. Confined to grassland in Arizona and Sonora, Mexico, the masked bobwhite was thought to be extinct by the mid-20th century, a victim of the degradation of its habitat through overgrazing.

In 1964 a small population was found in Mexico, and though biologists tried to reintroduce the quail to its former range and increase its numbers, they eventually realized the only way to save it was to set aside a large tract of land that could be managed specifically for its benefit. Hence, Buenos Aires National Wildlife Refuge, one of southern Arizona's most varied and appealing wildlife-viewing sites. As refuge habitats recover, a whole range of plants and animals other than the masked bobwhite also benefit, from native grasses to the rare Chiricahua leopard frog.

As you drive to the refuge visitor center, 8 miles north of Sasabe off Ariz. 286, keep alert for mule deer and pronghorn; both are frequently seen along the entrance road. At the visitor center, you can pick up maps, species lists, and advice about roads and trails. If nearby **Aguirre Lake** has water, you might want to walk its half-mile access trail to look for waterfowl or shorebirds.

Running south from the visitor center for 10 miles, **Antelope Drive** offers fine grassland birding and, with some luck, looks at other refuge wildlife as well. Look for pronghorn. In winter, the roadsides teem with sparrows. You might see (or at least hear) a masked bobwhite along the drive, but the chances are better for spotting a Gambel's or scaled quail, both common. The secretive Montezuma quail is also found here, which makes this refuge the only place in the United States with four species of quail present.

Antelope Drive is the designated wildlife route on the refuge, but more than 100 miles of dirt roads are open for driving *(many require four-wheel drive),* mountain biking, or walking.

Though grassland makes up the majority of Buenos Aires, other habitats offer a variety that no visitor should miss. On the eastern edge of the refuge, a 1-mile trail winds alongside **Arivaca Creek**

Birder scanning wetlands at Buenos Aires National Wildlife Refuge

under velvet mesquites, Arizona walnuts, and huge Fremont cottonwoods. A couple of miles east, just outside the small town of Arivaca (where a second refuge visitor center is open November to April), you'll find **Arivaca Cienega,** where a 2-mile loop trail circles a marsh fed by seven springs, creating a rare pool of permanent water.

Ask at either of the refuge visitor centers about visiting **Brown Canyon** in the Baboquivari Mountains, a beautiful area with a 47-foot natural bridge at its upper end, open only to guided tours.

■ 117,000 acres ■ South-central Arizona, 50 miles southwest of Tucson off Ariz. 286 ■ Best seasons winter and spring ■ Camping, hiking, mountain biking, bird-watching, wildlife viewing ■ Contact the refuge, P.O. Box 109, Sasabe, AZ 85633; 520-823-4251. http://southwest.fws.gov/refuges/arizona/

Organg Pipe Cactus National Monument

150 miles west of Saguaro West

Located away from the urban centers of Phoenix and Tucson, on a lonely road that leads only to Mexico, Organ Pipe Cactus National Monument is sometimes overlooked by travelers in the Southwest. That's a shame, because as a showcase of Sonoran Desert environment this park is unsurpassed. In 1976, the United Nations recognized that fact and listed it as a World Biosphere Reserve, a category that includes Amazonia and the Everglades.

You'll find no skyscraping peaks here, no dramatic canyons—the main attraction is a beautiful expanse of native plants and their associated wildlife, set amid rugged volcanic hills. Beauty is in the eye of the beholder, of course. Few would argue with applying that word to the display of wildflowers in Organ Pipe after a wet winter, when Mexican poppies, brittlebushes, globemallows, lupines, Ajo lilies, owl's clover, penstemons, and many other species dot the desert with color.

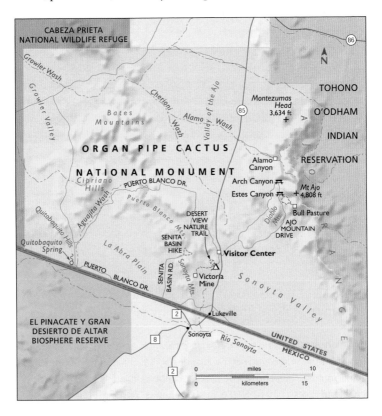

The monument is named for the organ pipe cactus, a common species farther south in Mexico, but in the United States confined to a small area along Arizona's southern border. It's just one of many notable species here, among them senita (another columnar cactus) and the distinctive-looking elephant tree. Two scenic drives explore Organ Pipe, but to appreciate it best you should get out and explore on foot. Short and medium-length trails offer a chance to see flora and fauna, especially early in the morning and around sunset.

As you drive south into the national monument along Ariz. 85, you're bound to note the striking peak standing above the ridgeline to the east. Called **Montezumas Head** today, it was known to Native Americans as "Old Woman With a Basket." At the **visitor center,** an audiovisual presentation introduces the Sonoran Desert and explains why the park is so exceptional. Just outside, a short wheelchair-accessible **nature trail** identifies a few common desert plants.

Drive south to the monument's campground to hike either the **Victoria Mine Trail,** 4.5 miles round-trip into granite hills to an abandoned gold and silver mine, or the **Desert View Nature Trail,** a 1.2-mile loop with vistas over the Sonoyta Valley in the southeastern part of the monument.

Exploring the Diablo and Ajo Mountains

Across Ariz. 85 from the visitor center is the start of the 21-mile **Ajo Range Drive,** an unpaved but well-graded loop around the Diablo Mountains to the edge of the Ajos. (*Be sure to buy road guide at visitor center.*) As soon as you begin the drive, heading northeast, you'll observe organ pipe cactus in abundance. These cold-sensitive plants live here at the northern edge of their range, and so favor south-facing slopes.

Organ pipe, saguaro, and cholla cactuses favor the looser, gravelly soils of the alluvial foothills known as bajadas over the flat low ground, where the soil is more tightly packed. Creosote bush and bursage, a shrub related to ragweed, dominate the flats. Along washes grow mesquite, foothills paloverde (the Arizona state tree), and ironwood, among other water-dependent plants.

Nine miles into the loop, watch for a natural rock arch 90 feet wide on a cliff far above the road. Less than 2 miles farther, you'll reach the Estes Canyon picnic area, where a fairly strenuous loop

trail ascends a canyon in the foothills of the Ajo Range. A spur
leads to **Bull Pasture,** where early ranchers grazed their cattle, making a round trip of 4.1 miles. In the higher elevation, you'll leave
the desert environment and enter a zone of oaks, junipers, and
jojobas, shrubs favored by bighorn sheep—which, with luck, you
might spot here. Those with stamina can continue 3 more hard
miles to the top of 4,808-foot **Mount Ajo.**

Exploring the Puerto Blancos

Back at the visitor center, you'll find the entrance to **Puerto
Blanco Drive,** named for the mountains it encircles on its 53-mile
loop. *(Plan on at least a half day to travel this unpaved route.)* At its
southwestern corner, the drive passes **Quitobaquito Spring,** an oasis
bordered by cattail, cottonwood, and mesquite located practically
on the Mexican border. Birding can be excellent here from fall
through spring. The pond is best known as the home of an endangered subspecies of the desert pupfish. Just over an inch long, the
pupfish has evolved to tolerate great fluctuations in water temperature, oxygen content, and salinity—necessities for survival in confined desert water holes.

As the drive heads back east toward Ariz. 85, watch for the
north spur to **Senita Basin,** one of the park's highlights. Look along
the road for senita cactus and elephant tree, both specialties of the
national monument. The former looks something like organ pipe
cactus but has deeper fluting and a dense growth of spines at the
top of its columns; the latter is named for the resemblance of its
thick trunk to the leg of an elephant.

Hiking Senita Basin

This 2.9-mile **loop trail** begins at the parking lot at the end of
Senita Basin Road, a spur near the end of the Puerto Blanco Drive.
It's an easy route with little elevation change, but like the rest of
Organ Pipe it can be brutally hot at midday in the warm months.
Morning and late afternoon are best, not only for temperature but
to increase your chances of seeing wildlife. The hills that surround
you as you start the hike are formed of pinkish granite. All around
are typical desert plants including ocotillos, creosote bushes, organ
pipe cactuses, paloverdes, and ironwoods.

Soon you'll cross a small rise with lots of white quartz scattered
over the ground. Old-time miners saw this mineral as an indication

that gold and silver might be present; you'll see evidence of mining in many places along the trail. Where the trail splits in 0.2 mile, bear right. You'll pass several saguaro cactuses growing up through the branches of the "nurse" trees that sheltered them in their infancy; later, the cactus roots may take so much water from the soil that the nurse can be killed.

At a junction a mile along the trail, turn left onto what was once a wagon road. In less than a half mile you'll descend slightly to cross a wash, a good spot for desert birds. In another few hundred yards you should reach another junction; turn left for the last mile back to the parking lot.

■ 330,690 acres ■ Southwest Arizona, 75 miles south of Gila Bend off Ariz. 85 ■ Best months mid-Nov.–mid-April. Intensely hot in summer ■ Adm. fee ■ Camping, hiking, bird-watching, wildlife viewing, scenic drives ■ Contact the monument, Route 1, Box 100, Ajo, AZ 85321; 520-387-6849. www.nps.gov/orpi

Senita cactus at sunset, Organ Pipe Cactus National Monument

Zion

R ising in Utah's high plateau country, the Virgin River carves its way to the desert below through a gorge so deep and narrow that sunlight rarely penetrates to the bottom. As the canyon widens, the river runs a gauntlet of great palisade walls rimmed with slickrock peaks and hanging valleys. The scale is immense—sheer cliffs dropping 3,000 feet, massive buttresses, deep alcoves. Nineteenth-century Mormon pioneers saw these sculptured rocks as the "natural temples of God." They called the canyon Little Zion after the celestial city.

A million years of flowing water has cut through the red and white beds of Navajo sandstone that form the sheer walls of Zion. The geologic heart of the canyon began as a vast desert millions of years ago; almost incessant winds blew one dune on top of another until the sands reached a depth of more than 2,000 feet. You can still see the track of these ancient winds in the graceful cross-bedded strata of Zion's mighty cliffs.

Unlike the Grand Canyon where you stand on the rim and look out, Zion Canyon is usually viewed from the bottom looking up. The vertical topography confines most of Zion's 2.5 million yearly visitors between canyon walls.

Streamside on the canyon floor grow thick stands of Fremont cottonwood, box-elder, willow, and, a short distance away, cactus and Utah juniper. Vegetation changes rapidly as the terrain rises almost a mile in elevation. The high plateaus support Douglas-fir and ponderosa pine.

Within the park's 229 square miles lies a landscape of remote terraces and narrow gorges. A number of these canyons are so well hidden that early surveyors overlooked some that are 20 miles long.

More than 100 miles of wilderness trails crisscross Zion's backcountry, while 15 miles of paved trails encourage more casual visits.

- Southwest Utah, near St. George, Cedar City, Kanab
- 146,578 acres
- Established 1919
- Best seasons spring and fall. Kolob Terrace Road closed in winter
- Camping, hiking, backpacking, rock climbing, tubing, mountain biking, horseback riding
- Information: 435-772-3256 www.nps.gov/zion

View from Angels Landing, Zion National Park

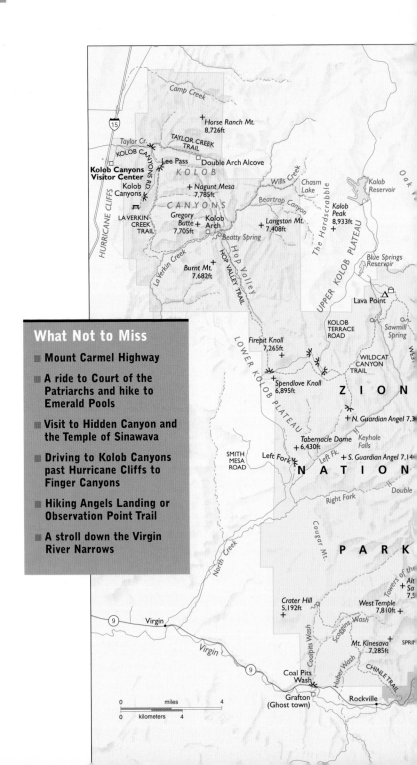

What Not to Miss

- Mount Carmel Highway

- A ride to Court of the Patriarchs and hike to Emerald Pools

- Visit to Hidden Canyon and the Temple of Sinawava

- Driving to Kolob Canyons past Hurricane Cliffs to Finger Canyons

- Hiking Angels Landing or Observation Point Trail

- A stroll down the Virgin River Narrows

Camp Creek

Horse Ranch Mt. 8,726ft

Taylor Cr.
TAYLOR CREEK TRAIL
KOLOB CANYONS RD.
Lee Pass Double Arch Alcove
Kolob Canyons Visitor Center
KOLOB
Kolob Canyons
Wills Creek
Chasm Lake
Kolob Reservoir

CANYONS

Nagunt Mesa 7,785ft
Beartrap Canyon
Kolob Peak 8,933ft

Oak

HURRICANE CLIFFS

LA VERKIN CREEK TRAIL
Gregory Butte 7,705ft
Kolob Arch
Langston Mt. 7,408ft
Beatty Spring

The Hardscrabble

La Verkin Creek
Burnt Mt. 7,682ft
Hop Valley
HOP VALLEY TRAIL

UPPER KOLOB PLATEAU

Blue Springs Reservoir

Lava Point

KOLOB TERRACE ROAD
Sawmill Spring

Firepit Knoll 7,265ft

LOWER KOLOB PLATEAU

WILDCAT CANYON TRAIL

West

Spendlove Knoll 6,895ft

Z I O N

N. Guardian Angel 7,3

SMITH MESA ROAD
Tabernacle Dome 6,430ft
Left Fork
Keyhole Falls
Left Fk.
S. Guardian Angel 7,14

N A T I O N

Double

Right Fork

North Creek

Cougar Mt.

P A R K

Towers of the

Alt Sa 7,5

Virgin
Virgin

Crater Hill 5,192ft

West Temple 7,810ft

Scoggins Wash

9

Coalpits Wash

Huber Wash

CHINLE TRAIL

Mt. Kinesava 7,285ft

SPRIN

9

Coal Pits Wash

Grafton (Ghost town)
Rockville

0   miles   4
0 kilometers 4

How to Get There

From Cedar City to the Kolob Canyons Entrance, take I-15 about 18 miles south. To Zion Canyon, take I-15 to Utah 17 then Utah 9 to the South Entrance (about 60 miles). From Kanab, take US 89 to Utah 9 (at Mt. Carmel jct.) to the East Entrance. From Las Vegas and St. George, take I-15 and Utah 9 to the South Entrance. Airports: Las Vegas, Nev., and St. George, Utah.

When to Go

Open all year, but main season is March through October. Mild spring and fall temperatures are ideal for hiking. Summer rains can bring spectacular clouds and numerous waterfalls. Rock colors are heightened by contrast with winter snows, green summer foliage, deep blue fall skies.

How to Visit

On a 1-day visit, take two scenic drives for the best overview of the park. These are the **Zion-Mt. Carmel Highway** and the **Zion Canyon Scenic Drive.** For longer stays, add one of the classic walks in **Zion Canyon,** then take a road tour of the **Kolob Canyons** in late afternoon.

EXPLORING THE PARK

Zion-Mt. Carmel Highway: 10 miles; 2 hours to half day

This spectacular route descends almost 2,000 feet from the high mesa country at the park's East Entrance to desert country at the South Entrance. Partway along, the road bursts into the heart of Zion in the most dramatic possible way—from the mouth of a tunnel 800 feet above a canyon floor.

Shortly after passing through the East Entrance, stop at the **Checkerboard Mesa** for a classic view of weathered sandstone beds crosshatched with vertical joints. Continue driving as the road winds along the normally dry creek bed.

For the full impact of the approaching canyon, turn off at the Canyon Overlook parking area. This is a good place to stretch your legs along the 1-mile round-trip **Canyon Overlook Trail,** which charts a course above the winding narrows of Pine Creek to an impressive vista of The West Temple and the Towers of the Virgin. A printed trail guide identifies plants typical of the pinyon-juniper forest which surrounds you.

Back in the car, follow the road right through the canyon wall via the **Zion-Mt. Carmel Tunnel,** which breaks into blue sky again in just over 1 mile, then switchback down the side of Pine Creek Canyon. You'll pass close to **The Great Arch,** which is 400 feet high and recessed into a cliff. Soon you enter **Zion Canyon,** where Pine Creek meets the North Fork Virgin River. The canyon has an average width of half a mile, with walls 2,000 to 3,000 feet high.

Zion Canyon Scenic Drive: 6 miles; 2 hours to full day

At **Zion Canyon Visitor Center,** catch a free shuttle for the 6.6-mile Zion Canyon Scenic Drive (*no private vehicles allowed during peak seasons*), which follows the winding Virgin River through the park's main canyon. In addition to alleviating parking shortages and traffic hassles and curtailing pollution, the buses sport big windows and skylights that afford far better views than you can get from most cars. The shuttles leave regularly from the visitor center and operate from early April through October. You can get on and off wherever you like.

At **Court of the Patriarchs,** a short trail leads up the slope to a view of the Three Patriarchs, sheer faces carved by wind and water from Navajo sandstone.

Farther along the road and opposite Zion Lodge, the **Emerald**

The Great White Throne, Zion National Park

Pools Trail makes a 2.3-mile loop through box elder, Gambel oak, and shrub live oak to three natural rock basins fed by small streams. The lowest of these pools is a tiny oasis tucked into the side of the cliff and sheltered by bigtooth maple trees.

After a sojourn at the pools, take the shuttle to the **Grotto picnic area,** another pleasant spot to relax. It's also the start of the strenuous 2.5-mile trail to **Angels Landing,** an open spire of rock perched midway between river and canyon rim that provides one of Zion's best overall views. The route climbs to a knife-edge ridge that joins the landing to the western wall. Sheer 1,500-foot drops surround the promontory on three sides and allow excellent cross-canyon views of **The Great White Throne** and down the deep cut of Zion

Canyon. It's not recommended for those with a fear of heights.

A bit farther along the scenic road, you'll find **Weeping Rock Trail,** which is suitable for everyone. This half-mile paved walk meanders along the bottom of a wet, shaded side canyon and explores a vastly different plant community from the one you'll find elsewhere in the park. Numerous trailside signs identify and discuss the plants, including hackberry, box elder, and bigtooth maple. Toward the end of the trail, you'll even pass through a "desert swamp" fed by nearby springs. The trail ends at Weeping Wall, a lovely "dripping cliff," enlivened by hanging gardens of moss, maidenhair fern, and flowers. The water that makes these gardens possible percolates through the overlying sandstone until it hits shale and then seeps through to the surface of the cliff—1,000 to 4,000 years after falling as rain on the high plateau above.

Hikers at The Narrows

Weeping Rock is the starting point for some ambitious hikes, including the 2-mile round-trip **Hidden Canyon Trail,** which climbs to a hanging valley, and the **Observation Point Trail,** a strenuous 8-mile round-trip that leads to the top of the East Rim. Along the way, it passes through a beautiful narrows, winds into slickrock country, then swings back to the main canyon, and cuts into the very edge of the cliff. Once atop the rim, the route crosses a sandy mesa through stands of pinyon pine and juniper to **Observation Point,** with its fine views of the main canyon.

Back on the road, continue your shuttle ride to superb views of **The Great White Throne,** rising some 2,500 feet above the river, and the **Temple of Sinawava,** at road's end. The temple was named for the coyote-spirit of the Paiute Indians. Here and elsewhere in the park, keep watch for the tiny creatures of Sinawava's realm—canyon tree frogs, pocket gophers, eastern fence lizards. There are also more than 270 species of birds, including greater roadrunner, Gambel's quail, and the water-skimming American dipper.

Road's end is also the trailhead for one of the park's classic day hikes: **Riverside Walk,** an easy 2-mile round-trip on a paved trail suitable for kids and those in wheelchairs. Always crowded, always worthwhile, the trail leads between sheer sandstone cliffs, passing hanging gardens of maidenhair fern and golden columbine and stands of shady cottonwood and ash. It ends at **The Narrows,** where the North Fork rushes from a defile so narrow the only way to look is up. Deeper in The Narrows the walls are 2,000 feet high but in places only 18 feet apart. Flash floods here are a real danger; in the 1960s, a sudden flood caught 26 hikers, drowning 5.

Kolob Canyons Area: 1 hour to a half day or more

Located in the far northwestern corner of the park, just off I-15, this spectacular, accessible, and lightly visited region contains sheer sandstone cliffs every bit as colorful and spectacular as those in the main canyon—they're simply a bit smaller and lack a lush river valley at their base.

The **Hurricane Cliffs,** forming the western boundary of the park, screen the great towers of the Kolob from I-15. Follow the Kolob Canyons Road past the Kolob Canyons Visitor Center and into Taylor Creek Canyon. Here you get a hint of what's to come when the jagged face of Tucupit Point appears.

Continue up the road, skirting the beautiful South Fork Taylor Creek. Each vista becomes more striking as you cross **Lee Pass,** the trailhead for routes into the hidden canyons of La Verkin Creek. If time and stamina allow, you can hike to **Kolob Arch,** one of the world's largest freestanding natural arches at 310 feet long. This 14-mile round-trip is usually done as an overnight *(backcountry camping permit required).*

The road continues south to **Kolob Canyons Viewpoint** with its dramatic vista of the **Finger Canyons.** Sheer cliffs of pale red sandstone lift more than 2,000 feet into the blue sky. Narrow canyons work deep into the sides of Timber Top Mountain, connecting Shuntavi Butte with Nagunt Mesa.

Here, the mile-long **Timber Creek Overlook Trail** offers a chance to stretch your legs and get additional cliff views (not to mention far-reaching vistas to the south and west).

INFORMATION & ACTIVITIES

Headquarters
State Rte. 9
Springdale, UT 84767
435-772-3256
www.nps.gov/zion

Visitor & Information Centers
Zion Canyon Visitor Center, near the South Entrance on Utah 9, and Kolob Canyons Visitor Center, in the park's northwest corner off I-15, are both open daily year-round.

Seasons & Accessibility
Park open year-round. Kolob Canyons Road and main roads in Zion Canyon are plowed in winter. Dirt roads are impassable when wet. Lava Point inaccessible in winter and early spring due to snow. Contact park headquarters for current weather conditions.

Free shuttle service on Zion Canyon Scenic Drive is mandatory during high season. Pick up shuttle at Springdale or at the Zion Canyon Visitor Center. Shuttles run April through October.

Entrance Fees
$20 per car per week, multiple entries; or $10 per person. Also, $10 fee charged for escorting oversize vehicles through the mile-long tunnel on East Entrance road.

Pets
Not permitted in backcountry, on shuttles, in public buildings, or on trails; elsewhere allowed on leashes.

Facilities for Disabled
Visitor centers, Zion Human History Museum, shuttles, some rest rooms and trails are wheelchair accessible. Handicapped sites available in campgrounds.

Things to Do
Free ranger-led activities include nature walks and talks, evening programs, children's programs. Zion Human History Museum. Also, hiking, horseback trail rides—inquire at Zion Lodge or call 435-772-3810—climbing, bicycling (bicyclists must transport their bikes through the long tunnel—check at entrance or visitor center), limited cross-country skiing.

Special Advisories
■ Summer temperatures in park can exceed 105°F. Always carry bottled or treated water when hiking—at least a gallon a day per person in summer.
■ Permits, $5, are required for overnight backpacking trips; they are available at either of the park's visitor centers.

■ Rattlesnakes live here; watch out!

Campgrounds

Three campgrounds, 14-day limit. Watchman open all year. South open May–Sept., 128 sites, $16 per night. Lava Point open May–Oct., depending on weather, 6 sites, no fee. Reservations for Watchman through the National Park Reservation Service *(800-365-2267; http://reservations.nps.gov)*, 160 sites, $16–$20. Others, first come, first served. Showers nearby but outside park. Tent and RV sites.

Hotels, Motels, & Inns

(Unless otherwise noted, rates are for two persons in a double room, high season.)

INSIDE THE PARK:

■ **Zion Lodge** (off Utah 9) Xanterra Parks & Resorts, Cedar City, UT 84767. 435-772-3213 (Lodge) 303-297-2757 (reservations) or 888-297-2757. 81 rooms with AC. 40 cabins. $124–$146. Restaurant. www.zionlodge .com/static/1.htm.

OUTSIDE THE PARK

In Springdale, UT 84767:

■ **Driftwood Lodge** 1515 Zion Park Blvd., P.O. Box 98. 435-772-3262 or 800-528-1234. 42 units. $82–$104. AC, pool, hot tub. www.driftwood.net.

■ **Bumbleberry Inn** 97 Bumbleberry Ln., P.O. Box 346. 435-772-3224 or 800-828-1534. 30 units. $78. AC, pool, restaurant. www.bumbleberry.com.

■ **Canyon Ranch Motel** 668 Zion Park Blvd., P.O. Box 175. 435-772-3357. 22 units, 4 with kitchenettes. $68–$88. AC, pool.

■ **Cliffrose Lodge & Gardens** 281 Zion Park Blvd., P.O. Box 510. 435-772-3234 or 800-243-8824. 36 units. $109–$165. AC, pool. www.cliffroselodge.com.

■ **Flanigan's Inn** 428 Zion Park Blvd., P.O. Box 100. 435-772-3244 or 800-765-7787. 35 units. $99–$119. AC, pool, restaurant. www.flanigans.com.

■ **O'Toole's Under the Eaves Guest House** 980 Zion Park Blvd. 435-772-3457. 6 rooms, 4 private baths. $75–$145. AC. www.undertheeaves.com.

In Kanab, UT 84741:

■ **Parry Lodge** 89 E. Center St. 435-644-2601 or 800-748-4104. 89 units. $73. AC, pool, restaurant.

■ **Shilo Inn** 296 W. 100 North. 435-644-2562 or 800-222-2244. 118 units. $55–$99. AC, pool.

For additional accommodations near Zion National Park, contact Kane County Travel, 78 S. 100 East, Kanab, UT 84741. 435-644-5033 or 800-733-5263.

Excursions from Arches

Coral Pink Sand Dunes State Park

45 miles southeast of Zion

One glimpse of the namesake dunes as you near Coral Pink Sand Dunes State Park will convince you that they are indeed pink (up close more red or orange). Sprawling beneath blue skies and set among steep red cliffs peppered with pinyon and juniper, these graceful dunes compose the only major dune field on the Colorado Plateau.

Located just 45 miles from Zion National Park, the dunes seem a world apart visually. Composed of 10,000- to 15,000-year-old iron-oxide crystals, the dunes were formed by the Venturi Affect—wind funneling through a crack in the Navajo sandstone rock between the Moccasin and Moquith Mountains

The place to start, once in the park (mountain bikers may decide the roads outside the park are the most fun), is with the 0.5-mile **nature trail** and accessible railed walkway, which provide an orientation to the dunes.

Then it's off to the dunes. The object is to enjoy them—run, jump, roll, build sand castles or just walk. Although you will be sharing the two high ones—110 foot and 90 foot—with off-highway vehicles (OHV), there is plenty of room for both the hiker and four-wheeler to coexist (*265 acres are off-limits to OHV at all times, and all vehicles are prohibited 10:00 p.m.–9:00 a.m.; so enjoy the dunes during quiet hours*). Despite the struggle to climb to the top of the larger dunes, do so, for the view is worth it. On a perfect day you might get a glimpse of the North Rim of the Grand Canyon (see pp. 177-178).

On a sweltering day, it's understandable if you assume that nothing lives here, but you couldn't be further from the fact. Look at the sand and note the prints of the creatures that survive here, among them the endangered Coral Pink Sand Dunes tiger beetle—*Cicindela limbata albissima*. It's about the size of a thumbnail. Other wildlife includes lizards and beetles, deer and fox. Be aware that it is easy to become disoriented among the dunes, so always carry water and a map.

■ **3,730 acres** ■ **Southwest Utah, Northwest of Kanab** ■ **Year-round, best seasons spring and fall** ■ **Adm. fee** ■ **Hiking, biking, horseback riding, photography, OHVs** ■ **Contact the park, P.O. Box 95, Kanab, UT 84741, 435-648-2800. www.utah.com/stateparks/**

Dixie National Forest

50 miles northeast of Zion

The Dixie National Forest covers a large area north of Grand Staircase-Escalante National Monument *(see pp. 79–81).* It consists mostly of the following wooded high plateaus: the Markagunt Plateau surrounding and to the east of Cedar Breaks; the Paunsaugunt Plateau around Bryce Canyon; the Sevier Plateau north of the Paunsaugunt; the Table Cliff Plateau east of the Paunsaugunt; and the Aquarius Plateau north of the towns of Escalante and Boulder. Aquarius Plateau soars to 11,328 feet at Boulder Mountain, making it North America's highest forested plateau.

Rising from desert expanses to high-altitude stands of aspen, spruce, and fir on the Aquarius Plateau, these lands were all formed at the same time. Fault lines between them have since eroded into valleys. Traveling this country today is a lesson in how vegetation changes with elevation. On Utah 12 *(see pp. 76–78)* heading south from Torrey over Boulder Mountain, for example, the route climbs from a pinyon-juniper forest through ponderosa pine, then into aspen, Douglas-fir, and Engelmann spruce.

Farther west, Utah 143 from Panguitch to **Cedar Breaks National Monument** *(see pp. 339–341)* offers a similar succession, and

Prickly pear cactus blooming in Dixie National Forest

includes limber pine above Panguitch Lake. You can also experience this shift by driving dirt roads such as the **Hell's Backbone loop** *(off Utah 12 between Boulder and Escalante)* or by mountain biking the **Wildcat-Cat Creek** trails on Boulder Mountain.

The **Red Canyon** area northwest of Bryce invites exploration on numerous hiking and biking trails through red-rock country and Bryce-like hoodoos. If the hoodoos here are smaller in height and girth than those at Bryce, so are the crowds. The mile-long **Pink Ledges Trail,** which starts directly behind the Red Canyon Visitor Center, offers an interpretive brochure. The trails at both **Losee Canyon** (3 miles long) and **Thunder Mountain** (8 miles) are good routes for either bikers or hikers.

Locals enjoy fishing for trout, especially in the many lakes on Boulder Mountain. To the west, **Navajo** and **Panguitch Lakes** are large, natural, high-altitude lakes with well-developed campgrounds and boat ramps. Canoeists must share the waters with powerboaters. In addition to rainbow and brook trout, some areas boast two species of rare trout—Bonneville cutthroats and Colorado River cutthroats.

An almost endless network of backcountry roads and single-track trails suitable for mountain biking winds through Dixie National Forest. Few areas are more astonishing than the **Brian Head** mountain region, which lies to the northeast of Cedar Breaks National Monument.

The terrain does honor to the term mountain biking: Hundreds of miles of trails and roads lead through chilled air and aspen groves, past tumbling streams and 10,000-foot peaks. Indeed, it's possible in this area to begin well above timberline, then make a long, dizzy descent through the woods all the way to the red rock country far below.

Several businesses in the town of Brian Head—at 9,600 feet, one of the highest communities in Utah—offer shuttle services that take you to the top of 11,307-foot Brian Head Peak, allowing long rides down the mountain to pick-up sites below.

For intermediate riders, a particularly fine route—full of wildflowers and soaring views—is the **Dark Hollow-Second Left Hand Canyon** ride, a 17-mile (one way) trek from Brian Head Peak to the small town of Parowan.

The small town of **Brian Head** also sponsors a series of nature walks on Saturdays in July and August. For information on these or other recreational opportunities, contact the Brian Head Chamber of Commerce *(888-677-2810. www.brianheadutah.com)*.

■ **1.97 million acres** ■ **Southern Utah** ■ **Best months April–Oct.** ■ **Camping, hiking, backpacking, rockhounding, boating, canoeing, fishing, mountain biking, horseback riding, wildlife viewing, scenic drives** ■ **Contact the national forest, 82 N. 100 East, Cedar City, UT 84720; 435-865-3700. www.fs.fed.us/outernet/dixie_nf/welcome.htm**

Cedar Breaks National Monument

Cedar Breaks is an amphitheater of sculpted rock formations called hoodoos *(see sidebar p. 72)*. These colorful columns and pillars are composed of limestone, eroded in the same ways and at roughly the same time as nearby Bryce Canyon *(see pp. 67–75)*. Clearly, however, Cedar Breaks has its own unique character. For one thing, many visitors find the colors more dramatic here than at Bryce. The amphitheater is also bigger and deeper. Moreover, the gradient at Bryce is about 1,000 feet over 10 miles; at Cedar Breaks it's a whopping 2,500 feet over just 3 miles.

The plateaus of this area are tilted blocks, which create a landscape that rises and falls in a pattern like a series of breaking waves. Cedar Breaks lies on the upside of the Hurricane Fault—the steep edge where the wave breaks. Bryce, on the other hand, is on the more gradual back side of its plateau.

Cedar Breaks' Markagunt Plateau is higher than Bryce's Paunsaugunt (the visitor center at Cedar Breaks sits at more than 10,000 feet elevation), and it supports more of an alpine ecosystem. Snow lingers until late June; wildflowers such as Indian paintbrush, lupine, yarrow, and penstemon peak in mid to late July.

Meadows atop the plateau get more moisture and suffer less heat than the surrounding areas, resulting in an explosion of plant life. The old-growth Engelmann spruce forest here fell victim to a beetle epidemic in the late 1990s; as a result, you will occasionally see dead trees standing amid healthy subalpine fir and ancient bristlecone pines.

Only 20 percent of the monument—the area atop the plateau with views down into the amphitheater—contains the usual visitor services such as roads and rest rooms; the rest has been proposed as wilderness. A remote area nearby, located roughly below the amphitheater, is already a Forest Service-administered wilderness known as **Ashdown Gorge.** Unlike most of southern Utah, this untrammeled land was never grazed by cattle or sheep, making it a rich region for research on so-called relic vegetation—species of plants that predate the arrival of pioneers.

The steepness of the amphitheater makes it difficult to hike among the hoodoos, but overlooks at the **visitor center** and at turnouts along the road provide glimpses of these amazing formations, along with excellent vistas to the west. From these view spots, you'll stand at the very edge of the Markagunt Plateau, looking out upon the Basin and Range ecoregion.

It's worth your while to walk two trails along the rim. The 2-mile **Alpine Pond Loop,** which has an interpretive guide, leads to a forest glade and pond; the 2-mile **Ramparts Trail,** on the other hand, leads past a grove of bristlecone pines at **Spectra Point** to a viewpoint of the amphitheater. Both trails begin at parking areas along the monument road.

Cedar Breaks National Monument at sunset

Backpackers who are willing to make the hard, 9-mile hike down into the wilderness can start from **Rattlesnake Creek Trail,** just north of the park boundary. Be sure to check with the visitor center before you go; this path is not regularly maintained. Camping is forbidden in the amphitheater, so you'll need to set up your camp in the Ashdown Gorge Wilderness, then day-hike back up into the monument.

During the summer season rangers offer hourly geological talks, as well as evening campground programs on wildlife, bristlecone pines, and Native American cultural history. On weekends they lead guided morning hikes to the bristlecone pine stand at Spectra Point.

■ **6,155 acres** ■ **Southwest Utah, near Brian Head and Cedar City** ■ **Best months late May–mid-Oct. Many services and roads closed in late fall and winter** ■ **Camping, hiking, backpacking, guided walks, scenic drives** ■ **Adm. fee** ■ **Contact the monument, 2390 W. Hwy. 56, Suite 11, Cedar City, UT 84720; 435-586-9451. www.nps.gov/ceb**

Resources

US Forest Service Regional Offices

Southwestern Region (Arizona and New Mexico)
333 Broadway SE
Albuquerque, NM 87102
505-842-3292
www.fs.fed.us/r3

Intermountain Region (Nevada and Utah)
324 25th St.
Ogden, UT 84401
801-625-5306
www.fs.fed.us/r4/

Rocky Mountain Region (Colorado)
740 Simms St.
Golden, CO 80401
303-275-5350
www.fs.fed.us/r2

Pacific Southwest Region (California)
1323 Club Drive
Vallejo, CA 94592
707-562-8737; 707-562-9130 (TTY)
www.fs.fed.us/r5

For information on recreation and camping opportunities within the national forests visit:
www.recreation.gov or
www.reserveusa.com

US Fish and Wildlife Service

Southwest Region (#2)
500 Gold Ave. SW
Albuquerque, NM 87102
505-248-6911
http://southwest.fws.gov/

Arizona

Road Conditions
888-411-7623
www.az511.com

Tourism Office
Arizona Office of Tourism

1110 W. Washington St., Suite 155
Phoenix, AZ 85007
602-364-3700 or 866-275-5816
www.azot.com

State Parks/Camping
Arizona State Parks
1300 W. Washington St.
Phoenix, AZ 85007
602-542-4174
www.pr.state.az.us

Fishing and Hunting
Arizona Game & Fish Dept.
2221 W. Greenway Rd.
Phoenix, AZ 85023
602-942-3000
www.gf.state.az.us

Hiking
Arizona Trail Association
P.O. Box 36736
Phoenix, AZ 85067
602-252-4794
www.aztrail.org
(Information source for the 750-mile trans-state trail.)

Educational opportunities
Grand Canyon Field Institute
P.O. Box 399
Grand Canyon, Az 86023
866-471-4435
www.grandcanyon.org/fieldinstitute

Bureau of Land Management
BLM-Arizona Office
222 N. Central Ave.
Phoenix, AZ 85004
602-417-9200
www.az.blm.gov

Other recreation and public lands
Public Lands Information Center
222 N. Central Ave.
Phoenix, AZ 85004
602-417-9300
www.publiclands.org

California

Road Conditions
800-427-7623 (in Calif.) or
916-445-7623 (outside Calif.)
www.dot.ca.gov/hq/roadinfo/

California Tourism
California Travel and Tourism
800-462-2543
www.visitcalifornia.com

State Parks
California Dept. of Parks
& Recreation
P.O. Box 942896
Sacramento, CA 94296
916-653-6995
http://parks.ca.gov

Camping in many of California's state
parks is operated by:
Reserve America
800-444-7275
www.reserveamerica.com

Fishing and Hunting Licences
California Dept. of Fish & Game
3211 F St.
Sacramento, CA 95816
916-227-2245
www.dfg.ca.gov

Hiking
Pacific Crest Trail Association
5325 Elkhorn Blvd., PMB # 256
Sacramento, CA 95842
916-349-2109 or 888-728-7245
www.pcta.org

Educational opportunities
Anza-Borrego Institute
595 Palm Canyon Dr., Ste. A
Borrego Springs, CA 92004
760-767-0446
www.theabf.org

The Desert Institute
Joshua Tree National Park Assoc.
74485 National Park Dr.
Twentynine Palms, CA 92277

760-367-5525
www.joshuatree.org/dihome.html

Bureau of Land Management
BLM-California
2800 Cottage Way, Ste. W1834
Sacramento, CA 95825
916-978-4400
www.ca.blm.gov

BLM-California Desert District
22835 Calle San Juan de los Lago
Moreno Valley, CA 92553
909-697-5200
www.ca.blm.gov/cdd

Colorado

Road Conditions
877-315-7623
www.co.blm.gov/conditions.htm

Colorado Tourism
Colorado Tourism Office
1625 Broadway, Ste. 1700
Denver, CO 80202
303-892-3885 or 800-265-6723
www.Colorado.com

State Parks
Colorado Tourism Office
1625 Broadway, Ste. 1700
Denver, CO 80202
303-892-3885 or 800-265-6732
www.Colorado.com

Camping in many of Colorado's state
parks is operated by
Reserve America
800-444-7275
www.reserve america.com

Fishing and Hunting Licenses
Colorado Division of Wildlife
6060 Broadway
Denver, Colorado, 80216
303-297-1192 or 800-244-5613
http://wildlifelicense.com/co/

Camping
Private campgrounds

Colorado Association of
Campgrounds, Cabins and Lodges
888-222-4641 or 303-499-9343

Bureau of Land Management
BLM–Colorado Office
2850 Youngfield St.
Lakewood, CO 80215
303-239-3600
www.co.blm.gov/

Nevada
Road Conditions
775-888-7000
www.nevadadot.com/traveler/roads

Nevada Tourism
Nevada Commission on Tourism
401 North Carson St.
Carson City, NV 89701
800-638-2328 or 775-888-7000
www.travelnevada.com

State Parks
Nevada State Parks
1300 South Curry St.
Carson City, NV 89703
775-687-4384
www.state.nv.us/stparks/

Fishing and Hunting Licenses
Nevada Division of Wildlife
1100 Valley Rd.
Reno, NV 89512
775-688-1500
www.ndow.org

Bureau of Land Management
BLM–Nevada Office
1340 Financial Blvd.
Reno, NV 89502
775-861-6400
www.nv.blm.gov

Other recreation and public lands
Public Lands Interpretive Assoc.
6501 Fourth St., NW, Suite I
Albuquerque, NM 87107
877-851-8946 or 505-345-9498
www.publiclands.org

New Mexico
Road Conditions
800-432-4269
www.nmshtd.state.nm.us

New Mexico Tourism
New Mexico Dept. of Tourism
491 Old Santa Fe Trail
P.O. Box 20002
Santa Fe, NM 87503
505-827-7400 or 800-733-6396
www.newmexico.org

State Parks
New Mexico State Parks
P.O. Box 1147
Santa Fe, NM 87504
888-667-2757
www.emnrd.state.nm.us/nmparks

Camping reservations for New Mexico's
state parks:
877-664-7787
www.icampnm.com

Fishing and Hunting Licenses
New Mexico Game and Fish
P.O. Box 25112
Santa Fe, NM 87504
505-827-7911 or 800-862-9310
www.wildlife.state.nm.us

Bureau of Land Management
BLM–New Mexico Office
1474 Rodeo Rd.
Santa Fe, NM 87505
505-438-7400
www.nm.blm.gov

Other recreation and public lands
Public Lands Information Centers
1474 Rodeo Rd.
Santa Fe, NM 87505
505-438-7542
www.publiclands.org

2909 W. 2nd St.
Roswell, NM 88201
505-627-0272

435 Montano Rd., NE
Albuquerque, NM 87107
505-761-8700 or 877-851-8946

Texas

Road Conditions
800-452-9292 or
www.dot.state.tx.us/hcr/
main.htm

Texas Tourism
Texas Dept. of Commerce
P.O. Box 12728
Austin, TX 78711
www.traveltex.com

State Parks
Texas Parks & Wildlife
4200 Smith School Rd.
Austin, TX 78744
800-792-1112, Opt. 3
www.tpwd.state.tx.us/park

Fishing and Hunting Licenses
Texas Parks & Wildlife
4200 Smith School Rd.
Austin, TX 78744
800-792-1112
www.tpwd.state.tx.us/publications
/annual/general/licenses.phtml

Utah

Road Conditions
800-492-2400 or
www.dot.state.ut.us/public/
traveler_info.htm;

Utah Tourism
Utah Travel Council
800-200-1160
www.utah.com

State Parks
Utah State Parks and Recreation
1594 West North Temple
Salt Lake City, UT 84114
801-538-7220
http://parks.state.ut.us

Camping in many of Utah's state parks
is operated by:
Reserve America
800-444-7275
www.reserveamerica.com

Fishing and Hunting Licenses
Utah Division of Wildlife Resources
Southern Regional Office
1470 North Airport Rd.
Cedar City, UT 84720
435-856-6100
www.wildlife.utah.gov

Biking
Bicycle Utah
P.O. Box 711069
Salt Lake City, UT 84171
801-278-6294
www.bicycleutah.com

Educational opportunities
Canyonlands Field Institute
P. O. Box 68
1320 South Hwy. 191
Moab, UT 84532
435-259-7750 or 800-525-4456
www.canyonlandsfieldinst.org

Four Corners School of Outdoor
Education
P.O. Box 1029
Monticello, UT 84535
435-587-2156
www fourcornersschool.org

Zion Canyon Field Institute
Zion Natural History Association
Zion National Park
Springdale, Utah 84767
800-635-3959
www.zionpark.org/index.php

Bureau of Land Management
BLM-Utah Office
P.O. Box 45155
324 South State Street
Salt Lake City, UT 84145
801-539-4001
www.ut.blm.gov/

INDEX

Abbreviations
National Forest = NF
National Monument = NM
National Park = NP
National Recreation Trail =
NRT
National Wildlife Refuge =
NWR
State Park = SP

A

Abajo Mountains, Utah 26,
94
Ajo Mountains, Ariz.
323–324
Alamosa NWR, Colo. 222
Alpine Loop Byway, Colo.
274–275
Anasazi Heritage Center,
Colo. 278
Anasazi SP, Utah 77–78, 81
Antelope Valley/California
Poppy Reserve, Calif.
163–164
Anza-Borrego Desert SP,
Calif. 258–261
Apache-Sitgreaves NF,
Ariz.-N.Mex. 128, 129
Aquarius Plateau, Utah 70,
78, 336
Arches NP, Utah 15–31;
Delicate Arch 16, 18, 19,
20–21, 22, 25; Devils Gar-
den 16, 18, 20, 21, 22;
Fiery Furnace 16, 19, 21;
Klondike Bluffs 16, 21;
Landscape Arch 20, 21;
map 16–17; Park Avenue
Viewpoint 18, 22; Skyline
Arch 21; Tower Arch 16,
21; The Windows 16, 18,
19; Wolfe Ranch 16, 18,
19, 20
Arizona-Sonora Desert
Museum, Ariz. 304, 306,
312
Ash Meadows NWR, Nev.
166

B

Barton Warnock Environ-
mental Education Center,
Tex. 47
Beaver Canyon Scenic
Byway, Utah 108
Big Bend NP, Tex. 33–47;
Boquillas Canyon 36, 40,
41; Casa Grande 37, 38;
Chisos Basin 36, 37–38,
41, 42; Hot Springs 41;
Lost Mine Peak 37; map
34–35; Panther Junction
36, 37, 40, 41, 42; Persim-
mon Gap 36, 41; Pulliam
Bluff 37; Rio Grande Vil-
lage 36, 41, 42; Ross
Maxwell Scenic Drive 36,
38–40; Santa Elena
Canyon 40, 41; Sotol Vista
39; the Window 38
Big Bend Ranch SP, Tex.
46–47
Big Bend Recreation Area,
Utah 24
Bighorn sheep 167
Bitter Lake NWR, N.Mex.
132–133
Black Canyon of the Gun-
nison NP, Colo. 49–65;
Balanced Rock 55, 56;
Cedar Point Nature Trail
54; Chasm View 52, 53, 55,
56; High Point 52, 54; map
50–51; North Rim 50, 51,
55, 56; North Vista Trail
55; Oak Flat Trail 53;
Painted Wall 54; Pulpit
Rock 53; Rim Rock Nature
Trail 52; South Rim 50, 51,
55, 56; Sunset View 52, 56;
Tomichi Point 52, 56;
Uplands Trail 52
Blue Mesa Lake, Colo. 61
Bluff, Utah 112–113
Boney Mountain State
Wilderness Area, Calif. 146
Bosque del Apache NWR,
N.Mex. 130–132
Boulder, Utah 77–78
Box-Death Hollow Wilder-
ness, Utah 77
Bryce Canyon NP, Utah
67–81, 100, 191, 337, 339;
Bristlecone Loop Trail 69,
72; Bryce Amphitheater 67,
69, 70, 70; Bryce Point 69, 70,
71, 72; Fairyland Point 69,
72; map 68–69; Natural
Bridge 72–73; Navajo Loop
Trail 70; Queens Garden
Trail 69, 70; Rainbow Point
69, 72, 73; Rim Trail 70;
Sunrise Point 70, 72;
Under-the-Rim Trail 69,
70, 74; Yovimpa Point 71
Buenos Aires NWR, Ariz.
320–321
Butterfield Overland Mail
Route Historical Monu-
ment, Calif. 260

C

Canyon de Chelly NM,
Ariz. 282–283
Canyon del Muerto, Ariz.
282
Canyonlands NP, Utah 24,
26, 83–97; Chesler Park
Trail 91; Confluence Overlook Trail 90; Druid Arch
Trail 91; Elephant Hill 90,
91; Horseshoe Canyon
Unit 91; Island in the Sky
28, 83, 85, 86, 88, 91, 92;
map 84–85; The Maze 83,
85, 86, 91; The Needles 25,
83, 85, 88–91, 92, 93;
Newspaper Rock 88–89;
Pothole Point 87, 90; Shafer Trail 91; Slickrock Trail
90; Upheaval Dome 86
Capitol Reef NP, Utah 68,
76, 78, 99–113; Burr Trail
Loop 100, 104–105, 106;
Cathedral Valley Circle

104–105; Fremont River 99, 100, 102, 103, 105; Fruita 102–103; map 101; Petroglyphs 103; Rim Overlook Trail 103; Scenic Drive 100, 102–103; Waterpocket Fold 87, 99, 100, 102

Carlsbad Caverns NP, N.Mex. 115–133, 242; Bat Flight 118, 121, 122; Big Room Tour 118, 119–121; Desert Nature Trail 118, 121, 122; Kings Palace Tour 118, 121, 122; Lechuguilla Cave 120; map 116–117; Natural Entrance Tour 118, 119, 122; Slaughter Canyon Cave 118, 121, 122; Walnut Canyon Desert Drive 118, 121, 122

Catalina SP, Ariz. 313

Cathedral Gorge SP, Nev. 207–208

Cave Creek Canyon, Ariz. 318

Cedars Breaks NM, Utah 337, 339–341

Channel Islands National Marine Sanctuary, Calif. 135–149; map 136–137

Channel Islands NP, Calif. 135–149; Anacapa Island 137, 138–141, 142; map 136–137; Santa Barbara Island 141, 142, 143; Santa Cruz Island 140, 142, 143; Santa Miguel Island 140–141, 142, 143; Santa Rosa Island 140, 142, 143

Chihuahuan Desert, Mexico-U.S. 33, 44, 115, 127, 132, 133, 246

Chimney Rock Archaeological Area, Colo. 277

Chisos Mountains, Tex. 33, 36, 37, 38

Cimarron Canyon SP, N.Mex. 229, 231

Coconino NF, Ariz. 192, 193, 194

Colorado Desert, Calif. 162, 249, 252, 262

Colorado NM, Colo. 62–63

Colorado Plateau, U.S. 26, 192, 283, 294, 300

Colorado River Scenic Byway, Utah 24–25, 26

Continental Divide Trail 274

Coral Pink Sand Dunes SP, Utah 336

Curecanti NRA, Colo. 55, 61

D

Davis Mountains, Tex. 238, 246–247

Dead Horse Point SP, Utah 94

Death Valley NP, Calif. 151–169; Death Valley Museum 152, 154; Furnace Creek 154, 158, 159; Golden Canyon Interpretive Trail 152, 154; Harmony Borax Works 152, 155; map 152–153; Salt Creek Interpretive Trail 156; Scottys Castle 152, 156, 158; Stovepipe Wells Village 156, 159; Ubehebe Crater 152, 156; Windy Point Trail 156; Zabriskie Point 152, 154

Desert, adaption 44–45; survival 157; trees 262; tortise 255

Desert NWR, Nev. 167

Diablo Mountains, Ariz. 323–324

Dinosaur NM, Colo.-Utah 97

Dixie NF, Utah 76, 81, 106, 337

Dog Canyon, N.Mex. 127, 130

Dolores River, Colo.-Utah 276–277

Durango, Colo. 278, 280

E

Eagle Nest Lake, N.Mex. 229

El Malpais National Monument and Conservation Area, N.Mex. 296–298

Elk Mountains, Colo. 55, 60, 61, 65

Enchanted Circle National Scenic Byway, N.Mex 228–229

Escalante SP, Utah 77, 81

F

Fish Lake Scenic Byway, Utah 108

Fisher Towers Recreation Site, Utah 24–25

Fishlake NF, Utah 108–109; Kimberly-Big John Rd. 109

Fort Davis National Historic Site, Tex. 246

Fort Leaton State Historical Site, Tex. 47

French Joe Canyon, Ariz. 319

G

Glen Canyon NRA, Ariz.-Utah 78, 110–111

Goblin Valley SP, Utah 30–31

Gooseneck SP, Utah 112–113

Grand Canyon NP, Ariz. 171–195; Bright Angel Trail 180; Canyon View Information Center 174, 184; Cape Royal Road 173, 177; Corridor Zone 180; Desert View Drive 173, 175–177; Grandview Trail 176; Hermit Road 173, 174–175; maps 172–173, 181, 186; North Kaibab Trail 177, 180; North Rim 72, 171, 172, 177–178, 180, 184; Rim Trail 174, 175; South Kaibab Trail 176,

180; South Rim 171, 172, 174–177, 184; Tonto Trail 181; Tusayan Museum 176–177

Grand Mesa, Colo. 55, 58–60, 63

Grand Staircase-Escalante NM, Utah 76, 79–81, 189

Great Basin NP, Nev. 197–209; Alpine Lakes Loop Trail 200; Baker Lake/Johnson Lake Loop 202–203; Bristlecone Forest Loop 200–201; Bristlecone/Glacier Trail 200; Lehman Caves 197, 199, 201–202, 204; Lexington Arch 203; map 198–199; Osceola Ditch 200; Wheeler Peak Scenic Drive 199, 200–201

Great Sand Dunes NP & Preserve, Colo. 211–231; Dunes 214–215, 218; High Dune 212, 215; map 212–213; Medano Creek 212, 214–215; Medano Pass Primitive Road 212, 216; Montville Nature Trail 212, 215–216; Mosca Pass Trail 212, 216; Star Dune 215

Green River, U.S. 28, 83, 86, 94, 96–97, 183

Guadalupe Mountains NP, Tex. 233–247; The Bowl 239; Bush Mountain Trail 239; Dog Canyon 236, 239, 240, 242; El Capitan 238; Guadalupe Peak 239; Headquarters Visitor Center 237, 240; map 234–235; McKittrick Canyon 236, 238–239, 240; Permian Reef Geology Trail 239; Pine Springs 236, 240; Smith Spring Trail 237

Gunnison River, Colo. 49–50, 52, 53–54, 55

H

Havasupai Indian Reservation, Ariz. 186–187

Hell's Backbone, Utah 77, 81

Henry Mountains, Utah 78, 86, 90, 94

Highline NRT, Ariz. 294

Hole-in-the-Rock Road, Utah 77, 81, 110

Hole-in-the-Wall, Calif. 163

Holy Cross Wilderness, Colo. 64

Homolovi Ruins SP, Ariz. 298–299

Hoover Dam, Ariz.-Nev. 187

Hovenweep NM, Utah 113

Humphreys Peak, Ariz. 194, 195

Hunter-Fryingpan Wilderness, Colo. 64–65

J

Joshua Tree NP, Calif. 249–263; Arch Rock Nature Trail 254; Boy Scout Trail 255; Cholla Cactus Garden 252–253; Cottonwood Visitor Center 252, 256; Desert Queen Ranch 254–255; Hidden Valley Trail 254; Keys View 251, 255, 256; map 250–251; Oasis of Mara 252, 256; Ocotillo Patch 253–254; Park Boulevard 251, 252–255; Pinto Basin Road 251, 252; Ryan Mountain Trail 255

K

Kachina Peaks Wilderness, Ariz. 194–195

Kaibab NF, Ariz. 172, 188–191

Kaibab Squirrel 176

Kaiparowits Plateau, Utah 81

Kartchner Caverns SP, Ariz. 315–316, 319

Kelso Dunes, Calif. 163

Kimberley-Big John Road, Utah 109

Kodachrome Basin SP, Utah 76, 78–79, 81

L

La Garita Wilderness, Colo. 274

La Sal Mountains, Utah 19, 21, 25–26, 86

Lake Mead NRA, Ariz.-Nev. 187–188

Lamoille Canyon Scenic Byway, Nev. 206–207

Latir Peak Wilderness, N.Mex. 228

Lechuguilla Cave, N.Mex. 120

Lincoln NF, N.Mex. 130, 131, 242–246

Little Wild Horse Canyon, Utah 30

Living Desert Wildlife and Botanical Park, Calif. 262

Living Desert Zoo and Gardens SP, N.Mex. 124–125

Lizard Head Wilderness, Colo. 274

M

Madera Canyon, Ariz. 319

Malibu Creek SP, Calif. 146

Manti-La Sal NF, Utah-Colo. 25–26

Marfa, Tex. 247

Maroon Bells-Snowmass Wilderness, Colo. 64

McDonald Observatory, Tex. 246–247

Mead, Lake, Ariz.-Nev. 182, 187

Mesa Verde NP, Colo. 265–283; Balcony House 269, 272; Chapin Mesa Museum 268, 269, 272; Cliff Palace 265, 269, 272; Far

View Visitor Center 268, 270, 272; Long House 270, 272; map 266–267; Mesa Top Loop Road 268, 269–270, 272; Petroglyph Point Trail 269; Spruce Tree House 268, 269, 272; Wetherill Mesa 270–271, 272
Meteor Crater, Ariz. 301
Mexian gray wolves 128-129
Mitchell Caverns, Calif. 163
Moab, Utah 24, 28–29, 85, 92
Mogollon Rim, Ariz. 294–295, 300
Mojave Desert, Calif. 44, 161, 162, 165, 168; see also Joshua Tree NP
Mojave National Preserve, Calif. 162–163
Monte Vista NWR, Colo. 222
Monument Valley, Ariz.-Utah 281–282
Monument Valley Navajo Tribal Park, Utah 281

N
National Solar Observatory, N.Mex. 242
Natural Bridges NM, Utah 95
Navajo Mountain, Utah 71, 73, 78, 110

O
Oliver Lee Memorial SP, N.Mex. 127-28
Organ Pipe Cactus NM, Ariz. 322–325

P
Painted Desert, Ariz. 285, 289
Painted Desert Inn National Historic Landmark, Ariz. 291, 292
Panguitch, Utah 76, 337
Patagonia-Sonoita Creek Preserve, Ariz. 316–317, 318-319
Paunsaugunt Plateau, Utah 67, 76
Petrified Forest NP, Ariz. 285–301; Agate House 286, 290; Blue Mesa 286, 288; Blue Mesa Trail 290–291; Giant Logs Trail 288, 292; Lacey Point 289; Long Logs 289; map 287; Newspaper Rock 288; Painted Desert Visitor Center 286, 289, 292; Painted Desert Wilderness 291, 292; Pintado Point 286, 289; Puerco Pueblo 288; Rainbow Forest Museum 286, 288, 292; The Tepees 288
Petroglyph NM, N.Mex. 225
Pintail Lake, Ariz. 300
Pipe Spring NM, Ariz. 189
Point Mugu SP, Calif. 146
Potholes 87
Powell, Lake, Ariz.-Utah 78, 110
Pronghorn 223
Providence Mountains SRA, Calif. 163
Puerto Blanco Mountains, Ariz. 324
Pusch Ridge Wilderness, Ariz. 313

Q
Quitobaquito Spring, Ariz. 324

R
Rainbow Bridge NM, Utah 110
Ramsey Canyon Preserve, Ariz. 318–319
Red Canyon, Utah 76, 338
Red Rock Canyon National Conservation Area, Nev. 168–169
Red Rock Canyon SP, Calif. 165
Rio Grande petroglyphs 225

Rio Grande Wild and Scenic River, N.Mex. 224–225
River Road (El Camino del Rio), Tex. 46–47
Rocky Mountains, Canada-U.S. 33, 183, 226
Ruby Crest NRT, Nev. 207

S
Sabino Canyon, Ariz. 309
Sabino Canyon, Ariz. 309
Sacramento Mountains, N. Mex. 127, 242
Saguaro NP, Ariz. 303–325; Bajada Loop Drive 304, 306; Cactus Forest Drive 304, 308; Cactus Garden Trail 306; Desert Discovery Nature Trail 304, 306; Desert Ecology Trail 304, 309; map 305; Mica View Picnic Area 304, 309; Red Hills Visitor Center 304, 306, 310; Rincon Mountain District 303, 304, 308–309; Saguaro East Visitor Center 308, 310; Sendero Esperanza Trail 306; Tanque Verde Ridge Trail 309; Tucson Mountain District 303, 304, 306; Valley View Overlook Trail 306
Salton Sea, Calif. 255, 263
San Francisco Mountain, Ariz. 192, 194–195
San Juan Mountains, Colo.-N.Mex 55, 60, 61, 63, 211, 226–227, 274–279
San Juan River, Utah 112–113, 282
San Juan Skyway, Colo. 274, 278–280
San Rafael Swell, Utah 26–27, 30
Sangre de Cristo Mountains, Colo.-N.Mex. 211, 212, 216, 219, 220–221; valley 230
Santa Catalina Mountains,

Ariz. 313–314

Santa Monica Mountains
NRA, Calif. 144–146

Santa Rosa Mountains, Nev.
260, 261, 263

Sauceda, Tex. 47

Scott M. Matheson Wetlands
Preserve, Utah 29

Senita Basin, Ariz. 324–325

Sierra Nevada, Calif. 165,
197

Silverton, Colo. 278, 280

Sky Island Scenic Byway,
Ariz. 313

Skyline National Scenic
Trail, Utah 109

Slick Rock Canyon, Colo.
276–277

Smokey Bear State Historical
Park, Ariz 131

Smugglers Gulch, Calif. 148

Solstice Canyon, Calif. 146

Sonoran Desert, Mexico-
U.S. 44, 249, 252, 253, 303,
306, 307

South San Juan Wilderness,
Colo. 274

Species, northern 226-227

Spooners Mesa, Calif. 148

Strawberry Crater Wilder-
ness, Ariz. 193

Sunset Crater Volcano NM,
Ariz. 192–193

Sunspot Scenic Byway,
N.Mex. 242

T

Telluride, Colo. 279

Tijuana River National Estuarine Research Reserve,
Calif. 148

Topanga SP, Calif. 145

Torrey Pines State Reserve,
Calif. 147

U

Uncompahgre Gorge, Colo.
280

Uncompahgre Plateau, Colo.
60, 62

Uncompahgre Wilderness,
Colo. 274

Utah 12 Scenic Byway
76–78, 79, 81, 337

V

Valle Vidal, N.Mex. 230

Valley of Fire SP, Nev.
208–209

W

Water 161

Weminuche Wilderness,
Colo. 274, 275–276

West Elk Wilderness, Colo.
65

Whales & whale watching
149

Wheeler Peak, N. Mex. 226

Wheeler Peak, Nev. 197, 200

Wheeler Peak Wilderness,
N.Mex. 228

White River NF, Colo. 64–65

White Sands NM, N.Mex.
125–127, 130

Wild Rivers Recreation Area,
N.Mex 225

Wupatki NM, Ariz. 192

Z

Zion NP, Utah 68, 191,
327–341; Canyon Overlook
Trail 330; Emerald Pools
Trail 330-331; Great White
Throne 331, 332; Hidden
Canyon Trail 332; Kolob
Canyons 329, 333, 334;
map 328–329; The Narrows
333; Observation Point
Trail 332; Riverside Walk
333; Temple of Sinawava
332; Timber Creek Over-
look Trail 333; Weeping
Rock Trail 332; Zion
Canyon Scenic Drive 329,
330–331, 334; Zion Human
History Museum 334;
Zion-Mt. Carmel Highway
329, 330

Zuni Mountains, N.Mex. 297

One of the world's largest
nonprofit scientific and
educational organizations,
the National Geographic Society was founded in 1888 "for
the increase and diffusion of
geographic knowledge." Fulfill-
ing this mission, the Society
educates and inspires millions
every day through its maga-
zines, books, television programs, videos, maps and
atlases, research grants, the
National Geographic Bee,
teacher workshops, and innovative classroom materials. The
Society is supported through
membership dues, charitable
gifts, and income from the sale
of its educational products.
This support is vital to National
Geographic's mission to
increase global understanding
and promote conservation of
our planet through exploration,
research, and education.

For more information, please
call 1-800-NGS LINE (647-
5463) or write to the following
address:

National Geographic Society
1145 17th Street N.W.
Washington, D.C. 20036-4688
U.S.A.

Illustration Credits

Cover, Galen Rowell/CORBIS
1 Erwin & Peggy Bauer. 2-3 Bruce Dale. 6 George H. H. Huey. 9 Bruce Dale. 14 George H. H. Huey. 18 Tom & Pat Leeson. 23-29 (all) George H. H. Huey. 32 Gordon Gahan. 43 Bruce Dale. 44-45 Ann Winterbotham. 46 Bruce Dale. 48, 52 George H. H. Huey. 57 Pat O'Hara/CORBIS. 58-75 (all), George H. H. Huey. 80 Diane Cook and Len Jenshel. 82, 87 George H. H. Huey. 88-89 Bruce Dale. 93, 97 George H. H. Huey. 98 Bob Krist. 102 George H. H. Huey. 107 Bob Krist. 108-114 (all) George H. H. Huey. 116-117 Tibor Toth.123 Walter Meayers Edwards. 124 George H. H. Huey. 126 Bruce Dale. 129, 133 George H. H. Huey. 134-164 (all) Phil Schermeister. 167 John Luke/Index Stock. 169 Melissa Farlow. 170 Bruce Dale. 175, 178 George H. H. Huey. 179 Ned Seidler. 182-195 (all) George H. H. Huey. 196-208 (all) Phil Schermeister. 210-224 (all) George H. H. Huey. 227 Michael S. Quinton/NGS Image Collection. 228-244 George H. H. Huey. 248-261 (all) Phil Schermeister. 264, 270-271 George H. H. Huey. 279 Tom Bean. 281 Bruce Dale. 284 George H. H. Huey. 290-291 Phil Schermeister. 293-301 (all) George H. H. Huey. 302 Bruce Dale. 307 George H. H. Huey. 308 Peter Essick. 311-341 (all) George H. H. Huey. Back cover, George H. H. Huey.

Staff credits

National Geographic Guide to the National Parks Southwest
Published by the National Geographic Society

John M. Fahey, Jr., *President and Chief Executive Officer*
Gilbert M. Grosvenor, *Chairman of the Board*
Nina D. Hoffman, *Executive Vice President, President, Books and School Publishing*
Kevin Mulroy, *Vice President and Editor-in-Chief*
Marianne Koszorus, *Design Director*
Elizabeth L. Newhouse, *Director of Travel Publishing*
Caroline Hickey, *Project Director*
Thomas Schmidt, *Editor*
Cinda Rose, *Art Director*
Carl Mehler, *Director of Maps*
Ruth Ann Thompson, *Designer*
Lise Sajewski, *Style/Copy Editor*
Gregory Ugiansky, The M Factory, *Map Production*
Lewis Bassford, *Production Project Manager*
Meredith Wilcox, *Illustrations Assistant*
Dianne Hosmer, *Indexer*
Ben Archambault, Ben Bodurian, Cindy Kittner, Barbara Noe, Larry Porges, Simon Williams, Jordan Zappala, *Contributors*

Library of Congress Cataloging-in-Publication Data

National Geographic guide to the national parks Southwest / [prepared by the Book Division].
    p. cm.
Includes bibliographical references and index.
    ISBN 0-7922-9539-0
    1. National parks and reserves--Southwest, New--Guidebooks. 2. Southwest, New--Guidebooks. I. Title: Guide to the national parks Southwest. II. National Geographic Society (U.S.). Book Division.
    F785.3.N375 2005
    917.904'34   2004020819

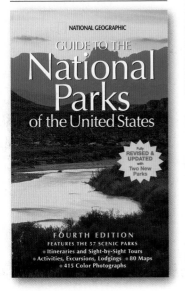